The 21st Century Webster's
Family Encyclopedia

The 21st Century
Webster's
Family Encyclopedia

Volume 10
Toxin - Zwo

1999 Edition

IMPORTED BY/IMPORTE PAR
DS-MAX CANADA
RICHMOND HILL, ONTARIO
L4B 1H7

ENGLAND
WENTWALK LTD.
278A ABBEYDALE ROAD, WEMBLEY
MIDDLESEX, HA0 1NT

MALAYSIA
PRO ENTERPRISE SDN BHD
LOT 605, SS13/1K, OFF JLN.
KEWAJIPAN, 47500 SUBANG JAYA
SELANGOR D.E., MALAYSIA

DS-MAX
IRVINE, CA 92618
IMPORTER: #16-1241510
949-587-9207

TRIDENT PRESS INTERNATIONAL

Copyright © 1999, Uitgeverij Het Spectrum BV, Utrecht

ISBN 1-55280-465-8

Printed in Peru

The 21st Century Webster's Family Encyclopedia
is based on the Spectrum Database

editors:
Bart Drubbel
Tjeerd van der Velde
Saskia van Iperen

Toxin, poisonous substance produced by a living organism. Examples of toxin-producing organisms include fungi, which secrete substances that destroy bacteria (and provide antibiotics), and poisonous spiders and snakes, which deliver their toxin via fangs. The symptoms of many infectious diseases (e.g., cholera, diphtheria, tetanus) are due to the release of toxins by the bacteria.

Toy dog, any of several small breeds of dogs kept as pets. Toy dogs are either naturally small or selectively bred to keep them small. In most cases they do not constitute a separate genus or species, but are related to larger dogs of various species. Examples include the Maltese, chihuahua, Pekingese, Pomeranian, shih tzu, toy poodle, and Yorkshire terrier.

Toynbee, Arnold Joseph (1889-1975), English historian. His principal work, *A Study of History* (12 vol., 1934-61), divides the history of the world into 26 civilizations and analyzes their rises and falls according to a cycle of "challenge and response."

Trace elements, minerals that make up all human, animal, and plant life. Small quantities of trace elements are needed to ensure the normal action of enzymes and hormones. In humans, lack of essential minerals such as iron may result in conditions such as pernicious anemia and goiter. Necessary minerals can generally be obtained from a healthy diet. Requirements vary among the different human, animal, and plant species.

Trachea, conduit by which air reaches the lungs from the pharynx. Air is drawn in through the mouth or nose and passes via the larynx into the trachea, which then divides into the major bronchi. It may be seen below the Adam's apple. In a tracheostomy, it is incised to bypass any obstruction to respiration.
See also: Respiration.

Trachoma, chronic conjunctivitis caused by *Chlamydia trachomatis*. Tetracycline eye ointments are usually effective.

Track and field, athletic sports including running, walking, hurdling, jumping for distance or height, and throwing various objects. The revival of the Olympic Games in 1896 gave international and national competition an enormous boost, and in 1912 the International Amateur Athletes Federation was set up.
Track events. Distances raced vary from the 50-m sprint to the 5,0000-m run. Hurdlers and steeplechasers have to clear a set number of obstacles. In relay races a baton is passed from one runner to the next.
Field events. In high jump and pole vault the contestant who clears the greatest height with the least number of attempts wins. A long jump running or triple jump (hop, step and jump) competitor is permitted six jumps. Throwing events also permit six throws. The javelin is a spear thrown by running up to a line and releasing. The shot, a solid iron ball, is "put" from the shoulder. The discus is a circular plate released with a sweeping sidearm action. The hammer throw consists of throwing an iron ball attached to a handle by a wire. All-around events include the 10-event decathlon and the 5-event pentathlon.

Tracy, Spencer (1900-67), U.S. film actor. During his career he appeared in more than 70 films over 37 years and won Academy Awards for *Captains Courageous* (1937) and *Boys' Town* (1938). His pairing with Katharine Hepburn in several movies, including *Woman of the Year* (1942) and *Adam's Rib* (1949), made them one of Hollywood's most famous cinematic couples.

Trade, buying and selling of commodities. It can take place within a nation (domestic trade) or between nations (foreign or international trade). Trade occurs because the people of a particular community or country do not produce all the goods they need. As a consequence, they must purchase these goods from another community or country. They may in turn sell their products to other communities or countries that need them. Trade among early peoples and civilizations usually involved an exchange of one product or service for another. For example, one group might have traded wood to another group for grain. As populations grew and their needs became more complicated, money became the medium of exchange and the boundaries of trade expanded. During the 13th, 14th, and 15th centuries, European merchants traveled to the Middle East and China in search of exotic goods. Overseas exploration created important trade between Europe and Africa and India, and between Europe and the colonies in both North and South America. Today in many countries, including the United States, trade occurs on many levels. People exchange money for services (subway or bus rides) and for goods (food, clothes, radios, and so on). Communities and states trade among one another, which explains why people in Ohio can buy California oranges. The United States also maintains a vast and active foreign trade with countries all over the world.

Trademark, name, symbol, or other device that identifies the product of one company. Strong trademarks, such as Tonka, are words with no apparent meaning which lessen the chance of them being used by another company. Weak trademarks, such as Bubbles, are ordinary words that often communicate the main feature of the product. Trademarks do not need to be registered with the U.S. Patent and Trademark Office to protect them from being duplicated, but such registration makes it easier to sue for infringement if the trademark is copied.

Trade route, land or water route used to transport goods from one area to another. Trade routes have historically led to the development of civilizations, the growth of cities, and the interchange of ideas. They have existed since ancient times and have increased in number and importance as civilizations have grown. The search for trade routes has contributed to the exploration of new territories and the establishment of colonial empires. Today an extensive network of air, land, and water routes covers all parts of the globe.

Trade union *See:* Labor movement.

Trade winds, persistent warm moist winds that blow westward from the high pressure zones at about 30°N and °S latitude toward the doldrums (intertropical convergence zone) at the equator. They are thus northeasterlies in the Northern Hemisphere and southeasterlies in the Southern Hemisphere. They are stronger and displaced toward the equator in winter.
See also: Horse latitudes.

Trafalgar, Battle of, decisive naval engagement of the Napoleonic Wars, fought on Oct. 21, 1805. The British fleet of 27 warships under Admiral Horatio Nelson met a combined French and Spanish fleet of 33 ships off Cape Trafalgar (southwestern Spain). By attacking in an unorthodox formation, Nelson surprised the enemy, sinking or capturing 20 vessels without loss, but was himself killed.
See also: Napoleonic Wars; Nelson, Horatio.

Tragedy, form of drama originating in ancient Greece, in which exceptional characters are led, by fate and by the very qualities that make them great, to suffer calamity and often death. Aristotle, in his famous definition, spoke of purification (*catharsis*) through the rousing of the emotions of pity and fear. The great classical tragedians were Aeschylus, Sophocles, and Euripides. Supreme in modern times is William Shakespeare. Great tragedians include Félix Lope de Vega, Pedro Calderón de la Barca, Pierre Corneille, Jean Racine, Johann Wolfgang von Goethe, and Friedrich von Schiller. In the 19th and 20th centuries, in which the heroic dimension of tragedy in drama is often shunned, the greatest exponents are probably Henrik Ibsen and Eugene O'Neill.

Tragopan, any of 5 species of birds in the pheasant family. These inhabitants of central and southern Asia mainly live on forested mountains. During courtship the colorful feathered folds of throat skin (the lappet) and blue fleshy horns on the sides of the head of the males enlarge for a brilliant display. Unlike many other kinds of pheasants, tragopans nest in trees rather than on the ground.

Trail of Tears *See:* Oklahoma.

Trajan (A.D. 53-117), Roman emperor responsible for great extensions of the empire and vast building programs. He conquered Dacia (Romania) and much of Parthia and rebuilt the Roman Forum. Adopted heir by Nerva (97), he became emperor in 98. He was known as a capable administrator and a humane and tolerant ruler.
See also: Rome, Ancient.

Tranquilizer, any of the agents that induce a state of quietude in anxious or disturbed patients. Minor tranquilizers are sedatives (e.g., benzodiazepines) valuable in treating anxiety. In psychosis, especially schizophrenia and (hypo) mania, major tranquilizers are required to suppress abnormal mental activity, as well as to sedate; phenothiazines (e.g., chlorpromazine) are often used.
See also: Depressant.

Transcendentalism, philosophical and literary movement that flourished in New England c.1835-60. Regarding rationalist Unitarianism and utilitarian philosophy as morally bankrupt and shallow, the transcendentalists took their inspiration from the German idealists, notably Immanuel Kant, from Samuel Coleridge, and from Eastern mystical philosophies. They believed in the divinity and unity of humankind and nature, and in the supremacy of intuition over sense perception as well as reason as a source of knowledge. The major figures were Ralph Waldo Emerson and Margaret Fuller, who edited *The*

Dial (1840-44), Henry David Thoreau, and Amos Bronson Alcott. The movement had considerable influence on U.S. literature (Nathaniel Hawthorne, Herman Melville, Walt Whitman) and politics (abolitionism, Brook Farm).

Transcontinental treaty *See:* Adams-Onís Treaty.

Transducer, device for converting an input of energy or information of one form into an output of another. Passive transducers require only the input signal to produce the output signal; active transducers require an additional source of energy. The light bulb and the microphone are examples of transducers.

Transformer, device for moving an alternating current by increasing or decreasing the voltage. This is an easy, inexpensive way for power companies to transport electricity over long distances. Transformers work by electromagnetic induction, where a magnetic field alters the voltage of the electric current. The current goes through a step-up transformer, which increases the voltage. High voltage electricity loses very little power when transported over long distance wires. When the current reaches its destination, step-down transformers are used to decrease the voltage to the level where it can be used by customers.

Transfusion, blood *See:* Blood transfusion.

Transistor, device in electronic equipment thast regulates the flow of electricity in such equipment. It works by controlling the flow of current between two terminals, the emitter and collector, by means of variations in the current flow between a third terminal, the base, and one of the other two. Transistors lower the voltage of the electricity to be used by a piece of electronic equipment, but keep the current strong. This provides items such as calculators, which require small voltages, with enough power to perform complex calculations. Transistor-transistor logic is a family of integrated circuits characterized by relatively high speed and low power consumption. Transistors are used in radios, television sets, and computers to control the flow of electric current.

Transkei, former independent homeland established by South Africa for the black Xhosa-speaking people. Located between the Indian Ocean and the Republic of Lesotho, it is 15,831 sq mi (41,002 sq km) and its capital is Umtata. Transkei, granted independence in 1976, was not recognized by any nation except South Africa. Many of Transkei's people are farmers and herders living in small villages, but the mining of the nation's rich mineral deposits is on the increase. With the abolishment of the apartheid policy, Transkei lost its independent status and fell under central South African rule.

Transmigration of the soul *See:* Reincarnation.

Transmission, automobile part that transmits the power generated by the engine to a driving axle. The power travels from the transmission to the drive shaft, then to the final drive. These 3 parts make up the drive train of an automobile. The transmission has several gears, which regulate the speed of the automobile by controlling the amount of power delivered to the driving axle. There are 2 types of automobile transmissions: manual, where the driver is responsible for shifting the gears, and automatic, where a device automatically shifts the gears when necessary.

Transmutation of elements, conversion of an atom of one element to an atom of another. Since atoms are identified by their atomic number (number of protons), any change in the number of protons will result in a different element. Atoms may change their number of protons by giving off or taking in atomic particles. Transmutation occurs naturally as a result of radioactive decay. Radioactive atoms are very unstable and give off atomic particles in order to become more stable. With one form of radioactive decay, alpha decay, the atom emits an alpha particle (2 protons and 2 neutrons). With beta decay the atom emits an electron, resulting in the production of a proton and the loss of a neutron. Sometimes, but less often, a positron (a positively charged electron) is emitted, so that a proton is lost and a neutron gained. Artificial transmutation may be accomplished by bombarding atoms with alpha particles so that the atom accepts an extra proton (1 of the 2 is immediately expelled). Transmutation is a by-product of fission (the splitting of nuclei) and fusion (the joining of nuclei).
See also: Radioactivity.

Transpiration, loss of water by evaporation from the aerial parts of plants. Considerable quantities of water are lost in this way, far more than is needed for the upward movement of solutes and for the internal metabolism of the plant alone. Transpiration is necessary for photosynthesis: In order to obtain sufficient carbon dioxide from the air, considerable areas of the plant's wet surface have to be exposed. But as a result, much water is lost through evaporation.

Transplant, organ removed from one person and surgically implanted in another to replace a lost or diseased organ. Autotransplantation is the moving of an organ from one place to another within a person, where the original site has been affected by local disease (e.g., skin grafting). Blood transfusions between those with compatible blood groups was the first practical form of transplant. In organ transplantation, tissue compatibility typing as well as blood grouping are needed to minimize the risk of rejection. Immunosuppressive drugs are also given to block the creation of antibodies that would attack the donor tissue. The most important, and now most successful, of organ transplants is that of the kidney. A single kidney is transplanted from a live donor who is a close relative or from a person who has recently suffered sudden death. Heart transplantation has been much publicized, but is limited to a few centers, and many problems remain. Liver and lung transplants have also been attempted, but there are still numerous difficulties. In corneal grafting the cornea of the eye of a recently dead person replaces that of a person with irreversible corneal damage leading to blindness. The lack of blood vessels in the cornea reduces the problem of rejection. Grafts from nonhuman animals are occasionally used (e.g., pig skin as temporary cover in extensive burns). Both animal and human heart valves are used in cardiac surgery.

Transportation, Department of, executive department of the U.S. government responsible for the development and coordination of national transport policies and agencies. Set up by the Department of Transportation Act (1966), it began operating the following year. It reports to Congress on the optimum use of federal transportation funds. It supervises the federal aviation, highway, railroad, and urban mass transportation administrations, the U.S. Coast Guard, the Saint Lawrence Seaway Development Corporation, and the National Transportation Safety Board.

Transsexualism, condition in which a person has a psychological urge to belong to the opposite sex. People who experience this condition are called transsexuals. In most cases, therapy is not an effective treatment. Surgical techniques in conjunction with certain hormones can be used to make transsexuals physically resemble a member of the opposite sex. Transsexuality is not the same as homosexuality.

Trans-Siberian Railroad, railroad in Russia, the longest in the world, stretching 5,787 mi (9,313 km) from Moscow to Vladivostock on the Sea of Japan. Its construction (1891-1916) had a dramatic effect on the development of Siberia.

Transuranium elements, elements of atomic number above 92. All transuranic elements are radioactive and are products of artificial nuclear changes.

Transvaal, former province in the Republic of South Africa, between the Vaal and Limpopo rivers in the northeast. It is mainly high veld, 3,000-6,000 ft (914-1,829 m) above sea level. The capital is Pretoria and the largest city is Johannesburg. Mineral wealth includes gold, silver, diamonds, coal, iron ore, platinum, asbestos, and chrome. Its farmlands are noted for their cattle, corn, and tobacco. In 1993 the province was split into four new provinces.
See also: South Africa.

Transylvania, province in central Romania near the Hungarian border, situated between the Transylvanian Alps and the Carpathian Mts. Transylvania has been in dispute between Romania and Hungary for several hundred years. Once part of the Roman Empire, Transylvania was conquered and ruled by the Magyars (Hungarians) from the 11th to the 16th centuries. The Ottoman Turks took control in 1526 but vied with Austria for prominence until 1711, when Austria dominated. From 1867 to 1918, it was part of the Austro-Hungarian Empire. Transylvania was absorbed by Romania after World War I and, though a portion of it went to Hungary in 1940, Romania regained control after World War II. The province is rich in iron and other minerals and is a fertile farming, grazing, and wine-making area. It is famous as the setting of the legend of Dracula, written by English author Bram Stoker in 1897.
See also: Romania.

Trappists, members of the clan of the Reformed, or Strict, Observance, a Roman Catholic monastic order founded (1664) by Armand de Rancé, abbot of La Trappe in Normandy, France. He instituted a rigorous discipline of silence, prayer, and work. There are 12 U.S. abbeys. The abbot general lives in Rome.
See also: Cistercians.

Travertine, type of limestone that forms in dense layers. It is easily cut and often used in construction for decorative purposes. It is found in places where limestone is in contact with evaporated water containing calcium carbonate, and around hot springs and streams. Stalactites and stalagmites are chiefly comprised of travertine, which is mostly white or cream colored.

Treason, behavior by a subject or citizen that could harm the sovereign or state. In many countries treason has been loosely defined and used as a political weapon. The U.S. Constitution, however, states that treason consists only in levying war against the United States or in adhering to it enemies, "giving them Aid and Comfort"; evidence of two witnesses or confession in open court is necessary to secure a conviction.

Treasury, Department of the, executive department of the U.S. government, established in 1789, responsible for federal taxes, customs, and expenditure. It also plays a major role in national and international financial and monetary policies. Its head, the secretary of the treasury, the second-ranking member of the president's cabinet, is an *ex officio* governor of the International Monetary Fund. The department's other responsibilities include the U.S. Secret Service and the bureaus of Customs, Mint, Engraving and Printing, Internal Revenue, and Narcotics.

Treaty, agreement between states. Treaties are bilateral (between two states) or multilateral (between several states), and cover matters such as trade, tariffs, taxation, economic and technical cooperation, diplomatic relations, international boundaries, extradition of criminals, defense, and control of arms and aggression. Some treaties, for example the North Atlantic Treaty Organization (NATO), are military; others set up international organizations, which have become an important part of modern international relations.

Treaty of 1783 *See:* Revolutionary War in America.

Tree, woody perennial plant with a well-defined main stem, or trunk, that either dominates the form throughout the life cycle (giving a pyramidal shape) or is dominant only in the early stages, later forking to form a number of equally important branches (giving a rounded or flattened form to the tree). The trunk of a tree consists almost wholly of thick-walled water-conducting cells (xylem) that are renewed every year, giving rise to annual rings. The older wood in the center of the tree (the heartwood) is much denser and harder than the younger, outer sapwood. The outer skin, or bark, insulates and protects the trunk and often shows characteristic cracks or falls off, leaving a smooth skin. Trees belong to the two most advanced group of plants. The gymnosperms include the cone-bearing trees such as pine, spruce, and cedar; they are nearly all evergreens and most live in the cooler regions of the world. The angiosperms (flowering plants) have broader leaves and much harder wood; in tropical climates they are mostly evergreen, but in temperate regions they are deciduous.

Tree frog, or tree toad, one of several hundred types of frogs belonging to the family Hylidae, commonly found in North and South America. Many varieties have adhesive pads on their fingers and toes that stick to trees and facilitate climbing and leaping. Males have a characteristic high-pitched call, which they use to attract their mates. Tree frogs are about 1-5 in (2.5-13 cm) long, eat insects, and change color.

Tree shrew, small, squirrel-like arboreal insectivore (family Tupaiidae) with a pointed snout. Tree shrews were once thought to be primates, related to the lemurs, but they are now considered a group of their own. They live in trees and bushes from India and China to the Philippines and Borneo. Except for the pen-tailed tree shrew they come out by day, and most species live in family groups. They feed on leaves, fruit, and small animals. The babies are born in a nest of leaves, and the mother visits them every two days to feed them.

Tree toad *See:* Tree frog.

Trench mouth, or Vincent's infection, disease of the mouth and throat, probably caused by bacteria, poor oral hygiene, and malnutrition. Initial symptoms include pain and bleeding of the gums and bad breath. Chewing and swallowing food is also painful. If not treated, trench mouth can lead to gum destruction and eventual tooth loss.

Trent, Council of, series of 3 conferences held in Trent, Italy, by leaders of the Roman Catholic church in the mid-16th century. Convened by Pope Paul III in 1545 to counteract the Protestant Reformation in Europe, the council did much to define Catholic doctrine and bring about a Counter-Reformation. The first council, which lasted until 1547, established the Catholic church's sole right to interpret the Scriptures and took issue with the Protestant interpretations of sin and salvation. The second council (1551-52) defined the nature of the sacraments and reaffirmed the validity of the rituals practiced in Holy Communion. The third council (1562-63) defended the controversial granting of pardons (indulgences) for the commission of certain sins, approved prayers to the saints, and established seminaries for training the priesthood. The council's actions became part of the Catholic doctrine by papal confirmation in 1564.
See also: Counter-Reformation.

Trent Affair, naval incident in the U.S. Civil War that nearly brought Britain to militarily support the South. In Nov. 1861, Charles Wilkes, commanding the Union ship *San Jacinto* stopped the British ship *Trent* and seized two southern agents, J.M Mason and John Slidell. Britain demanded an apology for this violation of the freedom of the sea and ordered 8,000 troops to Canada. The southerners were freed in December.
See also: Civil War, U.S.

Trenton (pop. 92,124), capital (since 1790) of New Jersey, situated at the head of navigation on the Delaware River, opposite Pennsylvania. The city was settled in 1679 by Quaker farmers under Mahlon Stacy. In 1714 Stacy's son sold part of the property to William Trent, for whom the city was named. During the American Revolution, Trenton was the site of Gen. George Washington's famous crossing of the Delaware at the head of his troops and the site of their victory over the Hessians (Battle of Trenton, 1776). Trenton, which served as the capital of the United States Nov.-Dec. 1784, developed as an industrial, transportation, and trade center in the 20th century.
See also: New Jersey.

Trenton, Battle of, American victory in the Revolutionary War, fought on Dec. 26, 1776. To forestall a British attack on Philadelphia, George Washington crossed the Delaware River at night and surprised a British force of 1,500 Hessians at Trenton, N.J. The battle was won in 45 minutes, rallying Washington's army and the American cause.
See also: Revolutionary War in America.

Trephining, surgical removal of a small, circular piece of skull. An ancient, even prehistoric, practice, it was probably first performed to release evil spirits from a person's head. Today it is used primarily to open the way for certain brain surgeries and to relieve pressure caused by bleeding between the brain and the skull. The operation is performed with a small saw called a trephine.

Trevelyan, George Macauley(1876-1962), English historian who rejected the "scientific" approach to history in favor of a more humanistic and literary approach. He taught at Cambridge (1927-51) and was best known for a colorful study of Garibaldi (3 vols., 1907-11), a one-volume *History of England* (1926), *England Under Queen Anne* (3 vols., 1903-34), and *English Social History* (1942).

Triage (French, "sorting"), allocation of limited medical or food resources by selecting those in need who would most benefit in the long run. During World War I (1914-18) the word was introduced to describe the classification of wounded soldiers. Medical help was first administered to those who would survive only with immediate treatment; help was delayed or, if necessary, withheld from those who were expected to die or to recover with or without treatment. By extension, a triage system is suggested to determine what countries in need of food are to receive supplies. A system of triage also is used in hospital emergency rooms to determine the order in which patients are attended.

Trial, method of settling disagreements of determining criminal guilt. In the United states, this involves a hearing before a judge, with or without a jury. In the United States the right of an accused person to a speedy and public trial by a jury of peers is guaranteed in the Constitution. Trials in common law countries, such as the United Kingdom and United States, are "adversary" proceedings, in which the court impartially decides between the evidence of two parties. Under civil law systems trials tend to be more "inquisitorial," allowing the court itself a greater role in the gathering of evidence. Under both systems the judge ensures that procedure is followed and that the rules of evidence are observed, and determines the guilty offender's sentence. Questions of fact are left to a jury, if there is one; jury trial is more expensive and time-consuming, and so it is reserved for more serious offenses.

Trial by combat, medieval method of settling disagreements. According to its tenets, the two disputing parties fought hand-to-hand combat, the belief being that God would intervene on behalf of the just participant. Nobles, women, and priests were usually represented by substitute fighters. Eventually the method was replaced by trial by jury.
See also: Divination.

Triangle, three-sided polygon. There are three main types of plane triangle: scalene, in which no side is equal in length to another; isosceles, in which two of the sides are equal in length; and equilateral, in which all three sides are equal in length. A right (or right-angled) triangle has one interior angle equal to 90° and may be either scalene or isosceles. The "corners" of a triangle are termed vertices (singular: vertex). The sum of the angles of a plane triangle is 180°. A spherical triangle is an area of the surface of a sphere bounded by arcs of three great circles, each arc being less than 180°, each side and interior angle being termed an element. The sum of the three sides is never greater than 360°; the sum of the three angles is always in the range of 180°-540°.

Trianon, Treaty of, World War I treaty that reduced Hungary's territory by almost two-thirds as punishment for its part in the war. Signed June 4, 1920 by Hungary and the Western Allies, including the United States, the treaty forced Hungary to relinquish almost 90,000 sq mi (233,100 sq km) to Romania, Czechoslovakia, and what is now Yugoslavia. As a result, the country lost all of its seaports as well as about 12 million inhabitants.
See also: World War I.

Triassic Period, first period of the Mesozoic Era (c.225-190 million years ago).

Tribe, people who live in a community in a particular area, sharing the same language, culture, and often kinship. The tribal system is one the earliest forms of society and still exists in most of Africa, on many Pacific islands, and among Australian aborigines and Native Americans. Tribes may be made up of only 50 to 60 people or, like the Kikuyu of East Africa, have more than a million members. Tribal rule may be by a local chief or, as in some large African tribes, by a king and councillors. Native American Plains tribes, such as the Arapaho and Cheyenne, were ruled by a council of chiefs. In earlier times, the kingdom of Israel united a number of Jewish tribes.
See also: Ethnic group.

Trichina, parasitic roundworm, belonging to the trichina family, that causes an infection known as trichinosis. Larval worms that infect the muscles of animals usually die by themselves; if an infected animal is eaten, however, the larvae can be set free from their cysts (sacs) to invade the intestine of the host and reproduce more larvae. The degree of infection in these cases ranges from mild to fatal. Preventative measures include sufficient cooking and freezing of meat.

Trichinosis *See:* Trichina.

Trier (pop. 93,500), city in southwestern Germany, on the Moselle River. Named for the Treveri, a people of ancient Gaul, the city produces steel, leather goods, and textiles. It is also an important railroad junction and the center of a famous wine district. Trier has been a center of Roman Catholic tradition since the Renaissance.
See also: Germany.

Trieste (pop. 228,400), city-seaport in northeastern Italy at the head of the Adriatic Sea, with steel, oil, and shipbuilding industries. A busy port in Roman times, it was part of Austria (1382-1919) and then of Italy. Claimed by Yugoslavia in 1945, it was made a Free Territory (1947-54), then restored to Italy.
See also: Italy.

Triggerfish, fish belonging to the Balistidae family, found in tropical coastal waters. It measures less than 1.5 ft (46 cm) in length, is colorful, and has a round, flat body. When threatened, it uses one of its spines to "trigger" a spinal enlargement, thus allowing it to lock itself into tight spaces.

Trigonometry, branch of geometry that deals with the ratios of the sides and angles of triangles, particularly of right-angled triangles and the applications of these ratios. Plane trigonometry deals with these relationships mapped on a plane surface. The principle ratios, when considering angle A of right-triangle ABC whose sides opposite the angles A, B, and C respectively are a, b, and c, and where c is the hypotenuse, are:

name	abbreviation	ratio
tangent	tan A	a/b
sine	sin A	a/c
cosine	cos A	b/c
cotangent	cot A	b/a
cosecant	cosec A	c/a
secant	sec A	c/b

As can be seen, the cotangent is the reciprocal of the tangent, the cosecant that of the sine, and the secant that of the cosine. The basis of trigonometric calculations is Pythagoras's theorem, $a^2 + b^2 = c^2$, which in trigonometric form reads $\sin^2 A + \cos^2 A = 1$; this is true for angle A. From these ratios are derived the trigonometric functions, setting y equal to tan x, sin x, etc. These functions are termed transcendental (nonalgebraic). Of particular importance is the sine wave, in terms of which many naturally occurring wave motions, such as sound and light, are studied. Spherical trigonometry studies triangles lying on a sphere, and thus can be used to calculate distances on a globe.

Trillium, colorful wildflower (genus *Trillium*) of North American woodlands and eastern Asia. A member of the lily family, trilliums have 3 sepals, petals, and leaves on each stem. They bloom in early spring, and are also called wake-robins because their flowers appear at the same time robins return north. Colors of the more than 40 varieties include white, pink, dark red, yellow, green, or a painted variety.

Trilobite, extinct marine animal (phylum Arthropoda) from the Paleozoic Era (570-240 million years ago). Scientists have identified about 10,000 species from the fossilized remains of these small (4 in/10 cm) invertebrates. Their name (Latin, "3 lobes") refers to the 3 sections created by 2 lengthwise grooves across their soft, horny shells. The thorax contained many sections, each bearing legs that had gills, enabling the trilobites to breathe.

Trinidad and Tobago

Capital: Port of Spain
Area: 1,980 sq mi
(5,128 sq km)
Population: 1,117,000
Language: English
Government: Presidential republic
Independent: 1962
Head of gov.: Prime minister
Per capita: U.S. $3,770
Mon. unit: 1 Trinidad and
Tobagodollar =
100 cents

Trinidad and Tobago, officially Republic of Trinidad and Tobago, independent republic in the West Indies, consisting of 2 separate islands in the Caribbean Sea north of Venezuela. The island of Trinidad is 1,864 sq mi (4,828 sq km) and Tobago is 116 sq mi (300 sq km). The capital is Port of Spain, on Trinidad.
Land and people. Trinidad is very fertile and mainly flat, rising to c.3,000 ft (914 m) above sea level in the north. Tobago is densely forested and is dominated by a mountain ridge some 1,800 ft (549 m) high. The climate of both islands is tropical. The majority of the people are of black African descent, but more than one-third are East Indian. The principal languages are English and a French patois.
Economy. The country is one of the more prosperous in the Caribbean, producing and exporting sugarcane, cocoa, and bananas, as well as chemicals and petroleum products. Tourism is a growing industry.
History. Trinidad was discovered by Christopher Columbus in 1498 and settled by the Spanish, but British rule was established in 1802. Tobago, once held by the Dutch and French, went to the British in 1803. Combined politically in 1888, Trinidad and Tobago joined the West Indies Federation in 1958 but left in 1962. Eric Williams was premier from independence in 1962 until his death in 1981. During this term, Trinidad and Tobago became a republic (1976). In 1990, a coup attempt against the government of Prime minister Arthur Napoleon Raymond Robinson was diffused when the government promised new elections and amnesty for the rebels. However, rebel leader Iman Yasin Abu Bakr and many of his followers were imprisoned upon their surrender. Economic troubles have recently plagued the country, and severe rioting has taken place in the capital, Port-of-Spain. In 1997 Robinson was elected president.

Trinitrotoluene *See:* TNT.

Trinity, central doctrine of Christian theology, that there is one God who exists in three Persons and one Substance. The definition of the doctrine, implicit in the New Testament, by the early ecumenical councils (notably Nicaea and Constantinople) was the product of violent controversy with heresies like Arianism, Monophysitism, Nestorianism, and Monarchianism.

It is classically summed up in the Athanasian Creed. The three Persons—the Father, the Son (incarnated as Jesus Christ), and the Holy Spirit—are each fully God: coequal, coeternal, and consubstantial, yet distinct. The Son is "eternally begotten" by the Father; the Holy Spirit "proceeds" from the Father and (in Western theology) from the Son. The doctrine is a mystery, being known by revelation and being above reason (though not unreasonable). Hence it has been challenged by rationalists and by sects like the Jehovah's Witnesses and the Mormons.
See also: Christianity; Religion.

Triple Alliance, defense arrangement between Austria-Hungary, Germany, and Italy in the late 19th and early 20th centuries. In 1882 the 3 nations pledged mutual help if any of them were attacked by 2 or more other nations. Germany and Austria-Hungary signed an agreement in 1879 at the prompting of German chancellor Otto von Bismarck, and Italy joined them 3 years later. Serbia also joined in 1882 and Romania in 1883; the name remained Triple Alliance because the 2 Balkan nations were not considered major powers. The alliance was renewed several times before the outbreak of World War I in 1914, but actually broke up when the war started: Italy and Romania fought on the side of the Allies—France, Great Britain, and Russia (the Triple Entente).
See also: World War I.

Triple Entente, defense pact originally formed between France and Russia in 1890 to counterbalance the threat posed by the Triple Alliance—Germany, Austria-Hungary, and Italy—8 years earlier. In 1907 Great Britain joined. Each nation agreed to help the others if attacked by any or all of the Triple Alliance nations. After World War I broke out in 1914, the Triple Entente nations became known as the Allies; they signed the Declaration of London in which each ally agreed not to make a separate peace with the Central Powers, as the Triple Alliance nations came to be called.
See also: World War I.

Tripoli (pop. 500,000), city located in northwestern Lebanon, second largest in the country. A manufacturing center and seaport, its industries include petroleum refining, sponge fishing, textiles and the growing of citrus fruits. The name Tripoli comes from the Arabic *Tarabulus* ("Three Cities") because the city was founded in the 300s B.C. by explorers from 3 different Phoenician cities.
See also: Lebanon.

Tripoli (pop. 990,700), capital and largest city of Libya, located in northwest Libya on an arm of the Mediterranean Sea. Founded in the 600s B.C. by the Phoenicians, it was captured by the Romans in the 1st century B.C. Control passed to the Vandals in the 4th century A.D., the Arabs in the 7th century, the Spanish in 1510, and the Ottoman Turks in 1551. In the early 1800s, Tripoli was a stronghold for the Barbary Pirates, who attacked ships in the Mediterranean and exacted money from their captains in exchange for their freedom. The United States went to war against Tripoli (1801-05) to end the practice. Tripoli was conquered by Italy in 1911 and remained in Italian hands until freed by the Allies during World War II. Today it is a major manufacturing center, shipping port, and oil-refining center. The city was

bombed by the United States in 1986 as a result of Libya's alleged condoning of terrorist activities.
See also: Libya.

Triticale (genus *Triticosecale*), hybrid grain produced by crossbreeding wheat with rye. When developed by botanists in 1876, it could not produce seeds; the development of seed-bearing triticale in the 1930s suggested commercial uses. It has a high yield and is high in protein. It can be bred for special soil and climatic conditions and resistance to disease, and may become an important food for humans and animals.

Tritium, hydrogen isotope that is 3 times heavier than ordinary hydrogen. One of 3 hydrogen isotopes (the others are protium and deuterium), tritium contains 1 proton and 2 neutrons in its nucleus. It is used in the release of nuclear energy through the fusion process. A radioactive gas and a key component of the hydrogen bomb, it is also used in luminous paints and as a tracer. Helium is formed when tritium decays.

Triton, in Greek mythology, sea god with human head and chest and a fishlike tail. Son of the sea god Poseidon and Amphitrite, he lived in a golden palace on the sea floor and stirred or calmed the seas by blowing on a conch shell. He is credited with helping Jason's Argonauts on their journey and with befriending sailors in the seas around ancient Greece. In Virgil's *Aeneid*, Triton is accused of drowning Misenus, a human trumpeter who challenged Triton's skill on the conch shell.
See also: Mythology.

Triumph, Arch of *See:* Arc de Triomphe.

Trogon, bird of the family Trogonidae. Male trogons have dark feathers of green, blue, or violet on their heads and backs and bright feathers of red, orange, or yellow on their undersides. Female trogons are similar but duller in color. Trogons inhabit warm regions in both the Western and Eastern hemispheres.

Trojan horse *See:* Trojan War.

Trojan War, conflict between Greece and Troy, made famous by Homer's *Iliad*. Paris, son of Priam of Troy, carried off Helen, wife of Menelaus of Sparta, and took her to Troy. The Greeks, led by Agamemnon, Menelaus, Odysseus, Achilles, and other heroes, swore to take revenge. They besieged Troy for 10 years; in seeming defeat they pretended to sail away, leaving a huge wooden horse outside the city, with Greek soldiers concealed in its belly. The Trojans took it into the city, and that night the soldiers opened the city gates to the Greek army. Most of the Trojans were killed, the city was burnt, and Helen reclaimed. The legend is thought to have been based on an actual conflict of 1250 B.C.
See also: Greece, Ancient.

Trollope, Anthony (1815-82), English author. His series of 6 books, known as "the Barsetshire novels," (1855-67) are satires that portray the lives of ordinary people in a fictional county (Barsetshire): *The Warden*, *Barchester*

Towers, Doctor Thorne, Framley Parsonage, The Small House at Allington,
and *The Last Chronicle of Barset.* In all he wrote more than 50 books,
including *The Bertrans* (1859), *The Eustace Diamonds* (1873), *The Way We
Live Now* (1875), and *Cousin Henry* (1879).

Trombone, musical instrument, one of the brass wind instruments. It has a
slide mechanism to alter the length of the playing tube and increase the note
range. Developed from a sackbut, it was first used in a symphony by Ludwig
van Beethoven in 1808. There is also a valve trombone, similar to the
trumpet.

Trona, carbonate mineral found in dry regions of the world or extracted from
evaporated brine. It is light-colored, has crystal formations, and is soluble in
water. Trona is a source of soda ash, which is used to manufacture paper,
glass, and chemicals.

Tropical fish, any of a variety of marine and freshwater fish native to the
tropics, but particularly those valued for use in aquariums because they are
ornamental, small, and able to reproduce quickly and easily. The tropical fish
most commonly found in home aquariums are guppies and other freshwater
fish of the Poeciliidae family, bearing live young (rather than eggs). Some
other popular aquarium fish are cichlids, which are egg bearing, and clown-
fish, a saltwater species. Tropical fish range in size from 1-12 in (2.5-30 cm)
and generally eat food made from grains, as well as insects, fish, aquatic
plants, and dried fish.

Tropical rain forest, regions of the world near the equator characterized by
high levels of rainfall and humidity. Vast numbers of unique animal and bird
species inhabit these regions. Vegetation includes many trees that have
significant commercial value. This has resulted in extensive deforestation,
especially in the Amazon rain forest region of South America. This practice
endangers many plant and animal species and poses a threat to the world's
climate system. The temperature in a rain forest ranges from 68°F (20°C) to
93°F (34°C).

Tropic bird, graceful seabird (genus *Phaethon*) with long, trailing tail
feathers. Tropic birds are found in all tropical oceans and are often seen far
out to sea. Their food is fish and squids, which they catch by diving. They
nest under rocks or in crevices on islands. Plumage is generally satiny and
white, with some black.

Tropic of Cancer, imaginary line of latitude showing the northernmost
point on the earth at which the sun can appear directly overhead. The sun's
rays shine straight down on the Tropic of Cancer on June 20 or 21, which is
the summer solstice and the first day of summer in the Northern Hemisphere.
Lying 23°27' north of the equator and encircling the earth, the Tropic of
Cancer also represents the northern boundary of the Tropical Zone.
See also: Latitude; Tropics.

Tropic of Capricorn, imaginary line of latitude showing the southernmost
point on the earth at which the sun can appear directly overhead. The sun's
rays shine straight down on the Tropic of Capricorn on December 21 or 22,

which is the winter solstice and the first day of winter in the Northern Hemisphere. Lying 23°27' south of the equator and running completely around the earth, the Tropic of Capricorn also marks the southern boundary of the Tropical Zone.

Tropics, land and water 1,600 mi (2,570 km) north and south of the equator, as defined by the Tropic of Cancer (23°27' north latitude) and the Tropic of Capricorn (23°27' south latitude). Because the sun's rays are more direct in these latitudes, the tropics generally have warm to hot climates year round with little variation in temperature, and receive sunshine for longer hours each day. Elevation, wind, and proximity to the ocean are also factors that affect weather conditions in the tropics, creating several climatic types, including tropical rain forests, steppes, deserts, and savannas.

Tropism, movement of a plant in response to external directional stimuli. If a plant is laid on its side, the stem will soon start to bend upward again; this movement (geotropism) is a response to the force of gravity. The stem is said to be negatively geotropic. Roots are generally positive geotropic and grow downward. Phototropisms are bending movements in response to the direction of light. Stems are generally positive phototropic (bend toward the light). Most roots are negatively phototropic. Some roots exhibit positive hydrotropism: They bend toward moisture. This response is more powerful than the response to gravity. Tropisms are controlled by differences in concentration of growth hormones.

Troposphere, lowermost zone of the earth's atmosphere, extending from the earth's surface up to 5-6 mi (8-9 km) over the poles and 8-10 mi (12.8-16 km) over the equator. In this zone normal lapse rates prevail, i.e., temperatures decrease with altitude. The top of the troposphere is called the tropopause.
See also: Atmosphere.

Trotsky, Leon (Lev Davidovic Bronstein; 1879-1940), Russian revolutionary Communist, a founder of the USSR. President of the Petrograd (Leningrad) soviet in the abortive 1905 revolution, he escaped from prison to France, Spain, and New York. In 1917 he returned, went over to Bolshevism, and led the Bolshevik seizure of power in the October Russian Revolution. As commissar of foreign affairs (1917-18) he resigned in protest over the Treaty of Brest-Litovsk and became commissar of war (1918-25), organizing the Red Army into an effective force. After V.I. Lenin's death (1924), he lost power to Joseph Stalin and was deported (1929). Bitterly opposed to Stalin's "socialism in one country," he continued to advocate international revolution, founded the Fourth International, and attacked Stalinism in *The Revolution Betrayed* (1937). He was murdered in Mexico City by a Stalinist agent.
See also: Union of Soviet Socialist Republics; Russian Revolution.

Troubadour, name for courtly poet-musicians of Provence, southern France (1100-1300). Their poems, written in Provençal, mostly on the theme of love, were sung. Troubadours developed the conventions of courtly love, and influenced poetry and music in Germany, Italy, Spain, and England. Courtly poets in northern France were called *trouvéres*.

Trout, any of several relatives of the salmon, native to the Northern Hemisphere. Trouts are prized as game and food fishes. Like salmon, trout can be recognized by the fleshy, adipose fin. Some trout spend all their lives in fresh waters, favoring clear, well-aerated streams or lakes, but others live in the sea and return to river beds to breed. Various species include the brown trout, imported from Europe, the rainbow trout of western states, and the red-spotted Dolly Varden. The lake, or mackinaw, trout of deep lakes used to be netted by the ton in the Great Lakes until the arrival of lampreys.

Trout lily *See:* Dogtooth violet.

Troy, city of ancient northwestern Asia Minor, near the Dardanelles, described in Homer's *Iliad* and rediscovered by Heinrich Schliemann in 1870. The earliest site (Troy I) dates from 3000 B.C. Troy II contained an imposing fortress and had wide trade contacts. Its famous treasure of gold, copper, and bronze indicates a wealthy community. Troy VI (2000-1300 B.C.) had a citadel surrounded by huge limestone walls and large houses built on terraces; it was destroyed by earthquake. The rebuilt Troy VlIa was probably Homer's Troy. It was looted and destroyed by fire (c.1250 B.C.). Troy VIII was a small Greek village. Troy IX was the Greek and Roman city of Ilium, or Ilion.
See also: Trojan War.

Trucial states *See:* United Arab Emirates.

Trudeau, Edward Livingston (1848-1915), innovator of tuberculosis treatment in the United States. He founded the Trudeau Sanitarium and in 1894, the Saranac Laboratory, the first U.S. laboratory for tuberculosis research.
See also: Tuberculosis.

Trudeau, Pierre Elliott (1919-   ), Canadian prime minister (1968-79, 1980-84). A law professor, he entered parliament in 1965, became minister of justice in 1967, and succeeded Lester Pearson as prime minister and Liberal Party leader (1968). He sought to promote a dialogue between the provincial and federal governments and to contain the Quebec separatist movement, giving the French language equal status with English. In 1970 he recognized the People's Republic of China. Briefly out of office (1979-80), he returned to cope anew with the constitutional issue that resulted in the Constitution Act (1982), giving Canada its independence from Great Britain.
See also: Canada.

Truffaut, François (1932-84), French film director and critic. A leading New Wave director, he attracted attention for his series of semi-autobiographical films, including *The 400 Blows* (1959) and *Stolen Kisses* (1968). His other films include *Jules and Jim* (1961), *Day for Night* (1973), and *The Last Métro* (1980).

Truffle, underground fungus (genus *Tuber*) that has long been regarded as a delicacy. Pigs and dogs are trained to find them by scent. Some grow up to 2.2 lb (1 kg) and resemble potatoes; most are much smaller. They have not yet been cultivated on a wide scale, but there are attempts underway.

Trujillo Molina, Rafael Leonidas (1891-1961), Dominican Republic dictator (1930-61) and president (1930-38, 1942-52). He introduced much material progress but savagely suppressed political opposition and feuded with neighboring countries. He was assassinated.
See also: Dominican Republic.

Truk Islands, group of islands in the western Pacific, part of the Caroline Islands. All of the major islands and many smaller ones lie within a lagoon almost 40 mi (64 km) wide surrounded by a coral reef. Nearly 40,000 people live on the islands, which were first explored by Europeans in 1825. Possession of the islands passed from Spain to Germany to Japan. After World War II, they came under U.S. control. Today, along with other Caroline Islands, they make up the Federated States of Micronesia.

Truman, Harry S. (1884-1972), 33rd president of the United States. The challenges of Truman's presidency, which began after the sudden death of Franklin D. Roosevelt, included the end of World War II, use of the first atom bomb, the Cold War, the Marshall Plan and NATO, the controversial McCarthy hearings, and the Korean War.
Early life. Truman's poor eyesight kept him out of West Point, so he worked at odd jobs in Kansas City, then on the family farm. During World War I, he served in France as a member of the Missouri National Guard. In 1919, he married Elizabeth Wallace, known as Bess; they had one child. Truman co-owned a men's clothing store that failed in the 1921 farm depression.
Politics. Truman left business to serve as a Jackson Co. judge (1922-24), attend Kansas City School of Law (1923-25), and serve as a chief judge (1926-34). As a U.S. senator (1934-44), Truman chaired a defense-related Senate committee, gaining influence and respect in Congress. In 1944, when a three-way contest developed, Truman became the compromise Democratic vice-presidential candidate. He was elected with incumbent Franklin D. Roosevelt. Only 83 days into his fourth term, President Roosevelt died and Truman became president.
President. Truman's first task was the resolution of World War II. With Stalin and Churchill, he made postwar arrangements for Europe. To end the war in Asia, he twice used the atom bomb on Japan—the first and only times that devastating weapon has been used in war.
Domestically, Truman's conflict with Congress contributed to rising inflation and a wave of strikes. Congress passed the antilabor Taft-Hartley Act

---

Harry S. Truman

33rd president of the United States

Born:	Lamar, Mo.; May 8, 1884
Term:	Apr. 1945-Jan. 1953
Vice president:	Alben W. Barkley (Jan. 1949-Jan. 1953)
Political party:	Democratic
Spouse:	Elizabeth (Bess) Virginia Wallace Truman
Children:	1
Died:	Kansas City, Mo.; Dec. 26, 1972

over Truman's veto, and buried his ambitious Fair Deal program, which included civil rights proposals, a medical insurance plan, and federal aid to education. But eventually he won a higher minimum wage, increased social security, and was able to pass aid-for-housing laws.

Overseas, a "cold war" was growing as the Soviet Union expanded its control over Eastern Europe. Truman announced the Truman Doctrine and the Marshall Plan, which pledged aid for nations resisting Communist takeover. He also supported the 1949 creation of the North Atlantic Treaty Organization (NATO), a military alliance that would defend Western Europe from Eastern-bloc attack.

Truman won the 1948 election to remain in office. In 1950 Sen. Joseph McCarthy launched a campaign to drive Communists, real and imagined, out of government. The investigations grew in fervor until it was finally discredited, but for a time it all but overwhelmed Truman's domestic attention. Also in 1950, Communist North Korea invaded South Korea. Truman immediately sent U.S. troops to Korea, winning UN approval of the "police action." His policy disputes with Gen. Douglas MacArthur, commander of the UN forces (of which 90% were from the United States), led him to dismiss MacArthur in 1951, sparking controversy at home. The Korean War ended by armistice in July 1953; loss of life was heavy on both sides.

Truman survived an assassination attempt in Nov. 1950 and, in 1950-51, congressional exposures of corruption and wrongdoing in some executive agencies. In 1952 he announced that he would not run for reelection.

Retirement. Truman retired to his home in Independence, Mo., to write his memoirs and plan Independence's Harry S. Truman Library and Museum. He died Dec. 26, 1972, in Kansas City, Mo.

Truman Doctrine, U.S. declaration (1947) stating the United States would "support free peoples who are resisting attempted subjugation by armed minorities or by outside pressures." Aimed at halting communist expansion and aggression, the Truman Doctrine provided substantial aid to Greece and Turkey, helping those nations defeat communist guerrillas.

Trumbull, John (1756-1843), U.S. painter. He studied with Benjamin West in London, where he started *The Battle of Bunker's Hill* (1786). He made 36 life-portrait studies for his best known work, *The Signing of the Declaration of Independence* (1786-94), one of his four monumental pictures on Revolutionary themes for the U.S. Capitol rotunda (1817-24). He is also well known for his portraits of George Washington.

Trumbull, Jonathan (1710-85), governor of Connecticut (1769-84). The only governor to support the patriotic cause before the Revolutionary War, he later helped supply colonial troops with ammunition, food, and clothing. A statue of Trumbull was installed at the Capitol Building in Washington, D.C., in 1872.

Trumbull, Lyman (1813-96), U.S. senator from Illinois who supported antislavery legislation. He was one of the originators of the Thirteenth Amendment, which made slavery unconstitutional. He also played an influential role in the passage of the Fourteenth Amendment, which guaranteed the rights of blacks.

Trumpet, musical instrument, one of the brass wind instruments. The modern trumpet comprises a cylindrical tube in a curved, oblong form that flares out into a bell. Three piston valves (first introduced in 1815) regulate pitch. The trumpet is a popular dance and jazz-band instrument, as well as an orchestral instrument.

Trust, in law, legal relationship in which property is administered by a trustee, who has some of the powers of an owner, for the benefit of a beneficiary; the trustee is obliged to act only in the beneficiary's best interest and can derive no advantage except an agreed upon fee. The trustee may be an individual, perhaps looking after the property of a child until it comes of age, or a corporate body; banks and trust corporations often act as trustees of larger properties. Under specialized form, called corporate trust, a group of trustees may hold the stock and thus control the operations of companies that would normally be competitors. The Sherman Antitrust Act (1890) attacked such trust, but enforcement was weakened by U.S. Supreme Court decisions. Enforcement of antitrust legislation has become complicated by the growth of huge conglomerates, which control many companies in different industries.

Trust territory, formerly dependent territory administered under United Nations supervision. A trustee nation was responsible for developing the trust territory and assisting it to independence. The Trusteeship Council helped the General Assembly and Security Council supervise trust territories. Of the 11 trust territories (mostly former mandates of the League of Nations), the U.S.-administered Pacific Islands was the last to be terminated.

Truth, Sojourner (1797?-1883), U.S. abolitionist and feminist. Born into slavery in New York State as Isabella Baumfree, she escaped shortly before slavery was declared unlawful in the state (1828). In 1843, after taking the name Sojourner Truth, she became a traveling preacher. Soon after, she began to speak out against slavery, the first black woman to do so. She was known for her passionate oratorical style, her great energy, and her ready wit. In 1864 she went to Washington, D.C., to work for improved living and working conditions for the black people who settled there after fleeing the South. In the 1870s she tried unsuccessfully to convince the U.S. government to set apart undeveloped land for farms for blacks.
See also: Abolitionism.

Truth table, systematic tabulation of all the possible input/output combinations produced by a binary circuit.

Trypanosome, microscopic unicellular parasite that infests the blood plasma of animals and humans, producing disease; it is transmitted by insects. Trypanosome protozoa are responsible for trypanosomiasis of the African (Changas's disease) varieties, carried by the tsetse fly and certain other bugs. They are relatively insensitive to chemotherapy in established cases; prevention is therefore important.

Tsar, or czar, English spellings of the Russian word for "emperor." The term is used for the rulers of Russia from 1547 to 1917. The last tsar, Nicholas II, was executed in 1918, during the civil war that followed the October 1917 revolution.

Tschaikowsky, Peter Ilich *See:* Tchaikovsky, Peter Ilich.

Tsetse fly, name for 20 species of muscoid flies (genus *Glossina*). They are true winged flies very like houseflies, except that the mouthparts are adapted for piercing the skin of mammals and sucking blood. Widespread in tropical Africa, some species act as vectors of the trypanosomes that cause sleeping sickness.

Tshombe, Moise Kapenda (1919-69), president (1960-63) of the Congolese breakaway state of Katanga. Backed by Belgian interests, he unsuccessfully opposed Prime Minister Patrice Lumumba and the UN. He returned from exile to be premier (1964-65) of the Congo (Zaïre). He died in prison in Algeria.

Tsimshian, Native American tribe, residing in British Columbia along the Nass and Skeena rivers. Known for their seaworthy canoes and elaborate totem poles, the tribe became wealthy during the late 18th and early 19th centuries through trade with European sea merchants exploring the west coast of North America. Tsimshian are known for the potlatch, a complex ceremony marking important events, such as marriages or deaths. There are about 12,000 Tsimshian in British Columbia today.

Tuamotu Islands, group of 75-80 small islands and atolls spanning nearly 1,000 mi (1,609 km) in the South Pacific Ocean. The first European to see the islands (1606) was Pedro Fernandes de Queivós, a Portuguese explorer in the service of Spain. Annexed by France in 1881, the islands now are part of French Polynesia. About 11,000 Polynesians inhabit the Tuamotu Islands, making their living primarily from the sale of pearls and coconut oil.

Tuareg, Berber tribe in the Sahara. Its people are fair skinned and its social system comprises noble families, a large number of vassal tribes, and black slaves. Adult men, but not women, wear a blue veil. Tuareg script is like that of the ancient Libyans.

Tuatara (*Sphenodon punctatus*), reptile resembling the lizard. Inhabitants of a few small islands off the coast of New Zealand, they are the last surviving members of the order Rhynchocephalia, which lived on earth more than 200 million years ago. Green-skinned tuataras have a row of scales down their backs and tails and grow to 2 ft (60 cm) in length. Females carry their eggs for up to a year before depositing them in the ground, where they take another year to hatch. Some tuataras live as long as 77 years.

Tuba, low-pitched brass musical wind instrument with three to five valves. It is held vertically. There are tenor, baritone, euphonium, bass, and contra-bass tubas. They are included in symphony orchestras and in marching bands.

Tuber, swollen, underground stem or root that contains stored food material; they are prennial. The potato is a stem tuber, swells at the tip of a slender underground stem (stolon) and gives rise to a new plant the following year. Dahlia tubers are swollen roots.

Tuberculosis (TB), group of infectious diseases caused by the bacillus *Mycobacterium tuberculosis*, which kills some 3 million people every year throughout the world. TB may invade any organ but most commonly affects the respiratory system, where it has been called consumption or phthisis. In 1906 it killed 1 in every 500 persons in the United States, but today it leads to only 1 in 30,000 deaths because of effective drugs and better living conditions. Symptoms of pulmonary tuberculosis include fatigue, weight loss, persistent cough with green or yellow sputum and possibly with blood. Treatment is mainly by triple drug therapy, with streptomycin, para-aminosalicylic acid (PAS), and isoniazid, together with rest. Recovery takes about 2 years. The tuberculin skin test can show whether a person has some immunity to the disease, though the detection of the disease in its early stages, when it is readily curable, is difficult. Control of the disease is accomplished by preventive measures such as X-ray screening, vaccination, isolation of infectious people, and food sterilization.

Tuberose (*Polianthes tuberosa*), tropical plant of the agave family, native to Asia and America but cultivated elsewhere for its use in perfumes and other products. The tube-shaped root produces a long stem up to 3 ft (91 cm) tall, with sword-shaped leaves and waxy, white, heavily fragrant flowers.

Tubman, Harriet (c.1820-1913), U.S. abolitionist. Born a slave in Maryland, she escaped in 1849. Using her wits, her knowledge of the woods, and her trusted contacts on the Underground Railroad, Tubman conducted 19 rescue missions that freed more than 300 slaves from Maryland. Despite a $40,000 reward for her capture, she was never caught. During the Civil War (1861-65) she served as a nurse and spy for the Union army in South Carolina; after the war, she helped raise money for African-American schools in Auburn, N.Y., and in 1908 she established a home for elderly and needy African Americans.
See also: Abolitionism; Underground Railroad.

Tubman, William Vacanarat Shadrach (1895-1971), president of Liberia (1944-71). He made extensive economic, social, and educational reforms and extended the rights of tribespeople and women.
See also: Liberia.

Tucker, Richard (1914-75), U.S. opera singer. In 1945 Tucker, a lyric tenor, made his debut at the New York Metropolitan Opera as the lead in Amilcare Ponchielli's *La Gioconda*, and went on to sing in the leading opera houses of North America and Europe. Equally versatile in French and Italian, he was a star at the Metropolitan until his death.
See also: Opera.

Tucson (pop. 415,100), city in southeast Arizona, inc. 1877. Founded as a Spanish presidio (walled military outpost) in 1776 by Juan Bautista de Anza, Tucson became part of Mexico in 1821, and, in 1853, control passed to the United States as a result of the Gadsden Purchase. A major research and educational center, Tucson is also a popular tourist destination, transporta-

tion hub, and home of the University of Arizona, several museums, and the San Xavier del Bac Mission, dating from the earliest days of the town. Situated in a valley with mountains on 3 sides, Tucson enjoys a year-round hot, dry, sunny climate that has made it a popular retirement center.
See also: Arizona.

Tudor, Antony (1909-87), English choreographer who introduced dramatic, emotional themes into U.S. ballet. Founder (1939) of the American Ballet Theatre (ABT), his works for the company include *Dark Elegies* (1937) and *Pillar of Fire* (1942). He was also ballet director of the Metropolitan Opera (1957-63) and associate director of the ABT (1974-80).

Tudor, House of, reigning dynasty of England (1485-1603). Of Welsh descent, Henry Tudor, earl of Richmond and heir to the House of Lancaster, ended the Wars of the Roses by defeating Richard III in 1485; he became Henry VII, first Tudor king. The succession included Henry VIII (r.1509-47), Edward VI (r.1547-53), Mary I (r.1553-58), and Elizabeth I (r.1558-1603). Under the Tudors England became a major power and enjoyed a flowering of the arts.
See also: England; United Kingdom.

Tuileries, former royal palace in Paris. Situated on the right bank of the River Seine, the palace was built by order of Catherine de Medici (1564) and was completed in the 1600s. Forced into use as a residence by King Louis XVI and his queen, Marie Antoinette, during the French Revolution (1789), it was also used during the 1790s by revolutionary leaders to hold session and by Napoleon, who made it his primary residence after taking power. After the Bourbon restoration (1814-15) it once again became a royal residence before being destroyed by fire during the Paris Commune uprisings of 1871. The 75-acre (30-hectare) Tuileries Gardens remain affiliated with the Louvre museum.

Tularemia, or rabbit fever, infectious disease due to bacteria (*Pasteurella tularensis*), causing fever, ulceration, lymph node enlargement, and sometimes pneumonia. It is carried by wild animals, particularly rabbits, and insects. Antibiotics are fully effective in treatment.

Tulip, name for plant (genus *Tulipa*) native to Europe and Asia, grown from bulbs. Cultivated tulips were introduced to Europe via Holland in the 16th century and have become popular spring-flowering garden and pot plants. They have deep, cup-shaped flowers; new varieties are continually being bred. Tulips come in a variety of colors and in some instances in a combination of colors.

Tuliptree *See:* Yellow poplar.

Tulsa (pop. 375,300), city in northeast Oklahoma, on the Arkansas River. Settled in the 1830s by members of the Creek tribe, Tulsa grew rapidly after the discovery of oil in 1901. Oil is still a major industry, along with airline, aerospace, and construction-material industries. Completion of the McClellan-Kern Arkansas River Navigation System in 1971, connecting Tulsa with the Gulf of Mexico, made Tulsa a major inland port. The city is also a major

education and cultural hub, with 4 colleges, 2 prominent museums, a ballet company, opera company, and philharmonic orchestra.
See also: Oklahoma.

Tumbleweed, common name for several plants native to North America that grow in clumps on waste land and dry into loose balls. These break from the soil and are blown by the wind, scattering seeds. Examples are the so-called Russian thistle (*Salsola kali*) and *Amaranthus albus*.

Tumboa *See:* Welwitschia.

Tumor, or neoplasm, abnormal overgrowth of tissue. These may be benign proliferations, such as fibroid of the womb, or they may be forms of cancer (lymphoma or sarcoma), which are generally malignant. The rate of growth, the tendency to metastasize (spread locally and to distant sites via the blood vessels and lymph system), and systemic effects determine the degree of malignancy. Tumors may present as a lump, by local compression effects (especially with brain tumors), or by systemic effects, including anemia, weight loss, false hormone actions, neuritis, etc. Treatments include surgery, radiation therapy, and chemotherapy.
See also: Cancer.

Tuna, high-speed fish with rows of finlets on the tail. Also called tunnies, they live in shoals in the warmer seas of the world. The bluefin tuna (*Thunnus thynnus*) of the North Atlantic and Mediterranean grows to 14 ft (4.3 m) long and weighs up to 1,800 lb (816.5 kg). Others, such as the Pacific albacore and yellow-fin tuna, are smaller, but all are important commercial fish. They are caught by net, hook, and harpoon, and their "white meat" is canned. Tuna feed on small fish, eating considerable amounts during the summer months in the northern parts of their ranges before migrating southwards to spawn.

Tundra, plains of the Arctic Circle. For most of the year the temperature is less than 32°F (0°C), and even during the short summer it never rises above 50°F (10°C). The soil is a thin coating over permafrost. Tundra vegetation includes lichens, mosses, and stunted shrubs. Similar regions on high mountains (but generally without permafrost) are called alpine tundra.
See also: Permafrost.

Tungsten, or wolfram, chemical element, symbol W; for physical constants see Periodic Table. Tungsten was discovered by brothers Fausto and Juan José de Elhuyar in 1783. It occurs in wolframite, scheelite, huebnerite, and ferberite. The element is prepared by reduction of the oxide with hydrogen or carbon. It is a steel-gray, hard, ductile, unreactive metal, and has the highest melting point and lowest vapor pressure of all metals. Alloys of tungsten have many high-temperature applications. Tungsten and its compounds are used in filaments for electric lamps and television tubes, fluorescent lighting, glass-to-metal seals, and high-speed tool steels.

Tunis (pop. 596,700), capital city of Tunisia, on the Lake of Tunis, in northeastern Tunisia. Probably established before Carthaginian times, the city was part of the ancient Carthaginian empire until Carthage was destroyed by the Romans in 146 B.C. Later rebuilt, Tunis became a major trading port

Tunisia

Capital:	Tunis
Area:	63,362 sq mi
	(164,150 sq km)
Population:	9,380,000
Language:	Arabic
Government:	Presidential republic
Independent:	1956
Head of gov.:	Prime minister
Per capita:	U.S. $1,820
Mon. unit:	1 Tunesian dinar =
	1000 millimes

that was captured by the Moslems in the 7th century. It was established as the country's capital by the Hafsid dynasty (13th-16th centuries) and was under Turkish rule from 1534 to 1881, when it became a center for piracy as well as trade. The French occupation of Tunisia lasted 1881-1956, after which time the country gained its independence. Today it thrives as a major port and is active in the manufacture of olive oil, textiles, and carpets. Since 1979 it has been the headquarters for the Arab League.
See also: Tunisia.

Tunisia, republic in North Africa. With an area of some 63,362 sq mi (164,150 sq km), Tunisia is bounded on the south by Libya, on the west by Algeria, and on the north and east by the Mediterranean Sea. The Cape Bon peninsula, in the extreme northeast, is only 96 mi (153 km) from Sicily. Tunis is the capital and chief port.

Land. Tunisia's irregular coastline has several good harbors, among them Bizerte. In the northwest, spurs of the Atlas Mountains enter the country from Algeria. The Medjerda River, Tunisia's only permanent river, flows through the northern mountains on its way to the Gulf of Tunis. The Medjerda River valley is a major wheat-producing area. The northern highlands also have dense forests of oak and cork oak, pines, and junipers. The Tabassah Mountains rise in west-central Tunisia and include the country's highest peak, Mt. Sha'nab (5,066 ft/1,544 m). In north-central Tunisia, the dry plain of the Sahel lies between the Atlas and Tabassah mountains and gives way to Tunisia's fertile, heavily populated coastal plain. To the south of the Sahel, beyond the Chott Djerid and other salt lakes, are the Saharan sands and date-palm oases of southern Tunisia. In coastal Tunisia, summers are generally hot and dry; winters are warm and wet. The Sahel has less than 10 in (25 cm) of rain yearly. Rainfall can be irregular and there are sometimes droughts.

People. The people of Tunisia, predominantly Berber and Arab, include small French, Italian, and Maltese minorities. Most people live in the fertile north and some 55% of the population live in towns. The people are overwhelmingly Muslim, and French is spoken, though Arabic is the official language.

Economy. Tunisia's economy is primarily agricultural. The main crops are wheat, barley, and other grains; olives, citrus fruits, dates, and wine grapes; and vegetables. Crude petroleum is the country's principal export, followed by clothing, olive oil, and phosphates. Industry has traditionally centered around food processing, but is expanding.

History. Once a colony of the Phoenicians, Tunisia was the state of the ancient city of Carthage, center of a rich and powerful commercial empire which was conquered by the Romans in 146 B.C. After several centuries of Roman rule, Tunisia was conquered by the Vandals in 439 A.D., by the Byzantines in 533, and by the Arabs in 670. Tunisia saw its heyday as a Muslim state under the Hafsid dynasty, from the 13th to the 16th centuries. Late in the 16th century, Tunisia came under the sway of the Ottoman Turks and the Barbary States were a haven for pirates until Tunisia was made a protectorate by the French in 1881. Tunisia achieved its independence from France in 1957 and became a republic under the presidency and virtual one-man rule of Habib Bourguiba. Bourguiba's dominance was not effectively challenged until 1987, when he was replaced by Gen. Zine al-Abidine Ben Ali.

Tunnel, underground passageway usually designed to carry a highway or railroad, to serve as a conduit for water or sewage, or to provide access to an underground working face. Although tunnels have been built since prehistoric times, tunneling methods remained primitive and hazardous until the 19th century. Modern softground tunneling was pioneered by Marc Brunel, who invented the "tunneling shield" (1824), a device subsequently improved (1869-86) by James Greathead, whose shield is basically a large steel cylinder with a sharp cutting edge driven forward by hydraulic rams. Tunneling through hard rock is facilitated by an array of pneumatic drills mounted on a "jumbo" carriage running on rails. Explosives are inserted in a pattern of holes drilled in the rock face and then detonated. Increasingly, however, automatic tunneling machines called moles, with cutting heads consisting of a rotating or oscillating wheel that digs, grinds, or chisels away the working face, are employed. Another common tunnel-building method— used in constructing the New York subway—is "cut-and-cover," which involves excavating a trench, building the tunnel lining, and then covering it. The world's longest vehicular or railroad tunnel is the 12.3-mi (19.8-km) Simplon II in the Alps, completed in 1922.

Tunney, Gene (James Joseph Tunney; 1898-1978), U.S. world heavyweight boxing champion (1926-28). In 1926 he beat Jack Dempsey in the controversial fight of the "long count." He retired in 1928, having lost only one of his professional bouts.

Tunny *See:* Tuna.

Tupelo, name of several trees belonging to the Nyssaceae family, found in Southeast Asia and in North America. The trees produce small white flowers and fruits, which provide food for many species of birds. The wood of the tupelo is used for making boxes, baskets, and other wooden products. The black tupelo, or Blackgum (*Nyssa sylvatica*), is found in moist areas of the United States and in parts of Canada and Mexico. It grows from 35-80 ft (11-24 m) tall. The water tupelo, or sourgum (*N. aquatica*), is found in swamps in the southeastern United States. It grows as tall as 115 ft (35 m).

Tupí-Guaraní, group of Native American tribes from central and eastern South America. The tribes inhabiting Paraguay and southern Brazil are called Guaraní; those in the Amazon Basin are of the Tupí, or Tupinabá, stock. Practitioners of ritual cannibalism in ancient times, they developed into farmers, hunters, fishers, and fruit gatherers. Under Spanish and Portuguese rule, which began in the 16th century, Jesuit missionaries organized the Tupí-Guaraní people into agricultural settlements, where many of them were converted to Christianity and assimilated into the Western cultural mainstream. Guaraní is still one of the major languages spoken in Paraguay today.

Tupper, Sir Charles (1821-1915), Canadian politican and one of the founders of the Dominion of Canada. He served temporarily as prime minister in 1896 following the resignation of Mackenzie Bowell; however, he lost the election largely due to his support of the reestablishment of French-language schools in Manitoba. Tupper was known as a skilled speaker and politician.
See also: Canada.

Turbine, machine for directly converting the kinetic and/or thermal energy of a flowing fluid (air, hot gas, steam, or water) into useful rotational energy. The working fluid either pushes against a set of blades mounted on the drive shaft (impulse turbines) or turns the shaft by reaction when the fluid is expelled from nozzles (or nozzle-shaped vanes) around its circumference (reaction turbines). Water turbines include the vast inward-flow reaction turbines used in the generation of hydroelectricity and the smaller-scale tangential-flow "Pelton wheel" impulse types used when exploiting a very great head of water. In the 1800s, Charles Alernon Parsons (1854-1931), a British engineer, designed the first successful steam turbines, having realized that the efficient use of high-pressure steam demanded that its energy be extracted in a multitude of small stages. Steam turbines thus consist of a series of vanes mounted on a rotating drum with sator vanes redirecting the steam in between the moving ones. They are commonly used as marine engines and in thermal and nuclear power plants. Gas turbines are not as yet widely used except in airplanes and for peak-load electricity generation.

Turbojet *See:* Jet propulsion.

Turbot (*Psetta maxima*), large flatfish found in the North Sea and Icelandic waters. It has an almost circular body up to 3 ft (91 cm) long, with a warty upper surface. Its an important food fish in Europe. Two American Pacific flatfish are also known as turbot: the curlfin turbot and the "C-O" sole.

Turgenev, Ivan (1818-83), Russian writer whose realistic portrayals of the peasants and nobility of his country helped bring about social reforms and influenced later Russian writers. *A Sportsman's Sketches* (1852), one of his earliest works, is believed to have led to Czar Alexander II's emancipation of the serfs. Other major works include *Rudin* (1856), *A Nest of Gentlefolk* (1859), *On the Eve* (1860), *Fathers and Sons* (1861), *Smoke* (1867), and *Virgin Soil* (1877). Also a playwright, his best-known drama is *A Month in the Country* (1850), which influenced Anton Chekhov. A member of the

Turkey

Capital:	Ankara
Area:	300,948 sq mi
	(779,452 sq km)
Population:	64,567,000
Language:	Turkish
Government:	Republic
Independent:	1923
Head of gov.:	Prime minister
Per capita:	U.S. $2,780
Mon. unit:	1 Turkish lira or pound
	= 100 kurus

landowning class who spent much of his time in Western Europe, Turgenev was one of a group of reformers who believed that Russia should adopt some of the best attributes of Western culture.

Turin (pop. 952,700), city in northwestern Italy. It is a major industrial center, with automobile (Fiat, Lancia), machinery, chemical and electrical industries. It was the capital of the kingdom of Sardinia (1720-1861) and the first capital of united Italy (1861-64).
See also: Italy.

Turkestan, or **Turkistan**, large region in Asia covering parts of China, the former USSR, and Afghanistan. It is so-called because peoples of Turkic ancestry have inhabited this region since the 6th century A.D. From the time of Marco Polo, the area has served as an important trade link between the Asian and European continents. The region, which has no distinct boundaries, has been officially divided into Chinese, Soviet, and Afghan Turkestan. Many of the region's people are Muslim.

Turkey, republic occupying Asia Minor and a small part of southeastern Europe. Lying between the Black and the Mediterranean seas, the Asian and European parts of Turkey are separated by the Straits, a waterway consisting of the Bosporus, the Sea of Marmara, and the Dardanelles. The Straits strategically link the Black Sea with the Mediterranean Sea. Covering 301,382 sq mi (780,574 sq km), Turkey is bounded by Iraq, Syria, and the Mediterranean Sea on the south; the Aegean Sea on the west; Greece and Bulgaria on the north; and Georgia, Armenia, Azerbaijan and Iran in the east. The capital is Ankara.
Land. Asian Turkey is mountainous inland and has an extensive semiarid plateau giving way to narrow coastal lowlands. Mt. Ararat, at 16,945 ft (5,165 m), is Turkey's highest peak, and the Tigris and Euphrates rivers rise in the east. Earthquakes are frequent. European Turkey, which is actually eastern Thrace, is fertile hill country and the site of the city of Istanbul, formerly Constantinople. The climate is Mediterranean around the coastal lowlands and the European section, but drier and subject to greater extremes inland on the Asian side, with harsh winters toward the northeast.

People. The Turks are largely descended from the Tatars, who entered Asia Minor in the 11th century A.D. There are small Kurdish, Arab, and Orthodox Christian minorities. The people are overwhelmingly Muslim. The official language is Turkish.

Economy. Agriculture is the basis of the economy. The chief crops are grains, cotton, fruits, and tobacco. Cattle are raised on the Anatolian plateau, in the western reaches of Asian Turkey. Turkish industry has been developed greatly since World War II and includes steel, iron, and textile manufacturers. There are large deposits of coal, iron, and other metals, and some oil.

History. Anatolia was the cradle of ancient civilizations, dating back to at least 7000 B.C. Its famous sites include Troy, Ephesus, and the Hittite capital of Hattusas. Turkey was, successively, part of the Hittite, Persian, Roman, Seljuk, and Ottoman empires. Its western coast was, for a time, the site of some of the most brilliant city-states of the ancient Greeks, including Halicarnassus and Miletus. The Ottoman Empire, with its center in Turkey, was founded in the 13th century and endured until it was formally dissolved after World War I. Modern Turkey was largely the work of Mustafa Kemal Atatürk, who declared the republic in 1923. Atatürk initiated an ambitious program of reform and modernization aimed at establishing Turkey as a modern nation-state on the European model. His reforms ranged from changing the alphabet to emancipating women. Atatürk died in 1938 and Turkey remained neutral for most of World War II. Afterwards, the country joined NATO and received substantial U.S. aid. Turkey has undergone 2 major military coups since the end of World War II, one in 1960 and another in 1980. Tension with Greece has almost led to war on several occasions. In 1974, Turkey invaded and occupied the northern third of the island of Cyprus. The central government has also fought intermittently with Kurds in Anatolia. Civilian rule returned to Turkey in 1983 with the election of Turgut Ozal to the presidency. In 1996, for the first time in Turkey a Muslim fundamentalist (Necmettin Erbakan) became prime minister. Entry into the EU became problematic.

Turkey, name of two species of large New World game birds, family Meleagrididae. The common turkey (*Meleagresi gallopavo*) is found in the open woodland and scrub of North America, and is the ancestor of the domestic turkey. The head and neck of both species are naked and have wattles; a fleshy caruncle overhangs the bill. The naked skin in the common turkey is red; in the ocellated turkey, blue.

Turkish, Turkic language, official language of Turkey, also spoken by minorities in eastern Europe and southwestern Asia. Evolved during the Ottoman Empire, it was written in Arabic script until Atatürk introduced a modified Latin alphabet in 1928.

Turkmenistan (Republic of), independent country in central Asia, bordering Kazakhstan and Uzbekistan in the north, Afghanistan in the southeast, Iran in the south, and the Caspian Sea in the west.

Land and climate. The Kara Kum desert covers about 90% of the landmass in this region. The country has a desert climate with hot summers and cold winters.

People. Most of the population are Muslims, who speak a Turkic language: Turkmen. Russians, Uzbeks, and Kazakhs are important minorities. The

Turkmenistan

Capital:	Ashkhabad
Area:	188,456 sq mi
	(488,100 sq km)
Population:	4,297,000
Language:	Turkmenian
Government:	Presidential republic
Independent:	1991
Head of gov.:	President
Per capita:	U.S. $920
Mon. unit:	1 Turkmenian manat =
	100 tenge

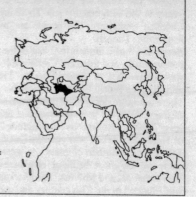

majority of the population lives in the southeast, where the capital city of Ashkhabad is located.

Economy. The major products are related to their herds of Karakul sheep and Turkoman horses. In the late 19th century Turkmenistan came under Russian rule; it became part of the USSR (Soviet Union) in 1920 and a constituent republic in 1925. Turkmenistan declared its sovereignity in 1990 and became fully independent in 1991. In spite of the large gas supplies the economy developed slowly. In 1997 a connection with the Iranian gasmain was established.

See also: Union of Soviet Socialist Republics.

Turks, family to Turkic-speaking, chiefly Muslim people extending from Sinkiang (west China) and Siberia to Turkey, Iran, and former East European USSR. They include the Tatars, Kazakhs, Uzbeks, Kirghiz, Turkmens, Vighurs, Azerbaijanis, and many others. The Turks spread through Asia from the 6th century onward and were converted to Islam in the 10th century. In the west they controlled vast lands under the Seljuks (1000s-1200s) and the Ottoman Empire (1300s-1923).

Turks and Caicos Islands, two British colonial island groups in the West Indies. They cover 166 sq mi (430 sq km) of land in the southeastern part of the Bahama Islands group. The chief economic activity is the exportation of lobster, hemp, and sponges. Many of the region's inhabitants fish for a living.

Turner, Frederick Jackson (1861-1932), U.S. historian. His view of the role of the frontier in shaping U.S. individualism and democracy was influential. *The Frontier in American History* (1920) reprinted earlier papers. He won a Pulitzer Prize for his study of sectionalism in the United States (1932).

Turner, John Napier (1929-   ), prime minister of Canada following the resignation of Prime Minister Pierre Trudeau. In 1984, after having served 2 1/2 months, Turner called a general election and lost to Progressive Conservative candidate Brian Mulroney. Turner had previously held a variety of posts in the cabinets of prime ministers Lester Pearson and Pierre

Trudeau. A Liberal Party member, he was interested in developing social programs to help the nation's poor and unemployed.
See also: Canada.

Turner, J(oseph) M(allard) W(illiam) (1775-1851), English Romantic landscape painter. His work is famous for its rich treatment of light and atmosphere, in oil, watercolor, or engraving. His paintings include *The Fighting Téméraire* (1839) and *Rain, Steam and Speed* (1844).

Turner, Nat (1800-31), U.S. slave and revolutionary. Born on a plantation in Southampton County, Va., he believed that God had chosen him to free the slaves. He gathered 60-70 other slaves and led them in what came to be known as the most serious slave rebellion in the nation's history. About 60 whites were killed, including the family of Turner's owner, Joseph Travis, before the Virginia militia suppressed the revolt 6 weeks later, capturing and hanging Turner and about 20 of his followers. Although the rebellion led to reprisals and stricter laws against slaves, Turner became a symbol for the abolitionist movement.

Turnip, plant (genus *Brassica*) native to Europe and Asia. It was developed into a root crop, mainly for cattle feed, in the 19th century. Its swollen, yellowish-white taproot is packed with starch and is fit for human consumption. If left in the ground over the winter, the turnip sends up a flowering stem, using food stored in the root during its first year.
See also: Starch.

Turnstone, one of two types of shore birds belonging to the sandpiper family. It characteristically uses its short bill to turn over stones in search of food. The ruddy turnstone is found in arctic regions of the world. The black turnstone is native to the Bering Sea region and migrates to southern Alaska and California for the winter.

Turquoise, $AL_2(OH)_3PO_4H_2O+Cu$, igneous (volcanic) mineral containing aluminum, copper, and phosphorus, found in arid regions of the earth, especially Iran, the Sinai Peninsula, and the North American Southwest. Varying in color from light blue (gem quality) to greenish-gray, turquoise has been used to make jewelry for thousands of years. Native American tribes of the Southwest, especially the Navajos, became skilled in fashioning turquoise-and-silver jewelry.

Turtle, reptile (order Chelonia) with a shell that almost encloses the body. A land turtle is sometimes called a tortoise, and some freshwater turtles are given the name terrapin. The turtle has existed for more than 175 million years, and there are now about 230 species spread over the warmer parts of the world, 44 of them in the United States. Some species are becoming rare because they are hunted for their flesh or for their shells. The turtle's shell is made of two parts—the upper carapace and the lower plastron. The vertebrae and ribs are fused to the carapace. The shell is covered with horny plates, except in the soft-shell and the leathery turtle, where it has a leathery covering. There are five kinds of marine turtles: the leathery turtle and the green, hawksbill, loggerhead, and ridley turtles. Except for the last, all are found in North American waters. All come ashore to lay their eggs in sandy beaches: Freshly hatched turtles have to rush down to the shore after hatching to avoid predators. The green turtle is the species most used for turtle soup, and the hawksbill provides tortoise shells. The land and freshwater turtles are smaller than the marine turtles. They range from 2-in (5-cm) mud turtles to the 2-ft (61-cm) 100-lb (45-kg) alligator snapping turtle or "stinkpot", the reptilian equivalent of the skunk. The box turtles have a hinged plastron so that they can completely shut themselves in their shells.

Turtledove, woodland bird belonging to the pigeon and dove family. It is native to Europe and parts of Asia and Africa. During the winter, it migrates south to the sub-Saharan continent. A small, shy bird, it is often recognized by its sad, cooing song.

Tuscany, region in west-central Italy, extending from the Apennine Mountains to the west coast. It is mostly mountainous, with fertile river valleys and coastal strip. Agricultural products include cereals, olive oil, and Chianti wine. Iron and other minerals are mined; the chief manufactures are textiles, chemicals, and machinery. Center of the ancient Etruscan civilization, Tuscany has many famous cities, including Florence, Lucca, Pisa, and Siena.

Tuscarora, North American Native American tribe. Driven from their lands in North Carolina by European-American settlers, the Tuscaroras joined the Iroquois League in 1722. Some hundreds now live in New York State and Ontario, Canada.

Tussock moth, type of moth belonging to the Lymantriidae family. Caterpillars of the species have brightly colored hair, but adults are whitish-gray in color. Some varieties, such as the gypsy moth, were brought to the United States from Europe. Tussock moths often cause extensive damage to trees and orchards.

Tutankhamen (fl.c.1350 B.C.), Egyptian pharaoh. Though he died at 18, he gained modern-day fame when his tomb was discovered in Thebes by Howard Carter and the earl of Carnarvon in 1922 with its treasures intact. His solid gold coffin, gold portrait mask, and other treasures are housed in the Cairo museum.
See also: Egypt, Ancient.

Tutu, Desmond (1931-   ), South African black minister, recipient of the 1984 Nobel Peace Prize. In 1957 Tutu was named the first black Anglican dean of Johannesburg. In 1978 he was appointed general secretary of the South African Council of Churches, elected bishop of Johannesburg in 1984, and archbishop of Cape Town in 1986. He has been a consistent opponent of apartheid. In 1995, he became chairman of the Commission for Truth and Reconciliation, which investigates violations of human rights during the apartheid era.

Tutuila *See:* American Samoa.

Tuva, republic of the Russian Federation between Siberia and Mongolia. Formerly a Russian protectorate, the region became the autonomous republic of Tannu Tuva in 1921. In 1944, it was annexed by the USSR and its name changed to Tuva. Most of the region's inhabitants are descended from

Tuvalu

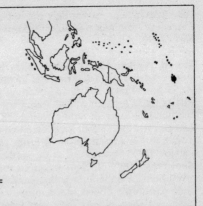

Capital:	Funafuti
Area:	10 sq mi
	(26 sq km)
Population:	10,444
Language:	Tuvaluan
Government:	Parliamentary
	monarchy
Independent:	1978
Head of gov.:	Prime minister
Per capita:	U.S. $330
Mon. unit:	1 Australian dollar =
	100 cents

Turkic-speaking peoples and raise animals for a living. Tuva exports animal hides and wool; its mineral resources include gold, asbestos, and cobalt. *See also:* Union of Soviet Socialist Republics.

Tuvalu (formerly Ellice Islands), independent Commonwealth nation composed of nine small atolls spread over more than 500,000 sq mi (1,295,000 sq km) in the West Pacific. The capital is Fongafale on Funafuti.
Land and climate. The largest island, Vaitupu, covers only 2 sq mi (5.2 sq km). No spot on these coral atolls rises more than 16 ft (4.9 m) above sea level. The soil is poor and there are no rivers and little vegetation besides coconut palms. The average annual temperature is 86°F (30°C); most of the rainfall occurs between Nov. and Feb.
People and economy. The inhabitants are Polynesian, with almost 30% living on the island of Funafuti. Copra is the only export, although the sale of postage stamps abroad also produces income.
History. The islands were largely ignored by Europeans until the 19th century, when whaling began in the area. The population was reduced from 22,000 to 3,000 between 1850 and 1875 because of disease and forcible recruitment for labor abroad. A British protectorate over both the Ellice and Gilbert (now Kiribati) islands was established in 1892. In 1974 Ellice Islanders voted for separate status, achieving independence in 1978.

TV *See:* Television.

TVA *See:* Tennessee Valley Authority.

Twain, Mark (Samuel Langhorne Clemens; 1835-1910), U.S. author and popular humorist and lecturer. After being a printer's apprentice (1848-53), he led a wandering life, becoming a Mississippi river pilot (1857-61) and then a journalist, establishing a reputation with his humorous sketches. In 1869 he produced his first best-seller, *The Innocents Abroad*, followed by *The Adventures of Tom Sawyer* (1876), *The Prince and the Pauper* (1882), his masterpiece *Huckleberry Finn* (1884), and the satirical *A Connecticut Yankee in King Arthur's Court* (1889). In later life, Twain lost most of his money through speculation and suffered the loss of his wife and daughters.

His works became increasingly pessimistic and bitingly satirical, as in *The Tragedy of Pudd'nhead Wilson* (1894) and *The Man Who Corrupted Hadleyburg* (1899).

Tweed, William Marcy 'Boss' (1823-78), U.S. politician. Born in New York City, Tweed was a member of the U.S. House of Representatives (1853-55). Afterwards, he held various powerful positions in New York City politics, including New York City school commissioner (1856-57) and commissioner of public works (1870). Through his control of the Tammany organization, he affected nominations and patronage in New York City Democratic politics. From 1867 to 1871, he served as a state senator. He is best known as the leader of the Tweed Ring, a group of New York City politicians infamous for swindling the city treasury out of millions of dollars through contracts for city improvements. Due in large part to the efforts of the magazine *Harper's Weekly* and political cartoonist Thomas Nast, the Tweed Ring was finally exposed, and Tweed himself was convicted and jailed in 1873 on charges of corruption. He died in jail.

Tweed River, waterway forming part of the Scotland-England border. It rises in southeastern Scotland and flows into the North Sea. In the 19th century, mills were built along the river to produce water power for local textile factories. The name of the cloth known as tweed may come from the name of the river.

Twelve Tables, Laws of the, earliest Roman code of laws. Created by decemvirs (members of a council of 10 men) who based the laws on earlier Roman customs, the Laws of the Twelve Tables were written on tablets (450 B.C.) and displayed in the forum. They contained civil, criminal, and sacred legal precepts and became revered as a prime source of law. Only fragments survive.
See also: Rome, Ancient.

Twelve-tone music, or serial music, type of music developed in the 1920s that rejects tonality as the basis for composition. Its most famous exponent, Arnold Schoenberg, laid down a method of composition that attempted to free music from the 8-note octave and its associated conventions. Twelve-tone compositions are constructed around a specific series of the twelve notes of the chromatic scale. Later 20th-century composers have used the twelve-tone construction with greater freedom. Composers of twelve-tone music include Igor Stravinsky, Roger Sessions, Walter Piston, Ernst Krenek, Domitry Shostakovich, and Schoenberg's pupils Anton von Webern and Alban Berg.

Twelve Tribes, twelve family groups into which the ancient Hebrews were divided. According to the Bible they were descended from and named for ten sons of Jacob and two sons of Joseph. Those descended from Jacob's sons were Asher, Benjamin, Dan, Gad, Issachar, Judah, Naphtali, Reuben, Simeon, and Zebulun; the two from Joseph's sons were Ephraim and Manasseh. When the Hebrews finally reached the Promised Land, they divided the country among these twelve family groups. A thirteenth tribe, Levi, third son of Jacob, had no portion of land set aside for it.

John Tyler

10th president of the United States
Born: Charles City Co.; Mar. 29, 1790
Term: Apr. 1841-Mar. 1845
Vice president: None
Political party: Whig
Spouses: Letitia Christian Tyler; Julia Gardiner Tyler
Children: 15
Died: Richmond, Va.; Jan. 18, 1862

Tyler, John (1790-1862), 10th president of the United States. Tyler, the first United States vice president to step into the presidency on a president's death in office, entered politics as a Democrat but was elected as a Whig. As president, however, he so opposed the Whigs' program that he was expelled from the party, burned in effigy, and threatened with impeachment. Most of his cabinet resigned in anger.

Early life. Tyler graduated from William and Mary College in 1807; studied law under his father, a former Virginia governor; then was admitted to the Virginia bar in 1809. At age 21, he was elected to the Virginia House of Delegates. In 1813, Tyler married Letitia Christian; they had eight children.

Politics. Tyler served in the U.S. House of Representatives (1816-21), in the Virginia legislature (1823-25), as governor of Virginia (1825-1827), and as a U.S. senator (1827-36). A political conservative, Tyler believed in a narrow interpretation of the Constitution, and that the powers of the federal government should be strictly limited. In 1836, when the Virginia legislature instructed him to support President Andrew Jackson, who stood for a powerful federal government, Tyler resigned from the Senate instead. Although Tyler had broken with the Democrats, he had always opposed favorite measures of the Whigs. Even so, the Whigs, seeking to rally all anti-Jackson forces, nominated Tyler for the vice presidency in 1840. He ran with William Henry Harrison under the slogan "Tippecanoe and Tyler too." The Whig ticket won. Within a month after the inauguration in 1841, however, Harrison died and Tyler became president. It was the first time a U.S. vice president succeeded a president in office.

President. Tyler soon angered his Whig supporters. When the Whigs presented a nationalist program, including a National Bank, Tyler vetoed the bill. When he vetoed another bill in September, his entire cabinet, except Secretary of State Daniel Webster, resigned. Tyler was expelled from the Whig party and there was an unsuccessful attempt to impeach him.

Under Tyler, the United States and Britain signed the Webster-Ashburton Treaty defining the Canadian border and committing both nations to police the illegal African slave trade. Tyler ended the Seminole War in Florida, backed Morse's telegraph system, reorganized the Navy, and signed the Preemption Act that helped settle much of the Midwest.

Tyler's determination to bring Texas into the Union reopened the slavery controversy, as the North opposed its entry as a slave state. With no hope of reelection in 1844, Tyler pushed hard to win annexation for Texas. On Mar. 1, 1845, after much debate and political wrangling, he signed the bill admitting Texas to the Union. Two days later, on his last day in office, he signed another bill, admitting Florida.

Retirement. Tyler's wife, Letitia, had died in 1842. In 1844, he had married Julia Gardiner; the couple had seven children. Tyler retired to Virginia, but continued to take part in politics. In 1861, he led a peace conference in Washington, hoping to avert civil war. When the Senate rejected the Southerners' terms, he returned to Virginia and voted for itss secession. He was elected to the Confederate House of Representatives in Nov. 1861, but died on Jan. 18, 1862, before taking his seat.

Tyler, Moses Coit (1835-1900), critic and historian of early U.S. literature. He was appointed professor of American history at Cornell University in 1881, the first such position in the United States. He helped to found the American Historical Association in 1884. His books include the 2-volume *The Literary History of the American Revolution 1763-1783*, published in 1897.

Tyler, Wat (d. 1381), leader of the English Peasant's Revolt (1381), England's first popular rebellion. Protesting high taxation after the Black Death, Tyler and his Kentish followers captured Canterbury, then took the Tower of London. Richard II promised abolition of serfdom and feudal service. At a second meeting with the king, Tyler was stabbed, and the revolt was brutally crushed.

Tylor, Sir Edward Burnett (1832-1917), British anthropologist. A pioneer in the field, he was an authority on animism and primitive mentality. His books *Research into the Early History of Mankind* (1865) and *Primitive Culture* (1871) were among the earliest works on anthropology as a social science. Additional theories were expounded in *Anthropology* (1881). *See also:* Anthropology.

Tyndale, William (c.1494-1536), English biblical translator. A Roman Catholic priest, he translated the New Testament from Greek and Hebrew to the English vernacular in his effort to stem church corruption, but he was unable to get his work published in England. He left for Germany in 1524, where he succeeded; he then had copies smuggled into England. While in Germany, he befriended Martin Luther and was strongly influenced by him. Despite the ban on his translated Bibles in England, Tyndale wrote tracts defending the English Reformation. In 1535 he was arrested by Roman Catholic authorities in Antwerp, Belgium, tried and convicted of heresy, and the following year was executed. His translations form the basis of the King James (Authorized) Version of the Bible, which is in common usage today. *See also:* Bible.

Type, characters, including letters, numbers, and punctuation marks, assembled to form words and sentences in the printing of books, magazines, and newspapers. Type consists of thousands of styles, or type faces (fonts), that fall into 4 categories: Roman type, with small finishing strokes (serifs) that extend outward from the characters; sans-serif type, lacking the serifs; script type, which closely resembles actual handwriting; and italic type, which is slanted to the right. Type size is measured by "points" in North America and England. One point equals 0.012837 in (0.3514598 mm) and most type ranges from 6 to 72 points. Movable type was invented in Asia in the 11th century and was introduced to Europe by Johannes Gutenberg in the 1440s.

Type was later cast in lead and set by hand or machine. Today most type is set on computers programmed for correct size, style, and line width.
See also: Printing.

Typewriter, writing machine activated manually or electrically by means of a keyboard. In the classic model, when a key is depressed, a pivoted bar bearing a type character strikes an inked ribbon against a sheet of paper carried on a cylindrical rubber "platen." The platen carriage then automatically moves a space to the left. In some electric models all type is carried on a single rotatable sphere that moves from left to right and strikes a fixed platen. The first efficient typewriter was developed in 1868 by C.L. Sholes.
See also: Sholes, Christopher Latham.

Typhoid fever, infectious disease due to *Salmonella typhosa*, causing fever, a characteristic rash, lymph node and spleen enlargement, gastrointestinal tract disturbance with bleeding and ulceration, and usually marked malaise or prostration. It is contracted from other cases or from disease carriers, with contaminated food and water as major vectors. Carriers must be treated with antibiotics (and have their gall bladder removed if this site is the source). Vaccination may help protect high-risk persons; antibiotics (e.g., chloramphenicol) form the treatment of choice.

Typhus, infectious disease caused by rickettsia and carried by lice, leading to a feverish illness with a rash. Severe headache typically precedes the rash, which may progress to skin hemorrhage; mild respiratory symptoms of cough and breathlessness are common. Death ensues in a high proportion of untreated adults, usually with profound shock and kidney failure. Recurrences may occur in untreated patients who recover from their first attack, often after many years. A similar disease due to a different but related organism is carried by fleas (murine typhus). Chloramphenicol or tetracyclines provide suitable antibiotic therapy.

Tyrannosaurus *See:* Dinosaur; Prehistoric animal.

Tyre, or Sur (pop. 23,000), town in southwest Lebanon, situated on the eastern end of the Mediterranean Sea. A thriving seaport under the Phoenicians, Tyre was ruled by Egypt before 1000 B.C. From 1100 to 573 B.C. it enjoyed its most prosperous period, which included the founding of Carthage (9th century), and was a major cultural, intellectual, and commercial center, famous for its purple dye and high-quality ceramics. In 332 B.C. Alexander the Great conquered Tyre and built a causeway that connected what was then the island of Tyre to the mainland, creating a peninsula, site of the present-day city of Tyre. The city later fell under the control of the Roman and Byzantine empires and was captured by the Crusaders in 1124, before being overrun and destroyed by the Muslims in 1291. Tyre was taken by Israeli forces in 1982 during their invasion of Lebanon.

Tyrol, or Tirol, state in western Austria. Over half its original area was ceded to Italy in 1919. Austria's highest peak, Grossglockner (12,461 ft/3,798 km), is located there. Farming, lumber, and tourism are its main sources of income. The capital is Innsbruck.

Tyron, William (1729-88), English governor of North Carolina (1765-71). In 1771, after harshly crushing the revolt of the Regulators at the Battle of Alamance, he was appointed governor of New York.

Tyrrhenian Sea, part of the Mediterranean Sea bounded by the west coast of Italy and by the islands of Corsica, Sardinia, and Sicily. The Strait of Messina in the south connects it with the Ionian Sea.

Tyson, Mike (1966-), U.S. boxer. He won the World Boxing Council heavyweight title in 1986 to become the youngest winner of a boxing championship to date. In 1987 he went on to win the World Boxing Association (WBA) and International Boxing Federation (IBF) titles. He lost his heavyweight titles after being knocked-out by James "Buster" Douglas in 1990. From 1992-95 he was imprisoned on charge of a sexual assault. Afterwards he returned into the boxing ring. In 1996 he was suspended after biting off a piece of his opponent's ear.
Sardinia, and Sicily. The Strait of Messina in the south connects it with the Ionian Sea.

Tyson, Mike (1966-), U.S. boxer. He won the World Boxing Council heavyweight title in 1986 to become the youngest winner of a boxing championship to date. In 1987 he went on to win the World Boxing Association (WBA) and International Boxing Federation (IBF) titles. He lost his heavyweight titles after being knocked-out by James "Buster" Douglas in 1990. From 1992-95 he was imprisoned on charge of a sexual assault. Afterwards he returned into the boxing ring. In 1996 he was suspended after biting off a piece of his opponent's ear.

U

U, 21st letter of the English alphabet, corresponding to the Semitic letter *waw*, meaning "hook," represented by a tenthook symbol and probably derived from an ancient Egyptian symbol for a pole support. The Greeks altered it to *Y*, and as the 20th letter of the Roman alphabet it became *V*, representing both *U* and *V* sounds. The use of *U* for the *U* sound dates from the Middle Ages. *U* is also the chemical symbol for the element uranium.

U-2, U.S. spy plane used during the 1950s and 1960s. The U-2 was effective because it could fly at extremely high altitudes of 70,000 ft (21,100 m) and photograph military installations on the ground. It became the focus of international attention when a U-2 was shot down while flying over the USSR in 1960, at the height of the Cold War between the United States and the USSR.
See also: Cold War.

U-235, any of the different forms of an isotope of the element uranium with a mass number of 235 (the number of protons and neutrons in the atom's nucleus). When found in minerals, U-235 is always combined with the isotopes U-234 and U-238. Separating the natural U-235 from the other isotopes produces a more potent form of U-235, which is used in atomic bombs and nuclear reactors because it easily undergoes fission. The use of

U-235 in nuclear reactors produces extremely toxic isotopes of other elements, such as strontium 90. U-235 was used in the atomic bombs that the United States dropped on Hiroshima and Nagasaki, Japan, in 1945.
See also: Nuclear energy; Radioactivity.

U-238 *See:* Uranium.

U.A.R.

Ubangi River, chief northern tributary of the Zaïre (Congo) River, in central Africa. Formed by the junction of the Mbomu and Uele rivers, it flows 700 mi (1,130 km) west and south, forming part of Zaïre's northwest border with the Central African Republic.

U-boat *See:* Submarine.

Ucayali River, chief headstream of the Amazon, in northern Peru. Formed by the junction of the Urubamba and Apurímac rivers in central Peru, it flows 1,000 mi (1,600 km) north to the Marañón River southwest of Iquitos.
See also: Amazon River.

Uccello, Paolo (c.1397-1475), Florentine early Renaissance painter, noted for his use of perspective. His best-known works are the *Creation* and *Noah* scenes (1431-50) in Santa Maria Novella, Florence, and the three richly decorative panels of *The Battle of San Romano* (1455-60).
See also: Renaissance.

Udall, Nicolas (1505-56), English schoolmaster, scholar, and playwright. Headmaster of Eton (1534-41) and of Westminster (1554-56), he wrote the first known English comedy, *Ralph Roister Doister* (c. 1553).

Uffizi Palace, 16th-century palace in Florence, Italy, built by Giorgio Vassari for Cosimo I de' Medici as a public office building. It houses one of the world's finest art collections, rich in classical, Dutch, Flemish, and Italian Renaissance paintings and sculptures.
See also: Florence.

UFO *See:* Unidentified flying object.

Uganda, landlocked republic in east-central Africa. Covering 93,070 sq mi (241,040 sq km), Uganda is bordered by Tanzania and Rwanda in the south, Sudan in the north, Zaïre in the west, and Kenya in the east. The capital is Kampala.
Land and People. More than 80% of the land area of Uganda consists of a fertile plateau some 3,000 to 5,000 ft (914-1,524 m) above sea level, with highlands to the east and west. About 16,386 sq mi (42,440 sq km) of Uganda consists of freshwater lakes and swamps. At the center of the plateau that dominates the country is Lake Kyoga. Other lakes are lakes Edward, Albert, George, and Victoria. Although Uganda is a tropical country, crossed by the equator, its altitude ensures a comparatively mild climate. Almost all Ugandans are black Africans, the majority belonging to one of several Bantu-spea-

Uganda

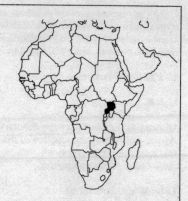

Capital:	Kampala
Area:	93,070 sq mi
	(241,040 sq km)
Population:	22,167,000
Language:	English, Swahili
Government:	Presidential republic
Independent:	1962
Head of gov.:	Prime minister
Per capita:	U.S. $240
Mon. unit:	1 Ugandan shilling =
	100 cents

king groups. The Baganda people of the south are the most numerous of these. More than half of the people are Christians, with a small minority of Muslims; the rest of the people adhere to animist beliefs. The official languages are English and Swahili.

Economy. Uganda's economy is agricultural and most farms are small, growing subsistence crops and raising livestock. Despite severe economic dislocation under Idi Amin Dada, Uganda remained one of the world's major producers of coffee, which accounts for almost all of its export earnings. Copper is the principal mineral.

History. The Bunyoro Kingdom of Bantu-speaking people that flourished in the 16th and 17th centuries and dominated Uganda was succeeded by the Baganda Kingdom, which came under the British in 1894. The British protectorate was gradually extended to other kingdoms, and by 1914 the present boundaries of Uganda became fixed. In 1962, Uganda became independent and was governed by Milton Obote until he was deposed by Maj. Gen. Idi Amin Dada in 1971. In 1972, Amin expelled Uganda's Asian population and established a brutal and bizarre reign of terror that cost some 300,000 Ugandans their lives and brought the nation to near total ruin. In 1979, Tanzania invaded Uganda and Idi Amin fled. By 1980, Milton Obote had been returned to power only to be replaced, 3 years later, by Gen. Tito Okello. Okello was overthrown by the National Resistance Army of Yoweri Museveni, who was sworn in as president in 1986. At the end of the 1990s, Ugandan troops were involved in armed conflicts in southern Africa.

Ugarit, ancient capital city of the Ugarit Kingdom of northwestern Syria, discovered in 1929 by French archeologists. Settled in the 5th millennium B.C., it flourished in the 15th and 14th centuries B.C. Numerous cuneiform tablets have revealed much information about the Ugarit language, related to biblical Hebrew.

UHF waves *See:* Ultrahigh frequency waves.

Ukraine (Republic of), independent country in Eastern Europe, bordered by Poland to the northwest; by Slovakia, Hungary, Romania, and Moldavia to

Ukraine

Capital:	Kiev
Area:	233,090 sq mi
	(603,700 sq km)
Population:	50,125,000
Language:	Ukrainian
Government:	Republic
Independent:	1991
Head of gov.:	Prime minister
Per capita:	U.S. $1,630
Mon. unit:	1 Hryvna = 100
	kopiyka's

the southwest; by the Black Sea and the Sea of Azov to the south; by Russia to the northeast and east; and by Byelorussia to the north. The capital is Kiev.
Land and climate. Ukraine consists for a large part of lowlands, with mountains on the Crimean and in the west: the Carpathian Mountains. The country has a moderate continental climate, with a subtropical climate in the Crimean peninsula.
People. About 75% of the population is Ukrainian, and Russians form the largest minority. The official language is Ukrainian. The population belongs to either the Ukrainian Orthodox Church or the Greek Orthodox Church.
Economy. The economy is based on heavy industry. Principal crops are sugar beets and potatoes. Important industrial cities include Kharkov, Donetsk, and Dnepropetrovsk. The chief Black Sea port is Odessa. Ukraine owns a number of nuclear plants; the explosion in the Chernobyl plant (1986) was the biggest nuclear disaster in history.
History. The region was ruled by the Mongols in the 13th century and by Poland and Lithuania from the 14th to the 17th century. In the late 18th century it came under Russian rule. After a brief period of independence (1918-22), it became part of the Soviet Union. It was almost completely destroyed by the Nazi occupation during World War II (1941-44), after which it was rebuilt. In the 1980s there was a rise in nationalist sentiment, especially in the western Ukraine. Together with the collapse of communism this resulted in independence in 1991. Relations between Ukraine and Russia strongly improved at the end of the 1990s.
See also: Union of Soviet Socialist Republics.

Ukranian, East Slavic language of the Slavonic group, closely related to Russian, from which it diverged c.1200. Written in a modified Cyrillic alphabet, it emerged as a literary language in the 18th century. It is the official language of the Ukraine.

Ukulele, small guitarlike instrument. Modeled after a small guitar of Portuguese origin, the ukulele became popular in Hawaii during the late 19th century. It was widely used throughout the United States and Europe in jazz bands and as accompaniment in folk songs.

Ulan Bator (pop. 619,000), capital and largest city of Mongolia. Located in the northeastern part of Mongolia along the Tuul Gol River, the city developed around a famous Buddhist monastery built in 1639. For years it served as an important trade center along a route between Russia and China. The city was known as Urga and Niislel Khureheh until it was renamed in 1924 in honor of the famous Soviet revolutionary leader Sukhe Bator. Today, Ulan Bator is Mongolia's cultural and industrial center. It is the home of the Mongolian State University and a science academy. Meat packing is an important industry along with the manufacture of furniture, textiles, and pharmaceutical products.
See also: Mongolia.

Ulanova, Galina (1910-98), Russian prima ballerina of the Bolshoi Theater, Moscow (1944-62). She excelled as a dramatic and lyric dancer, notably in Tchaikovsky's *Swan Lake* and Prokofiev's *Romeo and Juliet.*

Ulbricht, Walter (1893-1973), leader of post-World War II East Germany. A founding member (1918) of the German Communist Party, he spent 1933-45 in exile in the USSR. He became first deputy premier (1949) and head of state (1960-73) of the German Democratic Republic. An uncompromising Stalinist, he headed the Socialist Unity Party from 1950 until his replacement (1971) by Erich Honecker. He ordered the building of the Berlin Wall (1961) and had Eastern German troops participate in the invasion of Czechoslovakia, in 1968.
See also: Germany.

Ulcer, pathological defect in skin or mucous membrane caused by inflammation due to infection, loss of blood supply, failure of venous circulation, or cancer. Peptic, gastric, and duodenal ulcers may cause pain or acute hemorrhage, and may lead to perforation and peritonitis. Antacids usually provide effective treatment.

Ultima Thule, ancient Greek and Roman name for lands of the far north. Scholars believe that the Greek term referred to Norway, Iceland, and possibly the Shetland Islands. The Greek sailor Pytheas mentions the icy waters and long nights and days of a region he reached sometime during the 4th century B.C., but the location is not specified.

Ultrahigh frequency waves (UHF), radio waves with frequencies from 300 to 3,000 megahertz (1 megahertz equals 1 million cycles per second) and with short ranges, usually less than 50 mi (80 km). They are used primarily for television broadcasting, but are also used for air and naval navigation, for police radios, and for tracking spacecraft.
See also: Short waves.

Ultramicroscope, special microscope used for studying colloidal particles (particles in solution or suspension) too small to be seen with a regular-light microscope. A high intensity light beam originates not from the bottom of the instrument as with an ordinary microscope, but from the side. As this beam passes through the solution or suspension, the colloidal particles scatter the light, producing tiny dots of light that then can be seen against a dark background. The ultramicroscope, however, cannot provide the viewer with any structural detail of the particles.
See also: Microscope.

Ultrasonics, science of sound waves with frequencies above those that humans can hear (above 20,000 cycles per second). Modern piezoelectric techniques generate ultrasonic waves with frequencies above 24,000 cycles per second. These exhibit the normal wave properties of reflection, refraction, and diffraction, and are used to clean fine machine parts and, in medicine, to examine internal organs non-surgically.

Ultraviolet rays, invisible light lying beyond the violet end of the spectrum. It is produced naturally by the sun and lightning. Prolonged exposure to the sun's ultraviolet rays can result in sunburn and over a period of years, can cause skin cancer. Plants and animals are partially protected from the sun's ultraviolet rays by ozone, a form of oxygen formed in the upper atmosphere. Ultraviolet rays can, however, be beneficial. They are used by physicians to destroy some bacteria and viruses and by food manufacturers to disinfect food containers. Special lamps that produce ultraviolet rays have been successfully used to treat acne and other skin disorders.

Ulysses, or Odysseus, legendary hero of ancient Greece, son and successor of King Laertes of Ithaca, and husband of Penelope. He was the crafty counselor of the Trojan War (described in Homer's *Iliad*) and the subject of Homer's *Odyssey*, a recount of 10 years of adventures and obstacles faced by Ulysses in his effort to return home after the war.

Umbilical cord, in mammals, tubelike structure linking the developing embryo, or fetus, to the placenta through most of pregnancy. It consists of blood vessels that carry blood to and from the placenta, along with a gelatinous matrix. In humans, the cord is clamped at birth to prevent blood loss. It undergoes atrophy and its remains become the navel.

Umbrellabird, any of several crowlike birds (genus *Cephalopterus*) of tropical American forests, especially *C. ornatus*, whose crest can be expanded into an "umbrella." It also has a lappet of feathers hanging from the throat.

UN *See:* United Nations.

Un-American Activities Committee (HUAC), committee of the U.S. House of Representatives formed in 1938 to investigate subversive activities in the United States. The committee (officially designated the House Committee on Un-American Activities) won notoriety after World War II for its witch-hunt investigations of alleged Communist influence in government, unions, education, and the film industry. It was renamed Committee on Internal Security in 1969, but has been largely inactive.

Unamuno, Miguel de (1864-1936), Spanish philosopher and writer, rector of Salamanca University from 1900 to his death. Influenced by Kierkegaard, he explored the faith-reason conflict and the desire for immortality in *The Tragic Sense of Life in Men and Nations* (1913) and in essays and novels, such as *Mist* (1914). "The Christ of Velázquez" (1920) is his best-known poem.
See also: Philosophy.

Uncas (1588?-1683), chief of the Mohegans of Connecticut, celebrated in James Fenimore Cooper's *The Last of the Mohicans* (1826). He supported the British colonists in the 1637 war against the Pequot Native Americans.

Uncle Sam, popular figure developed by 19th-century cartoonists and officially adopted as a U.S. national symbol in 1961. He is portrayed as a white-haired, bearded gentleman dressed in the Stars and Stripes. The name possibly derives from Samuel "Uncle Sam" Wilson, an inspector of Army supplies in Troy, N.Y., during the War of 1812.

Unconscious, in psychology, that part of the mind the individual is unable to recall at will. The concept of the unconscious, or subconscious, was developed and studied by Sigmund Freud, the founder of psychoanalysis. He believed the unconscious included instinctual drives and repressed memory and desires. To this foundation of belief, C.G. Jung added the idea that there is also a collective unconscious, universal or cultural mental patterns and acts.
See also: Freud, Sigmund.

Underground, term generally used for any secret political movement that seeks to overthrow a country's existing government or military authority. Though undergrounds have operated in many nations throughout history, they came to wide public attention during World War II (1939-45). They were especially effective in German-occupied countries such as Yugoslavia, Poland, France, and the Netherlands.
See also: Guerrilla warfare.

Underground Railroad, secret network that helped U.S. slaves to escape from the South to the northern states and to Canada before the Civil War. Neither underground nor railroad, it was named for its necessary secrecy and for the railroad terms used to refer to its operation. Most of the "conductors" were slaves themselves, Harriet Tubman being one of the best known. Abolitionists, notably Quakers such as Levi Coffin, ran "stations" providing food and shelter along the way. Some 40,000-100,000 slaves escaped in this way.
See also: Abolitionism; Slavery.

Undset, Sigrid (1882-1949), Norwegian novelist. Largely known for her epic trilogy set in medieval Norway, *Kristin Lavransdatter* (1920-22), she won the 1928 Nobel Prize in literature. Her contemporary novels dealt with the position of women in society and with Roman Catholicism.

Undulant fever *See:* Brucellosis.

Unemployment, situation in which people who are normally part of the labor force are unable to find jobs. Seasonal layoffs occur because certain jobs are not available year round. Cyclical unemployment occurs during economic depressions or recessions, when production declines. Structural unemployment refers to permanent shifts in a nation's productive system such that certain groups become permanently unemployed.

Unemployment insurance, type of Social Security providing income to people involuntarily unemployed. Most modern industrial nations have

programs of this kind, financed by the governmnent, employers, employees, or a combination of these. In the 1800s some labor unions initiated unemployment benefits for out-of-work members. France introduced a voluntary national scheme in 1905, and Britain introduced the first compulsory insurance program in 1911. In the United States the first unemployment insurance law was passed in Wisconsin in 1932; three years later the Social Security Act established a federal-state program, now administered by the Department of Labor.
See also: Welfare.

UNESCO *See:* United Nations Educational, Scientific, and Cultural Organization.

Ungulate, term for any mammal with hoofs. Ungulates evolved to stand on their toes, and the toenails have become solid hoofs. The odd-toed ungulates (order Perissodactyla), with one or three toes per foot, include horses, rhinoceroses, and tapirs; the even-toed ungulates (order Artiodactyla), with two or four toes, include pigs, deer, antelopes, camels, cattle, and hippopotamuses.

UNICEF *See:* United Nations Children's Fund.

Unicorn, mythical creature with the body of a horse and one horn on its forehead. Unicorns have appeared in the art and legends of India, China, the Middle East, and medieval Europe, where they were associated with the Virgin Mary and Christ.
See also: Mythology.

Unicycle, single-wheeled vehicle with pedals, a seat mounted above the wheel, and no handlebars. The rider moves it by pedalling and can change direction by pedalling backward or forward or by shifting his or her weight. Unicycles were first used in the 19th century by circus performers, who often juggled objects as they rode.

Unidentified flying object (UFO), object or light reprotedly seen in the air during day or night that cannot always be explained by conventional phenomena. Though many UFOs are found to be objects, such as weather balloons or satellites, or the result of atmospheric conditions, there are certain sightings that do not fall into any known-phenomena categories. The U.S. government continues to investigate thousands of such reports and to sponsor scientific studies on the subject.

Unification Church, religious organization of Korean origin that became highly visible in the United States in the late 1960s. Based on the ideas of the Reverend Sun Myung Moon, who represents himself as an elect leader and seer, the organization recruits and regiments young people to dedicate their lives to the church in a highly disciplined fashion. Accused of "programming" its adherents ("Moonies") by brainwashing techniques, the Unification Church was investigated by Congress in 1977 and has been attacked by both business competitors and parents of involved youths. In 1982 Moon was convicted of conspiracy to evade taxes.

Uniform Code of Military Justice, body of law governing all members of the U.S. armed forces. It sets out procedures for court-martial and military justice. Enacted in 1950, it unified the codes of the army, navy, air force, and coast guard.

Uniformitarianism, doctrine in geology originally opposed to Catastrophism. Originated (1785) by James Hutton and championed by Charles Lyell in the 19th century, it holds that the same geologic processes are at work today as have always existed thoughout geologic time. Uniformitarianism emphasizes the relative slowness and gradual nature of geological change. *See also:* Geology.

Union, Act of, British Parliamentary act of 1840 that officially united Upper Canada and Lower Canada. Two separate Canadas had originally been established to appease the English and French inhabitants. The act not only joined the two Canadas but also stipulated that a government should be formed, consisting of a colonial governor and a legislative assembly composed of members elected by the people. Under the act, English became the official government language.
See also: Canada.

Union of South Africa *See:* South Africa.

Union of Soviet Socialist Republics (USSR) also known as the Soviet Union. Name of a union of 15 Soviet republics that desintegrated in 1991. Now independent countries, the constituent republics were Armenia, Azerbaijan, Estonia, Georgia, Kazachstan, Kirgizstan, Latvia, Lithuania, Moldova, Russian Federation, Turkmenistan, Ukraine and Uzbekistan. The union covered more than half of Europe and two-fifths of Asia. The capital was Moscow.

Land and People. The country comprises 15 constituent republics divided into 4 regions—European, Central Asian, Siberian, and Far Eastern. The Ural Mountains separate the European (west) sector from the Asian (east) sector. Most of the European sector is flatland, broken by the Urals, the Caucasus, and other highlands. To the east lie the great Siberian Plain and the deserts of central Asia; beyond them are the Siberian highlands and the Far Eastern mountains. Because it occupies about one-sixth of the land area of the world, the USSR has several different climatic regions, ranging from the polar north to the subtropical south. Long, cold winters and short summers are characteristic of much of the USSR's climate. Over 100 ethnic groups and nationalities make up the people of the country. Chief among them are Slavic-speaking peoples (Russians, Ukrainians, and Byelorussians); Turkic-speaking peoples (Uzbeks, Tatars, Kazakhs, and Azerbaijani); and the Armenians, Georgians, Lithuanians, and Moldavians. The official language is Russian. Approximately 75 percent of the people live in the European sector of the country. Religion is officially discouraged, but many people still follow the Russian Orthodox church. Other religions include Roman Catholicism, Protestantism, Islam, Judaism, and Buddhism. The ban on religion may be relaxed in the 1990s.

Economy. Under Communism, all industry is owned and operated by the government. Agriculture is organized around state farms (*collective farms*), with some small private plots permitted to farmers. A centralized economy has been a feature of the Soviet Union since 1917, but in the latter part of the 1980s, dissatisfaction with the performance of the economy has led to a time of turmoil and change. The USSR is a major producer of oil, coal, iron ore, natural gas, and timber, and it possesses a wealth of other natural resources. It is a major military power in the world, and a leader in space exploration and scientific research. In the 1990s the Soviet Union has begun to move away from top-down, centralized management in an attempt to form a market economy. Widespread strikes and demonstrations have been an early result of this transition.

History. Russia was ruled by tsars (emperors) for hundreds of years in an extremely autocratic manner. Under them the country was largely cut off from the industrially developing West. There were sporadic uprisings in the 19th and early 20th centuries against this despotic rule, and finally, due in large measure to the horrendous losses suffered by the Russians in World War I, the Russian Revolution of 1917 forced Tsar Nicolas II to abdicate. He was replaced by a provisional government, led by Alexander F. Karensky, a Socialist. The government proved ineffective and was itself overthrown in November 1917 by the Marxist Bolsheviks led by Vladimir I. Ulyanov, who took the name of Lenin. He was helped by Leon Trotsky in organizing the takeover and in successfully prosecuting the following civil war. Lenin and the Bolsheviks set Russia on the course of state ownership of the means of production (farms, factories, mills, mines, etc.). In 1922, the Communist government established the Union of Soviet Socialist Republics (then 4 union republics) with the Russian Republic the first and the largest, which it remains to this day. Lenin died in 1924, and, after some jockeying for power among his successors, Joseph Stalin emerged in 1927 as undisputed leader. He embarked on a far-reaching policy of collectivizing the farmland and of securing total government control over all economic planning. The followers of Trotsky and many other opponents of Stalin's rule were purged in the fierce repression of the 1930s. In 1941, Germany invaded the USSR despite having signed a nonaggression pact with it in 1939. The Great Patriotic War, as the Russians call World War II, lasted until the defeat of Germany in 1945, in which the Russian forces played a key role despite having sustained fearful losses. After World War II, the Soviet Union went on to establish Communist governments throughout eastern Europe and in Soviet-held East Germany. Friction between the Soviet Union and the United States and other West European democracies led to the Cold War, which effectively divided the world into competing East and West blocs, led by the Soviet Union and the United States, respectively. Stalin died in 1953 to be replaced by Nikita S. Khrushchev, who denounced the worst excesses of the Stalin era but who also continued the rivalry with the United States. Partly as a result of the dangerous confrontation with the United States over Soviet missiles in Cuba in 1962, where Russia was forced to turn back, Khrushchev was ousted by the party in 1964, replaced by Leonid I. Brezhnev. Relations with the West improved somewhat under Brezhnev (the period of détente), but the Soviet economy continued to stagnate and even deteriorate. The era of the old Bolsheviks, trained under Stalin, was coming to an end. Brezhnev died in 1982, to be replaced by Yuri V. Andropov. Andropov died in 1984 and was succeeded by Konstantin V. Chernenko, who died in 1985. Mikhail S. Gorbachev, at age 54, became head of the Communist Party, the first of the new generation of Soviet leaders to head the country. Faced with an unpopular war in Afghanistan, begun in the Brezhnev years, and with dire economic problems at home, Gorbachev embarked on a series of reforms he hoped would revitalize the country. He ended the Afghan war, allowed non-Communist governments to take power in Eastern Europe, approved the reunification of Germany by relinquishing control of East Germany, and set in motion new domestic policies such as *glasnost* (openness or freedom of expression for the people) and *perestroika* (reforms designed to transform the command economy of the USSR into one more receptive to free market forces). All these changes led to turmoil, where long-simmering disputes between ethnic groups and rival republics of the union broke into the open. With non-Communist parties allowed to participate in elections, various republics clamoring for independence, ethnic strife, and challenges mounted by powerful political leaders, the future existence of the Union of Soviet Socialist Republics was threatened and the union collapsed in 1991.

Unions, labor, workers' organizations formed to improve pay, working conditions, and benefits through collective power. Modern labor unions arose out of the concentrations of workers created by the Industrial Revolution. A craft (horizontal) union organizes workers by their particular skill; an industrial (vertical) union includes all workers in an industry. Unions negotiate contracts with employers by the process of collective bargaining. A closed (or union) shop increases bargaining strength by requiring that all workers belong to a union. Some states prohibit union shops by law. A dispute with employers may be referred to arbitration, or union members may resort to strikes, slowdowns, boycotts, or, more rarely, sit-downs. In the United States, local craft unions existed from the late 1700s. The influence of the socialistic Knights of Labor (1869-1917) gave way to that of the craft unions of the American Federation of Labor (AFL; founded 1886). In the early 1900s a wave of radicalism resulted in the formation of the Industrial Workers of the World, a revolutionary union across all industries. The industrial union-based Congress of Industrial Organizations (CIO) was formed in the 1930s, during the Depression. The AFL and CIO merged in 1955. The Taft-Hartley Act (1947) placed restrictions on unions, and the Landrum-Griffin Act (1959) curbed union corruption. In recent years, union organizing has lagged as the U.S. economy has become more service-oriented. Britain has a single Trades Union Congress, but many countries have rival unions with differing political outlooks.

Unitarianism, unorthodox Protestant faith that rejects the Trinity and the divine nature of Christ, and asserts the unipersonality of God. It developed out of views of such Reformation figures as Faustus Socinus, who influenced many 18th-century English Presbyterians to become Unitarians. Joseph Priestley gave it a great impetus in the United States, where liberal, rationalist Unitarianism, preaching toleration and universal salvation, developed among Congregational churches. The American Unitarian Association, led by William Ellery Channing, was founded in 1825. In 1961 the Unitarian and Universalist churches merged, creating the Unitarian Universalist Association.
See also: Protestantism.

Unitas, John (1933-), U.S. football player. A quarterback known for his accurate passing, he threw at least one touchdown pass in 47 consecutive National Football League (NFL) games. His achievements include 40,239 career passing yards (third on the all time list) and 253 career touchdown passes (second on the all time list). He played for the Baltimore Colts

United Arab Emirates

Capital:	Abu Dhabi
Area:	29,992 sq mi
	(77,700 sq km)
Population:	2,303,000
Language:	Arabic
Government:	Federal union of seven
	autonomous states
Independent:	1971
Head of gov.:	Prime minister
Per capita:	U.S. $17,400
Mon. unit:	1 UAE-dirham =
	100 fils

(1956-1973), winning 2 world championships (1958, 59) and 1 Super Bowl (1971). He finished his career with the San Diego Chargers (1974) and was inducted into the Pro Football Hall of Fame in 1979.

United Arab Emirates, federation of emirates in the eastern Arabian Peninsula, bordered in the north by the Persian Gulf, in the east by the Gulf of Oman, in the south by Oman, in the south and west by Saudi Arabia, and in the northwest by Qatar. It comprises Abu Dhabi, Ajman, Dubai, Fujairah, Ras al-Khaimah, Sharjah, and Umm al-Qaiwain. The city of Abu Dhabi is the capital. The indigenous population is Arab, and Arabic is the official language. Islam is the state religion, and most of the people are Sunni. The majority of inhabitants, however, are foreign workers, mostly from Asia. The country has a 400-mi (644-km) coastline and is mostly desert. In the east mountains rise to over 8,000 ft (2,438 m), giving way to a fertile coastal strip where dates, grains, and tobacco are cultivated. Herding, fishing, and pearling were the traditional occupations, but since the 1960s the country and its economy have been dominated by oil. The large oil income and small native population have made the Emirates one of the world's richest countries. Abu Dhabi, the largest emirate, is the site of the bulk of the oil production, but Dubai and Sharjah are significant oil exporters, too. Historically, the Emirates were dominated by Britain, to which they were bound by a formal truce (1820) that gave them the name Trucial States. After World War II, Britain granted the Trucial States autonomy. At that time they included Qatar and Bahrain, which chose separate statehood when the United Arab Emirates was formed as an independent state (1971). In 1981, the Emirates and other Gulf countries founded the Gulf Cooperation Council. During Iraq's occupation of Kuwait, the Emirates worked closely with the allied forces. In 1992, Iran confiscated 3 small islands off the coast. The Emirates received military aid from the United States, France, and the GCC-countries. The Emirates supported the peace agreements between Israel and Palestine and terminated the indirect economic boycot of Israel (1994).

United Arab Republic (UAR), union of Egypt and Syria proclaimed in 1958 as a step toward Arab unity. Cairo was the capital, and Egyptian president Gamal Abdul Nasser was president. The UAR effectively collapsed in 1961, when Syria withdrew. A 1963 attempt to unite Egypt, Syria, and Iraq failed. Egypt was still called the UAR until 1971, when its name was changed to Egyptian Arab Republic.

United Automobile Workers (United Automobile, Aerospace and Agricultural Implement Workers of America), second-largest U.S. industrial labor union, with local affiliates in Canada. Founded in 1935, it won recognition at General Motors, Chrysler, and Ford after major strikes and struggles (1937-41). Its members work in the automobile, space, aviation, and metal industries. The UAW cofounded the CIO, but left the AfL-CIO in 1968. Presidents have included Walter Reuther (1946-70), Leonard Woodcock (1970-77), and Douglas Fraser (1977-   ). UAW headquarters are in Detroit.
See also: Unions, labor.

United Church of Canada, Protestant church formed in 1925 by the union of Methodist and most Presbyterian and Congregationalist churches. Ecumenical, national, and missionary, it has a Presbyterian form of organization, stresses the rights of congregations, and has male and female ministers. It was joined in 1966 by Canada's Evangelical United Brethren Church, and has over a million adult members.

United Church of Christ, U.S. Protestant denomination set up by the 1957 union of the Congregational Christian Churches and the Evangelical and Reformed Church. It combines strong local autonomy with national services and organization.
See also: Congregational Church.

United Empire Loyalists, term for people of the original 13 American colonies who remained loyal to Britain during the Revolution and who emigrated to Canada. The largest group, some 50,000, left New York City in 1783 and founded New Brunswick (1784) and Upper Canada (now Ontario, 1791).

United Farm Workers of America (UFW), U.S. farm workers union. Several associations of agricultural workers merged in 1973 to form the UFW, which fights for better living and working conditions for farm workers, especially migrant workers in the southwest, south, and northeast, trying to ensure job security and better wages. The founding president is Cesar Chavez. To bring public attention to the needs of its members, the UFW of America often urges consumer boycotts of non-union products.
See also: Chavez, Cesar Estrada; Unions, labor.

United Food and Commercial Workers International Union (UFCW), large U.S. labor union formed in 1979 by the merger of the Amalgamated Meat Cutters and Butcher Workmen of North America and the Retail Clerks International. UFCW members include butchers, meat packers, canners, supermarket employees, department store clerks, and employees of pharmacies, shoe stores, hospitals, and nursing homes.
See also: Unions, labor.

United Kingdom, officially, United Kingdom of Great Britain and Northern Ireland, commonly known as Great Britain, constitutional monarchy consisting of most of the British Isles located off the northwestern coast of Europe.

With a total area of 94,251 sq mi (244,110 sq km), the United Kingdom is entirely surrounded by water, bounded on the east by the North Sea, on the west by the North Atlantic Ocean, and on the south by the English Channel. The island of Great Britain is separated from Northern Ireland, located in the northeast part of the island of Ireland, by the North Channel and the Irish Sea. The Strait of Dover is the narrowest part of the English Channel and is a passage of 21 mi (34 km) between Great Britain and France. In addition to Great Britain and Northern Ireland, the British Isles consists of thousands of smaller islands, including the Shetland Islands, the Orkneys, the Outer Hebrides, the Isle of Man, and the Scilly Islands. The capital is London.

Land and People. Geographically, the island of Great Britain is divisible into 7 distinct zones. The northernmost section of the island is the Scottish Highlands, a mountainous area and the site of Britain's highest mountain, Ben Nevis, 4,400 ft (1,343 m). Most of Scotland's people and its best farmland are in the Central Lowlands, a fertile plain just south of the Highlands. The Southern Uplands are the southernmost part of Scotland. It is hilly country culminating in Cheviot Hills, which separates England from Scotland.

The hilly country continues south of the Cheviot Hills in the Pennines of England, an area that includes England's famous Lake District. Below the Pennines and extending to the Channel are the English Lowlands. It is on this undulating plain that most of England's farms, villages, mines, industries, and major cities are located. West of the Central Lowlands lies Wales, dominated in the north by the Cambrian Mountains and in the south by fertile river valleys. The Bristol Channel separates Wales from the Southwest Peninsula, an uneven plateau that ends in cliffs facing the open seas. Northern Ireland, situated at the northeast end of the island of Ireland, has fertile land somewhat similar to the Central Lowlands of Scotland. Great Britain contains many bays and inlets, several navigable rivers, and numerous lakes. Though Britain is located in a relatively high northern latitude, its climate is comparatively mild, moderated by the influence of the Gulf Stream. In addition, the island gets regular and adequate rainfall.

The people of Great Britain have a mixed ancestry of Celtic peoples and Romans, as well as Germanic, Scandinavian, and Norman peoples. Over the centuries, the population has tended toward a certain homogeneity, but clear distinctions are still discernible and are reinforced by differences in language, religion, and custom. Welsh remains a distinct Celtic language. The native Scots and Irish speak varieties of Gaelic. And even the dominant English language has strong regional variants, though they began to disappear with the advent of television. Since World War II England has also become a racially varied society, thanks to a large influx of immigrants in the 1950s and 1960s, mostly from Asia, Africa, and the West Indies. The established church in England is the Church of England, headed by Archbishop of Canterbury. In Scotland, the established church is the Church of Scotland. Both churches are Protestant, but there are sizable minorities of Roman Catholics and Jews.

The United Kingdom is governed as a constitutional monarchy. In modern times, England's monarchs have reigned, but they have not governed. The monarch's role, though almost entirely symbolic, is important to England's social and political system and to the maintenance of the traditions that are the sources of authority. Power resides in the Parliament, a representative body divided into an upper and lower house. Members of the upper house,

United Kingdom

Capital:	London
Area:	94,251 sq mi
	(244,110 sq km)
Population:	57,721,000
Language:	English
Government:	Parliamentary monarchy
Independent:	1801
Head of gov.:	Prime minister
Per capita:	U.S. $18,700
Mon. unit:	1 Pound sterling = 100 pence

the House of Lords, hold their seats as privileges attached to rank; they are not elected. Members of the House of Commons must be elected. Effective political power is in the House of Commons. Elections must be held at least once every five years, but are usually held more often, and can be called at any time. After an election, the head of the winning party is designated prime minister and forms a government of ministers from among the most important members of the party. These leading ministers make up the cabinet, or inner council. Although Great Britain has a constitution, it is not in the form of a single written document as it is in the United States. It is made up, in part, of certain documents, like the Magna Carta, and, more loosely, of the vast body of Common Law, but it also consists, to a very large degree, of traditions that have continued over many generations. The British people are at liberty to reconstitute their government at any time. In addition to the monarchy and parliament, the system relies upon an independent judiciary with courts of appeal and judges who are appointed for life. It also relies upon a professional civil service to staff the government's many ministries. British civil servants hold their jobs regardless of the party in power.

Economy. Surrounded by water and with limited natural resources, England has long grown accustomed to and made a virtue of looking beyond its own borders for its economic well-being. Though not nearly as rich and powerful as it was in the 18th and 19th centuries, England remains a competitive manufacturing and trading economy. The country does not have enough arable land to meet all its farm needs: Agriculture accounts for just 2% of the gross national product. It has also used up the best of its once-rich coal reserves, though since the mid-1960s it has been self-sufficient in natural gas from the North Sea, and since the late 1970s it has also been self-sufficient in petroleum, also from the North Sea wells.

Trade is critical to the British economy. Britain ranks fifth in the world in foreign trade, after the United States, Germany, Japan, and France, and trades principally in manufactured goods, though one-third of its trade volume is given to food and raw materials. Britain has one of the world's largest merchant marine fleets. The country also continues to be a leading manufacturer, producing steel, automobiles and other vehicles, heavy machinery, appliances, machine tools, products of advanced technology (including jet engines and aircraft for military and civilian use), and electronic equipment.

The economy is aided by advanced scientific and technological research at its great universities. Great Britain also supplies markets in the chemical industries, pharmaceuticals, textiles and apparel, and food processing and beverages. Worldwide printing and publishing concerns are headquartered in England.

Government continues to be a strong presence in the British economy, and service industries are the major part of its economy, employing some two-thirds of its work force. The service sector includes education and the health-care system. It also includes wholesale and retail trade and the various institutions that provide financial services, including banks and insurance companies. The financial services industry contributes substantially to Great Britain's economy, and London continues to be one of the world's leading financial centers.

History. Evidence of Bronze Age civilization in England can be seen in the ruins of Stonehenge, but comparatively little is known about England before the arrival of the Romans in the 1st century B.C. The Romans were followed in the 5th century A.D. by Germanic tribes, the Angles, Saxons, and Jutes, who set up petty kingdoms. These in turn were overrun by Vikings, chiefly Danes, in the 9th and 10th centuries. The last successful invasion of England was in 1066, under William the Conqueror, of Normandy. The political and social organization the Normans imposed upon England laid the foundations of customs and traditions that would prove remarkably durable over the centuries and contribute much to the distinctive character of the people. In the 13th century, a group of English barons won concessions from King John set forth in the Magna Carta in 1215, marking an important development in the growth of Britain's unique political institutions. The 14th century was dominated by the Hundred Years War and the final unsuccessful bid by England's monarchs to establish effective control over their French lands and vassals. The 15th century witnessed the turmoil of the Wars of the Roses, dynastic struggles, which led to the rise of the Tudors, Henry VIII and Elizabeth I, whose combined reigns embraced the 16th century. Henry VIII embodied the English Renaissance and established England's independence from the papacy by seizing all church properties and establishing the Church of England. Elizabeth presided over the England of William Shakespeare and Sir Francis Drake. England, after destroying the Spanish Armada in 1588, claimed supremacy at sea and began expanding its overseas colonies and markets, an expansion that was to lead to a great empire. This was after nearly a century of civil and religious warfare centered upon the throne and, in particular, the Stuarts. The issue was finally put to rest with the Glorious Revolution and the accession of William III and Mary II in 1689, but only after bitter fighting and the Protectorate of Oliver Cromwell, leader of the Puritans. It was in the course of the conflicts of the 17th century that Parliament rose to prominence as a governing institution and the groundwork was laid for the governance of England in modern times. Modern Great Britain, with sovereignty residing in Parliament, was born with the Act of Union of 1707, which joined the formerly separate kingdoms of England and Scotland to form the United Kingdom. Through the laws of succession, the heirs to the British throne in the 18th century were German and this, as well as George III's disastrous policy leading to the loss of the American colonies, contributed to the reduction of the monarch to a symbolic head of state. Sovereignty resided in Parliament and the official leader of the government became the prime minister.

In the 18th century, Great Britain increased its power tremendously by using both the raw materials and markets of its growing empire to fuel the Industrial Revolution. Using modern technology, especially the steam engine, to build the first modern industries and turning its populace from agricultural work to industrial labor, Great Britain rapidly increased its wealth and power. At the end of the century, Great Britain faced a determined adversary in Napoleon Bonaparte of France. Defeated first at sea by Admiral Nelson in 1805 and on land by Lord Wellington at Waterloo in 1815, Napoleon, in fact, marked Britain's passage to world dominance. The 19th century also saw England's attempt to resolve the centuries' old hostilities with the Irish with the Act of Union of 1800, which created the United Kingdom of Great Britain and Ireland.

The 19th century was a period of political conflict and reform occasioned by Great Britain's wealth and power. There were bitter debates in Parliament over laws to ameliorate the harsh conditions in factories, and equally bitter disputes over the Corn Laws and the franchise. These debates would lay the foundations for the political parties that would dominate British politics throughout the 20th century, with the Whigs representing Liberal policies and the Tories conservative policies. These differences developed at the height of Britain's empire under Queen Victoria, who reigned from 1837 to 1901 and the rival views of politics were embodied in her two brilliant prime ministers, Benjamin Disraeli, the conservative, and William Gladstone, the liberal. By the time of Queen Victoria's death, the British empire consisted of about one-quarter of the world.

The 20th century proved much harder on England's fortunes. Great Britain entered World War I in 1914 against its economic rival, Germany. Great Britain helped win the war but lost 750,000 men in the fighting and did not adequately recover economically. The Irish problem continued to vex England, and in 1921 the British agreed to the independence of southern Ireland, but retained Northern Ireland. The worldwide depression hit England hard, and the 1930s saw the rise of fascism and the Nazis. Neville Chamberlain's policy of appeasing Hitler proved disastrous, and, led by Winston Churchill, England resisted Nazi ambitions. The English not only defended their own country, but in union with the United States and other allies, they destroyed the Nazis. England lost 360,000 men in World War II and its economy was in decline. In 1945, the Labour Party acceded to power and established England's welfare state with unemployment benefits, a comprehensive program of national health insurance, and the nationalization of key industries. The changes were dramatic, but the economy continued to lag. The same period saw the beginning of the breakup of Britain's empire. In 1947, India and Pakistan became independent, then in succession, one foreign policy and possession after another asserted its independence in Africa, Asia, and the Pacific.

In the 1950s Great Britain decided not to join the European Coal and Steel Community, nor would it join the European Economic Community, the Common Market. These proved costly decisions. The British economy expanded for a time but began to contract in the 1960s, and in 1963 and 1967 bids by Britain to gain admission to the Common Market were rejected, principally by France. Britain finally succeeded in joining the EEC in 1973, in the grip of the deepest economic downturn in the postwar years. In addition, the conflict in Northern Ireland turned violent. In May 1979 the Conservative Party, led by Margaret Thatcher, the first woman prime minister, came to power. The Conservatives drastically reduced government holdings, curbed the power of the unions, and strove to increase investment, all with some positive results. But after 11 years as prime minister, Mrs. Thatcher resigned in Nov. 1990 after losing Conservative Party leadership over her opposition to England's participation in European economic union, and in the late 1980s and early 1990s, the economy continued to be the major issue and challenge confronting England. Thatcher was succeeded by John Major as Conservative leader and prime minister. In 1997 the Constervative Party was defeated by Labour, led by Tony Blair. Blair contributed to the popularization of the British royal family, after Princess Diana's death.

United Methodist Church, largest Protestant denomination in the United States. Formed when the Methodist Church joined with the Evangelical United Brethren Church in 1968, it is the latest permutation of Methodism, a religious movement founded in England by John Wesley (1703-91). The church has around 10 million members nationwide and supports seminaries and colleges throughout the United States. It also supports many missionaries in foreign countries. A governing body made up of members from the laity and clergy meets every four years to elect bishops and determine church policy. The church opposes racism and the consumption of alcoholic beverages and supports the United Nations' peace-keeping efforts around the world.
See also: Methodists.

United Mineworkers of America *See:* Mineworkers of America, United.

United Nations (UN), international organization of the independent states founded after World War II, with the declared goals of promoting peace and international cooperation. It was launched at the 1945 San Francisco Conference prepared by the "Big Three" Allied Powers of World War II (the United States, Britain, and the USSR), and 51 states signed the charter. Membership had grown to 160 by 1989. The headquarters are in New York City. The UN has six major organs. The General Assembly, composed of delegates from all member states, meets once a year and provides a general forum but has little actual power. The Security Council has five permanent members, (China, France, Great Britain, the United States, and the USSR), each of which has the right to veto any resoltion, and ten rotating members. The Economic and Social Council, with 54 elected members, deals with "nonpolitical" matters, coordinating the work of the specialist agencies and operating commissions, such as those on children, refugees, and human rights. The Trusteeship Council is responsible for UN Trust Territories. The International Court of Justice, in The Hague, Holland, is the UN's principal organ of international law. The Secretariat is the administrative body headed by the Secretary General. Other UN institutions include the United Nations Conference on Trade and Development, the Office of the United Nations High Commissioner for Refugees, and the United Nations Children's Fund. Major specialized agencies affiliated with the UN include the Food and Agriculture Organization (FAO), General Agreement on Tariffs and Trade (GATT), International Atomic Energy Agency (IAEA), International Civil Aviation Organization (ICAO), International Labor Organization (ILO), International Monetary Fund (IMF), International Telecommunication Union (ITU), United Nations Educational, Scientific, and Cultural Organization

(UNESCO), Universal Postal Union (UPU), World Bank (IBRD), World Health Organization (WHO), and World Meteorological Organization (WMO). Initial enthusiasm regarding the role the UN would play on a global scale, has cooled off. This as a result of experiences in Somalia and Yugoslavia, where UN forces were hindered in their work and where their safety could not be guaranteed.

United Nations Children's Fund (UNICEF), UN organization formed (1946) as the UN International Children's Emergency Fund to help in countries devastated by World War II. It became a permanent body in 1953, retaining the UNICEF acronym and specializing in child welfare, family planning, and nutrition programs in disaster areas and in many poorer countries. It is financed voluntarily. In 1965 UNICEF was awarded the Nobel Peace Prize.
See also: United Nations.

United Nations Educational, Scientific, and Cultural Organization (UNESCO), UN agency established in 1946 to promote international collaboration through scientific, educational, and cultural activities. Its policy-making general conference meets biennially at its Paris headquarters. UNESCO has helped develop education in poorer countries and arranges scientific and cultural exchanges. Both the United States and Britain withdrew from UNESCO in 1985, charging that the organization was being manipulated for political purposes with an anti-American slant.
See also: United Nations.

United Nations University, research and training institution chartered in 1973 by the United Nations (UN). It is actually an agency through which institutions coordinate educational programs. Its aims are to provide information, research, and training opportunities for scholars and organizations around the world. Projects usually focus on the management of natural resources, hunger, and developing societies. University headquarters are in Tokyo.
See also: United Nations.

United Negro College Fund, nonprofit organization, founded 1944, that raises money to operate private colleges and universities for African Americans. It also provides counseling for students and staff for the member schools. The money comes from corporations, foundations, and individuals.

United Parcel Service (UPS), U.S. package delivery company. UPS delivers packages by truck or plane throughout the United States, Puerto Rico, and parts of Canada. Air service to Europe is also offered. The small delivery company that eventually became UPS was started in 1907 by James Casey and Claude Ryan to serve the Seattle area.

United Press International (UPI), world's largest independent news agency, created by the 1958 merger of United Press (founded 1892 by Edward W. Scripps) and the International News Service (founded by William Randolph Hearst in 1906). At its height in the 1950s, UPI had some 200 bureaus (half in the United States) that sent news and pictures to over 5,000 clients.

United Service Organizations (USO), independent, nonprofit grouping of organizations founded in 1941 to provide recreational, entertainment, religious, and social facilities for members of the U.S. armed forces. It is recognized by the U.S. Department of Defense and supported by contributions and volunteers.

United Society of Believers *See:* Shakers.

United States, government of the, consisting of various democratically elected governmental bodies in a federated union, with a judiciary both elected and appointed. The U.S. government relies for its day-to-day administration upon millions of employees and civil servants in numerous bureaucracies. Civil order is maintained by police forces, and national defense is the responsibility of the military. In the United States, both the police and the military as organs of government are under the ultimate authority and control of civilians holding elective office.

The government of the United States owes its fundamental character to the political practice and experience of the 13 original colonies. The colonists, in turn, were deeply influenced by their European heritage. The 3 major traditions that influenced the colonists in their political thinking were the parliamentary tradition of self-government and the principles of common law they brought with them from England; principles of governance contained in the Protestant, especially the Puritan, tradition of Biblical study; and the history of the ancient Roman republic. Against the background of the Europe they left behind, most of the early settlers were nonconformists. Their relation to the European tradition tended to be radical and unorthodox. Added to this was the experience of the New World. Its very existence was a challenge to assumptions and knowledge that had been taken for granted for centuries. It was separated from Europe by a long and dangerous ocean voyage. The country was wild. Settling and cultivating the land required hard work and resourcefulness, which eventually developed certain habits of mind, an independence from authority, practicality, and ingenuity, a willingness to experiment, and an openness to novelty. Well before the Revolutionary War, the American colonists had become a people with a separate and distinct character and sensibility, and with considerable experience in governing themselves. Added to that experience was confidence in their judgment, enough to pit themselves against the accumulated authority and force of a major European power. All these elements are the historical foundations of government in the United States.

The Revolution established that, for Americans, power and authority did not proceed from a monarch or a privileged aristocracy. Rather, government proceeded from the people. After the Revolution, America consisted of 13 independent states loosely united in a confederation. The arrangement did not work. A constitutional convention was called and the U.S. Constitution was drawn up, leaving substantial authority in each state but also establishing a central federal government. The principles of the Constitution are simple to state but were subject to intense debate and different interpretations even as they were being given their definitive written form. Government proceeds from the will of the people. The people have the right to make and unmake their government as they see fit. Power is divided so that it cannot easily be concentrated. The government is divided among a legislature that makes law, an executive that enforces it, and an independent judiciary that interprets the law when its meaning is in dispute. These branches check one another in various ways. Congress passes laws, but a president can veto. The president is commander-in-chief of the armed forces, but only Congress can levy taxes and declare war. No matter how promising the arrangement looked on paper, there were those who remained fundamentally critical and wary of concentrated governmental power. At their insistence, the constitution came to include the Bill of Rights with its list of basic liberties. Also firmly established in the Constitution were the strict separation of church and state and the supremacy of civilian authority over the armed forces. Profoundly influenced by English law and political traditions, the U.S. Constitution was a radical and revolutionary departure from the English model and, for that matter, from all others. It was ratified by two-thirds of the states and George Washington became the nation's first president. In doing so he not only filled a political office, but also fundamentally defined it. The Constitutional Convention was convened in Philadelphia in 1787 and went into effect on June 21, 1788.

Government in the United States is divided among several jurisdictions. There is the federal government, each separate state government, and local governments. The federal government has the power to collect taxes and custom duties, issue currency through the mint, borrow money, and issue bonds. It determines official weights and measures, issues patents and copyrights, controls immigration, and determines and confers citizenship. The federal government alone determines foreign policy, declares war, or negotiates with foreign states. Through its bureaucracies, it performs a wide range of regulatory functions touching on many industries and many aspects of the lives of its citizens. It has authority over interstate commerce, the environment, the national parks, labor-management disputes, and social security. Above all, and in the most basic terms, it is responsible for protecting the lives, property, rights, and liberties of its citizens. These include the right to vote, the right to trial by a jury of one's peers, freedom of speech and association, and freedom from arbitrary arrest or imprisonment.

Despite the considerable power and dominance of the federal government, authority is shared with the states, each of which has its own legislature, executive, and judiciary, each with its own written constitution and body of law.

Government has expanded and changed in the United States as rapidly as the country itself. Westward expansion in the 19th century required greater centralization of authority. The secession of the southern states provoked a constitutional crisis that ended in civil war. The South was defeated and the federal government emerged with more power and authority. Before the Civil War, Thomas Jefferson, Andrew Jackson, and James K. Polk enhanced the power of the presidency. During the Civil War, Abraham Lincoln became the most powerful president the republic had seen. For the balance of the 19th century, power shifted to Congress, but continued to accrue to Washington, D.C. The Spanish-American War in 1898, World War I, and World War II, under the successively more powerful presidencies of Theodore Roosevelt, Woodrow Wilson, and Franklin D. Roosevelt, saw the ascent of the United States as an international power and then a superpower. With the wars came a corresponding expansion in governmental power and responsibility. The U.S. government is now supported by vast bureaucracies, its budgets detail annual expenditures in the billions, it maintains huge standing military forces at home and around the world, but it continues to operate on much the same principles and organizational lines laid down in the Constitution.

The Congress makes laws; the executive branch, under the leadership of the president, enforces the laws and formulates national policies; the judiciary settles disputes at law. The relations within and among the branches of government are complex and change with new administrations and personalities, but the basic mechanics and principles remain much the same. Law is shaped by the needs or demands of organized citizens. Today there are many special interest groups (i.e., major industries, environmental groups), with money to employ lobbyists; these groups are outside of the main political parties and have some special policy goal or agenda. They influence lawmaking through newspapers, books, magazines, and television, demonstrations, and the use of lobbyists—paid professionals who actually seek out individual lawmakers and seek to persuade them to introduce certain legislation or to vote one way or another on pending legislation.

It is the elected congressional representatives and senators who draft bills and submit them to Congress for consideration. Bills are then assigned to various committees for study. Once out of a committee, a bill is returned for consideration and debate in the House or Senate before being voted upon. A simple majority is required to pass it. Then it must be signed by the president, who can veto the bill. The Congress may override the president's veto with a two-thirds majority. The process is lengthy, and from the time it is introduced to the time it becomes law, a bill goes through many changes, or amendments, in response to all of the competing and often conflicting interests that may be affected by the new law. The process has often been described as cumbersome and inefficient, but it was devised to ensure that laws would be made thoughtfully and with maximum input from those most affected. A more telling criticism of the current system is that in a society as large and complex as that of 20th-century United States, the only voices heard are those with the money needed to participate in government. More and more, it requires substantial sums of money to be elected to public office or to influence legislation.

In addition to elected officials, the government consists of vast bureaucracies without which the country could not function and elected officials could not effectively govern. In the executive branch, the major bureaucratic bodies include the departments of State, the Treasury, Defense, Justice, the Interior, Agriculture, Commerce, Labor, Health and Human Services, Housing and Urban Development, Transportation, Energy, Education, and Veterans' Affairs. The heads of these departments constitute what is known as the president's cabinet. In addition, there are a large number of independent agencies with various regulatory responsibilities, such as the Interstate Commerce Commission, the Federal Reserve, the Federal Communications Commission, the Selective Service System, and the National Labor Relations Board. The Congress also has a network of supporting bureaucracies that include 8 major administrative agencies. They are the Congressional Budget Office, the General Accounting Office, the Government Printing Office, the Library of Congress, the Office of Technology Assessment, the Copyright Royalty Tribunal, the Architect of the Capitol, and the U.S. Botanic Garden. The House of Representatives has 435 members and the U.S. Senate has 100 members. Representatives sit for 2 years, senators for 6. Presidents are elected for 4 years with a maximum of 2 terms. The number of representatives a state has depends upon its population. Population is determined by a census and reapportionment takes place every 10 years. Tax bills can only be initiated in the House of Representatives. The Senate has the authority to approve treaties and presidential appointments to major federal posts, including the Supreme Court. The federal judicial system is organized into 95 district courts, 13 federal appeals or circuit courts, and the Supreme Court. Federal judges are appointed for life by the president, but must be approved by the Senate. Nine justices sit on the Supreme Court. The United States has been traditionally a 2-party political system. Unlike other representative democracies, the U.S. system confers elective office upon the winner of a majority of the voters in a contested election. In proportional systems of representation, minority parties hold seats based upon the percentage of the electorate that supports them. In the United States the influence of third or minor parties tends to be temporary and usually takes the form of bringing forward to public attention and debate new grievances or political programs that are then taken up by one or another of the major parties.

United States Air Force *See:* Air Force, U.S.

United States Air Force Academy, federal institution for educating and training young men and women to be officers in the U.S. Air Force. Located in Colorado Springs, Col., and authorized by Congress in 1954, the academy offers a 4-year program consisting of academic work leading to a Bachelor of Science degree, military training (including flying instruction), physical education, and courses in ethics and honor. Candidates for the academy must be nominated by elected (or some appointed) U.S. officials.
See also: Air Force, U.S.

United States Army *See:* Army, U.S.

United States Border Patrol *See:* Border Patrol, United States.

United States Botanic Garden, national plant collection in Washington, D.C. Begun by a private organization in 1820, it was taken over by the government in 1843. The collection, which is open to the public, consists of over 10,000 plants, from the common to the rare and exotic. Guided tours and education courses are available.

United States capitals, cities that served as seats of the U.S. government until 1800, when Washington, D.C., became the permanent capital. After the Declaration of Independence (1776), the Continental Congress and subsequently the U.S. Congress met in various cities, moving every few years. Among these cities were Baltimore, Philadelphia, and New York City. Eventually, Virginia and Maryland negotiated with Congress to be the site of a permanent capital. In 1791, both states donated land to be set aside for its construction. The new capital was named after the nation's first president and is under direct federal jurisdiction, not being part of any state.

United States Coast Guard *See:* Coast Guard, U.S.

United States Coast Guard Academy, federal institution for the education and training of young men and women as commissioned officers in the U.S. Coast Guard. Created in 1876, it now is located in New London, Conn., on the Thames River. Candidates compete nationally on the basis of college entrance exams. The students, or cadets, participate in a 4-year program, during which they receive military training, training at sea, and academic instruction in courses ranging from marine engineering to government. *See also:* Coast Guard, U.S.

United States Congress *See:* Congress of the United States.

United States Constitution *See:* Constitution of the United States.

United States Forest Service *See:* Forest Service, U.S.

United States literature, literary works in English beginning in the original 13 English colonies and continuing in the present-day United States. Although the United States is a large continental country with varied influences, several strands or themes characterize its literature. The pioneer heritage of the country left its mark on later writers, primarily in their concern with individual values and liberties and a certain pervasive skepticism toward authority. Perhaps aligned with this, U.S. writers have shown a consistent tendency to break with literary traditions and strike out in new directions.
Colonial literature. The first writings in English in North America were by adventurers and colonists for readers back in England. While few of these could be called literature, some journals and accounts did manifest a lasting quality and interest. Capt. John Smith's vigorous *True Relation of Such Occurrences and Accidents...as Hath Happened in Virginia* (published in England in 1608) was the first personal account of life in the colonies. More sober histories of the period included John Winthrop's *Journal*, which described life in the Massachusetts Bay Colony from 1630 to 1649, and William Bradford's *History of Plimoth Plantation*. Religious and instructional works, however, dominated colonial writing, with sermons and religious tracts making up most of the colonists' reading matter. The first book published in the Puritan colonies was the *Bay Psalm Book* (1740). The most important of the early religious writers were Cotton Mather (a 2-volume ecclesiastical history of New England), Jonathan Edwards (sermons and books), and John Woolman (a journal reflecting on his life in the Quaker belief). Poetry in colonial times also largely reflected religious and pious themes. Among the early poets were Michael Wigglesworth, Anne Bradstreet, and Edward Taylor.
Revolutionary period literature. Not surprisingly, writing during the period of the Revolution concentrated on politics and on political philosophy. Benjamin Franklin encouraged writers by acting as a publisher and founder of newspapers. He also wrote political and satirical works, with his witty *Poor Richard's Almanac* (1733-58), one of the period's most popular publications. Political writing during this time reached new heights as men like Thomas Paine, Thomas Jefferson, Alexander Hamilton, and John Madison examined the nature of society. A formidable female writer of the late 18th century, Mercy Otis Warren, wrote not only plays and poetry but a history of the American Revolution—one of two contemporary histories considered significant. At war's end, as the new nation struggled to discover its identity, Hamilton, Madison, and John Jay wrote a brilliant series of letters called *The Federalist* in support of the new constitution. For style and content they are scarcely rivaled in political discourse.
Literature in the New Nation. The first U.S. novel was William Hill Brown's *The Power of Sympathy* (1789). Charles Brockten Brown, the first profes-

sional U.S. novelist, modeled his work after the English gothic romances, as exemplified in *Wieland* (1798) and *Edgar Huntly* (1799). Fame both in the United States and Europe was gained by Washington Irving with his *Sketch-Book* (1819-20) and by James Fennimore Cooper with his *Leatherstocking Tales* (1823-41). The leading poet of this time was William Cullen Bryant, who became known as the American Wordsworth for his deeply felt nature poems. Among his most important lyrics are "Thanatopsis" (1811), "To a Waterfowl" (1818), and "To the Fringed Gentian" (1832). Also notable was Henry Wadsworth Longfellow (*Evangeline*, 1847). The nation's attention turned to the problem of slavery in the 1830s with William Lloyd Garrison and his newspaper, *The Liberator*, leading the antislavery movement. The most influential antislavery work was Harriet Beecher Stowe's novel *Uncle Tom's Cabin* (1851-52), the best-selling book of the time.

Literature at mid-19th century. By the middle of the 19th century, U.S. literature had come of age. The transcendentalists were a group of New England writers who displayed in their works characteristics thought to be specifically American. They espoused a high moral seriousness and a sense that the individual was superior to tradition and social customs. They also called for a distinctly American literature, quite independent of European models. Chief among them was Ralph Waldo Emerson, who presented the group's theories in *Nature* (1836) and in his brilliant essays (e.g., "Self-Reliance," and "The Over-Soul," both 1841). Henry David Thoreau (*Walden*, 1855) was another transcendentalist who wrote observant, thought-provoking, and beautifully styled prose. Utterly American was the poet Walt Whitman (*Leave of Grass*, first edition published 1855), writing a free-form verse that broke with European models and celebrated the new country in the New World. Quite different, but equally untraditional, were the compact, emotionally intense lyrics of Emily Dickinson, almost all of which were published after her death in 1886. A darker strand in U.S. literature was evident in the eerie, haunting poetry and short stories of Edgar Allen Poe, for example, in lyrics such as "The Raven" (1845) and the sinister *Tales* (1840). Nathaniel Hawthorne's masterpiece *The Scarlet Letter* (1850) probed the psychological aspects of sin in the closed society of early New England Puritanism. In *Moby Dick* (1852), Herman Melville created an American epic, at once an adventure tale of the sea and a deep, enigmatic allegory.

Literature in the second half of the 19th century. After the Civil War, literature in the United States took on a national aspect in that writings of distinct regions gained a nationwide audience. The country eagerly read about the California gold rush and life in the West in the short stories of Bret Harte. Joel Chandler Harris retold the old black tales of the South. The greatest of the regionalist writers, however, Mark Twain, surpassed the genre and in *The Adventures of Tom Sawyer* (1876) and *The Adventures of Huckleberry Finn* (1884) wrote two American classics. By century's end, a new realism was taking hold in U.S. literature as was a reaching-out to European models and culture. Stephen Crane's *Red Badge of Courage* (1895), set in the Civil War, won acclaim for its realistic portrayal of warfare. Henry James went to Europe where he wrote novels of rare psychological insight about the clash of U.S. and European cultures (*The Portrait of a Lady*, 1881, and *The Golden Bowl*, 1904). William Dean Howells set out to depict the lives of average Americans (*The Rise of Silas Lapham*, 1885). Other noted realists included Frank Norris, Harold Frederick, Theodore Dreiser, Hamlin

Garland, Jack London, and James T. Farrell. A group of journalists and writers known as "muckrakers" employed realism to examine corruption and fraud in U.S. society. Among them were Lincoln Steffins, Ida M. Tarbell, and Upton Sinclair, whose novel *The Jungle* (1906) was instrumental in bringing about food and drug laws.

Literature after World War I. Disillusionment with the war stirred a generation of U.S. writers to become expatriates in Europe, in search of something to believe in. Labeled the "lost generation" by Gertrude Stein (*The Autobiography of Alice B. Toklas*, 1933), the group included Ernest Hemingway (*The Sun Also Rises*, 1925), F. Scott Fitzgerald (*The Great Gatsby*, 1925), and John Dos Passos (*U.S.A.*, 1930-36). One of the most powerful of U.S. novelists was William Faulkner (*The Sound and the Fury*, 1929). Social criticism continued with such writers as critic H. L. Mencken and Edmund Wilson and novelists Sherwood Anderson and Sinclair Lewis. Other novelists of the period include Willa Cather, Thomas Wolfe, and Nathanael West. The Great Depression fostered more socially aware writing, as evidenced in the works of John Steinbeck (*The Grapes of Wrath*, 1939). Notable U.S. poets of the 20th century include Edward Arlington Robinson, Edna St. Vincent Millay, Robert Frost, T.S. Eliot, Carl Sandburg, Hart Crane, Marianne Moore, Wallace Stevens, e.e. cummings, Langston Hughes, and, more recently, Robert Lowell, Elizabeth Bishop, Sylvia Plath, John Berryman, and John Ashberry. Among the most important playwrights of this period were Eugene O'Neill (*Long Day's Journey Into Night*, first produced in 1956), Elmer Rice, Maxwell Anderson, Lillian Hellman, Tennessee Williams, Arthur Miller, William Inge, and, in recent years, Edward Albee, David Rabe, Sam Shepard, and Neil Simon. Major novelists include Flannery O'Connor, Eudora Welty, J.D. Salinger, Norman Mailer, Saul Bellow, Philip Roth, Ralph Ellison, James Baldwin, Truman Capote, Mary McCarthy, Joyce Carol Oates, Thomas Pynchon, John Barth, Toni Morrison, and John Updike.

United States Marine Corps *See:* Marine Corps, U.S.

United States Merchant Marine Academy, government-sponsored educational institution (since 1943), located in Kings Point, N.Y. The academy prepares young men and women to become officers in the U.S. Merchant Marine. To be considered for admission into the school, a candidate must be nominated by a U.S. senator or representative and pass a competitive examination. The school program involves a 4-year undergraduate education, with some technical and naval training, as well as training on board a ship.
See also: Merchant marine.

United States Military Academy, oldest government-sponsored educational facility (founded in 1802), located in West Point, N.Y. The academy trains young men and women to become officers in the U.S. Army. An applicant must be nominated by an elected or appointed U.S. official, and must pass certain academic, medical, and physical requirements. The academy offers a 4-year undergraduate education with strong emphasis on military training.
See also: Army, U.S.

United States Naval Academy, federally funded and operated college for training men and women to be officers in the U.S. Navy and Marine Corps.

Founded in 1845, it is located at Annapolis, Md. Candidates must be nominated by elected or appointed officials, such as senators and representatives, and must be between the ages of 17 and 21 years. The four-year program includes academic studies leading to a bachelor of science degree, as well as required participation in varsity or intramural sports and training in professional skills such as navigation and sailing.
See also: Marine Corps, U.S.; Navy, United States.

United States Navy *See:* Navy, United States.

United States of America, country whose territory is principally on the continent of North America, but which includes islands of the Hawaiian archipelago in the Pacific Ocean. The United States is organized into 50 political subdivisions, or states, and the District of Columbia. In addition, the U.S. government maintains special political associations with various overseas territories including Puerto Rico and the U.S. Virgin Islands in the Caribbean, and Guam, American Samoa and Northern Marianas, all formerly parts of the Trust Territory of the Pacific Islands. Johnson, Midway, and Wake islands, also in the Pacific, are also dependent upon the United States. The contiguous states of the United States are bounded by the Atlantic Ocean to the east, the Pacific Ocean to the west, Canada to the north, and Mexico, the Gulf of Mexico, and the Caribbean Sea to the south. Alaska is separated from the 48 contiguous states by Canada and bounded by that country as well as the Pacific and Arctic oceans. The Hawaiian islands are in the central Pacific Ocean c.2,100 mi (3,380 km) from San Francisco, Calif. The nation's capital is Washington, D.C.
Land and People. With an area of 3,618,770 sq mi (9,372,614 sq km), the United States is geographically varied, and can be divided into approximately 6 regions. The Atlantic and Gulf Coastal Lowlands stretch south from Long Island to Florida and then west to Mexico. They extend inland an average of 200 mi (322 km) with many lagoons, sandbars, and good natural harbors. In southern Florida they include the Everglades and, on the Gulf Coast, the Mississippi River delta. The Appalachian mountain chain separates the Atlantic Lowlands from the western interior. The Appalachians run northeast to southwest from Nova Scotia in Canada to the southern United States. A low mountain system, the Appalachians include the White Mountains of New Hampshire, the Great Smoky Mountains, and the Blue Ridge Mountains of North Carolina, and give way to the Allegheny Plateau. The north-central section of the United States has the Great Lakes, among the world's largest freshwater lakes. The Great Lakes region forms a natural boundary between the eastern and western United States, and between the United States and Canada. Beyond the Alleghenies are the Central and Interior Plains, stretching to the Rocky Mountains and drained by the Mississippi-Missouri river system and its branches. Its uplands include the Ozarks in Arkansas and Missouri, and the Black Hills of South Dakota and Wyoming. The Rocky Mountains mark the western barrier of the Great Plains and are part of a mountain system extending from Alaska, through Canada and the United States and continuing down the length of South America. The highest mountain in the United States is Mt. McKinley in Alaska at 20,320 ft (6,194 m). Between the Rocky Mountains and the mountains of the Cascade and Sierra Nevada ranges farther west lies the Western Plateau and Basin, or the Intermontane Region. It contains the Great Salt Lake and Grand Canyon.

United States of America

Capital:	Washington, D.C.
Area:	3,618,770 sq mi
	(9,372,614 sq km)
Population:	270,312,000
Language:	English
Government:	Federal presidential
	republic
Independent:	1776
Head of gov.:	President
Per capita:	U.S. $26,980
Mon. unit:	1 Dollar = 100 cents

Finally, beyond the western mountains, are the Pacific Coastlands extending south from Puget Sound in the state of Washington to Central Valley in California. The lowest point in the United States is Death Valley in California, one of several desert regions to be found in the southwestern United States.

Climate in the continental United States is greatly influenced by geographic position. Winter temperatures vary greatly, being relatively high along the sheltered Pacific coast, but often extremely low in the interior and the east. Summer temperatures are mainly high in most areas with the southeast becoming subtropical and humid. Tornadoes can occur in spring, especially in the Mississippi valley, and summer thunderstorms and hurricanes are frequent along the south Gulf and Atlantic coasts.

The original inhabitants of the Unites States were the Native Americans, racially distinct and consisting of various peoples of different languages and cultures. Displaced and decimated by successive waves of migration from Europe beginning in the 16th and 17th centuries, remnant populations now live for the most part on reservations, principally in the Great Plains and Western states. The majority of the people of the United States are immigrants or descendants of immigrants who came to the United States in 2 distinct groups. From 1600 to 1820, most settlers were from England and Scotland. From the 1820s to the present, newcomers arrived from Ireland, Germany, and Scandinavia before the U.S. Civil War, then from Eastern Europe, the Mediterranean, and Asia. The U.S. population also includes a significant number of citizens who are descendants of the Mexicans who originally settled what is now the U.S. Southwest. African Americans are the descendants of men and women who were brought to North America as slaves as early as 1619. An exhaustive list of the origins of all U.S. citizens would include peoples from all over the world. Despite their varied origins, they have combined sufficiently to constitute an identifiable people with a common language, culture, and outlook. There is no established religion in the United States, but a majority of the people are Christians, chiefly Protestants but also Roman Catholics. The country's language is English, though many immigrants speak their own native languages.

Economy. In 1989, the gross national product of the United States was in excess of $5.2 trillion dollars, making it by far the world's richest country.

The United States can grow nearly all temperate and subtropical crops and is not only self-sufficient in essential foods but regularly produces surpluses. About half the land surface is given to farming, including dairy farming and the raising of livestock. The country contains valuable forests, particularly in the northwest and Alaska, and rich fisheries in the Atlantic, the Pacific, and the Gulf. Its considerable mineral wealth includes coal, iron ore, petroleum, and natural gas, but the needs of its vast economy and the consumption it generates have led to a decline in the reserves of some minerals, and the United States has increasingly become an importer of ores and of oil. Its enormous manufacturing sector produces steel, automobiles, aircraft, and aerospace technology, electronic equipment, textiles, and most kinds of consumer goods. The United States not only manufactures in quantity, but it also has long been a leader in setting standards for quality and efficiency in modern industrial production. In addition, a large sector of the economy is committed to research, development, and production in sophisticated weaponry and aerospace systems. Banking and the interrelated institutions that provide financial services and products worldwide are also major contributors to the economy.

History. The first permanent European settlement in the United States was St. Augustine, Fla., founded by the Spanish in 1565. Early English settlements were in Jamestown, Va., in 1607; Plymouth, Mass., in 1620; Maryland in 1634, Connecticut in 1636, and Pennsylvania in 1681. There were also French, Dutch, and Swedish settlements. By the 18th century, Britain was the paramount power on the new continent with prosperous, flourishing colonies in what was later to become the United States. Opposition to Britain's policy toward its North American colonies led to the Revolutionary War in which the forces of the 13 colonies under the generalship of George Washington, and with timely and substantial assistance from France, defeated Britain's armies. The war lasted from 1775 to 1783. Independence was declared in 1776, and after the war the separate states joined to form a federal republic with George Washington as its first president, in 1789. Expansion westward followed.

The area of the United States was doubled by the Louisiana Purchase, made in 1803. Florida was purchased from Spain in 1819. U.S. ambitions for expansion into Canada ended with the War of 1812 between Britain and the United States. Settlers moved over the Alleghenies and west over the Great Plains. Texas was annexed in 1845 and much of the territory of the U.S. Southwest was acquired through the Treaty of Guadalupe Hidalgo, which ended the Mexican-American War of 1848. Five years later, southern New Mexico and southern Arizona were added to the United States with the Gadsden Purchase in 1853 and, at the other end of the continent, Alaska was purchased from Russia in 1867.

As the country expanded, differences deepened between the cultures and economies of the northern and southern states. The southern states eventually elected to secede from the union and the result was the Civil War (1861-65), the bloodiest single conflict in the nation's history. Following the war came a period known as Reconstruction (1865-77). What was Reconstruction for the South was development and expansion for the rest of the country. The North became more and more industrialized and urbanized and the settlement of the West was hastened with the completion of the transcontinental railroad in 1869. As the nation became richer, more powerful, and more self-confident, its presence began to be felt abroad.

In 1898 Hawaii was annexed and other overseas territories came under U.S. control as a result of its victory in the Spanish-American War. The United States completed its entry into international affairs by participating (from 1917) in World War I (1914-18) and tipping the scales in favor of the Allies, the British and the French. Power and prosperity were soon followed by the Great Depression of the 1930s, an economic breakdown so complete that many felt the country was on the brink of revolution. Franklin D. Roosevelt became president and instituted his New Deal reforms, which halted the economic decline. Worldwide economic frustration and ambition led to World War II (1940-45) and the Japanese attack on Pearl Harbor on Dec. 7, 1941, marked the entrance of the United States into the war.

The United States emerged from World War II a military and economic superpower, leader of the Western, or free, world, and locked in rivalry with the Communist bloc led by the Soviet Union. With an ideology of anti-communism, which it pursued relentlessly at home and abroad, and a policy of resisting and containing what it saw as the spread of communism, the United States committed itself to the Cold War. It participated in the Korean War (1950-53) and, later, in the Vietnam War (1961-73).

Domestically, the Congressional hearings and investigations of Sen. Joseph McCarthy and his staff into Communist subversion, the unofficial purges of people who had been slandered or blackballed, and the trial and execution of Ethel and Julius Rosenberg for spying for the Soviet Union dominated much of the postwar decade. In the 1960s, at the same time the country was engaged in the Vietnam War, the government pursued its war on poverty, a combination of programs meant to alleviate poverty and equalize access to equal economic opportunity. The country also faced the profound social and legal crisis generated by the civil rights movement led by the Rev. Martin Luther King, Jr. The turmoil and unrest of the period was marked at the very outset by the assassination of President John F. Kennedy and later of Dr. King, and then Robert Kennedy.

Richard Nixon's election to the presidency signalled the end to the Vietnam War, but not before Cambodia had been embroiled in the widening regional disaster. Defeat in Vietnam was followed by economic recession at home. The Nixon presidency saw a major diplomatic breakthrough in its recognition of Communist China, but lost its credibility and authority with the Watergate domestic political scandal. Rather than face impeachment, Nixon resigned the presidency in disgrace. Both Gerald Ford and his Democratic successor, Jimmy Carter, worked to restore the sagging economy. The last year of Carter's presidency witnessed a further blow to the international standing of the United States with the ouster of the Shah of Iran by Iranian Muslim fundamentalists under the leadership of Ayatollah Khomeini, whose followers held the U.S. embassy staff in Teheran hostage for more than a year.

The Republican administration of Ronald Reagan sought to revive the economy by radically reducing governmental regulation. The policy proved stimulating in the short run, but left the nation deep in debt, with a great part of its banking system in disarray, and the gap between rich and poor wider than it was before Reagan's program was initiated. Internationally, the Reagan presidency struck a more militant anti-Communist tone. Defense spending was increased and the administration was determined to regain ground from communism, particularly in Nicaragua. The result was the Iran-contra scandal, in which it was discovered that the executive branch had been selling arms to Iran to finance forces seeking to overthrow the Marxist regime in Nicaragua. The president denied knowledge of the transactions or involvement in any wrongdoing, but the hearings into the matter raised serious questions, among them, whether or not the president was competent to govern.

Ronald Reagan was succeeded by George Bush, whose administration inherited the severe economic consequences of his predecessor's policies, in particular the collapse of the savings and loan institutions and the weakening of the U.S. banking system. In foreign policy, President Bush urged a continuation of normalizing relations with China despite pressure from many quarters to censure China for the Tiananmen Square massacre of dissident students and workers. In 1993 Bush was succeeded by the Democrat Bill Clinton. Clinton stood for a better social policy, but was often frustrated by the Republican majority in the Congres and Senate. In 1998 Clinton was threatened with impeachment.

United States Postal Service *See:* Postal Service, U.S.

United States President *See:* President of the United States.

United States Seal *See:* Great Seal of the United States.

United States Supreme Court *See:* Supreme Court of the United States.

United Steelworkers of America *See:* Steelworkers of America, United.

United Way of America (UWA), U.S. umbrella organization founded in 1918 to raise funds for charitable agencies working on health, recreation, and welfare projects. Over 200 major national organizations have been helped by the United Way's funds. It has 1,200 local chapters.

Unit rule, U.S. voting rule used at many political conventions. Under the rule, all the votes in a state delegation are thought of as a single unit. When a majority of the delegation members vote for a certain candidate during a convention, all the delegation votes go to that candidate. Unit rule was used by the Democratic party until 1968.

Universalism, Christian doctrine that holds that everyone will ultimately be saved by divine grace. The Universalist Church in the United States, initially Calvinistic, was formed (1779) by Hosea Ballou and other New England nonconformists. Liberal and syncretist, in 1961 it joined the Unitarians to form the Unitarian Universalist Association.
See also: Unitarianism.

Universal language, proposed language that people of all nations could speak and understand. Since the 1600s, the idea of a universal language has attracted philosophers, educators, politicians, and businesspersons alike. Its advocates believe that it would aid both cultural and political understanding among the disparate nations of the world. Its detractors claim that the idea of such a language is impractical. Several universal languages, including Volapuk and Esperanto, have been developed and used with some success. During the Middle Ages and Renaissance, Latin almost achieved the status of a universal language as it was used as a common language by diplomats and other educated people throughout Europe. Today, English is fast becoming a universal language.

Universe, general term for all of space and everything in it.

Universities and colleges, schools that are designed for the continuation of education beyond high school and that emphasize the study of liberal arts, arts, and sciences. A university generally offers courses in many subjects, including agriculture, art, history, literature, philosophy, and science. It may be divided into different departments, or colleges. For example, a university may have a College of Education within it. A college may also be a separate school, which usually emphasizes study in one area, such as liberal arts. Most U.S. universities and colleges are sponsored either privately (often by a church) or by local, state, or federal government. Most universities and colleges offer students a course of study leading to an undergraduate degree, a bachelor of arts or science degree. Most also have various graduate programs in which a student may continue to work toward a master of arts or science degree or a doctor's degree. Though the oldest university in the world is probably Al-Azhar University in Egypt (founded in A.D. 970), the prototypes for U.S. universities sprang up in Europe during the 12th century. These universities were usually associated with the Church, though by the 14th century, they were designed to train students in medicine and law as well as theology. The earliest U.S. university is Harvard, which was founded in 1636. Like their European models, the first U.S. universities and colleges were training centers for ministers. They soon, however, expanded their curricula to include engineering, art, medicine, science, and law. Today the population of the student body in these schools can range from several hundred, as might be found in a small liberal college, to many thousands (Ohio State University in Columbus, Ohio, has an enrollment of over 50,000).

Unknown soldier, in the United States and some European countries, an unidentified soldier killed in action in war whose tomb serves as a national shrine honoring all war dead. Unknown soldiers of World War I, World War II, the Korean War, and the Vietnam War are buried in the Tomb of the Unknown Soldier in Arlington National Cemetry, Arlington, Va.

UN Peacekeeping Forces, multinational forces under UN command, deployed around the world since 1948 to settle conflicts between and within countries. Such forces include armed troops as well as unarmed observers monitoring the implementation of political agreements. Peacekeeping forces are put in place when requested by the countries in conflict, with the agreement of the UN Security Council; personnel is then supplied voluntarily by UN member states. Primary areas of activity have been the Congo, Central America, and the Middle East. UN forces have been active in the Israeli-Arab conflict and in conflicts between Iran and Iraq, India and Pakistan, and parties within Cyprus, Angola, Cambodia, Somalia, and former Yugoslavia. Particularly after the failures in Somalia and Yugoslavia, a debate has been brought on regarding the usefulness of peacekeeping operations. After the Cold War the number of peacekeeping operations has increased and, as a result, organizational and financial problems have increased as well. *See also:* United Nations.

Untermeyer, Louis (1885-1977), U.S. writer and editor. Though he published many volumes of poetry and two novels, he is better recognized today as having been the editor of several poetry anthologies: *Modern American Poetry* (1919 and subsequent revision), *Modern British Poetry* (1920), and *A Treasury of Great Poems, English and American* (1942). From 1961 to 1963, he served as the poetry consultant for the Library of Congress.

Upanishads, group of philosophical treaties that make up the final part of the Veda, a collection of Hindu scriptures. They are thought to have been written from 900 to 600 B.C. Most of the existing 112 Upanishads are in dialogue form, and their speculative nature has inspired the formulation of several concepts central to the Hindu religion. One puts forth that the soul of an individual is one with the soul of the universe, or God.
See also: Hinduism; Vedas.

Upas, forest tree (genus *Antiaris*) of tropical Asia and Indonesia. Ancient tales describe this tree as yielding a juice that was used as arrow poison by ancient peoples; this accounts for a lot of the superstition and mysticism that surrounds this tree.

Updike, John (1932-   ), U.S. novelist, short-story writer, poet, and critic. He has dealt with the trials of contemporary life in such novels as *Rabbit, Run* (1960), *Couples* (1968), *Bech: A Book* (1970), *The Coup* (1978), *Rabbit is Rich* (1981, Pulitzer), *The Witches of Eastwick* (1984), *S.* (1988), *Rabbit at Rest* (1990; Pulitzer), *Brazil* (1994), and *Toward the End of Time* (1997). He published a book of memoirs, *Self-Consciousness*, in 1989.

Upjohn, Richard (1802-78), English-born U.S. architect, noted for his Gothic Revival churches, such as Trinity Church, New York City (1846). He was one of the founders and the president of the American Institute of Architects (1857-76).
See also: Architecture.

Upland sandpiper (*Bartramia longicauda*), also called upland plover, North American bird of the sandpiper family. For most of the year, it lives on the prairies and meadows of Canada and the northern United States, but it migrates for the winters to the grassy plains of Argentina and Brazil. It is usually about 12 in (30 cm) long, with dark- and light-brown feathers and a white belly. It eats locusts and other insect pests.

Upper Volta *See:* Burkina Faso.

UPS *See:* United Parcel Service.

Upshaw, Eugene, Jr. (1945-   ), U.S. football player. Upshaw played for the Oakland Raiders (1967-81) and was captain of the team (1970-81). Upon retirement as an active player, he became president of the National Football League Players' Association (1981-83). He was appointed to executive director in 1984 and supported the players in the football strike of 1987. He was inducted into the Pro Football Hall of Fame in 1987.

Upsilon particle, unstable subatomic particle without electrical charge. With a mass almost 10 times that of a proton, it is the heaviest known subatomic particle.
See also: Quark.

Ur, ancient Sumerian city that lay in what is now southern Iraq along the Euphrates River. An important port as well as religious and trade center, Ur thrived from about 3500 B.C. until the 4th century B.C. At that time, the Euphrates River changed its course and the then useless port city was abandoned. According to the Bible, the Hebrew leader Abraham was born in Ur. Some important architectural ruins of Ur have been found in southern Iraq. These ruins include the remains of a ziggurat, an ancient pyramid-like structure.
See also: Sumer.

Ural Mountains, mountain chain about 1,500 mi (2,400 km) long in western Russia, running north-south from the Kara Sea toward the Caspian. The Urals are the traditional boundary between Europe and Asia. Mt. Narodnaya (6,214 ft/1,894 m), in the northern section, is the highest peak. The Urals are heavily forested and rich in minerals.

Ural River, river in former USSR. Originating in the Ural Mountains of west-central Russia, it flows some 1,570 mi (2,527 km) south to the Caspian Sea. Several important Russian cities lie along it, including Magnitogorsk, a steel-making center. It is a rich source of salmon and sturgeon.

Uranium, chemical element, symbol U; for physical constants see Periodic Table. Discovered by Martin H. Klaproth in 1789, it occurs in the minerals pitchblende, uraninite, carnotite, autunite, and uranophane, among others. It is prepared by reduction of the tetrafluoride in a Thermit type of reaction. Uranium is a silver-white, lustrous, radioactive, reactive metal, a member of the actinide series. It is pyrophoric. Uranium-235 is fissionable and is used as fuel in nuclear reactors, and in atomic and hydrogen bombs. One pound of uranium has the fuel value of 1,500 tons of coal. Uranium-238 is fertile and used to produce plutonium-239, which is fissionable in breeder reactors. Uranium and its salts are highly toxic.

Uranium-235 *See:* U-235.

Uranus, third-largest planet in the Solar System and the seventh from the sun. Physically very similar to Neptune, but rather larger, Uranus orbits the sun every 84.02 years at a mean distance of 1.78 billion mi (2,87 billion km), rotating on its axis once every 10.75 hours. Since the plane of its equator is tilted 98° to the plane of its orbit, the rotation of the planet and the revolution of its five known moons (Titania, Oberon, Ariel, Umbriel, and Mirando), which orbit closely parallel to the equator, are retrograde. In 1977 the planet was found to have five rings, like those of Saturn but much fainter. In 1998 American and Canadian scientists discovered that Uranus has two more moons.
See also: Planet; Solar System.

Uranus, god of the sky in Greek mythology. His union with Gaea, the earth, produced a race of giants known as the Titans. Because Uranus hated and

feared his offspring, he forced them to live deep within the earth. The Titan Cronus rebelled against his father's decree, attacking and emasculating Uranus, a wound that separated Uranus from Gaea. (The myth may have originated as an explanation for the separation of the sky and earth.) The function of Uranus as god of the sky was eventually taken over in Greek mythology by Zeus, a son of Cronus.
See also: Mythology.

Urban, name of eight popes. **Urban II** (c.1042-99; r. 1088-99) continued the struggle against the emperor Henry IV begun by his predecessor, Gregory VII. At the Council of Clermont (1095) he initiated the Crusades. **Urban III** (r. 1185-87) was absorbed in a struggle with Emperor Frederick Barbarossa and his son Henry IV. **Urban IV** (c.1200-64; r. 1261-64) continued the struggle against the Hohenstaufen emperors and gave the crown of Naples and Sicily to Charles I. **Saint Urban V** (c.1310-70; r. 1362-70) attempted to return the papacy to Rome from Avignon and to effect a reconciliation with the Eastern Church. **Urban VI** (1318?-89; r. 1378-89) was involved in disputes with his cardinals that precipitated the Great Schism. **Urban VIII** (1568-1644; r. 1623-44) played an ambiguous role in the Thirty Years War through political opposition to the Roman Catholic Hapsburgs.

Urban Coalition, National, U.S. organization that works to solve problems of city dwellers. Formed in 1970, members include religious and civic leaders as well as business and labor representatives. Members identify problems related to education, health care, housing, and employment, and try to make local, state, and federal governments, as well as private organizations, aware of them. The coalition has about 40 local chapters operating throughout the United States.

Urban League, or National Urban League, voluntary organization established to end racial discrimination and to help minorities achieve political equality. Founded in 1910, the League works through its more than 100 local groups throughout the United States to provide job training and employment opportunities for minorities. It also implements health care and counselling programs. It funds research aimed at identifying the problems facing minorities and works to ensure that state and national governments are made aware of such problems. Headquarters are in New York City.

Urban renewal, removal of city slums and their replacement with improved residential or commercial facilities. Ideally, the federal government grants a city a certain amount of money to replace a slum neighborhood. The city then uses the funds to buy and demolish derelict property, relocating families and businesses to new areas. Next, the land is sold to private or public developers at a low price. Schools, parks, office centers, and so on are then to be built where the slum once stood. The program as a whole has been only moderately successful. In many cities cleared land has remained unsold and undeveloped for years. Federal funding of urban renewal has also been greatly cut, shifting the financial burden to the state and city governments.

Urea, organic compound, $CO(NH_2)_2$, that is the end product of the metabolism of nitrogen in protein in many animals. It is excreted in the urine. Urea's major uses are as a nitrogenous fertilizer and to make urea-formaldehyde resins.

Uremia, biochemical disorder often seen in cases of kidney failure, consisting of high levels of urea and other nitrogenous waste products entering the blood. Nausea, vomiting, malaise, itching, pigmentation, anemia, and acute disorders of fluid and mineral balance are common.
See also: Kidney.

Urey, Harold Clayton (1893-1981), U.S. chemist awarded the 1934 Nobel Prize in chemistry for his discovery of deuterium, an isotope of hydrogen. He was a leading theorist of the nature and origin of the moon.
See also: Deuterium.

Urine, waste product consisting of a dilute solution of excess salts and nitrogenous material, such as urea and deaminated protein, excreted by many animals. The wastes are filtered from the blood by the kidneys or equivalent structures and stored in the bladder until excreted. The passage of urine not only serves to eliminate wastes, but also provides a mechanism for maintaining the water and salt concentrations and pH of the blood. While all mammals excrete nitrogenous wastes in urine, other animals—birds, insects, and fish—excrete them as ammonia or in solid crystals as uric acid.

Uris, Leon (1924-   ), U.S. author of modern historical fiction. His most famous novel, *Exodus* (1958), follows the development of the state of Israel. His first novel, *Battle Cry* (1953), is a personalized account of service in the Marine Corps during World War II. Other works include *QB VII* (1970), *Trinity* (1976), and *Mitla Pass* (1988). Uris, in collaboration with his wife, Jill, has also written two photoessays, *Ireland: A Terrible Beauty* (1975) and *Jerusalem: Song of Songs* (1981).

Ursa Major and Ursa Minor *See:* Big and Little Dippers.

Ursulines, Roman Catholic religious order of women, the first devoted exclusively to the education of girls. The order was founded in Brescia, Italy (1535), by St. Angela Merici, with St. Ursula as patron saint.
See also: Roman Catholic Church.

Uruguay, officially the Oriental Republic of Uruguay. Covering 68,037 sq mi (176,215 sq km), which makes it the smallest republic in South America, Uruguay is bordered by Brazil to the north and northeast, the Atlantic Ocean to the east, Argentina to the west, and the Rio de la Plata to the south. The capital and chief port is Montevideo, where about 40% of the people live.
Land and People. Uruguay is a country of rolling grasslands and low hills, fringed by sands, lagoons, and bays. In the south, the Rio de la Plata estuary forms an alluvial plain called the Banda Oriental. From the narrow coastal plain the land rises gently to the Cuchilla Grande and other highlands, reaching their highest point in the Sierra de las Animas at 1,644 ft (501 m). Uruguay has a pleasantly mild climate. The people are mostly of Spanish and Italian descent with some 300,000 mestizos, persons of mixed European and Native American descent, forming a significant minority. Spanish is widely spoken, and most people are Roman Catholic.

Uruguay

Capital:	Montevideo
Area:	68,037 sq mi
	(176,215 sq km)
Population:	3,284,000
Language:	Spanish
Government:	Presidential republic
Independent:	1828
Head of gov.:	President
Per capita:	U.S. $5,170
Mon. unit:	1 Uruguay peso = 100
	centesimos

Economy. The economy of Uruguay is based on cattle and sheep raising with meat, wool, and hides providing 80% of the country's exports. Wheat, oats, flax, oilseeds, grapes, fruit, and sugarbeets are grown. Meat packing and tanning are the chief industries. There are important fisheries, but few mineral resources.

History. The region was visited by the Spanish in 1516 and settled by them in 1624. Resisting Portuguese incursions, they founded Montevideo in 1726. José Artigas led the independence movement from 1810 to 1820. Uruguay was then occupied by Brazil for several years, but finally expelled the invaders and became independent in 1828. A period of prolonged political instability was followed, in the early 20th century, by government under José Battle y Ordóñez. His economic and social reforms made Uruguay one of the most developed Latin American countries with a comprehensive social welfare system and advanced labor legislation. Labor unrest and the terrorism of the leftist Tupamaro guerrillas in the late 1960s led to a military takeover in 1973. Repression in the decade following was widespread, but eventually gave way to a return to civilian government in 1985. By means of industrialization, the government tries to switch from exporting live animals and animal products to new export products.

Uruguay River, southern South American river. Originating in southern Brazil, it flows for 1,000 mi (1,600 km) first west and then south before finally emptying into the Rio de la Plata, a huge estuary on the Atlantic coast. It forms part of the Argentine-Brazil border and all of the Argentine-Uruguay border.

U.S. *See:* United States of America.

USO *See:* United Service Organizations.

USSR *See:* Union of Soviet Socialist Republics.

Utah, state in the Rocky Mountain region of the western United States bordered by Utah to the north, Wyoming to the northeast, Colorado to the east, Arizona to the south, and Nevada to the west.

Land and climate. Utah has three main land regions. The state's northeast corner is part of the Rocky Mountains, primarily the Uinta and Wasatch

Utah

Capital:	Salt Lake City
Statehood:	Jan. 4, 1896 (45th state)
Familiar name:	Beehive State
Area:	84,899 sq mi (219,889 sq km); ranks 11th
Population:	2,059,000 (1997); ranks 34th
Elevation:	Highest—13,528 ft (4,123 m), Kings Peak; Lowest—2,000 ft (610 m), Beaverdam Creek
Motto:	Industry
Flower:	Sego lily
Bird:	Sea gull
Tree:	Blue spruce
Song:	"Utah, We Love Thee"

ranges. Eastern and southern Utah lie in the Colorado Plateau region, where rivers have cut hundreds of deep canyons and erosion has created spectacular land formations.The Basin and Range Region of western Utah, one of the nation's driest areas, has dry plains and the broad, barren salt flats of the Great Salt Desert. The Colorado and the Green are the state's chief rivers. Great Salt Lake, the largest natural lake west of the Mississippi River, is saltier than the ocean; only the Dead Sea is saltier. Deserts cover about a third of the state and forests another third. Utah has cold winters and warm summers.Principal cities are Salt Lake City, Provo, and West Valley City.

Economy. Manufacturing and service industries are the economy's mainstays, and Utah is a leading mining state. Chief manufactured goods are machinery, transportation equipment, processed foods, electrical equipment, and fabricated metals. Chief mining products are oil, coal, natural gas, uranium, copper, gold, magnesium, and natural salts. Agriculture is less important than in the past. Chief farm products are beef and dairy cattle, turkeys, hay, wheat, barley, corn, apples and other fruits, potatoes, and greenhouse and nursery products.

Government. Utah's constitution was adopted in 1895. The governor serves a 4-year term. The state legislature consists of 29 senators serving 4-year terms and 75 representatives serving 2-year terms. In the U.S. Congress, Utah is represented by 2 senators and 3 representatives.

History. When two Spanish Franciscan monks led an expedition into Utah in 1776, it was inhabited by Native American tribes that included the Ute, Paiute, and Shoshone. European-American fur traders soon followed, but no permanent white settlement occurred until the Mormons, led by Brigham Young, arrived at present-day Salt Lake City in 1847. The Mormons, members of the Church of Jesus Christ of Latter-Day Saints, sought refuge from religious persecution. In 1848, the United States acquired Utah as part of the settlement of the Mexican War. Utah applied for statehood as the state of Deseret in 1849, but Congress refused, instead creating the Utah Territory (which was larger than present-day Utah). In the 1850s and 1860s, fighting—including the Black Hawk War—erupted between Mormons and the Native Americans they displaced. The first transcontinental railroad, completed at Promontory Point, Utah, in 1869, brought new settlers. Utah won statehood in 1896, after clashes between Mormons and U.S. authorities, especially over the practice of polygamy, which the Mormons discontinued in 1890. Utah was hit hard by the Great Depression, but World War II renewed demands for its mining and manufacturing. Industry's importance grew in the 1950s and 1960s, as did the rise of tourism. In recent years, Utah has sought new businesses to avoid too much dependence on oil and mining. It also has worked to clean up pollution and protect its deserts and other land and water resources.

Ute, Native American tribe speaking a Shoshonean language and having a nomadic culture common in the Western plains, particularly Utah, Colorado, and New Mexico. Originally peaceful hunter-gatherers, they became marauders and buffalo hunters after obtaining Spanish horses in the 1800s. Some 4,000 now live in Colorado and Utah.

Uterus, or womb, female reproductive organ that is specialized for implantation of the fertilized egg and development of the embryo and fetus during pregnancy. The regular turnover of its lining under the influence of estrogen and progesterone is responsible for menstruation.
See also: Reproduction.

U Thant *See:* Thant, U.

Utica (pop. 75,632), industrial city of central New York State and the seat of Oneida County. Lying in the Mohawk River Valley, Utica is an important terminal on the New York State Barge Canal System. Its factories turn out electrical tools and machinery, textiles, metal products, foodstuffs, paper products, and clothing. The city is also an important market for the surrounding farm region.

Utica, ancient Phoenician colony on the coast of North Africa on the Mediterranean Sea. Founded about 1100 B.C., it was an important port and helped give the Phoenicians control over sea trade on the Mediterranean. A rival of its neighbor Carthage, Utica sided with Rome against Carthage in the Third Punic War (149-146 B.C.). With the Roman victory and the destruction of Carthage, Utica became the capital of the province. It fell to the Vandals (A.D.439), was recaptured by the Byzantine Empire (534), and destroyed by the Arabs (c.700).

Utilitarianism, theory of ethics that holds that the rightness or wrongness of an action is determined by the happiness its consequences produce. The theory dates from the 18th-century thinker Jeremy Bentham, who believed that actions are motivated by pleasure and pain and that happiness can be assessed by the quantity of pleasure. His follower John Stuart Mill later argued in *Utilitarianism* (1863) that some pleasures should be sought for their intrinisic quality. He interpreted the principles of utilitarianism as a basis for the struggle for political and social reforms.
See also: Bentham, Jeremy; Mill; Watson-Watt, Sir Robert Alexander.

Uzbekistan

Capital:	Tashkent
Area:	172,740 sq mi
	(447,400 sq km)
Population:	23,784,000
Language:	Uzbek
Government:	Presidential republic
Independent:	1991
Head of gov.:	Prime minister
Per capita:	U.S. $970
Mon. unit:	1 Som = 100 chin

Utopia, term used to denote any imaginary ideal state. Based on the Greek words meaning "no place," it was coined by Sir Thomas More as the title of his *Utopia* (1516), in which he described a just society free of internal strife.

Utrecht (pop. 234,000), city in the central Netherlands. Built on the site of a Roman fort, it was during its early history the residence of several German emperors. Until the 15th century, it was the region's most important cultural and industrial center, a role eventually taken over by Amsterdam. In 1579, representatives from the northern provinces met in Utrecht and signed the Union of Utrecht, uniting them against Spain and setting up the eventual formation of what is now the Netherlands. Today Utrecht is an important cultural center and the site of many historical buildings, medieval churches, museums, and universities. It is also the headquarters of the Netherland's rail network. Chief industries include construction and metalworking.
See also: Netherlands.

Utrecht, Peace of (1713-14), series of treaties among England, France, the Netherlands, Portugal, Prussia, Spain, and the Holy Roman Empire concluding the War of the Spanish Succession.
See also: Succession wars.

Utrillo, Maurice (1883-1955), French painter best known for his Paris street scenes. His finest works capture in modified cubism the atmosphere of old Montmartre, as in *Sacré Coeur de Montmartre* (1937).

Uxmal, ancient city in Yucatán, Mexico. Built by the Mayas, it flourished c.600-900 and has some fine examples of the late classical Mayan style of architecture.
See also: Mexico.

Uzbekistan (Republic of), independent country in central Asia, surrounded by Kazakhstan (north), Kirghizstan and Tajikistan (east), Afghanistan and Turkmenistan (south), and the Aral Sea (west). The capital is Tashkent.
Land and climate. The major part of the country is flat, there are mountains only in the east. The Aral Sea diminishes every year, as a result of the fact

that it does no longer receive any water from rivers such as the Amudarja. The climate is continental, with little precipitation.

People. The inhabitants are mostly Uzbeks (74%), an Islamic people. Russians (6%), Tartars, Kazakhs, and Tajiks are minorities.

Economy. Farming (especially cotton, rice, and fruit), horse breeding, and cattle raising are its chief industries. This country also has rich deposits of coal and oil. Tashkent is the industrial centre of Central Asia.

History. Before the 4th century, it was a province of the Persian Empire. Control of the region then shifted to the Arabs and to other groups, including the Turks, until it finally fell to the Russians toward the end of the 19th century. In 1991 the country gained independence. Since then the government has pursued a policy to liberalize the economy.

See also: Union of Soviet Socialist Republics.

V

V, 22nd letter in the English alphabet, corresponding with the Semitic letter *waw*, meaning "hook," represented by a tenthook symbol probably derived from an ancient Egyptian symbol for a pole support. The Greeks altered it to *Y*, and as the 20th letter of the Roman alphabet it became a *V*, representing both *V*, and *U* sounds. The use of *V* for the *V* sound dates from the Middle Ages, though the old confusion persisted longer. *V* represents 5 in Roman numerals, and serves as an abbreviation for words including *vanadium*, *verb*, *versus*, and *volt*.

Vaccination, method of inducing immunity to infectious disease due to bacteria or virus.Early methods of inducing immunity consisted of the deliberate innoculation of material from a mild case. The vaccinated body forms antibodies and is able to produce large quantities of them rapidly thereafter. This gives protection equivalent to that induced by an attack of the disease. It is occasionally followed by a reaction resembling a mild form of the disease, rarely by the serious manifestations. Persons on steroids, with immunity disorders, or eczema may suffer severe reactions and should generally not receive vaccinations.

See also: Immunity.

Vacuum, region of space devoid of matter. Such a region will neither conduct heat nor transmit sound waves. Because all materials that surround a space have a definite vapor pressure, a perfect vacuum is an impossibility and the term is usually used to denote merely a space containing air or other gas at very low pressure.

Vacuum cleaner, electric appliance that cleans dirt from surfaces such as carpets, rugs, and bare floors by suction. The first vacuum cleaning machines were developed about 1900 by several different inventors.

Vacuum tube, glass or metal envelope that controls electronic currents that are necessary to operate electronic equipment like radios, televisions, and computers. It gets its name from the fact that almost all air is removed from the tube for it to work. Between 1920 and 1950, all electrical equipment used vacuum tubes. They have now been replaced by a newer device, the transistor, which is smaller and more reliable and consumes less power.

Vaduz (pop. 5,000), capital of Liechtenstein, a principality in the Alps between Switzerland and Austria. Many medieval buildings still stand. Within walking distance of the picturesque town is the famous castle of the Liechtenstein princes.

Vagina, female reproductive organ consisting of a tubeshaped canal leading from the external genital orifice to the uterus. It measures 4 in (10 cm). The muscular walls, which are covered with a mucous membrane, fall together to give the vagina a slitlike appearance. During sexual intercourse, the male's penis is inserted into the vagina. During birth the vagina serves as the passage through which the baby leaves the mother's body.
See also: Reproduction.

Vaginitis, inflammation of the vagina, occurring particulary in women of childbearing age. Under normal circumstances, balanced quantities of various bacteria, fungi, and protozoa are present in the vagina. When the balance of these organisms is disrupted and larger amounts of organisms are allowed to reproduce at larger and faster rates, vaginitis occurs. Vaginitis can be triggered by pregnancy, lack of sleep, and poor health and diet. Common symptoms include swelling, itching, and vaginal discharge.

Valence, ability of an atom to form compounds, expressed as the number of electrons an element gives up or accepts from other elements. The meaning of the term has undergone several changes over the past century. One of the first definitions of valence referred to the number of hydrogen atoms with which an atom of a different element could combine. The term then came to encompass the bonding capabilities of ionized (electrically charged) atoms.
See also: Bond, chemical.

Valencia (pop. 752,900), third-largest Spanish city, in eastern Spain on the Turia River. A Roman settlement (138 B.C.), it came under the rule of the Moors (750-1238). Today it is a commercial and industrial center.

Valens (A.D. 328-378), Roman emperor from 364 to 378. He was actually co-emperor, ruling the eastern part, while his brother Valentinian ruled the western part. During his reign the Visigoths, a tribe living along the empire's northern borders, rebelled against the Romans. The Visigoths met and defeated the Romans in the battle of Adrianople. Valens was killed during the fighting.
See also: Rome, Ancient.

Valentine, Saint (d.A.D. 270), Roman martyred priest. His traditional association with love probably reflects the near-coincidence of his feast day (Feb. 14) with the ancient Roman fertility festival of Lupercalia (held Feb. 15). The practice of sending Valentine cards dates from the 19th century.

Valentinian I (A.D. 321-375), Roman emperor who ruled 364-375 in conjunction with his younger brother Valens. Valentinian succeeded the Emperor Jovian and appointed his brother to rule the eastern part of the empire while he ruled the west. During his reign, he subdued the Germanic tribes threatening the western provinces and built fortifications along the Rhine. *See also:* Rome, Ancient.

Valentinian III (A.D. 419-455), Roman emperor 425-455. Though declared emperor at the age of 6; he never ruled the empire in his own right, since political power was wielded in his youth by his mother, Galla Placidia, and later by the patrician Flavius Aëtius. The invasion of the Vandals and Huns occurred during his reign. Hostilities between Valentinian and Aëtius led to the murder of Aëtius by Valentinian (454), who was himself murdered the following year. *See also:* Rome, Ancient.

Valentino, Rudolph (Rodolfo d'Antonguolla; 1895-1926), Italian-born U.S. film star, one of the greatest romantic male stars of the silent film era. Valentino's films included *The Four Horsemen of the Apocalypse* (1921), *The Sheik* (1921), and *Blood and Sand* (1922).

Valera, Eamon de *See:* De Valera, Eamon.

Valerian (d.A.D. 269), Roman emperor 253-60. In 257 he campaigned against the Persians, but was defeated and captured (260) by the Persian emperor, Shapur I, and died in captivity. *See also:* Rome, Ancient.

Valéry, Paul (1871-1945), French poet, essayist, and critic. His early verse, *Album de Vers Anciens* (1920), was influenced by Stéphane Mallarmé. His best-known works are *La Jeune Parque* (1917) and *Le Cimetière Marin* (1920). He wrote on poetry in *Monsieur Tetse* (1896) and also on philosophical and critical themes.

Valhalla, in Scandinavian mythology, paradise hall of the dead where slain warriors live under the leadership of the god Odin. Valhalla is depicted as a magnificent palace built of battle shields, spears, and gold. The chosen heroes are wounded in battle daily and are restored each evening, until led by Odin to battle the giants at the time of Ragnarok, or Doomsday. *See also:* Mythology.

Valkyrie, in Scandinavian mythology, warriorlike maidens sent by Odin to escort dead heroes to Valhalla. The armored Valkyries rode on horseback to the battlefields to choose slain warriors worthy of afterlife. Valkyries were often portents of war in a supernatural or a human form who had the power to cause death. *See also:* Mythology.

Valle, José Cecilio Del (1780-1834), Guatemalan political leader and author of the Central American Declaration of Independence (1821). Valle led Guatemala's fight for independence from Spain, and when the country was annexed by Mexico (1822), he was imprisoned. Although elected vice president of the Central American Confederation (1823), Valle declined to serve. *See also:* Guatemala.

Valletta (pop. 9,200), seaport capital of Malta, on the northeastern coast of the island. A commercial and cultural center, Valletta is the site of the

Royal Malta Library, the Royal University of Malta, and the Manoel Theatre.
See also: Malta.

Valley, long, narrow depression in the earth's surface, usually formed by
glacier or river erosion. Young valleys are narrow, steep-sided, and V-
shaped; mature valleys are broader, with gentler slopes. Rift valleys are the
result of collapse between faults. A hanging valley, of glacial origin, is a side
valley whose floor is considerably higher than that of the main valley.

Valley Forge, area in Pennsylvania about 21 mi (34 km) north of Philadel-
phia where George Washington and his Revolutionary troops camped during
the winter of 1777-78, often called "The Winter of Despair." Washington
had suffered defeats at Brandywine and Germantown, Pa., and Philadelphia
was under British control. The Continental Congress was unable to keep his
troops supplied, and about 10,000 men endured cold and near starvation.
Although publicly criticized for holding this position, Washington remained
steadfast, and with Baron von Steuben, a Prussian military expert, reorgan-
ized the Continental Army. The soldiers were taught new drills and troop
formations, and by winter's end the army was highly disciplined. Valley
Forge National Historic Park now covers the campsite.
See also: Revolutionary War in America.

Valley of the Kings, or Valley of the Tombs of Kings, narrow canyon on
the west bank of the Nile near Thebes, Egypt. It is the site of over 60 ancient
tombs, including the burial places of most of the Pharaohs of the 18th, 19th,
and 20th dynasties (1550-1085 B.C.). Among the tombs are those of Tutank-
hamen, Set I, Thutmose III, Ramses II, Ramses III, and Queen Hatshepsut.
See also: Egypt, Ancient.

Valois, royal house of France that ruled 1328-1589. The first Valois king
was Philip VI; under his rule and that of his descendants, the Valois region
of France was a Duchy held by family members. The rule of the Valois
Dynasty survived the Hundred Years War (1337-1453), and other conflicts.
With the death of Henry III (1589), the crown passed to the house of Bourbon.
See also: France.

Valparaíso (pop. 301,600), seaport city in central Chile, capital of Val-
paraíso province. The city, founded in 1536, lies on the Pacific Ocean about
70 mi (110 km) northwest of Santiago. It is a major center for manufacture.
Chief products include chemicals, textiles, tobacco, sugar and machinery.

Value added by manufacture, statistical measurement of the gain in value
of raw materials after being processed into a finished commodity. This is
computed by subtracting the overall cost of manufacture—including mate-
rials, supplies, storage, fuel, and labor—from the value of the finished
product.

Value-added tax (VAT), tax on the value added to goods or services at each
stage in their production and distribution. It originated in France in 1954 and
was later extended throughout the European Economic Community; it has
been considered at various times in the United States. In effect, VAT is a
sales tax computed on the difference between what a producer pays for a raw

material or semifinished product and what he or she sells it for. The cost of the tax is borne ultimately by consumers. It is a regressive tax because it bears most heavily on low-income people, who spend more and save less than those with high incomes. For government, VAT has the advantage of being broader than most sales taxes and thus producing large revenues even at low rates. The tax is virtually self-enforcing; producers who make tax payments submit claims for credit for the taxes included in their suppliers' prices, and this tends to discourage nonpayment along the line.
See also: Taxation.

Valve, mechanical device that, by opening and closing, enables the flow of fluid in a pipe or other vessel to be controlled. Common valve types are generally named after the shape or mode of operation of the movable element—cone, or needle, valve; gate valve; globe valve; poppet valve; and rotary plug cock. In the butterfly valve a disk pivots on one of its diameters. Self-acting valves include safety valves, usually spring-loaded and designed to open at a predetermined pressure; nonreturn valves, which permit flow in one direction only; and float-operated valves, set to shut off a feeder pipe before a container overflows.

Vampire, in folklore, spirit of the dead that leaves its grave at night to suck the blood of living persons. A victim who dies must be decapitated or buried with a stake through his or her heart, to keep from becoming a vampire.
See also: Dracula.

Vampire bat, South and Central American bat (genera *Desmodus* and *Diphylla*) that feeds on the blood of larger mammals and birds; the only parasitic mammal. The bat cuts a slit with its teeth and laps blood from the wound; anticoagulants in its saliva ensure a constant flow.

Vanadium, chemical element, symbol V; for physical constants see Periodic Table. Vanadium was discovered by A.M. del Rio in 1801. It occurs in the minerals carnotite, roscoelite, vanadinite, and patronite. It is obtained commercially from patronite, a sulfide. The element is prepared by reduction of the trichloride with magnesium. Vanadium is a bright white, soft, ductile metal, resistant to corrosion. It has a low thermal neutron cross section. It is used to bond titanium to steel. Vanadium and its compounds are used in special steels and ceramics and as catalysts and superconductive magnets. Vanadium and its compounds are toxic.

Van Allen, James Alfred (1914-), U.S. physicist and inventor who discovered two zones of radiation surrounding the earth (1958). This led to new knowledge of the effects of cosmic radiation on the earth. Van Allen developed the research rocket Aerobee. He was also instrumental in organizing the International Geophysical Year (1957-58), a program promoting worldwide cooperation in research.

Van Allen belts, 2 belts of high-energy charged particles, mainly protons and electrons, surrounding the earth, named for U.S. physicist James Van Allen, who discovered them in 1958. They extend from a few hundred to about 40,000 mi (65,000 km) above the earth's surface and radiate intensely enough that astronauts must be specially protected from them. The mecha-

nisms for their existence are similar to those involved in the production of the aurora borealis.
See also: Radiation; Van Allen, James Alfred.

Van Buren, Martin (1782-1862), eighth president of the United States. Van Buren was a shrewd judge of people and affairs and a consummate politician who virtually created the Democratic party and made Andrew Jackson president. Van Buren's skill in political maneuvering and in using patronage and the power of the press earned him the nickname "The Little Magician" and "The Fox of Kinderhook." But what he could do for others, he could not do as well for himself. His presidency did not lack achievement, but his do-nothing attitude in the face of the United States' first major depression cost him reelection.

Early life. With a rudimentary education, Van Buren studied law from an early age under a local lawyer. He was admitted to the bar in 1803. He began a successful legal career in Kinderhook, N.Y., entering local politics at about the same time. In 1807, he married Hannah Hoes. She died in 1819; he never remarried.

Politics. Van Buren served as surrogate of Columbia County, N.Y., then as New York senator and attorney general. His industry and political astuteness soon won him influence within the Republican Party. In 1821, he was elected to the U.S. Senate.

He stood for state's rights and opposed a strong central government, began to bring together other powerful Republicans who shared his sentiments. These "new" Republicans became the Democratic Party. In 1828, the year Jackson won the presidency, Van Buren was elected governor of New York. But within a few months, he resigned to become Jackson's secretary of state (1829-31). He served Jackson more as a political manager than as a cabinet member and became one of the most powerful men in Washington. He drafted Jackson's speeches, smoothed his relations with Congress, and continued to build up the Democratic Party. When Jackson won reelection in 1832, Van Buren was his running mate. In 1836, Jackson supported Van Buren for the presidency as his "hand-picked" successor; Van Buren defeated Whig candidate William Henry Harrison.

President. Within days of Van Buren's inauguration, the Panic of 1837 broke. Banks and business failed, specie payments were suspended, and rents, fuel and food prices soared. The Panic had been caused by unchecked speculation in western lands, manufacturing, transportation, and banking. A firm hand was needed to control it, but Van Buren, who believed that "the

---

Martin Van Buren

8th president of the United States

Born:	Kinderhook, N.Y.; Dec. 5, 1782.
Term:	Mar. 1837-Mar. 1841.
Vice president:	Richard M. Johnson.
Political party:	Democratic.
Spouse:	Hannah Hoes.
Children:	4.
Died:	Kinderhook, N.Y.; July 24, 1862.

less government interferes with private pursuits the better for the general prosperity," did almost nothing. Inevitably, he was blamed for the depression, as well as for the costly war against the Seminoles in Florida. He also antagonized the South by opposing the annexation of Texas. He was nominated for reelection in 1840, but had little chance of winning. The rough campaign tactics used to elect Jackson were used against Van Buren, and he lost to Harrison.

Retirement. Van Buren retired to his country estate at Kinderhook. He ran for president as a Democrat in 1844 but failed to win nomination; he ran again in 1848 on the Free-Soil ticket and lost. He died on July 24, 1862.

Vance, Cyrus (1917-), U.S. public official. A Wall Street lawyer, he was secretary of the army (1962-63) and deputy secretary of defense (1964-67). An experienced diplomatic troubleshooter, he served as President Carter's secretary of state (1977-80), resigning in protest over the abortive attempt to rescue U.S. diplomatic hostages in Iran. In 1993 Vance and Lord Owen (former Brittish foreign minister) devised a peace keeping plan for Yugoslavia, which was rejected by the Bosnian Serbs. After several futile attempts to establish peace in former Yugoslavia, Vance resigned as EU-mediator.

Vancouver (pop. 42,800), city in southwestern Washington, seat of Clark County. Founded by the Hudson's Bay Company as a trading fort (1825), the city is a port on the Columbia River.
See also: Washington.

Vancouver (pop. 1,602,500), largest city in British Columbia and third-largest in Canada, located on the Burrard Inlet, Strait of Georgia. Originally known as Granville, in 1886 it was renamed for the English explorer George Vancouver. It is an important Pacific port and a major manufacturing center for wood, paper, iron, steel, and chemical products. Other industries are shipbuilding, oil refining, and fish processing. After becoming the terminus of the trans-Canada railroad (1886), it rapidly expanded.
See also: British Columbia.

Vancouver, George (1757-98), English explorer. He took part in Captain Cook's voyages (1772-80) and in 1791-94 led an expedition that explored the Pacific and surveyed the American coast from San Luis Obispo, Calif., to British Columbia. He made surveys of Vancouver Island and the Strait of Georgia, visited Cook's Inlet, Alaska, and failed to find a Northwest Passage. The city of Vancouver, in British Columbia, Canada, was named after him in 1886.

Vancouver Island, largest island on the Pacific North American Coast, off southwestern British Columbia, Canada. Vancouver is separated from mainland Canada by a series of straits. The island is the southernmost end of a partially sunken mountain range called the Vancouver Range. It has a particularly mild climate due to the flow of the Japan Current. The mountain slopes are covered with extensive cedar and fir forests. Major industries include lumber, farming, and tourism. Victoria, Vancouver Island's largest city, is the capital of British Columbia.

Vandals, ancient Germanic people. They gradually migrated from south of the Baltic to Pannonia and Dacia. In the 5th century they invaded the Roman Empire, ravaging Gaul and Spain. Under Genseric they established a strong

Vandal kingdom in northern Africa (429) that extended to Sicily, and in 455 they sacked Rome. The Vandals were finally defeated by the Byzantine Belisarius, after which they disappeared as a unified people.

Van de Graaff, Robert Jemison (1901-67), U.S. physicist and inventor of the electrostatic generator, used in nuclear research. While a student at the Sorbonne, Van de Graaff attended lectures given by Marie Curie. He formed the idea for his generator when he realized that the study of atomic behavior requires a source of energetic beams of subatomic particles. In 1946 he became a founder of the High Voltage Engineering Corporation (HVEC).

Van de Graaff generator, or electrostatic generator, device for generating a high voltage charge, important in the study of nuclear power. Invented in the 1930s by Robert Van de Graaff, the machine operates by carrying electrical charges from a collection of high-voltage points on a moving belt into a hollow metal casing. A metallic brush transports the charge to the surface of the casing, and as the charge accumulates, the voltage increases. *See also:* Particle accelerator; Van de Graaff, Robert Jemison.

Vanderbilt, Cornelius (1794-1877), U.S. transportation mogul. Known as Commodore, he began with a ferry service that grew into an international steamship business. In the 1860s, he purchased a number of small eastern railroads. His group dominated the Northeast by the 1870s and controlled the New York-Chicago route. He established Vanderbilt University at Nashville, Tenn.

Van der Goes, Hugo (1440?-82), Flemish painter of religious subjects. He was influenced by Jan van Eyck and Rogier van der Weyden. Among his works are the *Portinari Altarpiece* (c.1476) and *Death of the Virgin* (c.1480).

Van der Meer, Simon (1925-), Dutch physicist who shared the 1984 Nobel Prize for physics with Carlo Rubia for their leading roles in planning and executing the experiments, reported in 1983, that demonstrated the existence of the elementary particles called intermediate vector bosons. *See also:* Boson; Physics.

Van der Waals, Johannes Diderik (1837-1923), Dutch physicist who investigated the properties of real gases. Noting that the kinetic theory of gases assumed that the molecules had neither size nor interactive forces between them, in 1873 he proposed **Van der Waals' equation**, in which allowance is made for both these factors. The weak attractive forces between molecules are therefore named Van der Waals forces. He received the 1910 Nobel Prize for physics. *See also:* Physics.

Van der Weyden, Rogier (1399?-1464), Flemish painter of religious subjects. He was probably influenced by Robert Campin and Jan van Eyck. He masterfully captured intangible emotion, while also distancing the viewer, in such works as *The Descent from the Cross* (c.1435).

Van Devanter, Willis (1859-1941), associate justice of the U.S. Supreme Court (1911-37). His opinions were staunchly conservative, and he was opposed to social welfare legislation and the New Deal. *See also:* Supreme Court of the United States.

Van Doren, Carl (1885-1950), U.S. author, educator, and literary critic. Van Doren taught at Columbia University (1911-30) and was an editor of the *Cambridge History of American Literature* (1917-21); *The Nation* (1919-22); and *Century Magazine* (1922-25). He is best known for his biographies, including *Swift* (1930), *Sinclair Lewis* (1933), and *Jane Mecom* (1950). He was awarded the Pulitzer Prize in 1939 for his biography *Benjamin Franklin* (1938).

Van Doren, Mark (1894-1972), U.S. poet and critic. His *Collected Poems* (1939) earned him the Pulitzer Prize in 1940. As a critic, Van Doren began his career with a study of Henry David Thoreau in 1916. His major critical writings appear in *Private Reader* (1942) and *The Happy Critic* (1961). Van Doren was a renowned professor of English at Columbia University (1920-59), where his students included John Berryman and Lionel Trilling. He also wrote plays, novels, and short stories.

Van Dyck, Sir Anthony (1599-1641), Flemish baroque portrait and religious painter. He was a pupil of Peter Paul Rubens, and his portrait style, influenced by Venetian art, was one of elegantly posed figures and rich but refined color and handling, particularly of materials. He painted Italian and English nobility and was court painter from 1632 to Charles I of England. *See also:* Baroque.

Van Eyck, Jan (1390-1441), Flemish painter. The first leading artist from the Netherlands, he collaborated with his older brother, Hubert (c.1370-1426), on the Ghent altarpiece. Completed in 1432, it comprises more than 250 figures in 20 panels. Van Eyck's other important works include a number of portraits, such as *Giovanni Arnolfini and His Bride* (1434). All are remarkable for realistic, closely observed details. He was the first painter to develop effects of richness, brilliance, and intensity in oil paint.

Van Gogh, Vincent (1853-90), Dutch postimpressionist painter. His early, dark-toned work, done in the Netherlands, focuses on peasant life. Later (1886-88), in Paris, he met Paul Gauguin and Georges Seurat. In 1888 he moved to Arles, in southern France, where—among many other paintings—he produced the brilliantly colored *Sunflowers* in a direct style and the symbolic *The Night Café*, using color suggestively. After a fit of insanity, in which he cut off his left ear (1889), he painted at the asylums of St. Rémy and Auvers. In *Portrait of Dr. Gachet* (1890) he attempted to express ideas and emotion in and through paint. He committed suicide.

Vanilla, any of various tropical vines (genus *Vanilla*) of the orchid family; the term also refers to the extract made from the vine's pods and used for flavoring. The plants grow to about 50 ft (15.2 m) and bear yellow-green flowers that produce the pods, 5-10 in (13-25 cm) in length. Vanilla extract is obtained by a process of pulverization of the cured vanilla pods which are then heated in alcohol and water. Vanilla is widely used to flavor chocolate, candy, ice cream, baked goods, and beverages.

Van Leeuwenhoek, Anton *See:* Leeuwenhoek, Anton van.

Van Leyden, Lucas (1494?-1533), Dutch engraver and painter. Van Leyden's engravings are finely executed compositions without any particular

Vanuatu

Capital:	Port Vila
Area:	4,707 sq mi
	(12,190 sq km)
Population:	185,000
Language:	English, French,
	Bislama
Government:	Republic
Independent:	1980
Head of gov.:	Prime minister
Per capita:	U.S. $1,200
Mon. unit:	1 Vatu = 100 centimes

central character. His engraving technique, utilizing precise cutting strokes, created depth and the illusion of light and shadow. His works include *Abraham and Isaac*, *Ecce Homo*, and *The Milkmaid* (all early 1500s).

Van Rensselaer, Kiliaen (1595-1643), Dutch colonizer and leading *patroon* (landowner). A member of the Dutch West India Company, he established the manor of Rensselaerswyck on the banks of the Hudson River, south of Albany.

Vanuatu, officially the Republic of Vanuatu, formerly the New Hebrides, independent republic consisting of 80 small islands, situated east of Australia and extending over some 500 mi (805 km) of the South Pacific Ocean.
Land. The overall area of the islands of Vanuatu is 4,707 sq mi (12,190 km). Espíritu Santo, the largest island, has an area of 1,542 sq mi (3,994 sq km). The capital, Vila, is on the second-largest island, Efâte. The islands are of volcanic origin and there are 6 active volcanos. The rugged mountainous interiors, densely covered with tropical rain forests, give way to narrow coastal strips where most of the islands' inhabitants live.
People. Almost all the people of Vanuatu are Melanesians. There are also small Chinese, British, and French minorities. The official languages are Bislama, English, and French.
Economy. About 70% of the people live in rural villages and pursue traditional subsistence farming. They grow coconuts and other fruits, yams, and taro; pigs are raised for food and ceremonial purposes. Local industries process copra, fish, and beef for export. Manganese has been mined since 1961, and tourism is increasing. Special tax laws have made Vanuatu a banking center and corporate haven.
History. There is evidence of human settlements on the islands as early as 1300 B.C., but the islands were not discovered by Europeans until the arrival of the Portuguese in 1606. The British and French explored the islands in the 18th century. During the 19th century, strife broke out between native inhabitants and British and French settlers. In 1906 a joint British-French condominium was established to rule the islands. In 1980, on the eve of independence, fighting broke out on Espíritu Santo where guerrillas were mounting an armed struggle for that island's secession. The fighting ended after British peacekeeping forces arrived. A 1987 hurricane caused much

death and destruction. In the 1990s Vanuatu agreed to destroy a number of American chemical weapons on Johnston, a remote coral island.

Vanzetti, Bartolomeo *See:* Sacco-Vanzetti case.

Vapor, substance that, though present in the gaseous phase, generally exists as a liquid or solid at room temperature.
See also: Evaporation.

Varanasi (pop. 932,400), formerly Benaras, ancient city in Uttar Pradesh State, on the Ganges River in northern India. The city is of great religious import as a center for Hindu pilgrimage, with over 1,500 temples and shrines. Varanasi has miles of riverfront ghats, or stairways, from which pilgrims may bathe in the holy Ganges River before praying. Industries include textiles and brassware. Varanasi is the site of Benaras Hindu University (1916) and the Mosque of Aurangzeb.
See also: India.

Varèse, Edgard (1883-1965), French-born U.S. composer of non-traditional music and sound techniques. *Ionisation* (1931), his most famous composition, is written for numerous percussion instruments and two sirens. Other works include *Hyperprism* (1923), and *Density 21.5* (1935). After 1950 Varèse concentrated mainly on electronically produced music.

Vargas, Getúlio Dornelles (1883-1954), president of Brazil (1930-45,1951-54). He set up a "New State" (1937), strongly centralized government-promoted industrial, economic, and social development. Opposition from the army during his second term led him to commit suicide.
See also: Brazil.

Vargas Llosa, Mario (1936-), Peruvian author of novels depicting modern Peruvian social and political life. His novels include *The Time of the Hero* (1962), *The Green House* (1966), *Conversations in the Cathedral* (1969), *The War of the End of the World* (1984), *Who Killed Palomino Molero?* (1987), and *The Storyteller* (1989). Vargas Llosa was an unsuccessful candidate for the presidency of Peru in 1990. In 1994, he received the Cervantes Prize for his complete works.

Varicella *See:* Chickenpox.

Varicose vein, enlarged or twisting vein, usually occuring in the legs, resulting from incompetent or damaged valves in the veins. Unpleasant in appearance, they cause venous stagnation, with skin eczema and ulcers on the inside of the ankle, hemorrhage, and edema (swelling). Treatment includes support stockings and, in more serious cases, removal through surgery.
See also: Vein.

Varnish, solution of resin that dries to form a hard, transparent film. It is widely applied to wood, metal, and masonry to improve surface properties without changing appearance. There are two main types: spirit varnishes, consisting of natural or synthetic resins dissolved in a volatile solvent such

Vatican City

Area:	109 acres (44 hectares)
Population:	840
Language:	Latin, Italian
Government:	Sovereign state
Independent:	1929
Head of gov.:	Pope
Mon. unit:	1 Italian lira = 100 centesimi

as alcohol, and oleoresinous varnishes—more resistant to heat and weather—which are mixtures of resins and drying oils dissolved in turpentine or a petroleum oil. Lacquer, the original wood varnish, is the sap of the varnish tree.
See also: Resin.

Varying hare *See:* Snowshoe hare.

Vasco Da Gama *See:* Da Gama, Vasco.

Vasectomy, sterilization procedure for men. The vas deferens are cut to prevent sperm from reaching the seminal vesicles and hence the urethra of the penis. It does not affect ejaculation.
See also: Sterilization.

Vásquez de Coronado, Francisco *See:* Coronado, Francisco Vásquez de.

Vassal *See:* Feudalism.

Vatican City, independent state, the world's smallest. It occupies 108.7 acres (44 hectares) of territory within the city of Rome, Italy. Vatican City serves as the spiritual, administrative, and political center of Roman Catholicism, and it is ruled by the pope, as head of the Roman Catholic church. It has a population of c.1,000 and its official languages are Italian and Latin. Vatican City is dominated by Saint Peter's basilica and the Vatican Palace, one of the world's largest residential palaces. Among the city's treasures are the frescoes of the Sistine Chapel executed by Michelangelo Buonarroti as well as the paintings, sculpture, and other artifacts in the Vatican Museum collection. The Vatican Archive and Library contain many priceless manuscripts and, reputedly, the world's most extensive holdings of erotic literature, including a collection that once belonged to Benjamin Franklin.
The Vatican has its own bank, mints its own coins, and oversees the administration and investment of the church's assets worldwide. The city has no income tax and no restriction on the import or export of funds. It has its own broadcasting facilities, railroad station, and the newspaper *L'Osservatore Romano*. The Swiss Guard, the pope's personal bodyguard, are Vatican

City's army. The city maintains diplomatic relations with many countries throughout the world by means of ambassadors, called nuncios, and sends apostolic delegates to other countries to represent the church's interests. As a matter of tradition and practice, the U.S. government did not post an ambassador to the papal court in the 18th and 19th centuries, nor to the Vatican City for most of the 20th century. Under President Ronald Reagan, the United States broke with a long-standing tradition and appointed an ambassador to Vatican City.

The official independence of Vatican City from Italy was established in 1929 following a long period of estrangement between the papacy and Italy over the papacy's loss of its once extensive territorial holdings, known as the Papal States, on the Italian peninsula. The issue was finally resolved in the Lateran Treaty negotiated that year between Cardinal Pietro Gasparri for the papacy and the Fascist dictator Benito Mussolini. In 1993 official ties with Israel were established and in 1994 with Jordan. The latter step was taken in order to improve relations with the Arab world.

See also: Roman Catholic Church.

Vatican Councils, the two most recent Roman Catholic ecumenical councils, held at the Vatican. Vatican Council I (1869-70), summoned by Pius IX, restated traditional dogma against materialism, rationalism, and liberalism. It also declared the pope to be infallible when, speaking *ex cathedra*, he defines a doctrine of faith or morals. Some dissenters seceded as Old Catholics. Vatican Council II (1962-65), summoned by John XXIII, aimed at renewal of the church, the updating of its organization and attitude to the modern world, and the ultimate reunion of all Christian churches. Protestant and Orthodox observers attended. Along with calling for a reform of the ministry and liturgy, including increased lay participation and use of vernacular languages, the council decreed that the bishops with the pope form a body ("collegiality") and that the Virgin Mary is "Mother of the Church."

Vatican Library, official library of the Roman Catholic Church in Vatican City. It was founded by Pope Nicholas V (r.1447-55) as a library for handwritten manuscripts. Open to scholars, the library contains about 1 million printed books and more than 70,000 manuscripts.

Vaudeville, term for variety shows deriving from Vau de Vire, a French valley and source of 15th-century songs, or from *voix de ville*, French street songs. It was applied from the 1880s to U.S. shows with musical, comic, dramatic, acrobatic, and juggling acts. Noted artists included Eddie Cantor, Will Rogers, and W. C. Fields. Vaudeville declined in the 1930s.

Vaughan Williams, Ralph (1872-1958), English composer famous for his use of traditional English folk music. The three *Norfolk Rhapsodies* (1906) were the first major works characteristic of his distinctive style. Other works include nine symphonies.

VD *See:* Venereal disease.

Veal, meat of young cattle or calves. The calves are fed on milk and the meat is drained of blood. As a result, veal is light in color and in flavor. Consumption in the United States averages about 4 1/2 lb (2 kg) per person yearly.

Veblen, Thorstein Bunde (1857-1929), U.S. economist and author. A social theorist known for his study of economic evolution and social change, Veblen produced sharp analyses of the wealthy classes. His *Theory of the Leisure Class* (1899), coined such terms as "conspicuous consumption" and "pecuniary emulation." Other works include *The Theory of Business Enterprise* (1904), a criticism of capitalism; and *The Engineers and the Price System* (1921).
See also: Economics.

Vecellio, Tiziano *See:* Titian.

Vector *See:* Force.

Vedanta (Sanskrit, "end of knowledge"), system of Hindu philosophy, based at first on the Upanishads (the final part of the Veda) and later on the Brahma Sutras, commentaries on the Upanishads, that date from the 1st century A.D. The Vedanta concern the relation of the individual (*atman*) to the Absolute (*Brahman*).
See also: Upanishads.

Vedas (Sanskrit, "knowledge"), most ancient of Indian scriptures, believed to have been inspired by God and basic to Hinduism. There are 4 *Samhitas* or collections of mantras (hymns)—the *Rig, Yajur, Sama*, and *Atharva-Veda*. The oldest may date from 1500 B.C. Vedic literature consists of the Veda itself, the *Brahmanas* and *Aranyakas, and the Upanishads.*
See also: Hinduism.

Veery (*Catharus fuscescens*), brownish bird of the thrush family, found in the northeastern United States and Canada. It is about 7 in (18 cm) long and nests in the lower branches of bushes or small trees.

Vega, or Alpha Lyrae, brightest main-sequence star in the constellation Lyra in the northern hemisphere, the fourth-brightest star in the night sky. The star is surrounded by a shell of solid particles indicating that it may be a solar system in a formative state. Vega is 26 light years away and is expected to become earth's polar star c.A.D. 14,000.
See also: Star.

Vega, Lope de (1562-1635), Spanish dramatist and poet credited with founding Spain's national drama. A prolific writer, Lope produced 426 plays of which 42 short ones survive. He also wrote narrative poetry, prose romances, and a poetical essay, *The New Art of Writing Plays* (1609), that expounded his theories of drama. His main themes were the friction between the masses and a corrupt nobility and the conflicts of honor and passion.

Vegetable, general term for the edible part of a plant. Vegetables are excellent sources of vitamins, iron, and calcium. They are sometimes grouped according to the part of the plant they represent: flower clusters (e.g. cauliflower), fruits (tomatoes), leaves (spinach), roots (carrots), seeds (peas), stems (asparagus), tubers (potatoes), and bulbs (onions).

Vegetable oil, substance obtained from the seeds of plants and the fleshy part of fruits. It consists almost entirely of fat, an important part of a healthy diet. It is used in both the production and the cooking of many foods. Soybean oil is the most commonly used vegetable oil in the United States, followed by corn, cottonseed, olive, peanut, safflower, and sunflower oil. Most margarines are made with soybean or sunflower oils as the main ingredient.

Vegetarianism, restriction of one's food to substances of vegetable origin. Vegetarianism is practiced variously for health and fitness and because of ethical or religious beliefs. A vegetarian is a person who abstains from eating meat, either keeping strictly to a diet of vegetables, grains, nuts, and fruit, or including eggs, milk, butter, and cheese. The latter is called an ovo-lacto-vegetarian.

Vein, thin-walled collapsible vessel that returns blood to the heart from the tissue capillaries. Veins contain valves that prevent back-flow, especially in the legs. Blood drains from the major veins into the inferior to superior vena cava.

Velázquez, Diego (1599-1660), Spanish painter. In 1623, he became court painter to King Philip IV of Spain. His style was influenced strongly by his Flemish contemporary, Peter Paul Rubens, and also by Italian artists of the High Renaissance. His masterpieces include *The Drunkards*, *Christ on the Cross*, and *The Maids of Honor*.
See also: Renaissance.

Velocity, vector quantity expressing the direction and speed of any moving object. Velocity may be uniform, in which case both speed and direction remain constant, or variable, in which case speed and/or direction change.
See also: Falling bodies, Law of.

Velvet leaf *See:* Indian mallow.

Venerable Bede, The *See:* Bede, Saint.

Venereal disease, name for infectious diseases transmitted mainly or exclusively by sexual contact. *Gonorrhea* is an acute bacterial disease that is frequently asymptomatic in females, although they may suffer mild cervicitis or urethritis. In males it may be asymptomatic also, but it usually causes a painful urethritis with urethral discharge of pus. Gonorrhea is best treated with penicillin. *Syphilis*, due to *Treponema pallidum*, a spirochete, is a disease with 2 stages. A painless genital ulcer, or chancre, develops in the weeks after contact. Secondary syphilis, starting weeks or months after infection, involves fever, malaise, and a characteristic rash, as well as organ disease (hepatitis, meningitis). If the disease is treated with a full course of penicillin in the early stages, its progression is prevented. Tertiary syphilis takes several forms. Gummas—chronic rubbery tumors affecting skin, epithelium, bone, or internal organs—may develop. Tertiary syphilis causes heart disease. Syphilis of the nervous system may cause tabes dorsalis, primary eye disease, chronic meningitis, or paralysis, with mental disturbance, personality change, failure of judgment, and muscular weakness. Penicillin may only partially reverse late syphilis. Other venereal diseases include Reiter's disease (in males only), genital trichomoniasis, thrush, *Herpes simplex* virus, and "nonspecific urethritis." Tropical venereal dis-

Venezuela

Capital:	Caracas
Area:	352,144 sq mi
	(912,050 sq km)
Population:	22,803,000
Language:	Spanish
Government:	Federal presidential
	republic
Independent:	1830
Head of gov.:	President
Per capita:	U.S. $3,020
Mon. unit:	1 Bolívar = 100
	céntimos

eases include chancroid, lymphogranuloma venereum, and granuloma inguinale.

Venezuela, republic in northern South America. Covering an area of 352,134 sq mi (912,050 sq km), Venezuela extends along the Caribbean coast from Colombia in the west and southwest to Guyana in the east. It is bordered by Brazil to the south and the Caribbean Sea in the north. The capital is Caracas.

Land. Venezuela may be divided into 4 contrasting geographical regions: the Venezuelan Highlands in the west and north; the coastal lowlands; the great central plain called the Llanos, dominated by the Orinoco River; and the Guiana Highlands. The Venezuelan Highlands are an extension of the Andes. Entering the country in the southwest, they contain Venezuela's highest mountains, including Pico Bolívar rising to 16,411 ft (5,002 m) to dominate the Sierra Nevada de Mérida. The central highlands with their fertile valleys form the most important part of the country and contain several large cities, including the capital, Caracas. The coastal lowlands, almost completely enclosed by mountains and centered on swamp-fringed Lake Maracaibo, are known as the Maracaibo Lowlands. They constitute one of the world's great oil-producing regions. The lowlands are known for their hot and humid climate. Inland lies the great central grassland plains called the Llanos. Covering some 120,000 sq mi (310,800 sq km) and drained by many streams descending from the mountains to the Orinoco River, they are the great cattle-grazing region of Venezuela. Finally, the Guiana Highlands, south of the Orinoco River, cover about half of Venezuela and are very thinly populated. Much of the region is covered with tropical forests and parts have yet to be explored. Angel Falls, the highest falls in the world at a height of 3,212 ft (979 m), are located in the Guiana Highlands.

People. Nearly 70% of the people of Venezuela are mestizo, a mixture of whites and Native Americans. About 20% of the population is white, mostly of Spanish descent; another 10% of the people are of black African descent; and 2% are Native Americans. The official language is Spanish and the dominant religion is Roman Catholicism.

Economy. Oil was first discovered in Venezuela in 1918. Since then, the country has been a major oil producer, although its share of the world market declined in the 1970s. Venezuela now accounts for 4% of the world's output. It also produces natural gas and iron ore. The country's chief agricultural products are coffee, rice, and cocoa. Oil revenues have been used to finance irrigation projects, industrial diversification, public works, and social welfare programs.

History. Venezuela was discovered by Columbus in 1498, but may have been named by the Italian navigator Amerigo Vespucci, who sailed the north coast of South America in 1501. When the first Spanish settlement was founded at Cumaná in 1521, the country was inhabited by Arawaks and Caribs. The Spanish had to overcome fierce resistance in establishing dominion. Venezuelan independence, unsuccessfully attempted by Francisco de Miranda in 1806, was proclaimed by a national congress in 1811. Miranda became dictator in 1812, but was imprisoned by the Spanish. Simón Bolívar, who was born in Venezuela, led the independence struggle and triumphed in 1821. He made the country part of Greater Colombia, but it later broke free and became an independent republic in 1830 under José Antonio Páez. Dictatorships followed, the longest and most successful under Juan Vicente Gómez, who ruled the country from 1908 to 1935. It was under Gómez that Venezuela's oil riches were first developed and concessions granted to foreign companies. In 1958, the corrupt dictatorship of Marcos Pérez Jiménez was brought down by a military junta under Rómulo Betancourt and the country was restored to democracy. The petroleum industry was nationalized peacefully in 1976. Venezuela's economy suffered in the early 1980s with the drop in oil prices, but new discoveries of oil fields and higher oil prices brought on by the crisis in the Persian Gulf (1990) have led to a boost in oil production. In 1998 saw an economic recession , when prices on the world market plummeted.

Venezuela Boundary Dispute, chiefly from 1841, Anglo-Venezuelan dispute over the location of the British Guiana-Venezuela border. In 1895 U.S. president Grover Cleveland, invoking the Monroe Doctrine, demanded arbitration supervised by the United States. This initially strained Anglo-U.S. relations almost to the point of war, but Britain submitted to arbitration, and a boundary was agreed upon in 1899.
See also: Monroe Doctrine.

Venice (pop. 305,600), city in northeastern Italy, seaport capital of the Veneto region and Venezia province. It comprises 118 islands in the Lagoon of Venice at the head of the Adriatic Sea. Transport is mainly along the famous canals by motorboat and gondola. Venice is built on piles sunk deep into the mud and is linked by a causeway to the mainland. The first *doge* (duke) was elected in 697. Venice rose to control trade between Europe and the East. At its height (15th century), Venice ruled many areas along the coast of the eastern Mediterranean, the Aegean, and parts of the Black Sea. Its power weakened during the long struggle with the Ottoman Empire (1453-1718). It fell to Napoleon Bonaparte in 1797 and became part of Italy in 1866. Venice is now a major tourist resort, boasting unique beauty and a magnificent cultural heritage.
See also: Italy.

Venkataraman, Ramaswamy (1910-), Indian statesman and president of India (1987-92). Venkataraman was an attorney and pro-labor advocate and social worker who was elected to parliament (1950). He served as minister

of finance (1980-84), and as minister of defense (1982-84). He was active in the United Nations and then served as Indira Gandhi's vice president (1984-87).
See also: India.

Ventricle *See:* Heart.

Ventris, Michael George Francis (1922-56), English architect and cryptographer who deciphered (1953) Linear B, a semipictorial Minoan-Mycenaean script, and showed it to be an ancient form of Greek. Following World War II, during which he was trained as a decoder, Ventris established a Committee of Correspondents, a group of scholars worldwide. With their advice, he set about deciphering the script, discovered on a number of clay tablets at Knossos, Crete (1900-08). Ventris used statistical analysis to plot a tentative syllabary. The results were published as "Evidence for Greek Dialect in Mycenaean Archives" (1953) and are significant for proving the Greek world to be literate some 500 years before Homer.

Venturi, Robert (1925-), U.S. architect. A controversial critic of the purely functional and spare designs of modern orthodox architecture, he set forth his "counterrevolutionary" views in *Complexity and Contradiction in Architecture* (1966) and *Learning from Las Vegas* (1972).
See also: Architecture.

Venus, in Roman mythology, goddess of love and beauty. Originally a minor deity associated with gardens, fruits, and flowers, Venus was adopted by Latin soldiers (c.217 B.C.) who enlarged her image to symbolize the life force. Venus was closely identified with the Greek Aphrodite. The Julii family, ancestors of Julius Caesar, were her priests.
See also: Mythology.

Venus, second planet from the sun in the solar system. Its diameter is 7,700 mi (12,392 km), slightly smaller than that of the earth. Its face is completely obscured by dense clouds containing sulfuric acid, although the USSR's spaceprobes *Venera-9* and *Venera-10* (Oct.1975) landings provided photographs of the planet's rocky surface. Venus revolves about the sun at a mean distance of 67.2 million mi (108.2 million km) in 225 days, rotating on its axis in a retrograde direction in 243 days. Its atmosphere is 97% carbon dioxide, and its surface temperature is c.850°F (455°C). Venus has no known moons and could not support life.
See also: Planet; Solar System.

Venus de Milo, armless statue of the Greek goddess Aphrodite. It was carved in marble c.150 B.C. and was discovered (1820) on the island of Melos. It is now in the Louvre in Paris.

Venus's-flytrap (*Dionaea muscipula*), insect-catching plant that lives in the sandy country of the Carolinas and neighboring states. Its leaves form a rosette against the ground, and the outer part of each forms a pad hinged in the middle. Around the edge of the pad are stiff teeth and 3 spines stick up from the middle of the pad. When an insect brushes the spines, the pad rapidly folds up so that the insect is caught behind the teeth. Secretions digest the soft parts of the insect's body. The Venus-flytrap's speed is remarkable. It has even been recorded catching a small frog.

Veracruz (pop. 295,300), port city in east central Mexico on the Gulf of Mexico. Once the site of a Native American village, Veracruz is now an important shipping center handling much of Mexico's foreign trade. It exports sugar, coffee, vanilla, chicle, and petroleum products. The city manufactures tiles, chocolate, liquor, footwear, and textiles. Gallega Island protects the harbor and is the site of the Spanish fortress of San Juan de Ulua (1565).
See also: Mexico.

Verbena, genus (*Verbena*) of the vervain family of herbaceous plants, especially several cultivated species with blue, white, crimson, purple, or striped flowers.

Verdi, Giuseppe (1813-1901), Italian opera composer. He rose to fame during the struggle for Italian unification and independence; early operas, such as *Nabucco* (1842), express these political ideals. By the time of *Rigoletto* (1851), *Il Trovatore* (1853), and *La Traviata* (1853), he had developed his powerful individual style well beyond the conventions inherited from Gioacchino Rossini, Gaetano Donizetti, and Vincenzo Bellini. *Don Carlos* (1867), *Aïda* (1871), and the *Requiem* (1874) honoring the novelist Alessandro Manzoni are works of his maturity. The 2 great Shakespearian operas of Verdi's old age, *Otello* (1887) and *Falstaff* (1893), were written to libretti by Arrigo Boito.
See also: Opera.

Verdin (*Auriparus flaviceps*), songbird common in low deserts and brush-lands of the U.S. Southwest and northern Mexico. The verdin is gray, with a yellow head, long tail, and sharp, black bill. It makes an oblong, thorny nest with a small side opening and the female lays 3 to 6 blue-green eggs. The verdin feeds on small insects and is usually seen singly but may travel in pairs or small family groups.

Verdun, Battle of (Feb.-Dec. 1916), major World War I engagement. The Germans launched a concentrated offensive against the fortified line of Verdun. The French logistically could not abandon this position, and the Germans hoped to exhaust France's forces during the battle. Total casualties were well over 700,000. No significant advantage was gained by either side.
See also: World War I.

Verdun, Treaty of, pact (A.D. 843) concluding the civil war between the heirs of Louis I, by which Charlemagne's empire was divided between his 3 grandchildren (Louis's sons). Lothair I kept the title emperor and received Italy and a narrow strip of land from Provence to Friesland. Louis the German received the lands between the Rhine and Elbe. Charles the Bald held the area west of the Rhine.
See also: Charlemagne.

Vergil, or **Virgil** (Publius Vergilius Maro; 70-19 B.C.), Roman poet. Maecenas became his patron and Octavian (later the Emperor Augustus) his friend. He won recognition with his *Eclogues* or *Bucolics*, pastoral poems reflecting the events of his own day. The *Georgics*, a didactic poem on farming, uses the world of the farmer as a model for the world at large. His last 10 years were spent on his epic masterpiece, the *Aeneid*, about the wanderings of the Trojan War survivor Aeneas and his struggle to found Rome.

Verlaine, Paul (1844-96), French poet, an early and influential exponent of symbolism. While imprisoned (1873-75) for shooting and wounding his friend and lover, the poet Arthur Rimbaud, he wrote *Romances sans Paroles* (1874), one of his finest volumes. After a period of religious piety, he returned to his life of bohemian dissipation and died in poverty.

Vermeer, Jan (1632-75), Dutch painter who spent his entire life in Delft. His interior scenes are noted for superb control of light, precise tonality, cool harmonious coloring, and classical composition. Of the fewer than 40 works attributed to him, his masterpieces include *The Letter* and *Head of a Girl* (both 1665).

Vermiculite, foliated clay mineral formed as a change in biotite. Vermiculite is soft, yellow or brown in color, with a monoclinic crystal structure. When heated, it can expand to a lightweight, highly absorbent, fireproof material about 16 times its original volume. Deposits occur in the United States, Australia, the USSR, South Africa, and Brazil. Vermiculite is used in construction as a sound and thermal insulator, as a fireproofing element, and as a potting medium for plants.

Vermont, state in New England, the northeastern region of the United States; bordered by Canada to the north, the Connecticut River (with New Hampshire on the other side) to the east, Massachusetts to the south, and New York and Lake Champlain to the west.

Land and climate. Vermont has 6 main land regions. The Northeast Highlands are part of the White Mountain range of New Hampshire. In the Western New England Upland, which lines most of the state's eastern border, lies the broad, fertile Connecticut River Valley. In the Green Mountains region, rounded peaks run north-south through the center of the state. The Champlain Valley is a fertile lowland area bordering Lake Champlain. In the southwest lie the Taconic Mountains region, part of a mountain range running from Massachusetts into Vermont, and the Vermont Valley, a narrow region of river valleys. The Connecticut is the state's major river; others include Otter Creek and the Winooski, Missisquoi, and Lamoille rivers. Forests cover about four fifths of the state. Vermont has short, cool summers and long, cold winters. Principal cities are Burlington and Rutland.

Economy. Vermont's economy is led by service industries and manufacturing. Chief manufactured goods are electrical equipment, fabricated metal products, books and other printed materials, processed foods, transportation equipment, and furniture. Agriculture and mining account for a small share of the state's economy. Chief farm products are milk and dairy products, apples, maple syrup, potatoes, corn, and hay. Granite is the chief mining product.

Government. Vermont's present constitution was adopted in 1793. The governor serves a 2-year term. The state's legislature, called the General Assembly, consists of 30 senators and 150 representatives; all serve 2-year terms. In the U.S. Congress, Vermont is represented by 2 senators and 1 representative.

History. Several Native American tribes lived in the area before the first Europeans—an expedition led by French explorer Samuel de Champlain—arrived in 1609. The first permanent white settlement was established at present-day Brattleboro in 1724. Parts of Vermont were battlegrounds during the French and Indian wars. In 1770, Ethan Allen organized the Green

Vermont

Capital:	Montpelier
Statehood:	Mar. 4, 1791 (14th state)
Familiar name:	Green Mountain State
Area:	9,614 sq mi (24,900 sq km); ranks 43rd
Population:	589,000 (1997); ranks 49th
Elevation:	Highest—4,393 ft (1,339 m), Mt. Mansfield; Lowest—95 ft (29 m), Lake Champlain
Motto:	Freedom and Unity
Flower:	Red clover
Bird:	Hermit thrush
Tree:	Sugar maple
Song:	"Hail, Vermont"

Mountain Boys to resist New York's claims to Vermont lands. When the American Revolution broke out, the Green Mountain Boys joined other patriots to fight the British. In 1777, Vermont's settlers declared it an independent territory; it is one of 3 states (with Texas and Hawaii) that were recognized by the U.S. government as being independent republics before they joined the Union. Vermont's 1777 constitution prohibited slavery and was the first to provide for universal male suffrage (the right to vote). After the War of 1812, which was unpopular in Vermont, hard times drove many Vermonters to the Midwest. During the 1800s, Vermont switched from a sheep-raising to a dairying state. During the Civil War, Vermont supported the

Union cause. From the late 1800s until the Great Depression (1930s), the importance of agriculture and the state's textile industries declined while that of tourism and manufacturing grew. World War II revived manufacturing. In the 1960s, 1970s, and 1980s, Vermont sought new industries while trying to preserve the scenic beauty that attracts tourists to the area.

Vernal equinox *See:* Equinox.

Verne, Jules (1828-1905), French novelist, pioneer of the genre of science fiction. He often incorporated genuine scientific principles in his imaginative adventure fantasies and anticipated the airplane, submarine, television, space travel, etc. His most famous novels include *Journey to the Center of the Earth* (1864), *Twenty Thousand Leagues Under the Sea* (1870), and *Around the World in Eighty Days* (1873).

Verrazano, Giovanni da (1485?-1528?), Italian navigator and explorer in the service of France. Verrazano explored the Atlantic coast of North America from

Newfoundland to the Carolinas (1524). He is believed to have been the first European to explore the Hudson River and Manhattan Island regions.

Verrazano-Narrows Bridge, world's longest suspension bridge (4,260 ft/1,298 m), spanning the Narrows at the entrance to New York harbor, completed in 1964.

Verrocchio, Andrea del (1435-88), Italian sculptor, painter, and architect. Verrocchio trained as a goldsmith and probably learned painting under Fra Filippo Lippi. Many of Verrocchio's sculptures survive, but only 1 or 2 paintings are positively identified as his. His works are characterized by naturalistic poses, strong forms, and careful craftsmanship. His most famous works include the bronze sculptures *Christ and Saint Thomas* and *David* and an equestrian statue, the Colleoni Monument. Leonardo da Vinci and Il Perugino were among Verrocchio's students.

Versailles (pop. 95,200), French city, residential suburb 12 mi (19 km) southwest of Paris, capital of Yveline department. It is world-famous for its magnificent Palace of Versailles, built for King Louis XIV in the mid-1600s. The seat of the French court for over 100 years, it was made a national museum in 1837, and the palace and its formal gardens are among France's greatest tourist attractions.
See also: France.

Versailles, Treaty of, agreement ending World War I, imposed on Germany by the Allies on June 28, 1919. It set up the League of Nations. Under the treaty, Germany lost all her colonies and Lorraine was given to France, Eupen-Malmédy to Belgium, and Posen and West Prussia to Poland. Gdansk became a free city, the Saar (with its coalfields) was to be under international administration for 15 years, and the Rhineland was to be demilitarized and occupied by the Allies for 15 years at German cost. Heavy reparations were imposed, and Germany's armed forces were drastically reduced. German resentment of the treaty's harshness was a factor in the rise of Nazism and the eventual outbreak of World War II.
See also: World War I.

Vertebra *See:* Spine.

Vertebrate, subphylum of the chordates, containing all those classes of animals that possess a backbone—a spinal column made up of bony or cartilaginous vertebrae. The classes of vertebrates are fish, amphibians, reptiles, birds, and mammals.

Vertical take-off aircraft *See:* V/STOL.

Vertigo, disturbance in which the individual has a subjective impression of movement in space or of objects moving around him or her, usually with a loss of equilibrium. As distinguished from faintness, lightheadedness, or other forms of dizziness, vertigo results from a disturbance somewhere in the body's equilibratory apparatus, e.g., the inner ear.

Vervain *See:* Verbena.

Verwoerd, Hendrik Frensch (1901-66), Dutch-born South African politician and premier (1958-66). A professor of psychology from 1927, he became editor of the Afrikaans nationalist newspaper *Die Transvaaler* (1937). A senator from 1948, he was appointed minister of native affairs (1950), and enforced apartheid rigorously, stressing "separate development" and creating the homelands. He was assassinated.

Very high frequency waves (VHF), electromagnetic radio waves falling between high frequency and ultra high frequency. VHF waves are from 30 million to 300 million cycles per second, and the wavelengths range from 1 to 10 meters. They are used for television and FM (frequency modulation) radio broadcasts and by amateur radio operators.
See also: Radio.

Vesalius, Andreas (1514-64), Flemish biologist regarded as a father of modern anatomy. After considerable experience of dissection, he became one of the leading figures in the revolt against Galen. In his most important work, *On the Structure of the Human Body* (1543), he described several organs for the first time.
See also: Anatomy.

Vesey, Denmark (1767?-1822), free African American who planned a slave revolt at Charleston, S.C. (1822). Vesey was a carpenter who had purchased his freedom with money won in a street lottery. Dissatisfied with his inability to achieve full citizenship, with his children's status as slaves, and with the oppressive treatment of slaves in general, he gathered as many as 9,000 slaves and free blacks, who armed themselves with homemade weapons and prepared to attack Charleston. The plot was betrayed, and Vesey and 35 other leaders were hanged; 32 others were exiled.
See also: Slavery.

Vespasian (Titus Flavius Vespasianus; A.D. 9-79), Roman emperor from 69. The son of a tax collector, he rose in the army under Nero and was sent in 66 to suppress a rebellion in Judaea. His reign began an era of order and prosperity. He began the building of the Colosseum.
See also: Rome, Ancient.

Vespucci, Amerigo (1454-1512), Italian navigator for whom America was named. In 2 voyages (1499-1500, 1501-2) he explored the coast of South America and deduced that the New World must be a continent and not part of Asia. The name *America* first appeared on a map published in 1507.
See also: America.

Vessel, Blood *See:* Artery; Blood; Vein.

Vesta, in Roman mythology, goddess of the hearth and home. She was the daughter of Saturn and Ops and the sister of Jupiter and is portrayed as young and virginal. Vesta's symbol, that of fire, evolves from the Roman necessity of maintaining a perpetual fire in the home as a sacred obligation. Vesta's temple, in the Forum in Rome, housed a public flame guarded by the six vestal virgins.
See also: Mythology.

Vestal virgins, in ancient Rome, priestess, chosen very young, who served the shrine of Vesta, goddess of the domestic hearth, for 30 years. Punishment for breaking the vow of chastity was burial alive. The virgins' chief responsibility was to tend to the sacred flame in Vesta's temple.
See also: Vesta.

Vetch, climbing or trailing vine (genus *Vicia*) of the pea family. At the tip of each leaf stem is a pair of slender tendrils that curl around other plants. They have attractive flowers like those of peas, and their seeds are carried in pods. There are several native vetches in North America, but the most common ones are of European origin. In Europe they are grown as crops for hay or pasture or to hold the soil on embankments.

Veterans Administration *See:* Veterans Affairs, Department of.

Veterans Affairs, Department of (VA), formerly the Veterans Administration, U.S. government executive department consolidated (1989) to administer the various health, rehabilitation, education, loan, compensation, and insurance programs provided to veterans of the military services. The VA operates hospitals throughout the country, provides educational assistance and training programs under various GI Bills, lends money for home purchases, and administers 113 national cemeteries.

Veterans Day, U.S. holiday, celebrated on Nov. 11, to honor the members of the U.S. military forces, past and present. Originally known as Armistice Day, it was designated by President Woodrow Wilson to commemorate the end of World War I.

Veterans of Foreign Wars of the United States (VFW), one of the largest veterans' organizations in the United States. It assists needy veterans and their families, fosters patriotism, promotes community service, and lobbies for legislation. The VFW was formed in 1913. There are some 2.1 million members in about 9,800 local posts. Officers and enlisted men and women on active duty or honorably discharged, who have fought in any foreign military campaign of the United States, are eligible to join the VFW.

Veterans' organizations, groups formed to foster the spirit of comradeship developed during war and to demonstrate support for the government. The groups are politically influential due to the size of their memberships, and they lobby for legislation beneficial to veterans such as pensions, education, and services for disabled veterans. In the United States, the first veterans' organization was the Society of the Cincinnati. Formed in 1783, with George Washington as its first president, it consisted of veterans who had fought in the Revolutionary War. The Grand Army of the Republic, formed in 1866, was an organization of veterans of the Union Army that wielded great political power for over 40 years. The American Veterans of World War II, Korea and Vietnam (AMVETS) was founded in 1944.

Veterinary medicine, medical care of sick animals, sometimes including the delivery of their young. It is practiced separately from human medicine since animal diseases differ largely from those affecting humans. Veterinarians treat domestic, farm, sport, and zoo animals. General medical advances—e.g., in vaccines and antibiotics—have been aided by veterinary research.

Veto, in politics, the power of the executive to reject legislation. It is a Latin word meaning "I forbid," pronounced by the Roman tribunes when they exercised their right to block laws passed by the Senate. Under the U.S. Constitution (Art. I, Sect. 7), the president can veto any bill passed by Congress, but this can be overridden by a two-thirds majority in both houses. In the Security Council of the United Nations, the 5 permanent members (China, France, Great Britain, the United States, and Russia) possess a veto over proceedings.

VFW *See:* Veterans of Foreign Wars of the United States.

VHF waves *See:* Very high frequency waves.

Vibraphone, electric percussion instrument resembling a xylophone but having metal rather than wooden bars. The vibraphone has 37 bars (keys), each attached to a frame above a tuned resonator that can be opened or closed to produce a vibrating note. The player uses hard or soft cloth-headed beaters to strike the keys and can control the length and loudness of the notes with a sustaining pedal. The vibraphone was invented (1921) by Hermann Winterhoff and was first used orchestrally in the opera *Lulu* (1937).

Vice president of the United States, second-highest elected official. Constitutionally and politically, this office does not carry great power. The vice president was originally intended as the neutral presiding officer in the Senate and as the constitutional successor on the death or resignation of the president. Eight vice presidents have succeeded to the presidency during their time in office, taking over for presidents who have died or resigned. The increase in presidential duties with World War II has been partly responsible for giving the vice president a greater share in political and legislative matters, in particular as a member of the National Security Council. The 25th Amendment (1967) permits the president to fill a vacancy in the office of vice president, subject to the approval of Congress. The amendment permits the vice president to act as president when the president is disabled. For 8 hours in 1985, while President Reagan was in surgery, Vice President George Bush served as acting president, the first vice president to do so.

Vichy (pop. 30,500), health resort in south-central France, famous for its mineral springs. Its chief industry is bottling Vichy water. In World War II it was the seat of the Vichy government of Marshal Henri Pétain, which was set up in unoccupied France in 1940. After Germany occupied the whole of France in 1942, the Vichy government under Pierre Laval continued to collaborate with the Nazis, until the Allies liberated France.
See also: France.

Vicksburg (pop. 25,434), city in western Mississippi, seat of Warren County and site of a crucial campaign in the U.S. Civil War. Built in 1791 on the site of a Spanish outpost on the Mississippi River, it had a strategic position that made it a key Confederate bastion, until it was taken by Union forces under Gen. Ulysses S. Grant in 1863 after a 6-week siege. The port produces chemicals, machinery and metal, lumber and food products.

Vicksburg, Battle of *See:* Civil War, U.S.

Victor Emmanuel, name of 3 Italian kings. Victor Emmanuel I (1759-1824) was king of Sardinia (1802-21). He recovered his mainland possessions after Napoleon I's fall (1814), but his harsh rule provoked a revolt in Piedmont led by the Carbonari, and he abdicated. Victor Emmanuel II (1820-78) was king of Sardinia (1849-61) and the first king of united Italy (1861-78). With the Conte di Cavour and Giuseppe Garibaldi he played a major part in Italy's unification. Victor Emmanuel III (1869-1947) was king of Italy (1900-46), emperor of Ethiopia (1936-43), and king of Albania (1939-43). After appointing Benito Mussolini premier in 1922, he became a mere figurehead. His unpopular association with Fascism ultimately obliged him to abdicate.

Victoria (1819-1901), queen of Great Britain and Ireland from 1837 and empress of India from 1876. As a young queen she depended heavily on the counsel of Lord Melbourne. Her life was transformed by marriage in 1840 to Prince Albert, who became the greatest influence of her life. She mourned for the rest of her life after his death in 1861. She had strong opinions and believed in playing an active role in government, and her relations with a succession of ministers colored the political life of her reign. Her dislike of Palmerston and Gladstone and fondness for Disraeli, for example, were notorious. In old age she became immensely popular and a symbol of Britain's imperial greatness.
See also: United Kingdom.

Victoria (pop. 66,300), city in southwestern British Columbia, Canada, on the southeastern tip of Vancouver Island. Victoria is the capital of British Columbia, a tourist and retirement center, and a shipping point for the island's products. It is the site of the University of Victoria and the Royal Roads Military College. The Dominion Astrophysical Observatory and the British Royal Navy base at Esquimalt Harbor are nearby.

Victoria (pop. 1,184,000), capital of the colony of Hong Kong. The city is located on the slopes of Victoria Peak on the island of Hong Kong. It is commonly referred to as the Central District or merely as Hong Kong. Victoria is the government, banking, and commercial center of the island and home to the University of Hong Kong.
See also: Hong Kong.

Victoria, state in southeast Australia, the second-smallest and most densely populated in the country. It is divided east-west by an extension of the Australian Alps, with lowlands, hills, and valleys in the south and low plains north and west. The climate is temperate. Agriculture is important: wheat, oats, barley, and grapes are grown, and cattle and sheep are raised. Automobiles, textiles, and processed foods are produced, and coal and some gold are mined. Melbourne is the capital and largest city.
See also: Australia.

Victoria Falls, waterfall on the Zambesi River in south-central Africa between Zimbabwe and Zambia, where the 1-mi- (1-km-) wide river plunges 400 ft (122 m) into a narrow fissure. The falls were named for Britain's Queen Victoria by the explorer David Livingston in 1855.

Vicuña (*Lama vicugna*), member of the camel family living in the western High Andes at up to 16,400 ft (c.5,000 m). They are believed to be the original of the domesticated alpacas. Vicuñas are graceful animals living in family groups of a stallion and up to 20 mares, occupying a fixed territory.

Video camera, device that converts images into electronic signals for television viewing. The first video cameras, developed in the 1930s, were used for live telecasts. Color video cameras were developed in the 1950s. By the 1970s portable video cameras were being manufactured for use in the home. In the mid-1980s the videotape recorder was small enough to be combined with a video camera in a single unit.

Video cassette recorder *See:* Videotape recorder.

Videodisc, flat, round, plastic platter on which both picture and sound are reproduced on a television set. Unlike a video cassette recorder (VCR), a videodisc cannot record television programs off the air. Videodiscs do, however, offer superior picture and sound quality. There are 2 different videodisc systems: one employs a mechanical stylus and the other a laser. Originally developed in the 1970s for use as home entertainment, videodiscs are now used widely in education and industry.

Videotape, magnetic tape used to record television programs. In order to record the vast amounts of information necessary to reconstruct a television picture, 2-in- (5-cm-) wide tape must be run through the tape heads at 15 in (38 cm) per sec. The tape heads rotate to record the track crosswise on the tape.

Videotape recorder (VTR), mechanism that records visual images and sounds on magnetic tape. The recorded picture and sound can be played back and seen on the television screen. Home videotape recorders, also known as video cassette recorders (VCRs), are used largely by a consumer population to record television programs.

Vienna (German: *Wien*; pop. 1,539,800), capital of Austria, on the Danube River, one of the world's great cities. Associated with Josef Haydn, W. A. Mozart, Ludwig von Beethoven, and the various Strausses, it is a celebrated musical, theatrical, and cultural center and has many famous buildings and museums, including the Hofburg, Schönbrunn, and Belvedere palaces, the Cathedral of St. Stephen, the State Opera, the Art History Museum, and the City Hall. A Roman town, it became the residence of the Hapsburgs in 1282. It was besieged by the Turks in 1529 and 1683. A great period of prosperity and building began in the 18th century, and Vienna was capital of the Austro-Hungarian empire until 1918, when the modern republic of Austria was formed. In World War II it was occupied by the Nazis and bombed by the Allies. The modern city, population 1,500,000 (1987 est), is also a commercial and industrial center, producing machinery, metals, textiles, chemicals, furniture, handicrafts, and food products.
See also: Austria.

Vienna, Congress of, assembly held in Vienna (1814-5) to reorganize Europe after the Napoleonic Wars. Effective decision making was carried

out by Metternich of Austria, Tsar Alexander I of Russia, Castlereagh and Wellington of Britain, von Humboldt of Prussia, and Talleyrand of France. Among other territorial adjustments, the Congress established the German Confederation and the kingdoms of the Netherlands and Poland (under Russian rule), and restored the Papal States and the kingdoms of Sardinia and Naples. Austria gained parts of Italy, Prussia gained parts of Austria, and Britain gained overseas territories to achieve a new balance of power, ignoring the nationalist aspirations of the peoples concerned.
See also: Napoleonic Wars.

Vientiane (pop. 442,000), capital and largest city of Laos, located on the Mekong River. Vientiane is the commercial center of Laos and produces livestock, rice, cigarettes, silk and other textiles, and plastics. It is the site of the Royal School of Medicine and the Royal School of Public Administration and is noted for its many Buddhist pagodas.
See also: Laos.

Vietnam, officially the Socialist Republic of Vietnam, located in southeast Asia. With an area of 127,545 sq mi (330,341 sq km), Vietnam is bordered by Kampuchea (formerly Cambodia), and Laos on the west; China to the north and east; and the Gulf of Tonkin, the South China Sea, and the Gulf of Thailand to the east and south. The capital is Hanoi.
Land and climate. Narrow and S-shaped, Vietnam is a 1,000-mi (1,609 km)-long strip on the Indo-China peninsula. The country's major cities and economic centers are located in the Red River delta in the north and the Mekong River delta in the south. More than 90% of the people live in the delta regions. Between them lies a heavily forested mountainous backbone giving way to a narrow coastal strip along the South China Sea and the Gulf of Tonkin. Vietnam has a tropical monsoon climate with high humidity and rainfall.
People. About 85% of the people are Vietnamese. There are also urban Chinese minorities, though many Chinese fled the country in 1979 when hostilities flared up between Vietnam and China. There are also several distinct peoples in the highlands, such as the Meo, also called the Hmong, who preserve their own cultures. The major cities are Hanoi, Ho Chi Minh City (formerly Saigon), Hue, Da Nang, and Haiphong. The official language is Vietnamese and the dominant religions are Buddhism and Roman Catholicism, though the Vietnamese government discourages both.
Economy. Vietnam has an agricultural economy based principally upon rice growing in the Mekong and Red River deltas. Other crops include corn, cotton, hemp, sugarcane, rubber, coffee, and tea. Fishing and forestry are locally important. Minerals, including coal, iron, tin, zinc, lead, and phosphates are found mainly in the north, where most of the country's industry, chiefly the manufacture of iron and steel, chemicals and textiles, is concentrated. There is also some manufacturing around Ho Chi Minh City. Offshore oil deposits have been found.
History. Established as a distinct people by the 2nd century B.C., the Vietnamese now occupy what were formerly the distinct regions of Tonkin in the north, Annam in the center, and Cochin China in the south of their country. Tonkin and Annam were conquered by China in 111 B.C. In the 2nd century A.D., the Champa kingdom emerged in central Vietnam. The Chinese were eventually driven out in 939. The Annam empire then grew, eventually

Vietnam

Capital:	Hanoi
Area:	127,512 sq mi
	(330,341 sq km)
Population:	118,236,000
Language:	Vietnamese
Government:	Socialist republic
Independent:	1954
Head of gov.:	Prime minister
Per capita:	$240
Mon. unit:	1 Dong = 100 xu

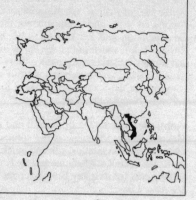

defeating and displacing the Champas in 1471 and expanding south into Cochin China. European traders and missionaries began arriving in the 1500s. French forces captured Saigon in 1859 and in 1862 the French annexed Cochin China and merged it with present-day Kampuchea to form French Indochina. During the Japanese occupation of Indochina (1941-45), the Vietnamese resisted. After the defeat and withdrawal of the Japanese, a republic was proclaimed under Ho Chi Minh in 1945. The French attempted to reassert their authority by establishing Bao Dai as emperor and became embroiled in a war between nationalist and communist guerrillas beginning in 1946. The French were finally defeated in 1954 at Dien Bien Phu. At the Geneva Conference held that same year, the country was divided, pending nationwide free elections, into Communist North Vietnam under Ho Chi Minh, and non-Communist South Vietnam. The French withdrew and, with U.S. backing, the regime of Ngo Dinh Diem declared an independent republic in South Vietnam in 1955 and, in 1956, refused to hold free elections. The Vietnam war ensued with South Vietnam being aided by the United States. At the height of its involvement, the United States had committed some 550,000 ground troops to the war. Despite a major military effort, the United States were unable to contain or defeat the Viet Cong guerrillas consisting of South Vietnamese opposed to the regime and North Vietnamese guerrillas reinforced by regulars of the North Vietnamese army. Successive South Vietnamese regimes proved unable to win popular backing and to provide the necessary political and military leadership. In addition, the United States suffered substantial setbacks to its international standing as the object of widespread criticism and resistance to the war at home and abroad. A cease-fire agreement was finally signed in 1973 and U.S. troops were withdrawn, but only at the end of a prolonged bombing campaign and the invasion of Cambodia. Upon the withdrawal of U.S. troops, Communist forces launched a major offensive and by 1975 had won control of all of South Vietnam, effectively ending 35 years of fighting. The unified Socialist Republic of Vietnam was proclaimed in 1976. Since then, Vietnam has attempted to rebuild its society and economy but was further distracted by war with neighboring Kampuchea in 1979 when its forces overthrew the regime headed by Pol Pot. Years of war and economic dislocation have resulted in harsh living conditions and a large number of refugees. In the early 1990s the economy was liberalized and economic growth boomed. Vietnam, like other Asian countries, experienced a currency crisis (1997/98).

Vietnam Veterans Memorial *See:* Washington, D.C.

Vietnam War, conflict in South Vietnam (1957-75) between South Vietnamese government forces, backed by the United States, and Communist guerrilla insurgents, the Vietcong, backed by North Vietnam. The conflict originated in 1941 when a Viet-minh guerrilla force was formed under Hi Chi Minh to fight the Japanese. After 1946 it fought the French colonial government, defeating them at Dien Bien Phu. The Geneva Conference then temporarily divided Vietnam at the 17th parallel between the Communists (North) and the Nationalists (South). Ngo Dinh Diem, the South Vietnamese premier, canceled national elections and declared the South independent in 1956. The Viet Nam Cong San (Vietnamese Communists), or Vietcong, was then formed to oppose his increasingly corrupt regime. The Vietcong fought a ferocious guerrilla campaign that led Diem to call in U.S. support forces under the U.S.-South Vietnamese military and economic aid treaty of 1961. In 1963 he was overthrown by his officers; after a period of turmoil, Nguyen Van Thieu became president in 1967. In 1965 the United States had begun bombing the North in retaliation for the use of northern troops in the South. Increasing numbers of U.S. combat troops, many of them drafted, began to arrive in 1965 and totaled nearly 550,000 by 1968, when fruitless peace talks began in Paris. The large-scale U.S. campaign proved unable to do more than hold back the highly motivated Vietcong. Vietnamese civilians suffered terribly at the hands of both sides. The American people were sharply divided by severe uncertainties about U.S. goals and participation in the war. In November 1969 President Richard M. Nixon announced the "Vietnamization" of the war by building up South Vietnamese forces and withdrawing U.S. combat troops, but ever mounting, sometimes violent U.S. anti-war demonstrations reached their peak later that month when 250,000 protesters marched on Washington. The war had spread to Cambodia and Laos before a cease-fire was signed in Jan. 1973, followed by the total withdrawal of U.S. troops a few months later. The South was then overrun by Vietcong and North Vietnamese forces; the war effectively ended with the fall of the South Vietnamese capital of Saigon in May 1975. In the late 1980s the government began an economic restructuring plan with the purpose of stimulating private enterprise. In 1990 the Vietnamese Foreign Minister, Nguyen Co Thach, met with U.S. Secretary of State James A. Baker III in the first high-level meeting since the 1970s. They discussed Vietnam's involvement in Cambodia and U.S. MIAs, 2 issues that have kept the countries from establishing diplomatic relations.

Vikings, or Norsemen, Norwegian, Swedish, and Danish seafarers who raided Europe from the 9th to the 11th centuries. Expert shipbuilders and navigators, they were capable of long sea voyages, and their ferocity made them the terror of Europe. The Norwegians raided Scotland, Ireland, and France and colonized the Hebrides, Orkneys, the Faroes, Iceland, and Greenland. They may also have discovered America. The Danes raided England, France, the Netherlands, Spain, and Italy. The Swedes went down the eastern shores of the Baltic, through what is now western Russia, and reached the Bosporus and Byzantium. In addition to being raiders, the Vikings traded and created permanent settlements. They united the Hebrides and the Isle of Man into a kingdom. The Shetlands, the Orkneys, and Caithness became an earldom. Kingdoms were also set up in Ireland and Russia.

Villa, Pancho (Francisco Villa; 1877-1923), Mexican revolutionary leader. Originally a bandit in northern Mexico, Villa joined (1910) the insurgent forces of Francisco Madero fighting against the dictator Porfirio Díaz. After the successful campaign, he remained in the irregular army. When Madero was assassinated (1913), Villa joined forces with another revolutionary, Venustiano Carranza, and together they took Juárez (1914). Villa became governor of the state of Chihuahua and with Carranza continued his rebellion against Madero's successor, Gen. Victoriano Huerta (1914). In 1914-15 Villa and Emiliano Zapata took control of Mexico City but were later defeated by Gen. lvaro Obregón. Competition between Villa and Carranza forced a break in their alliance, and Villa, embittered by U.S. recognition of Carranza's government, attacked and burned the town of Columbus, N.M., killing 16 people. U.S. Gen. John Pershing then led an unsuccessful 11-month expedition into northern Mexico in pursuit of Villa. The invasion strained U.S.-Mexican relations, and Pershing was recalled. When Carranza's government was overthrown (1920), Villa was awarded a grant of land. He was assassinated at his ranch (1923).
See also: Mexico.

Villa-Lobos, Heitor (1887-1959), Brazilian composer, conductor, and teacher, known for his research on and use of folk music. He composed over 2,000 works, many of which combine indigenous melodies with the counterpointing of Johann Sebastian Bach. His compositions include 9 instrumental suites called the *Bachanias Brasileiras* (1930-45), 14 *Serestas* (1925-41) for voice and piano, 12 symphonies, and 16 string quartets. Villa-Lobos founded the Brazilian Academy of Music (1945).

Villard, Henry (1835-1900), German-born U.S. journalist and financier. Correspondent for the *New York Herald* and *New York Tribune* in the Civil War, he later (1881) acquired the New York *Evening Post* and *The Nation*. Entering the railroad business in 1873, he created the Oregon Railway and Navigation Co. (1879), and became president of Northern Pacific (1881-84, 1888-93). In 1890 he formed the Edison General Electric Co.

Villella, Edward Joseph (1936-), U.S. dancer who performed his first solo within a year of joining the New York City Ballet (1957). He is noted for his bravura style, with powerful leaps. Villella's most famous performances include the title role in Balanchine's *The Prodigal Son*, and Oberon in *A Midsummer Night's Dream*.
See also: Ballet.

Vilnius, or Vilna, capital and largest city of Lithuania (pop. 590,100). Settled in the 10th century, Vilnius was named the Lithuanian capital in 1323. The city later came under Polish rule (1569) and then was annexed by Russia (1795) which retained power until 1918. Between that year and 1938, control was contested by Poland and Lithuania. In 1939 Lithuania recovered control, but the country (and the city) was occupied by the USSR until 1991. The Nazi occupation (1941-45) destroyed the large Jewish population. Today

Vilnius is an important trade center for grain, timber, chemicals, machinery, leather goods, paper, and textiles. It is noted for its public buildings and churches reflecting Roman, Byzantine, and Gothic influences.
See also: Lithuania.

Vimy Ridge, Battle of, World War I battle (April 9, 1917) in which the Canadian Corps of the British Army impressively defeated the German forces in northern France. The capture of Vimy Ridge by the Canadian forces helped to symbolically identify Canada as an independent nation.
See also: World War I.

Viña del Mar, leading resort and second largest city in Chile, located on the Pacific coast just northeast of Valparaíso. The city is noted for its pleasant climate, beaches, hotels, and nightclubs.

Vincennes, city on the Wabash River in southwestern Indiana. Founded in 1732 by François-Marie Bissob, sieur de Vincennes, the city was Indiana's first permanent settlement. In 1779 it was taken over by U.S. forces under George Rogers Clark. The Northwest Ordinance (1787) brought settlers from Kentucky, Virginia, and Pennsylvania. Today, Vincennes is the seat of Knox County. It is an agricultural, industrial, and coal-mining center.
See also: Indiana.

Vinci, Leonardo da *See:* Da Vinci, Leonardo.

Vine, general name for plants with climbing or trailing stems that cannot grow upright without support. Vines have either woody or herbaceous (nonwoody) stems. They can be evergreen or deciduous. Some have tendrils (the sweet pea, the grapevine, and the cucumber), and others have adhesive disks (the woodbine or Virginia creeper) or small roots (English ivy) to anchor them to their support. Some twine their stem around the support (the convolvulus and hop), and others simply ramble over the surrounding area, with no means of holding themselves up (the blackberry and the rambler rose). By far the most important vine economically is the grapevine, from which the wine grape is harvested.

Vinegar, sour liquid, consisting mainly of acetic acid and water, used for seasoning and preserving foods. Vinegar is produced by the action of yeast and bacteria on fruits and grains. It is made from alcoholic beverages such as wine and cider.

Vinegar eel (*Turbatrix aceti*), tiny roundworm, about 1/16 in (1.6 mm) in length, found in fermenting cider vinegar. Vinegar eels feed on fruit pulp and the bacteria that produce the vinegar from the cider. They are harmless if swallowed.

Vinland, region of eastern North America discovered A.D. 1000 by Viking explorers, probably led by Leif Ericson, and briefly settled (1004) by Thorfinn Karlsefni. Some scholars believe it was in New England, others favor Newfoundland (where Viking remains have been found). The Norse sagas describe the discovery of a fertile region where grapes grew, hence "Vin(e)land."

Vinson, Frederick Moore (1890-1953), chief justice of the U.S. Supreme Court (1946-53). A Kentucky Democrat, he was a member of the House of

Representatives (1923-9, 1931-7) and secretary of the treasury (1945-6). While he was chief justice, the Supreme Court made important civil liberty rulings. *See also:* Supreme Court of the United States.

Vinyl, durable and useful plastic material used in making a variety of products. Vinyl plastics were first manufactured commercially in 1927. By 1973 the production of vinyl plastics in the United States totaled 4.6 billion lb (2.1 billion kg). One of the strongest vinyl plastics is polyvinyl chloride (PVC), produced by combining vinyl with chloride to form vinyl chloride gas, and then putting the gas through a process known as polymerization. Research in the 1970s showed that serious illness, including a form of liver cancer, can result from breathing air polluted by vinyl chloride. The Environmental Protection Agency now requires that manufacturers install equipment to eliminate vinyl chloride from the air breathed by workers.

Vinyl chloride *See:* Vinyl.

Viol, forerunner (15th-17th centuries) of the violin. Viols have sloping shoulders, frets, a low bridge, and a soft, mellow tone. The 6 strings are tuned in fourths. The treble, alto, tenor, and bass (*viola da gamba*) viols are all held upright, as was the double-bass *violone*, which became today's double-bass. Interest in the viol has revived in the 20th century.

Viola, stringed musical instrument, the tenor voice of the violin family. It is 14.5-17 in (37-43 cm) long, has 4 strings, and is played with a bow. The viola originated in the 1500s. The composers Hector Berlioz, Richard Strauss, and Sir William Walton wrote for the viola as a solo instrument.

Violet, low herbaceous plants (genus *Viola*) that produce characteristically shaped flowers on slender stalks. Most species occur in the Andes, but many are found in North America and Europe. Several species, including the pansy, are cultivated as garden ornamentals. They grow mainly in moist woods.

Violin, smallest, most versatile member of the bowed, 4-stringed violin family (violin, viola, cello, double bass). Violins succeeded the viol in the 17th century, differing in their flexibility, range of tone and pitch, arched bridge, squarer shoulders, narrower body, and lack of frets. The violin proper, derived from the 16th-century arm viol, is tuned in fifths and ranges over 4 1/2 octaves above G below middle C. Perfected by the craftsmen of Cremona, it became a major solo instrument. The principal violinist leads the orchestra. Classical string quartets have 2 violins.

Violoncello *See:* Cello.

Viper, family of snakes with highly developed venom apparatus, found in Europe, Africa, and Asia. Vipers are short, stoutly built, and typically terrestrial. One of the best-known species is the common European viper, or adder (*Vipera berus*).

Viper's bugloss, or blue thistle (*Echium vulgare*), plant found in dry areas of the eastern United States. It has bright blue flowers and grows to about (90 cm) tall. It was once thought to be a cure for viper bites.

Virchow, Rudolf (1821-1902), Pomeranian-born German pathologist. His most important work was to apply knowledge concerning the cell to pathology. He was the first to document leukemia and embolism. He was also distinguished as an anthropologist and an archeologist.
See also: Leukemia; Pathology.

Vireo, small, greenish, insectivorous bird (family Vireonidae) of tropical and temperate America. Vireos live in thick undergrowth except for the red-eyed vireo. This species is also noted for its rambling song. The white-eyed vireo mimics other birds. The nest is built near the ground and is anchored by cobwebs. Most species are migratory.

Virgil *See:* Vergil.

Virginal, type of small harpsichord, its strings parallel to the single keyboard. There is 1 wire per note. Encased in a small rectangular box, the virginal was popular c.1550-1650.

Virginia, state in the southeastern United States; bordered by Maryland to the northeast, the Atlantic Ocean to the east, North Carolina and Tennessee to the south, Kentucky to the west, and West Virginia to the west and northwest.
Land and climate. Virginia has 5 main land regions. The Atlantic Coastal Plain, also called the Tidewater, is a low-lying area of tidal waterways with some swamps or salt marshes. Covering most of central Virginia is the Piedmont, a low, rolling plateau that rises into the mountain peaks and valleys of the Blue Ridge region. The Appalachian Ridge and Valley region, covering most of western Virginia, consists of a series of parallel ridges separated by river valleys and lowlands. The rugged Appalachian Plateau, in the state's southwestern corner, contains extensive coal deposits. Virginia's major rivers are the James, Rappahannock, and Potomac. The state's largest lake, Kerr Reservoir, is artificial. Forests cover nearly two thirds of the state. Virginia has mild winters and warm summers. Principal cities are Norfolk, Virginia Beach, and Richmond.
Economy. Virginia's economy is based on service industries and manufacturing. Chief manufactured goods are chemicals, tobacco products, processed foods, electrical and transportation equipment, and textiles. Agriculture and mining account for a small share of the state's economy. Chief livestock products are beef and dairy cattle and turkeys; chief crops are tobacco, soybeans, peanuts, corn, and hay. Chief mining products are coal and crushed stone. Virginia is the nation's leading producer of kyanite.
Government. Virginia's present constitution was adopted in 1971. The governor serves a 4-year term. The state's legislature, called the General Assembly, consists of 40 senators serving 4-year terms and 100 delegates serving 2-year terms. In the U.S. Congress, Virginia is represented by 2 senators and 11 representatives.
History. The Virginia area was home to various Native American tribes when the first European settlers—Spanish Jesuits—arrived in 1570. In 1607, the first permanent English settlement in the New World was established at Jamestown. In 1612, John Rolfe, a Jamestown settler, began raising tobacco, which became the basis of Virginia's economy. The first blacks came to Virginia as indentured servants in 1619; by 1715, blacks constituted about 25% of the population. Also in 1619, the House of Burgesses, the country's

---

Virginia

Capital:	Richmond
Statehood:	June 25, 1788 (10th state)
Familiar name:	Old Dominion
Area:	40,767 sq mi (105,586 sq km); ranks 36th
Population:	6,734,000 (1997); ranks 12th
Elevation:	Highest—5,729 ft (1,746 m), Mt. Rogers; Lowest—sea level, along the Atlantic coast
Motto:	Sic Semper Tyrannis (Thus Always to Tyrants)
Flower:	Flowering dogwood
Bird:	Cardinal
Tree:	Flowering dogwood
Song:	"Carry Me Back to Old Virginia"

---

first representative legislature, was established. Virginia became a royal colony in 1624. It took a leading role in the American Revolution and events leading to it; distinguished Virginia patriots included Patrick Henry, Thomas Jefferson, George Washington, and James Madison. In 1776, Virginia became the first American colony to adopt a constitution and a declaration of rights. During the Civil War, a Virginia convention voted to secede, but western Virginians supported the Union. The split led to the 1863 formation of the state of West Virginia. Virginia was readmitted to the Union in 1870. In the late 1800s and early 1900s, Virginia became industrialized and urbanized. Desegregation and school integration became major issues in the 1950s and 1960s.

In the 1970s and 1980s, major issues included antipollution and conservation efforts and problems related to falling demand for coal and tobacco, once key to Virginia's economy.

Virginia Beach (pop. 417,000), resort city on the southeastern edge of Virginia, bordered by the Atlantic Ocean and Chesapeake Bay. Over 2 million tourists visit its warm climate and attractive beaches annually. Many of its residents are employed at 4 nearby military installations. Virginia Beach was incorporated in 1963 and has a council-manager form of government.
See also: Virginia.

Virginia City, "ghost town" in western Nevada, a leading tourist attraction, c.20 mi (32 km) south of Reno. The town was founded in 1859, and the exploitation of the Comstock Lode of gold and silver turned the community into a boom town overnight. A fire destroyed most of it in 1875, and the ore gave out by the 1890s.
See also: Nevada.

Virginia Company, name of 2 companies of merchant-adventurers granted patents by the English crown (1606) for colonizing America. The London Company, authorized to settle anywhere from present-day South Carolina to New York, founded Jamestown (1607). The Plymouth Company, granted rights from present-day Virginia to Maine, fared badly. It was reorganized (1620) into the Council for New England, which made the original grant to the Pilgrim Fathers and the Puritan settlers.

Virginia creeper (*Parthenocissus quinquefolia*), rambling, viny plant that grows in eastern North America. A member of the vine family, it resembles poison ivy. Its leaves turn red and yellow in autumn.

Virginia Resolutions *See:* Kentucky and Virginia Resolutions.

Virgin Islands, westernmost group of the Lesser Antilles in the West Indies, east of Puerto Rico. The western islands belong to the United States and the eastern group to Britain. Discovered and claimed for Spain by Christopher Columbus (1493), the Virgin Islands were settled chiefly by English and Danes in the 1600s. England secured the British Virgin Islands in 1666. The Danish West Indies were acquired by the United States for strategic reasons in 1917 and became the U.S. Virgin Islands. The economy of both groups now depends on tourism, but farming (food crops, livestock) and fishing are also important. The Virgin Islands of the United States, a U.S. territory covering 133 sq mi (344.5 sq km) include St. Thomas, St. John, St. Croix, and some 65 islets. Charlotte Amalie, the capital and only city, stands on St. Thomas. The British Virgin Islands are separated from the American islands by a strait called The Narrows. Covering 59 sq mi (153 sq km), the group consists of about 30 mainly uninhabited islands. The largest island is Tortola, which has the capital and chief port, Road Town.

Virgin Islands National Park, national park, authorized in 1956, located on most of St. John (19 sq mi/49 sq km) Virgin Island of the United States, comprising 15,000 acres (6,070 hectares) with interesting marine flora and fauna and remnants of prehistoric Native American civilization.

Virginius Massacre, seizure of a merchant ship, the *Virginius* (1873), by Spain during its conflict with Cuba. Spanish authorities executed 53 passengers and crew members, including the commander, John Fry, a U.S. citizen. The event almost involved the United States in a war with Spain. It was later discovered that the *Virginius* was a Cuban-owned ship fraudulently flying the U.S. flag and carrying a U.S. registration. Spain returned the ship, paid an indemnity to the families of those executed, and denied any hostile intent.

Virgin Mary *See:* Mary.

Viroid, class of infectious agents, causing several plant diseases. Made up of a complex chain of RNA (ribonucleic acid) molecules, they are replicated by the host cell's enzymes. Viroids affect such plants as potatoes, tomatoes, hops, and avocadoes, among others.

Virus, submicroscopic parasitic microorganism comprising a protein or protein/lipid sheath containing nucleic acid (DNA or RNA). Viruses are inert outside living cells, but within appropriate cells they can replicate (using raw material from the cell), causing viral diseases in the host organism. Various viruses infect animals, plants, and bacteria (in which case they are bacteriophages). Few drugs act specifically against viruses, although immunity can be induced against particular viruses. Various pathogenic organisms formerly regarded as large viruses are now distinguished as *bedsonia*.

Viscosity, resistance of a fluid to shape change or relative motion within itself. All fluids are viscous, the viscosity arising from internal friction between molecules. The viscosity of liquids decreases as they are heated, but that of gases increases.

Vishinsky, Andrei Yanuarievich (1883-1954), Soviet diplomat and jurist. Chief state prosecutor in the purge trials of 1936-38, he was deputy commissar (1940-9) and commissar (1949-53) for foreign affairs, and USSR's chief UN delegate (1953-54).
See also: Union of Soviet Socialist Republics.

Vishnu, in Hinduism, second deity in the Trimurti (divine trinity, including Brahma, the creator, and Shiva, the destroyer), representing the preserving and protecting aspect of the godhead. The ancient *Vishnu Purana* text describes him as the primal god, as do his followers (Vaishnavas), who also worship his many avatars, such as Rama, Buddha, and Krishna. Vishnu is often represented dark blue in color, holding in his 4 hands a lotus, mace, discus, and conch. His consort is Lakshmi.
See also: Hinduism.

Visigoths (West Goths), Germanic people. In the 3rd century A.D. they invaded Roman Dacia (Romania). Under Fritigern they defeated the Romans at Adrianople (378) and, led by Alaric I, they invaded Thrace and Italy, sacking Rome (410). They founded a kingdom in Gaul and Spain (419), but Alaric II lost the northern lands to Clovis, king of the Franks (507). Roderick, last Gothic king of Spain, lost his throne to the Moors (711).

Vision *See:* Eye.

Vistula River, largest (678 mi/1,091 km long) and most important river in Poland. Through a system of canals, it connects the Oder, Dmepr, and Neman rivers, all of which are navigable. It empties into the Baltic Sea. The Vistula is frozen 2 to 3 months of the year.

Vital statistics, data related to the important events, such as birth, marriage, and death, in a person's life. Registration of many such statistics, including birth dates filed on birth certificates, is required by law. The Vital Statistics Division of the National Center for Health Statistics, a division of the U.S. Dept. of Health and Human Services, analyzes and publishes U.S. data.

Vitamin, specific nutrient compounds essential for body growth or metabolism and which can be supplied by a balanced diet or, when necessary, in the form of supplements. Enzymes and coenzymes are necessary for metabolism, especially the processes by which the body absorbs and utilizes nutrients. But there are certain coenzymes the body can obtain only from vitamins. Vitamins are denoted by letters and are often divided into fat-soluble and water-soluble kinds. Fat-soluble vitamins can be stored in the body's fat; water-soluble vitamins pass out of the body through urine. The A, D, E, and K vitamins are fat soluble; the B and C vitamins are water soluble.

Vitamin A, or retinol, is essential for skeletal growth, healthy epithelial tissue, and eyesight. It is found in milk, butter, and egg yolks. Green leafy or yellow vegetables contain a substance called carotene, which the body converts to Vitamin A. Vitamin A deficiency can cause skin, eye, or mucous membrane lesions. Overdoses can be harmful to the skin. Vitamin D, or calciferol, is a crucial factor in calcium metabolism, especially the growth and maintenance of bone. It is found in human skin and is activated with exposure of the skin to sunlight. Vitamin D deficiency can cause rickets or bow legs. An overdose can cause kidney damage. Vitamin E, or tocopherol, appears to play a role in blood cell and nervous system tissues, but its precise functions and properties have yet to be determined. It is found in peanuts, vegetable oils, wheat germ, and green leafy vegetables. Vitamin K provides essential cofactors for the production of certain clotting factors in the liver. It is used to treat some clotting disorders. Vitamin K is contained in liver and green leafy vegetables.

Important members of the B group include B_1 or thiamine; B_2 or riboflavin; niacin; B_6 or pyridoxine; folic acid; and B_{12} or cyanocobalamin. Thiamine acts as a coenzyme in carbohydrate metabolism. It occurs naturally in whole grains, yeast, nuts, and lean pork. Its deficiency, seen in rice-eating populations and alcoholics, causes beriberi. Riboflavin is also a coenzyme active in oxidation reactions. It is found in milk, green leafy vegetables, and liver and organs. A deficiency will cause lesions of the skin, mouth, or eyes. Niacin is a general term for nicotinic acid and nicotinamide, coenzymes in carbohydrate metabolism. Niacin occurs in wheat germ, lean meat, fish, and peanuts. A deficiency causes pellagra and, if the deficiency is extreme, it can cause death. Pyridoxine provides an enzyme important in energy storage and its deficiency can lead to anemia. It occurs naturally in lean meat, whole grains, milk, and egg yolks. Folic acid is an essential cofactor in the metabolism of nucleic acid and a deficiency of the vitamin, which is not uncommon in pregnancy, can cause anemia. Folic acid occurs naturally in yeast and in green leafy vegetables. Cyanocobalamin is essential for all the body's cells and a deficiency can lead to pernicious anemia. It occurs naturally in bivalves and fish, eggs and lean meat, and rigorous vegetarians are at particular risk of deficiency. Pantothenic acid, biotin, choline, inositol, and para-aminobenzoic acid are other members of the B-group. Vitamin C, another of the water-soluble vitamins, is also known as ascorbic acid and plays an important role in the healing process, blood cell formation, and bone and tissue growth. It occurs naturally in citrus fruits, cabbage, berries, peppers, and tomatoes. Deficiency leads to scurvy, and extreme and prolonged deficiency causes death. The beneficial effects of Vitamin C in the prevention and treatment of the common cold have yet to be conclusively determined.

Vivaldi, Antonio (c.1680-1741), Venetian baroque composer. He wrote vocal music, sonatas, some 450 concertos for violin and other instruments (helping establish the 3-movement form), and *concerti grossi*, including the famous *Four Seasons*. His work has a sparkling clarity, strong rhythms, and a wealth of melody.
See also: Baroque.

Vivisection, dissection of living animals, usually in the course of physiological or pathological research; the use of the term is often extended to cover all animal experimentation. The practice remains the subject of considerable public controversy.

Vizsla, or Hungarian pointer, breed of hunting dog. It was probably first brought to central Europe by the Magyars about 1,000 years ago. The vizsla weighs about 50 lb (23 kg) and has a rusty or sandy yellow coat.

Vladimir I (?-1015), Russian grand duke who established Christianity as the country's official religion. Born a pagan, he converted to Christianity about 988. He built churches, schools, and libraries and promoted trade with European countries. He was declared a saint after his death.

Vladivostok (pop. 643,000), capital of Primorski Kray, in the eastern Russian Federation, chief Pacific naval port of Russia, on Peter the Great Bay near North Korea. Founded in 1860, it has shipbuilding, manufacturing, chemical, and fish-canning industries. It is the east terminus of the Trans-Siberian Railway. *See also:* Union of Soviet Socialist Republics.

Vlaminck, Maurice de (1876-1958), French artist who, along with André Derain and Henri Matisse, was a leader of the fauvist movement. Vlaminck was strongly influenced by Vincent van Gogh and adopted his slashing brushstrokes and brilliant colors for dramatic effect. He moved gradually to a style close to that of Paul Cézanne. Notable works include *The Storm*.

Vocal cord *See:* Larynx.

Vocational education, courses of study that prepare students for a range of occupations that do not require baccalaureate or higher degrees, in areas such as agriculture, business, trades, industry, health services, home economics, and various technical fields. Instruction takes place in high schools, trade schools, community colleges, and correspondence schools and through formal apprenticeship programs and on-the-job training. Many vocational education programs have been funded by the U.S. government.

Vocational rehabilitation, service designed for persons, usually 16 years of age and older, with mental and/or physical handicaps, to become employable. The three components of vocational rehabilitation are rehabilitation counseling, vocational evaluation, and job placement. Specialists in each of these areas work as a team, matching job skills and performance against standards in a career field. In the United States, vocational rehabilitation first developed in the late 1800s to assist disabled veterans. In Canada, the Vocational Rehabilitation of Disabled Persons Act of 1961 established vocational rehabilitation guidelines. Counselors in vocational rehabilitation are usually required to have a bachelor's degree and preferably a master's degree with a concentration in counseling, human relations, industrial psychology, statistics, and testing.

Vogelweide, Walther von der *See:* Walther Von der Vogelweide.

Voice, sound emitted in speech, the method of communication exclusive to *Homo sapiens*. Dependent upon the passage of air from the lungs through the trachea, larynx, pharynx, and mouth, its quality is largely determined by the shape and size of these structures and the resonance of the nose and nasal sinuses. Phonation is the sounding of the elements of speech by the action of several small muscles on the vocal cords of the larynx. Articulation consists in the modulation of sounds by the use of the tongue, teeth, and lips in different combinations. Vowels are produced mainly by phonation, while consonants derive their characteristics principally from articulation.

Voice of America (VOA), radio division of the International Communications Agency (formerly the U.S. Information Agency), established in 1942 to explain the U.S. role in World War II. Its network now broadcasts, in English and other languages, a favorable view of life in the United States to many (chiefly Communist) countries.
See also: Information Agency, U.S.

Voiceprint, or speech spectrogram, visual record of the sound waves of a human voice made by running a tape recording of a voice through an instrument called a sound spectrograph. The sound spectrograph was developed in the 1940s by U.S. scientists at Bell Research Laboratories. Voiceprints are used in the study of speech and hearing disorders. Police use voiceprints for evidence in the prosecution of criminal cases.

Volapük, universal language created in 1879 by Johann Martin Schleyer, a German priest. It combined elements of English, German, Latin, French, and Italian. It proved difficult to learn because of the unfamiliar appearance of the words and its grammatical complexity. Few people speak Volapük today.

Volcano, fissure or vent in a planet's crust through which magma and associated material may be extruded onto the surface. This may occur with explosive force. The extruded magma, or lava, solidifies in various forms soon after exposure to the atmosphere. In particular it does so around the vent, building up the characteristic volcanic cone, at the top of which is a crater containing the main vent. There may be secondary vents forming "parasitic cones" in the slopes of the main cone. If the volcano is dormant or extinct, the vents may be blocked with a plug (or neck) of solidified lava. Classifying volcanoes in order of increasing violence, the main types are Hawaiian, Strombolian, Vulcanian, Vesuvian, and Peléan. Volcanoes are generally restricted to belts of seismic activity, particularly active plate margins, but some intraplate volcanic activity is also known, as in the case of Hawaii. At midocean ridges magma rises from deep in the mantle and is added to the receding edges of the plates. In mountain ranges, where plates are in collision, volatile matter ascends from the subducted edge of a plate, perhaps many kilometers below the surface, bursting through the overlying plate in a series of volcanoes. Around 500 active volcanoes are known of on earth; active volcanoes have also been found on Mars and on Jupiter's satellite Io.

Volcker, Paul Adolph (1927-), U.S. economist and chairman of the Federal Reserve Board (1979-87). He served as undersecretary for monetary affairs in the Treasury Department (1969-74) and president of the New York Reserve Bank (1975-9) before being appointed to head the Federal Reserve by President Jimmy Carter. He was architect of the Board's tight-money

policy, which kept interest rates on borrowing high in order to contract the money supply and dampen inflation. In 1983 President Ronald Reagan appointed him to a second term.
See also: Economics.

Vole, mouselike member of the New World rat and mouse family, closely related to the lemming. Voles are about 5 in (13 cm) long with short, shaggy, grayish-brown fur. Most inhabit fields and meadows. There are over 40 species of vole. The most common North American species is the meadow vole (genus *Microtus*).

Volga River, chief tributary of Russia and the longest in Europe. It rises in the Valdai Hills, northwest of Moscow, and flows 2,293 mi (3,690 km) through Gorki, Kazan, Kuibyshev, Saratov, Volgograd, and Astrakhan to its Caspian Sea delta. Draining an area of some 530,000 sq mi (1,372,700 sq km) it is the main artery of the world's greatest network of commercial waterways linking the White, Baltic, Caspian, Azov, and Black seas.

Volgograd (pop. 1,005,000), important manufacturing city in Ukraine located on the west bank of the Volga River. It was founded in the 1200s as Tsaritsyn and renamed Stalingrad (after Joseph Stalin) in 1925. During World War II the city was devastated by the battle between the advancing German army and the defending forces. It was completely rebuilt after the war and renamed Volgograd in 1961, after Stalin was downgraded.

Volkswagen (German, "the people's car"), one of the world's largest producers of passenger cars. It was established by the German government in 1937 and is now owned privately. The Volkswagen beetle, designed by the Austrian engineer Ferdinand Porsche in the mid-1930s, became the most popular car ever built. Volkswagen builds over 2.5 million cars annually in countries throughout the world. In 1998 Volkswagen took over Rolls-Royce.

Volleyball, game for 2 teams of 6, who volley (using any part of the body above the waist) an inflated ball (8.25 in/21 cm in diameter) across an 8-ft (2.4-m) high net, conceding points by failing to return the ball or by hitting it out of bounds. Invented at the Holyoke (Mass.) YMCA in 1895 by W. G. Morgan, it became an Olympic event in Tokyo (1964).

Volstead Act, law passed by the Congress of the United States in 1919 to enforce the 18th Amendment to the Constitution, which prohibited the manufacture, sale, or transportation of alcoholic beverages within the United States. The amendment was introduced by Representative Andrew J. Volstead of Minnesota. The 21st Amendment repealed the Volstead Act (1933).
See also: Prohibition.

Volta, Alessandro (1745-1827), Italian physicist. The volt was named for him. He invented (1800) the voltaic pile (the first battery) and thus provided science with its earliest source of continuous electric current. Volta's invention demonstrated that "animal electricity" could be produced using solely inanimate materials, thus ending a long dispute with the supporters of Luigi Galvani's view that it was a special property of animal matter.
See also: Electric current.

Voltaire (François-Marie Arouet; 1694-1778), French author, philosopher, and major figure of the Enlightenment. An enemy of tyrants, he spent much of his life in exile, including 23 years at his property on the Swiss border. His *Letters Concerning the English Nation* (1733) extolled religious and political toleration and the ideas of Sir Isaac Newton and John Locke. The satire *Candide* (1759), a rational skeptic's attack on the optimism of Gottfried von Leibniz, shows Voltaire's astringent style at its best. A friend of Frederick II of Prussia, Voltaire contributed to Denis Diderot's *Encyclopedia* and wrote his own *Philosophical Dictionary* (1764).
See also: Age of Reason.

Volunteers of America, voluntary philanthropic society founded in New York City (1896) by Ballington and Maud Booth after a split with the Salvation Army. It aims to win converts to Christianity and provides many social services. Though it retains military forms and titles, it is run democratically.

Vomiting, return of food or other substance (e.g., blood) from the stomach. It may be induced by drugs, motion sickness, infection, uremia, or stomach or pyloric disorders. Morning vomiting may be a feature of early pregnancy. Drugs may be needed to control vomiting, along with fluid and nutrient replacement.

Von Braun, Wernher (1912-77), German rocket engineer who designed the first self-contained missile, the V-2, which was used against the United Kingdom in 1944. In 1945 he was brought to the United States, where he led the team that put the first U.S. artificial satellite in orbit (1958). He later developed the Saturn rocket used in the Apollo moon-landing program, and he pioneered the concept of the space shuttle.
See also: Rocket.

Vonnegut, Kurt, Jr. (1922-), U.S. fiction writer. Vonnegut writes dark and humorous science-fictionalized novels of life with little purpose. His works portray societal, religious, political, and scientific systems as unavoidably destructive. His first novel, *Player Piano* (1952), is a study of technology in modern society. *Mother Night* (1961), *Cat's Cradle* (1963), and *God Bless You, Mr. Rosewater* (1965), explore the morals and social conventions in America. *Slaughterhouse Five* (1969), ruminates on the compulsion humans have to impose devastation on themselves, and suggests that this be accepted with resignation and humor. Other works include *Breakfast of Champions* (1973), *Deadeye Dick* (1982), *Galapagos* (1985), *Bluebeard* (1987), *Hocus Pocus* (1990), and *Timequake* (1997).

Von Neumann, John (1903-57), Hungarian-born U.S. mathematician who put quantum mechanics on a rigorous mathematical foundation. He created game theory, and made important contributions to the theory of computers, as well as to many branches of abstract mathematics.
See also: Quantum mechanics.

Von Sternberg, Josef (1894-1969), Austrian-born U.S. motion-picture director famous for his films starring Marlene Dietrich. The first film, *The Blue Angel* (1930), was made in Germany. It was followed by *Morocco* (1930),

Dishonored (1931), *Shanghai Express* (1932), *Blond Venus* (1932), *The Scarlet Empress* (1934), and *The Devil Is a Woman* (1935), all filmed in Hollywood.

Von Willebrand's disease, hereditary disease in which there is prolonged bleeding when the skin is injured. Unlike hemophilia, Von Willebrand's disease causes external bleeding; internal bleeding is rare. It affects both males and females and occurs most commonly in Scandinavian countries. The disease is caused by the absence of one of the clotting factors in the blood. Erik von Willebrand, a German professor of medicine, first identified the disease in 1926.

Voodoo, folk religion, chiefly of Haiti, with West African and added Roman Catholic and native West Indian elements. It involves worship of the spirits of saints and ancestors, who may "possess" participants. Prayers, drumming, dancing, and feasts are part of the ritual. A cult group's priest or priestess is believed to act as a medium, work charms, lay curses, and recall zombies (the "living dead").
See also: Religion.

Vorster, Balthazar Johannes (1915-83), South African political leader and prime minister (1966-78). On the right of the Nationalist Party, he was in charge of education (1958-61) and minister of justice (1961-66), responsible for some of the most repressive of the apartheid laws. He sought later to improve relations with black Africa. Elected president in 1978, he resigned in 1979 after being accused of false testimony on expenditure of government funds.
See also: South Africa.

Voting, formal collective expression of approval or rejection of a candidate for office or a course of action. The election of officers is a basic feature of democracy, but universal adult suffrage is recent: U.S. women obtained the vote only in 1920. Sometimes voting is compulsory, as in Australia and in Communist states. In the United States, voting originally followed English parliamentary practice, with the addition of the New England town meeting. Ballot papers first appeared in Massachusetts in 1634. Most U.S. states now use voting machines to ensure secrecy, speed, and accuracy.

Voting Rights Act of 1965, U.S. law aimed at eliminating local laws and practices that served to prevent blacks and other minorities from voting. It was strongly backed by President Lyndon B. Johnson, who signed it into law.

Voyager Program, two unmanned U.S. probes of the outer solar system. *Voyager 1* made close approaches to Jupiter in March 1979 and to Saturn in Nov. 1980. *Voyager 2* bypassed Jupiter in July 1979, swung around Saturn in Aug. 1981, continued to Uranus in 1986 and Neptune in 1989. The probes provided remarkable close-up views of the two giant gas planets and their satellites, revealing, among other things, the existence of a ring around Jupiter, active volcanoes on Jupiter's moon Io and a completely unexpected complexity in Saturn's ring system.
See also: Space exploration.

Voyageurs National Park, scenic 219,431-acre (88,804-hectare) park in northern Minnesota (authorized in 1971), with lakes, forests, and interesting glacial features.

Vuillard, Édouard (1868-1940), French painter, printmaker, and decorator who, along with his friend Pierre Bonnard, developed the intimist style of painting. His subjects were scenes from his private world, chiefly domestic scenes from his mother's home. Vuillard received commissions to do decorative works also. He painted the foyer of the Théatre des Champs-Elysées (1913) and the murals in the Palais de Chaillob (1937) and the League of Nations, Geneva (1939).

Vulcan, in Roman mythology, god of fire. He was also the blacksmith of the gods, skilled in metalworking. Vulcan is identified with the Greek god Hephaestus. He was a son of Jupiter and Juno and was married to Venus.
See also: Mythology.

Vulgate, Latin version of the Bible, so called because it became the most widespread (Latin: *vulgata*) in use. Largely the work of St. Jerome, who revised earlier Old Latin translations, it was collected in the 6th century and universally established by 800. In 1546 the Council of Trent confirmed the Vulgate as the sole official version of the Roman Catholic church.
See also: Bible.

Vulture, any of 2 families of large, soaring, diurnal birds of prey. The New World vultures are a primitive family, Cathartidae; the Old World vultures are a branch of the Accipitridae, being most closely related to certain eagles. All vultures are adapted to feed on animal carrion. Their heads and necks are wholly or partially naked; several have specialized tongues to feed rapidly on liquid flesh or bone marrow.

V/STOL (*V*ertical/ *S*hort *T*ake-*O*ff and *L*anding), type of aircraft that can take off and land vertically or on a short runway. While large conventional planes need about 5,000 ft (1,500 m) of runway, a V/STOL plane needs less than 500 ft (150 m). V/STOLs have great military value because they can land on small airfields near the scene of battle as well as on small aircraft carriers and military ships without large flight decks. Both the United States and Great Britain have a combat V/STOL called the Harrier. There are commercial STOLS that can operate from small airports.
See also: Airplane.

W

W, 23rd letter of the English alphabet. Its origins have been traced to the Semitic letter *waw* (meaning "hook"), which was a symbol resembling a tent peg or hook, itself perhaps derived from a *y*-shaped Egyptian hieroglyph. This letter reached the Roman alphabet as a *v*, though it was used both for *u* and *v*. Medieval Norman scribes began writing *vv* or *uu* ("double *u*") to represent the Anglo-Saxon *w* sound for which Norman French had no equivalent.

Wabash River, river running through Ohio, Indiana, and Illinois. Rising in Grand Lake, in western Ohio, the Wabash flows west and southwest across Indiana for about 475 mi (764 km) before emptying into the Ohio River in southwestern Indiana. The river forms a major segment of the border between

Indiana and Illinois. The Wabash was used as a transportation route by Native Americans as early as the 12th century.

Waco (pop. 189,123), industrial city in central Texas, situated on the Brazos River nearly 100 mi (161 km) south of Dallas. Besides being a major market for cotton and other agricultural products, Waco is home to factories producing clothing, glass products, textiles, and machinery. Waco was the residence of the Branch Davidians, a religious cult that made headlines in 1993, when, after a 6-week standoff with the FBI, its compound was burned and at least 75 cultists died.

Wages and hours, income derived from labor, figured on the basis of the number of hours worked. Wages, the rate of which is determined by supply and demand, are the leading source of income in the United States and may be calculated for work completed by the hour, day, week, month, or by individual job or service performed. In addition to wages, workers may also receive remuneration in the form of overtime payments, bonuses, paid vacations, holidays, sick or maternity leave, and retirement benefits. Wages are categorized as either money wages or real wages. Money wages are the actual amount paid to workers; real wages represent the buying power of the money wages. Economists gauge economic change by investigating the fluctuations in money wages and making real-wage comparisons.

Wagner Act *See:* National Labor Relations Act.

Wagner, Honus (John Peter Wagner; 1874-1955), U.S. baseball player. Wagner, considered to be baseball's greatest shortstop, won 8 National League batting titles (1900, 03, 04, 06-09, 11) and holds the National League record for triples (252 career). Wagner's hit over .300 for 17 consecutive seasons (1897-1913), a major league record. He played for the Louisville Colonels (1897-99) and Pittsburgh Pirates (1900-17) and was among the first group of players inducted into the National Baseball Hall of Fame (1936).

Wagner, Richard (1813-83), German composer. His adventurous and influential music marks the high point of German romanticism. A conductor in provincial opera houses, he achieved his first successes as a composer with the operas *Rienzi* (1838-40), *Der Fliegende Holländer* (1841), *Tannhäuser* (1844), and *Lohengrin* (1846-48), in which he pioneered his new ideas in fusing music and drama. The culmination of his creative principles is found in the myth cycle, *Der Ring des Nibelungen*, comprising *Das Rheingold* (1853-54), *Die Walküre* (1854-56), *Siegfried* (1856-69), and *Götterdämmerung* (1874). Involved in the 1848 Dresden revolution, Wagner fled (with the help of Franz Liszt) to Switzerland, where he wrote *Tristan und Isolde* (1857-59) and the comic opera *Die Meistersinger von Nürnberg* (1862-67), in addition to part of the Ring cycle. He next moved to Bavaria (1872), where Ludwig II helped him found the Bayreuth Festival. *Parsifal* (1877-82) was his last opera. His second wife, **Cosima** (1837-1930), the daughter of Liszt, was largely responsible for the continuing success of the Bayreuth Festival.

Wagner, Robert Ferdinand (1877-1953), German-born U.S. politician. As a Democratic senator (1927-49) from New York, he helped create the New

Deal program, particularly influencing programs involving labor, social
security, and housing.

Wagner, Robert Ferdinand, Jr. (1910-91), U.S. politician and administra-
tor. Son of senator Robert F. Wagner, he served 3 terms as mayor (1954-66)
of New York City, introducing controversial reforms in housing, education,
and civil rights. He was U.S. ambassador to Spain (1968-69).

Wagon, wheeled vehicle of primary importance to transportation and com-
merce. The invention of the wagon coincided with that of the wheel, over
5,000 years ago, when solid wooden wheels were fixed to a simple axle
attached to a sledge. Wheeled transport vehicles, hauled by oxen, developed
in Mesopotamia. The Greeks and Romans improved vehicle design until after
the fall of the Roman Empire, when little was done to advance the design of
wheeled conveyance. Farm carts remained the most widely used transport
until the development of 4-wheeled coaches in Germany in the Middle Ages.
By the 17th century, in western Europe, a period of mechanical and scientific
enlightenment had begun. Spring suspension came into use permitting
longer-distanced travel at higher speeds. This led to development and im-
provement of commercial and passenger coaches and carriages, freight-
transport vehicles, and ultimately to the invention of the automobile.

Wagtail, any of several small Old World birds (family Motacillidae) related to
the pipits. Wagtails have long tails that they wag up and down to keep their balance.
The yellow wagtail has spread across the Bering Strait and nests in Alaska.

Wahoo, swift-swimming sport and food fish (*Acanthocybium solandri*), of
the mackerel family. The wahoo is found worldwide in warm waters,
particularly tropical areas of the Atlantic, Pacific, and Indian oceans. The
wahoo has a slender, elongated body with a pointed nose, long backfin, and
crescent-shaped tail. Its back is dark gray-blue, with silvery, irregularly
striped sides. Wahoos may grow to 8 ft (2.4 m) in length and attain a weight
of about 180 lb (82k).

Wailing Wall, part of the western wall of the ancient Temple in Jerusalem,
destroyed by the Romans in A.D.70. It is held sacred by the Jews, who gather
there to pray and mourn the Temple's destruction.
See also: Jews.

Wainwright, Jonathan Mayhew (1883-1953), U.S. general. A veteran of
World War I, he was commander of the defense of the Philippines during
World War II. Despite great courage, he had to surrender Bataan and
Corregidor to the Japanese in 1942, upon which he was taken as a prisoner
of war until 1945. He was awarded the Medal of Honor on his return.
See also: World War II.

Waite, Morrison Remick (1816-88), seventh chief justice of the U.S. Su-
preme Court (1874-88). Appointed by Pres. Ulysses S. Grant, Waite became
the principal interpreter of post-Civil War amendments to the Constitution,
including that of the due process clause of the 14th Amendment, limiting
state power. In the Granger Cases (1877), which involved state legislation
intending to establish maximum rates charged by the operators of grain

elevators and railways, he maintained that only businesses that were "affected with a public interest" could be subject to state regulation. In several cases concerning newly freed slaves, Waite held that the privileges and immunities due U.S. citizens under the 14th and 15th amendments had not provided Congress the power to safeguard civil rights, but that suffrage for freed slaves must come from the states. Waite was one of the founders of the Republican Party.
See also: Supreme Court of the United States.

Wake, tradition in which people gather at the home of a dead person before burial. This is a popular custom, especially in Western cultures. Its purpose in part is to console the family and friends of the deceased, but it is also assumed that long ago a consensus of people was needed to confirm the status of the corpse.

Wake Island, atoll in the central Pacific Ocean, an unincorporated territory administered by the U.S. Air Force. An important commercial and military airbase, it consists of 3 islets (Wake, Wilkes, and Peale), totalling 3 sq mi (7.8 sq km) situated around a shallow lagoon. It was occupied by Japan from 1941 to 1945.

Wake-robin *See:* Trillium.

Waksman, Selman Abraham (1888-1973), U.S. microbiologist. Waksman, an authority on soil microbiology, developed a controlled system to discover antibiotics among microbes, particularly actinomycetes. Antibiotic activity was tested on about 10,000 soil microbes, leading to the discovery of the antibiotic streptomycin (1943), the first truly effective agent in the treatment of tuberculosis. Waksman was awarded the Nobel Prize in physiology or medicine in 1952.
See also: Microbiology.

Walata, important trade city of West Africa in the 11th-16th centuries, now the town of Oualata in Mauritania. Settled by the Muslims in the late 11th century, it was successively controlled by the Mali Empire, the Tuareg, and the Songhai Empire. Trade was conducted in copper, gold, swords, and slaves.

Wald, George (1906-), U.S. chemist and prominent pacifist. His work on the chemistry of vision brought him a share, with Haldane K. Hartline and Roger A. Granit, of the 1967 Nobel Prize in physiology or medicine.
See also: Chemistry.

Wald, Lillian D. (1867-1940), U.S. nurse, public health services pioneer, and social worker, founder of the Henry Street Settlement (1893). Wald organized a visiting nurse service that led to the inception of the first public school nursing system. She became an advocate for children and others with special health needs, and was responsible for initiating both an American Red Cross nursing service to rural areas (1912) and The Children's Bureau (1912), a national group. Wald, as a member of the American Union Against Militarism as well as several other national and international commissions of the same nature, promoted world peace, public welfare, and supported worker's unions. Written works include *The House on Henry Street* (1915) and *Windows on Henry Street* (1934).

Waldenses, or Waldensians, reforming Christian sect founded by Peter Waldo in Lyons, France, in the 12th century. They preached poverty, rejected the papacy, and took the Bible as their sole authority, for which they were excommunicated (1184) and persecuted. The survivors united with the Protestants in the Reformation. The Waldensian Church still exists, with several offshoots in the United States.
See also: Protestantism.

Waldheim, Kurt (1918-   ), Austrian diplomat and minister of foreign affairs (1968-70), and secretary general of the United Nations (1972-81). As secretary general he worked to strengthen the UN's peacekeeping role and to increase aid to poor countries. In 1986 he was elected to the Austrian presidency, up to 1992, in spite of his history as a German intelligence soldier and Nazi officer (World War II).
See also: Austria; United Nations.

Wales (Welsh: *Cymru*), historic principality of Great Britain, politically united with England since 1536. It is a large, roughly rectangular peninsula projecting into the Irish Sea west of England. Covering 8,016 sq mi (20,761 sq km), it is dominated by the Cambrian Mountains (Mt. Snowdon, 3,500 ft/1,085 m), and its rivers include the Severn, Wye, Usk, Taff, Dee, and Teifi. The climate is mild and wet. The majority of the population lives in the south, near the rich coalfields. Less than 20% speak both Welsh and English. The largest cities are Cardiff, the capital, and Swansea. Major industries, including coal mining, steel, oil refining, manmade fibers, and electronics, are also concentrated in the south. Agriculture, mostly cattle and sheep raising, predominates elsewhere. In a referendum in 1997 a small majority (53%) voted for the introduction of a parliament for Wales. The parliament will have control of British government funds intended for Wales.
See also: England.

Walesa, Lech (1943-   ), president of Poland (1991-95). In 1980 he led the Polish labor movement in its struggle to win government recognition of Solidarity (an umbrella labor group composed of about 50 trade unions)—the first time a Communist government had recognized an independent labor organization. In a 1981 military crackdown, the Polish government banned Solidarity and interned Walesa. He was released in 1982 and awarded the Nobel Peace Prize in 1983. In the upheavals of 1989, Solidarity was revived, and Walesa played a key role in establishing the new non-Communist Polish government.
See also: Poland.

Walker, Alice (1944-), U.S. author of poetry and novels examining the life experiences of African Americans. Walker was awarded the Pulitzer Prize for *The Color Purple* (1982), the story of Celie, a poor girl growing up in the rural South. Other works include *Once* (1968) and *Revolutionary Petunias and Other Poems* (1973), both volumes of poetry; a biography, *Langston Hughes, American Poet* (1974); the novel *The Third Life of Grange Copeland* (1970), *Meridian* (1976), and *Possessing the Secret of Joy* (1992).

Walker, David (1785-1830), radical African-American abolitionist. Walker, a free man, educated himself, became an abolitionist speaker, and

contributed to *Freedom's Journal*, a newspaper dedicated to the anti-slavery movement. In 1829 Walker wrote the anti-slavery tract *An Appeal to the Colored Citizens of the World*, which was a strong indictment of all pro-slavery advocates, and which exhorted slaves to revolt against their bondage. Copies of Walker's treatise were smuggled into Southern states in the pockets of second-hand clothing. Legislation was soon introduced outlawing the circulation of all abolitionist literature and making it illegal for slaves to be educated.
See also: Abolitionism.

Walker, Herschel, Jr. (1962-   ), U.S. football running back. Walker, a 3-time All-American player from the Univ. of Georgia, won the Heisman Trophy in 1982. He played for the New Jersey Generals (U.S. Football League), the Dallas Cowboys, and the Minnesota Vikings.

Walker, Mary Edwards (1832-1919), U.S. physician, writer, and advocate of women's rights. The Medal of Honor bestowed upon Walker (1865) for her work as a surgeon for the Union forces during the Civil War was revoked (1917) because of her official non-military status. The medal was rightfully reinstated many years later (1977). To protest restrictions placed upon women, she chose to wear clothes unacceptable in her time—trousers. She further discussed women's rights in her books *Hit* (1871) and *Unmasked, or the Science of Immortality* (1878).
See also: Women's movements.

Walkie-talkie, portable 2-way radio frequently used by police, hunters, and others on the move to communicate over short distances (up to a few kilometers). In the United States, walkie-talkies operate on 1 or more of 23 channels lying between 26.960 MHz and 27.255 MHz.

Walking, or race-walking, competitive track-and-field sport. This form of racing utilizes a precise heel-and-toe gait: The leading foot touches the ground heel first advancing the walker quickly forward onto the toe, which provides a pushing momentum to each stride. The leg is locked in a straight position momentarily while the foot is still touching the ground. An expert race-walker can walk 1 mi (1.6 km) in about 6.5 minutes while an ordinary walker would take about 15-20 minutes to cover the same distance. Walking competitions, particularly in the Olympic Games, are held at distances of about 12-31 mi (20-50 km).

Walking stick, or stick insect, insect (*Diapheromera femorata*) that resembles a twig, camouflaging it from its enemies. There are several species of these insects of the family Phasmidae; the common walking stick has long, slender legs and a body of about 2-3 in (5-8 cm). They are usually a green or brownish color, may have sharp spines, and release a noxious scent. Walking sticks harm trees by eating the leaves; however, few survive the larval stage because the female lays her eggs where she stands and most fall to the ground.

Wallaby, rabbit-sized member of the kangaroo family (especially genus *Macropus*), native to Australia, Tasmania, and New Guinea. Like kangaroos, wallabies have large, strong hind feet and limbs and long tails. They are herbivores. All wallabies produce a single offspring, suckling it in the marsupium, or pouch.

Wallace, Alfred Russel (1823-1913), English naturalist and evolutionist. He formulated a theory of natural selection (survival of the fittest) simultaneously with, but independent of, Charles Darwin. Wallace explored at length the Malay Archipelago and the Amazon, where the idea of natural selection occurred to him, and where he formulated a basis for geographically categorizing animals. Wallace published "On the Law Which Has Regulated the Introduction of New Species" (1855), which he shared with Darwin. Together they presented their theory before the Linnaean Society (1858). Other works include *The Malay Archipelago* (1869), *Contributions to the Theory of Natural Selection* (1870), and *The Geographical Distribution of Animals* (2 vols, 1876), a systemization of the science of biogeography. *See also:* Darwin, Charles Robert.

Wallace, George Corley (1919-98), U.S. political leader, governor of Alabama (1963-67, 1971-79, 1983-86). Wallace, a segregationist, achieved notoriety in 1963 with his unsuccessful attempt to prevent racial integration at the University of Alabama. He ran for president 3 times, and in 1972 was shot and paralyzed in an attempted assassination while campaigning for the Democratic presidential nomination. Unable by Alabama law to succeed himself as governor, he had his wife, Lurleen, run for office to replace him (she won the election). He won the 1982 gubernatorial election with black support, and retired in 1986.

Wallace, Henry Agard (1888-1965), 33rd vice president of the United States (1941-45). A distinguished agricultural economist and plant geneticist, he was secretary of agriculture under President Franklin D. Roosevelt (1933-41). His success with New Deal farm programs led to the vice presidency. He became secretary of commerce (1945) but was dismissed (1946) for criticizing Truman. He ran unsuccessfully in 1948 as presidential candidate of the Progressive Party.

Wallace, Lew (Lewis Wallace; 1827-1905), U.S. military leader, lawyer, and author. Wallace is best known for his novels, particularly *Ben Hur* (1880), about the advent of Christianity in the Roman Empire. Wallace served in the Mexican War, and while a Union Army major general in the Civil War, captured Fort Donelson, Tenn. Wallace had studied law before the wars and became a practicing attorney in Indianapolis after military service. He headed courts of inquiry investigating wartime conduct of some Union and Confederate leaders, and served on the trial of Abraham Lincoln's assassins. He was appointed governor of New Mexico (1878-81) and minister to Turkey (1881-85).

Wallboard, fibrous building material made in rigid sheets and used to cover walls and ceilings for temperature and sound insulation, fire protection, and decoration. Types of wallboard include *fiberboard*, made of compressed cane or wood fibers; *hardboard*, a denser, more compressed board of similar composition; and *plasterboard*, used in building as a substitute for plaster, made of heavy paper, fiberboard, or other material bonded to a gypsum core.

Wallenberg, Raoul (1912-47?), Swedish diplomat. While representing Sweden in Budapest during World War II, he issued Swedish passports to 20,000 Hungarian Jews to prevent their deportation into Nazi hands. Soviet

authorities arrested him as a spy in 1945 and reported his death in prison in 1947. In 1981 an international association found evidence indicating he might be alive and urged the former Soviet Union to investigate (his death was never verified). In the same year the U.S. Congress declared him an honorary U.S. citizen.
See also: Sweden.

Waller, Fats (Thomas Wright Waller; 1904-43), U.S. jazz and blues pianist, composer, and entertainer. Waller began his career working in cabarets and theaters, where he accompanied various singers. He was one of few jazz musicians to become widely popular, and by the late 1920s his music, which was often witty and animated, was heard in many Broadway revues. From 1929 to 1943 Waller recorded hundreds of songs, including "Ain't Misbehavin'," "Honeysuckle Rose," and "Blue Turning Gray Over You." Waller also appeared in films, including *Stormy Weather* (1943).
See also: Jazz.

Walleye *See:* Perch.

Wallflower, or gillyflower, fragrant flowering plant (*Cheiranthus cheiri*) of the mustard family. Wallflowers, native to southern Europe and now widely cultivated, are so named for their tendency to grow on walls or on the sides of cliffs. The plants are biennial or perennial, grow to about 28 in (70 cm), and have stalks bearing clusters of maroon or purple flowers. The western wallflower (*Erysimum asperum*), a perennial, produces golden, orange, or brown flowers.

Walloons, French-speaking people (chiefly Celtic), inhabitants of southern Belgium and adjacent areas of France. The Walloons, who make up about 40% of Belgium's population, have often been at odds with the Flemish-speaking majority, who have resented French political and cultural domination. Separate regional administrations were set up in 1974.

Wallpaper, printed, painted, or embossed wall covering used to finish interior walls. Wallpaper, which is hung with glue or paste on the undecorated side, is utilized mainly as a decorative feature, and may be from any of 5 categories: ceiling papers, border papers, scenic or panel papers, papers of imitative design, or relief-surfaced papers made of ricepaper, burlap, straw fibers, or thin wood. It is thought that wallpapers originated in Europe in the 1500s to imitate expensive tapestries. Other wallpapers evolved in China (1600s) and in France (1700s). The first U.S. wallpapers were produced in Philadelphia (1739).

Wall Street, financial center of the United States, located in lower Manhattan, New York City. Wall Street is the home of the New York Stock Exchange, many other commodity exchanges, and head offices of many banks and insurance and brokerage firms. The term "Wall Street" also refers to the nation's aggregate financial interests.
See also: Stock exchange.

Walnut, deciduous tree of the genus *Juglans*, prized for its wood and nuts. In the United States the black walnut (*J. nigra*) grows to 150 ft (45.7 m), its wood being used for furniture, musical instruments, and gun stocks. The English walnut (*J. regia*), which provides edible walnuts, is naturalized throughout the world. The walnut tree is a member of the family Juglandaceae and is related to the hickory and pecan.

Walpole, Sir Robert (1676-1745), English politician often described as Great Britain's first prime minister. A Whig, he held ministerial posts from 1708 to 1717. He was rewarded for his role in salvaging the government from the South Sea Bubble (a speculation scandal) with an appointment as first lord of the treasury and chancellor of the exchequer (1721), during which time he dominated Parliament and created political and financial stability. Facing opposition and unpopularity as Britain became involved in European wars from 1739, he resigned in 1742, becoming first earl of Orford.
See also: United Kingdom.

Walrus, either of 2 subspecies of seal-like marine mammals (*Odobenus rosmarus*), distinguished by upper canines that extend into long tusks (up to 3.5 ft/1.1 m) and wrinkled brown hides. Adult males may weigh up to 3,000 lb (1,400 kg). Walruses are found in shallow waters around Arctic coasts, often hauling themselves out onto rocks or ice floes to bask. They feed almost exclusively on mollusks.

Walter, Bruno (Bruno Walter Schlesinger; 1876-1962), German-born U.S. conductor. He was a protégé of Gustav Mahler, but his career in Europe was cut short by the Nazis (they forced him to leave), and he lived in the United States from 1939. He was renowned for his interpretations of Mahler, Wagner, Beethoven, and Brahms with the Metropolitan Opera and the New York Philharmonic.

Walter, Thomas Ustick (1804-87), U.S. architect known for the classical Greek influence in his designs. Walter was professor of architecture at Franklin Institute in Philadelphia; president of the American Institute of Architects (1876-87), and designer of Founder's Hall, Girard College, Philadelphia. Walter is best known for his designs of the additions and new dome for the U.S. Capitol in Washington, D.C. (1851-65). Other examples of his architectural designs are Andalusia, the home of Nicholas Biddle, and Moyamensing, a Philadelphia county prison.
See also: Architecture.

Walter Reed Army Medical Center, military hospital and care facility in Washington, D.C. The center, named for U.S. Army pathologist Walter Reed, researcher of typhoid and yellow fevers, provides medical care for military personnel and their families; conducts medical and scientific research; and provides advanced education for medical personnel. The center covers a combined area of 253 acres (103 hectares) in Washington, and Forest Glen and Glenhaven, Md. Facilities include the Walter Reed Army Inst. of Research, the Armed Forces Inst. of Pathology, and the Inst. of Dental Research.
See also: Reed, Walter.

Walther Von der Vogelweide (c.1170-c.1230), most renowned medieval German lyric poet, or minnesinger. Walther's poetry was more politically oriented than that of other minnesingers, with about one-half of his 200 poems being moral, political, or religious in nature. These didactic poems encouraged such virtues as self-discipline, charity, and fidelity, and extolled the benefits of pilgrimage. The other half were love poems, which were fresh in their appraisal of courtly love and of the society of his time. Walther was a poet in the Viennese court of Leopold V, and later wandered from court to court until German Emperor Frederick II granted him a small fief in Wurzburg, where it is assumed that he lived out the remainder of his life.

Walton, Ernest Thomas Sinton (1903-95), Irish nuclear physicist. He shared with John D. Cockcroft the 1951 Nobel Prize in physics for their development of the first particle accelerator, with which they initiated the first nuclear-fission reaction applying nonradioactive substances.
See also: Cockcroft, Sir John Douglas; Particle accelerator.

Walton, George (1741-1804), colonial politician from Georgia. He signed the Declaration of Independence and served on the Continental Congress (1776-81). While defending Savannah against the British, he was taken prisoner (1778). He served his state as a chief justice and governor as well as a senator in the federal government (1795-96).

Walton, Izaak (1593-1683), English writer. His famous *The Compleat Angler* (1653), written as a dialogue between a fisherman, Piscator, and a hunter, Venator, combines praise for simple living with sound advice on the sport of fishing. His biographies include *John Donne* (1640), *Sir Henry Wotton* (1651), *George Herbert* (1670), and *Bishop Sanderson* (1678).

Walton, Sir William Turner (1902-83), English composer. He had a brilliant early success with *Façade* (1923), a chamber work set to poems by Edith Sitwell. Other works include the oratorio *Belshazzar's Feast* (1931), film scores (notably for films of Shakespeare plays), and the opera *Troilus and Cressida* (1954).

Waltz, ballroom dance in 3/4 time, probably originating from the *ländler*, a folk dance; also, music in 3/4 time. Its popularity in the 19th century was due largely to the music of the Strauss family.
See also: Strauss.

Walvis Bay, or Walvisbaai, South African exclave district within Namibia's boundaries, on the Atlantic coast. Walvis Bay has an area of about 434 sq mi (1,124 sq km) and is Namibia's only deep-water seaport. The harbor is a major one with links to most leading overseas shipping centers, and has been a point of controversy since the 1970s, with South Africa and Namibia in dispute over the area's jurisdiction. When Namibia became independent of South Africa (March 21, 1990), Walvis Bay was adjudged to remain under the dominion of South Africa. After two years of mutual administration, Walvis Bay was delegated to Namibia. Industries include fishing and fish processing.
See also: Namibia; South Africa.

Wampanoag, Native Americans of the Algonquian language family who lived east of Narragansett Bay, R.I. Their chief, Massasoit (c.1580-1661), made friends with the Pilgrims (1620). His second son, known as King Philip, was the leader during King Philip's War (1675), his attempt to rid his land of foreign settlers. After their defeat the Wampanoag were nearly exterminated.

Wampum, strings of shell beads and disks made by Native Americans, used as ornaments and as money in trading. Early European settlers accepted wampum as currency (a purple variety was especially valuable), but the production of counterfeit glass beads undermined their value in the early 18th century.

Wandering Jew, or striped inch plant, any of several trailing plants that are grown indoors for their flowers and foliage. *Tradescantia fluminensis variegata* has green leaves, irregularly striped with white; *Callisia elegans* has green leaves with white pinstripes; and *Zebrina pendula* has purple, green, and silver striped leaves. They grow best in sunny windows and are extremely easy to propagate by taking cuttings and rooting them in water and wet sand.

Wandering Jew, legendary man (identified as a Jew in the 17th century) doomed to wander the earth until the Second Coming of Christ as punishment for taunting Jesus as He struggled to His Crucifixion. This tale has been chronicled several times, in the medieval tale *Flores historiarum*; in "A Brief Description and Narration Regarding a Jew Named Ahasuerus" (1602); and in the play "Le Juif errant" (1844-45).

Wang Wei (699-759), Chinese poet, landscape painter, and calligrapher of the T'ang dynasty (618-907). Wang Wei is credited with the creation of the broken ink (*p'o-mo*) method of wash brushstrokes, and was a master of monochromatic landscape paintings, particularly snowscapes. The lyric poetry of Wang Wei often related nature's attributes. He was revered in later years, probably for uniting poetry, painting, and calligraphy in a single art form.

Wankel engine, internal-combustion engine that produces rotary motion directly. Invented by the German engineer Felix Wankel, who completed his first design in 1954, it is used in automobiles and airplanes. A triangular rotor with spring-loaded sealing plates at its apexes rotates eccentrically inside a cylinder, while the 3 combustion chambers formed between the sides of the rotor and the walls of the cylinder successively draw in, compress, and ignite a fuel-and-air mixture. The Wankel engine is simpler in principle, more efficient, and more powerful weight-for-weight than a conventional reciprocating engine, but it is more difficult to cool.
See also: Internal combustion engine.

Wapiti (*Cervus canadensis*), North American subspecies of the red deer, called elk in the United States. It is larger than the typical European red deer, and, unlike the red deer, the terminal points of its antlers are in the same plane as the beam and do not form a crown. Once the most abundant deer in North America, wapiti are now severely reduced in number and range.

War, organized armed conflict between groups of people or states. War is not found elsewhere in the animal kingdom. Since recorded history began, people have been involved in hostility for different aims: power, territory, wealth, ideological domination, security, or independence. Until modern times most wars were fought with limited means for limited aims, but modern weapons threaten mass destruction with their ability to eliminate whole populations, thus endangering the survival of the human race.

War aces, combat pilots with at least 5 "victories" or "kills," confirmed downings of enemy aircraft. Famous aces of World War I, the first air war, included Baron Manfred von Richthofen of Germany (the "Red Baron") and Captain Eddie Rickenbacker of the United States. The leading ace of World War II was Captain Erich Hartmann of Germany (a record 352 kills); Lieutenant Colonel Heinz Bär of Germany was the first jet ace.

War Between the States *See:* Civil War, U.S.

Warble fly, also cattle warble or heel fly, large, beelike fly of the family Hypodermatidae that deposits its eggs on the legs or feet of cattle. There the larvae (cattle grub) enter the skin and migrate within the body for several months. This produces a characteristic painful lump, or warble. At maturity, the cattle grub emerges and pupates wherever it drops. The warble fly is a pest in Europe and North America, causing economic losses due to damaged hides and meat.

Warbler, small songbird native to the Americas. Warblers (family Parulidae) are seen throughout the United States and Canada during the temperate months, and migrate south to winter in South and Central America. Among the many species of warblers are the American redstart (*Setophaga ruticilla*), the yellow warbler (*Dendroica petechia*), and the hooded warbler (*Wilsonia citrina*). The feathers of warblers vary in color. The birds grow to about 3.5-10 in (9-25 cm), and they are noted for their lively movements and song. Warblers are beneficial to farmers and gardeners as they feed on harmful insects.

Warburg, Otto Heinrich (1883-1970), German biochemist. He was awarded the 1931 Nobel Prize in physiology or medicine for discovering the chemistry of cell respiration. He was director of the Kaiser Wilhelm (now Max Planck) Institute for Cell Physiology, Berlin, from 1931 to 1953. *See also:* Biochemistry; Cell.

War correspondent, news reporter who sends information from a war front to print or broadcast media, to provide accurate, up-to-date coverage. The Mexican War (1846-48) was probably the first war to be reported on systematically by getting information immediately from the front. U.S. writers who have been important war correspondents include Walt Whitman (Civil War, 1861-65) and Stephen Crane (Spanish-American War, 1898).

War crime, in international law, violation of the laws and rules of war. The first systematic attempt to frame laws for warfare was by Hugo Grotius (1625). Since 1864 various agreements have laid down principles for the treatment of combatants and civilians and have attempted to outlaw certain weapons. Among the few people convicted of war crimes was Confederate officer Henry Wirz, executed in 1865. An attempt was made to try the

German Kaiser after World War I, and some German officers were tried (mostly acquitted) by a German court. One major war crimes trial, conducted by the United States, USSR, France, and Britain, was at Nuremberg, Germany, in which 3 categories of war crimes were defined: crimes against peace (planning and waging aggressive war); "conventional" war crimes (murder of civilians or prisoners of war, plunder, etc.); and crimes against humanity (murder, enslavement, or deportation of whole populations). The principle of individual responsibility was also established. A tribunal of 11 nations in Tokyo, Japan (1946-47), sentenced alleged Japanese war criminals.
See also: Nuremberg Trials.

Ward, Aaron Montgomery (1843-1913), U.S. businessperson. In 1872, with capital of $2,400, he and his partner, George Thorne, started the mail-order house that became the vast firm of Montgomery Ward & Co. Annual sales had risen to $40 million at the time of his death.

Ward, Artemus (1727-1800), leader in the American Revolutionary War. As governor of Massachusetts (1774-75), he besieged Boston until George Washington arrived, and he was second in command of the Continental army (1775-76). He served in Congress (1791-95).
See also: Revolutionary War in America.

Ward, Barbara (1914-81), British writer, economist, and commentator on the relations between the Western powers and developing nations. She was foreign editor of *Economist* magazine (from 1946), governor of British Broadcasting Corp. (1946-50), and a professor at Columbia Univ. (N.Y.C.; 1968-73). In her writings she stressed the importance of economic aid and international cooperation in such books as *The Rich Nations and the Poor Nations* (1962), *Nationalism and Ideology* (1967), and *Progress for a Small Planet* (1979).
See also: Economics.

Ward, Joseph (1838-89), U.S. educator, Congregational minister, and missionary. As a young minister he moved to the Dakota Territory (1869) and worked as a missionary. In conjunction with the Congregational Church, he established Yankton College (1881). For the duration of his life he was president and professor of philosophy of the college. He worked for the statehood of South Dakota and organized a group to pursue that goal (1879).

Ward, Lynd Kendall (1905-85), U.S. artist, writer, wood engraver. His works include *God's Man* (1929) and other novels created in woodcut (the first such text-less novels published in the United States), and watercolors, oil paintings, and lithographs. He illustrated such children's books as *The Little Red Lighthouse and the Great Gray Bridge* (1942) and *The Biggest Bear* (1952), for which he won the 1953 Caldecott Medal.

Ward, Robert (1917-), U.S. composer. He studied at both the Eastman and Juilliard schools of music. The influence of jazz and U.S. folk melodies is heard in his works, which include the Pulitzer Prize-winning opera *The Crucible* (1961).

War debt, financial obligations to the United States incurred by foreign countries during World War I. The United States lent its allies $11.5 billion

when the expense of war became unaffordable for many of them. The war debt was paid in part by reparations levied against Germany at the Treaty of Versailles, and in part by the borrower nations. The entire war debt was never paid due to worldwide post-war economic depression.
See also: World War I.

War Department, United States, former executive department (1789-1947) created to govern all phases of the military. The War Department was headed by the secretary of war, an administrator who was under military advisement by the War Council. The principal task of the War Department was to ensure the proper functioning of the Army, including recruitment, transportation, weapon maintenance, and education and welfare of the troops. At times the War Department was involved in nonmilitary functions, such as managing the U.S. Island possessions and supervision of Reconstruction in the post-Civil War South. In 1947 the Natl. Military Establishment came into being (it later became the Dept. of Defense) and the War Department became the Dept. of the Army, within the Dept. of Defense.
See also: Defense, Department of.

Warhol, Andy (1927-87), U.S. artist and filmmaker, famous for his pop art silk-screen paintings that incorporated everyday objects (e.g., soup cans). His highly innovative, often erotic, and often lengthy films include *Chelsea Girls* (1966) and *Lonesome Cowboys* (1969).

Warm-blooded animal, or homoiotherm, animal whose body temperature is not dependent on external temperature but is maintained at a constant level by internally generated metabolic heat. This constant temperature enables the chemical processes of the body, many of them temperature dependent, to be more efficient. Mammals and birds have developed this homoiothermy, and it is now believed that pterodactyls, therapsids, and many other extinct reptiles may also have been warm-blooded.

Warner, Jack L. (1892-1978), U.S. film producer who, with his 3 brothers, founded Warner Brothers, one of the largest and most successful Hollywood film studios. Warner Brothers produced the first sound film, *The Jazz Singer* (1927), and was the first studio to produce for television.

Warner, Pop (Glenn Scobey Warner; 1871-1954), U.S. football coach. He coached at Georgia (1895-96), Cornell (1897-98), Carlisle (1899-1903), Cornell (1904-06), Carlisle (1907-14), Univ. of Pittsburgh (1915-23), Stanford (1924-32), and Temple (1933-38), winning 313 games (third winningest coach in Division I-A). Warner pioneered both the single- and double-wing formation and led Standford to a Rose Bowl victory (1928).

Warner, Seth (1743-84), hero of the American Revolutionary War and a leader of the Green Mountain Boys. He helped capture Fort Ticonderoga, took Crown Point, N.Y. (1775), and was largely responsible for the victory at Bennington (1777).
See also: Green Mountain Boys; Revolutionary War in America.

War of 1812, conflict between the United States and Great Britain (1812-15). Due to the maritime policies of Britain and France during the French

Revolutionary Wars and the Napoleonic Wars, U.S. trade slumped. At the same time, the British were confiscating U.S. ships and impressing U.S. crewmen (as in the *Chesapeake* incident, when the British impressed 4 crew members from a U.S. frigate), to which the United States responded with the Embargo Act (1807) and the Noninterference Act (1809), banning trade with the belligerents. Anti-British feeling, fed by war hawks and by the conviction that British support of the Native Americans in the West was hindering U.S. expansion, led to declaration of war on June 18, 1812. However, the United States was unprepared for such a conflict, and its attempted invasion (1812) of Canada (Britain's main North American possession) was a failure. Early U.S. naval successes, which led to a retaliatory British blockade, include Capt. Oliver Perry's victory in 1813 at the battle on Lake Erie. In 1814 U.S. troops held their own at Chippewa and Lundy's Lane, and the victory of the Battle of the Thames at Plattsburgh halted a British advance on the Hudson Valley. In Chesapeake Bay a British force that had captured and sacked Washington, D.C., was repelled in its attempt to take Baltimore. There was a military stalemate, and peace negotiations were begun in June 1814. The Peace of Ghent, signed on Dec. 22, 1814, was essentially a return to the situation before the war. Two weeks later, Andrew Jackson defeated the British at the Battle of New Orleans, which took place before word of the treaty reached the United States. The war had several far-reaching effects on the United States: The military victories promoted national confidence and encouraged expansionism, while the trade embargo encouraged home manufactures.

War on Poverty *See:* Johnson, Lyndon Baines.

War Powers Resolution, also called War Powers Act, U.S. law that describes the procedure that both the President and the Congress must follow in order to legally declare war. According to this law, the President may send military forces to an area where conflict arises, but the legislative branch must be informed by the executive branch within 48 hours. For the forces to remain in place for more than 90 days, the President must seek approval from the Congress. The law was created in response to the Vietnam War (1957-75), during which time both President Nixon and President Johnson approved military actions without the consent of Congress. This law was employed to initiate military action in the Persian Gulf (1991).

Warrant, judicial order (signed usually by a judge or court clerk) authorizing arrest of a suspect, seizure of goods, or search of premises. Strict procedures govern the issuing of a warrant. There are also tax warrants and warrants of attorney and of attachment.

Warren, Earl (1891-1974), chief justice of the U.S. Supreme Court (1953-69). Attorney general (1939-43) and governor (1943-53) of California, he was Republican vice presidential candidate in 1948. Appointed to the Supreme Court by President Eisenhower, his leadership of the court resulted in a number of landmark liberal judgments concerning individual and civil liberties, notably *Brown* v. *Board of Education of Topeka* (1954), declaring racial segregation in schools unconstitutional. Warren also led the commission assigned to investigate Pres. John F. Kennedy's assassination.
See also: Supreme Court of the United States.

Warren, Joseph (1741-75), U.S. politician and physician. A patriot, he became a leader in the Revolutionary War when his sympathies for the effort were aroused by the passage of the Stamp Act. Warren became a Whig in Massachusetts and spoke and wrote in protest of unfair parliamentary actions. He was selected president of the Provincial Assembly (1775) and was major general of the Massachusetts troops. Warren was killed at the Battle of Bunker Hill.
See also: Revolutionary War in America.

Warren, Mercy Otis (1728-1814), U.S. author of patriotic works. Warren, who knew several Revolutionary War leaders, wrote to express her own political beliefs. She encouraged pro-Revolutionary sympathy with her satirical, anti-Tory plays: *The Adulateur* (1773), *The Defeat*, and *The Group* (1775). Her major work was a history of the American Revolution titled *History of the Rise, Progress, and Termination of the American Revolution* (3 vols., 1805). Warren advocated equal rights for women and the conservation of rights of individuals.

Warren, Robert Penn (1905-89), U.S. novelist, poet, and critic. One of the poets associated with the *Fugitive* magazine (1922-23), Penn's poetry and novels are often set in the South and address political and moral themes. He won Pulitzer prizes for his novel *All the King's Men* (1946),and his poetry collections *Promises* (1957) and *Now and Then* (1979). In 1986 he was appointed the first U.S. poet laureate.

Warren Report, findings of the commission established (Nov. 1963) by President Lyndon Johnson to investigate the assassination of President John F. Kennedy. The commission comprised Supreme Court Chief Justice Earl Warren, U.S. Representatives Hale Boggs and Gerald Ford; U.S. Senators Richard Russell and John S. Cooper; Allen Dulles; and John J. McCloy. The report; released in Sept. 1964, concluded that neither assassin Lee Harvey Oswald nor his killer, Jack Ruby, was part of a conspiracy. It criticized the FBI and Secret Service and recommended reforms in presidential security. The work of the commission has been widely challenged since its findings were published, and in 1979 a congressional committee announced its determinations, based on acoustical evidence, that 2 gunmen had shot at Kennedy.

Warsaw (pop. 1,644,500), largest city and capital of Poland, on the Vistula River. It is a commercial, industrial, cultural, and educational center, and transportation hub. Chief products are machinery, precision instruments, motor vehicles, electrical equipment, textiles, and chemicals. Warsaw has frequently been a focal point in European history. It replaced Kraków as Poland's capital in 1596 and subsequently fell into Swedish, Russian, Prussian, and German hands. Much of the city, which was razed in World War II, has been carefully reconstructed, including Warsaw's medieval old town, Stare Miasto.
See also: Poland.

Warsaw Pact, or Warsaw Treaty Organization, mutual defense pact signed in 1955 in Warsaw by the USSR and its Communist neighbors (Albania, Bulgaria, Czechoslovakia, East Germany, Hungary, Poland, and Romania)

after the formation of the North Atlantic Treaty Organization (NATO). Its unified command has headquarters in Moscow. In 1968 (when Albania formally withdrew) pact forces invaded Czechoslovakia to overthrow its independent-minded regime. In 1980-81 the USSR used pact maneuvers and threats of intervention by pact members to discourage labor unrest in Poland. Following the conventional arms treaty signed with NATO (1990), which drastically reduced the number of soldiers and weapons on the European continent, and the breakup of the Soviet-led Communist bloc, the Warsaw Pact was officially dissolved (1991).
See also: North Atlantic Treaty Organization.

Warship, ship armed and employed for combat. Ships have been used in battle since antiquity, when cargo carriers became warships when necessary. The oar- and sail-powered galley ships of the Romans and Greeks, and the Viking long ships attacked enemy vessels by ramming them. By the 1500s ships were larger and heavier, and when armed became floating artillery depots. Spain had such a fleet—galleons built for their explorers' long expeditions; however, when England, with lighter galleons, destroyed the Spanish Armada, heavier-armed but more maneuverable warships (called capital ships) were built and ruled the seas for the next 200 years. In the early 1800s steam-powered warships with rotating gun turrets were invented and outfitted with explosive shells, which replaced cannonballs. But ironclad ships, the precursors of modern warships, proved able to withstand their attack, as was attested in the Civil War battle between the *Monitor* and the *Merrimack* (neither lost in battle). The English ship *Dreadnought* was the first truly modern battleship, and in the early 1900s designers improved battleship capabilities using it as a model. This type of massive battleship, as well as the submarine, were the most effective of the World War I warships. By the end of World War II there were great advances in the design and capabilities of combat ships. Aircraft carriers, destroyers, cruisers, frigates, amphibious ships, and minesweepers led the way into modern warfare. Advances in technology yielded further specialization, and with the advent of the *Nautilus* submarine, warships entered the nuclear age.

Wars of Succession *See:* Succession wars.

Wars of the Roses, fight between the House of Lancaster and the House of York for the English throne (1455-85). A white rose stood for the House of York and a red rose stood for the House of Lancaster. The throne of England changed hands 5 times after the beginning of the war, at which time Henry VI, a Lancaster, ruled. When Henry Tudor, King Henry VII, took the throne (1485), he married Elizabeth, a York. This union dissolved the conflict between both houses and created a new dynasty, the House of Tudor.

Wart, scaly excrescence on the skin caused by a virus. Warts may arise without warning and disappear equally suddenly. Numerous remedies have been suggested, but local freezing or cauterization are often effective. Warts that grow on the soles of the feet, pushed inward by the weight of the body, are called verrucas.

Wart hog, wild hog (genus *Phacochoerus*) distinguished by large, gristly facial warts and 1-ft (30.5-cm) curling tusks. Wart hogs are found in Africa south of the Sahara. They prefer plains and open scrub and live in family groups, feeding on grass, leaves, sometimes fruit, roots, and carrion.

Warwick (pop. 87,123), city in east-central Rhode Island, on Pawtuxet River and Narragansett Bay. The township government of Warwick was organized in 1647, and became an industry-based settlement when mills were built on the Pawtuxet River. The city's major industries include production of textiles, clothing, and metal products.
See also: Rhode Island.

Warwick, Earl of (Richard Neville; 1428-71), British soldier and influential leader. He is known as "the Kingmaker" for having put Edward IV and Henry VI on the throne. In 1453 Warwick aided the duke of York in his attempt to seize the power of the Lancastrian duke of Somerset, chief adviser to Henry VI. In 1455, during the War of the Roses, when the 2 sides fought at the Battle of Saint Albans, Warwick and the Yorkists were victorious over the Lancastrians. In 1460 the 2 sides fought again at the Battle of Northampton. Warwick won again, this time capturing the king, who was allowed to keep his throne because he was deemed such an ineffectual leader. Later that same year, the Lancastrians captured and killed York, and a few months later, regained King Henry. Warwick managed to enter London with York's son, Edward, proclaim him king in March of 1461, and, in effect, rule England for the first 3 years of Edward's reign. That same month Warwick and Edward defeated the Lancastrians at the Battle of Towton. Warwick gradually became disenchanted with the independent-minded Edward, who married against his wishes, and so in 1470, Warwick teamed with Lancastrian Henry VI and his wife, Margaret, in France and brought them back to England, where he deposed Edward and restored the crown to them. In 1471 Warwick was killed at Barnet in a battle against Edward.
See also: United Kingdom.

Wasatch Range, part of the Rocky Mountains that stretches southward from northern Utah into southern Idaho. The range is about 140 mi (225 km) long and its height averages about 10,000 ft (3,000 m). Its highest peak is Mt. Timpanogos, at 11,750 ft (3,581 m). West of the Wasatch Range lies a lake valley in which the Great Salt Lake and Salt Lake City are located. Streams from the Wasatch Range are used to irrigate farmlands in the valley.
See also: Rocky Mountains.

Washakie (1804?-1900), chief of Eastern Shoshone Indians, a tribe from Utah and Wyoming. Because the Sioux, Cheyenne, and Blackfoot, among other tribes, were already the enemies of the Eastern Shoshone, Washakie and his people became allies of the U.S. government during the Indian Wars of the 1870s. He signed a treaty with the United States to allow the railroad through his tribe's territory. Later he voluntarily moved his people to the Wind River Reservation of Wyoming.

Washburn, Sherwood Larned (1911-), U.S. anthropologist. An expert on ape behavior and anatomy, he was one of the first scientists to study apes in their natural environments. Washburn was editor of *American Journal of Physical Anthropology* (1955-57). Previously on the faculties of Columbia University and the University of Chicago, he has been on the faculty of University of California, Berkeley, since 1959.
See also: Anthropology.

Washington

Capital:	Olympia
Statehood:	Nov. 11, 1889 (42nd state)
Familiar name:	Evergreen State
Area:	68,139 sq mi (176,479 sq km); ranks 20th
Population:	5,610,000 (1997); ranks 15th
Elevation:	Highest—14,410 ft (4,392 m), Mt. Rainier; Lowest—sea level, along the Pacific coast
Motto:	Alki (Bye and Bye)
Flower:	Coast rhododendron
Bird:	Willow goldfinch
Tree:	Western hemlock
Song:	"Washington, My Home"

Washing machine, machine that washes clothes. Most washing machines work automatically through the power of an electric motor. The temperature and amount of wash and rinse water as well as the strength of agitation used to clean the clothes is controlled through settings selected by the operator. The last cycle of most washing machines removes excess water by spinning the clothes. Although an electric-powered machine was invented in 1910, it took 27 more years to develop the automatic washer. The first patented washing machines (1860s) mechanically pushed clothes through water by use of a paddle.

Washington, Pacific Coast state in northwestern United States; bordered by Canada to the north, Idaho to the east, Oregon and the Columbia River to the south, and the Pacific Ocean and Puget Sound to the west.
Land and climate. Washington has six main land regions. The Rocky Mountains, in the northeast, is an area of mineral-rich ridges and valleys. The Columbia Plateau, in central and eastern Washington, is a semiarid, treeless lava basin with many coulees (steep, dry canyons). The Cascade Mountains, which split the state in two, has high, rugged peaks and volcanoes (most long-extinct) covered by glaciers and snowfields. The Puget Sound Lowland, between the Cascades and the Pacific coast, is a fertile, low-lying plain. The Olympic Mountains region, in the northwestern corner, has high, rug-  ged, snowcapped peaks, many of which are still unexplored. The hilly, heavily forested Coast Range lies in the southwestern corner. The vast Puget Sound, dotted with more than 170 islands, cuts deep into western Washington. The Columbia is the state's major river. Forests cover more than 50% of the state. Western Washington has cool summers and relatively mild winters; eastern Washington has warmer summers and colder winters. Principal cities are Seattle, Spokane, and Tacoma.

Economy. Manufacturing and service industries lead Washington's economy. Chief manufactured goods are transportation equipment (aircraft, aerospace vehicles, and ships), processed foods, lumber and wood products, aluminum, paper products, and chemicals. Agriculture and mining account for a small share of the state's economy. Lumber is the most valuable agricultural product; chief crops are wheat, apples, potatoes, hops, hay, and flower bulbs; chief livestock products are dairy and beef cattle. Chief mining products are sand and gravel and coal.

Government. Washington's constitution was adopted in 1889. The governor serves a 4-year term. The state legislature consists of 49 senators serving 4-year terms and 98 representatives serving 2-year terms. In the U.S. Congress, Washington is represented by 2 senators and 9 representatives.

History. The area was long-populated by various Native American peoples, including Nez Percé, Spokane, and Chinook, before the first Europeans— Spanish and English explorers—sailed along the coast in the 1500s. The first recorded European landing was in 1775, by the Spanish. The Lewis and Clark expedition explored the area in 1805; fur traders gradually moved in. In 1846, the 49th-parallel boundary with Canada was established. The area was included in the Oregon Territory (1848); Washington Territory (larger than present-day Washington) was created in 1853. War raged between European-American settlers and the area's Native Americans (1855-58); the coming of the railroad (1883) brought new white settlement. In 1889 Washington became the 42nd state. The Alaska and Klondike gold rushes (1897-98) brought new prosperity, as did World War I. The Great Depression (1930s) caused economic collapse, but World War II and new hydroelectric plants attracted the airline, aerospace, and other new industries. An economic slump in the 1970s forced state leaders to seek more diverse industries. In 1980 a devastating volcanic eruption at Mt. St. Helens killed 57 people and caused billions of dollars' worth of damage. In recent years, Washington has worked to attract new industries, and to conserve its natural resources without damaging valuable lumber-related industries.

Washington, Booker T. (1856-1915), U.S. educator. Born into a Virginia slave family, he was educated and chosen in 1881 to head a new school for blacks, the Tuskegee Institute, Ala. Under his guidance the institution expanded from 2 unequipped buildings to a complex with over 100 buildings and 1,500 students. Washington urged industrial education as the way to economic independence, which he believed to be an essential prerequisite to the demand for social equality. His writings included an autobiography, *Up from Slavery* (1901).

Washington, D.C. (pop. 3,923,574), capital of the United States, coextensive with the federal District of Columbia, which is the seat of the U.S. federal government. (The "D.C." in the city's name stand for District of Columbia.) It lies in the eastern United States on the west-central edge of Maryland on the Potomac River, with Virginia on the river's opposite side.

Important sites. The city's focal point is the domed Capitol, home of the Congress of the United States. The Capitol lies on a small rise; for this reason the area is referred to as Capitol Hill. To the northwest lies the White House, official office and residence of the President. Other important buildings are the headquarters of government departments and agencies, the U.S. Supreme Court, the Federal Bureau of Investigation (FBI), and the Library of Congress. Also a cultural and educational center, Washington, D.C., is the site

Washington, D.C

Area:	69 sq mi (179 sq km)
Population:	529,000 in the city
Motto:	Justitia omnibus (Justice for All)
Flower:	American beauty rose
Bird:	Wood thrush
Tree:	Scarlet oak

of the Smithsonian Institution, the National Gallery of Art, the John F. Kennedy Center for the Performing Arts, the National Archives, and the Folger Shakespeare Library. Among the city's famous monuments, parks, and memorials are the Lincoln Memorial, the Washington Monument, the Jefferson Memorial, and the Vietnam Veterans Memorial.

Economy. The city's economy is based largely on the federal government and related services; many important organizations also have offices there. There is little industry.

Government. The city's present system of government was established in 1973 by an act of Congress and approved by the people in 1974. Washington, D.C., is run by an elected mayor and city council. However, the federal government has final authority over all the city's government concerns. The mayor serves a 4-year term. The city council consists of 13 members serving 4-year terms. Washington, D.C., is represented in the U.S. Congress by 1 nonvoting representative.

History. In 1783 the Continental Congress voted for a federal city. In 1791 President George Washington chose the present site as a compromise between North and South. Washington, D.C., is one of the few cities to be planned before being built. In 1800 Congress moved to Washington, which replaced Philadelphia as the national capital. In 1814, during the War of 1812, the government buildings were burned down by British troops; new and more splendid plans were made and carried out. Since then, the city's population has risen steadily. Washington has long served as a gateway for blacks emigrating north; since the 1950s, blacks have made up a majority of the city's population. Since the 1970s, there has been a growing call among Washingtonians for statehood for the District of Columbia, but the U.S. Congress would have to vote approval of statehood and the proposed state constitution written by a 1982 constitutional convention. As the nation's capital, Washington, D.C., is a focal point for tourism, government, and political demonstrations.

Washington, George (1732-99), first president of the United States. As a soldier, Washington led the Continental Army in the revolution to win American independence from Britain. As one of the founders of the new

George Washington

1st president of the United States

Born:	Westmoreland Co., Va.; Feb. 22, 1732.
Term:	Apr. 1789-Mar. 1797.
Vice president:	John Adams.
Political party:	None.
Spouse:	Martha Dandridge Custis Washington.
Children:	None (2 stepchildren).
Died:	Mount Vernon, near Alexandria, Va., Dec. 14, 1799.

republic, he headed the Constitutional Convention. He was president during the most crucial years of his country's formation as a new nation. Washington's reputation for honesty, his strength of character, and his qualities as a leader won him the admiration of all Americans and a permanent place in history as "the Father of Our Country."

Early life. Washington spent his first 11 years on the family estate near Fredericksburg, Va. In 1743, after his father's death, George moved to Mount Vernon, home of his half-brother, Lawrence. Educated at home, Washington became interested in land management and surveying. At age 16 he went on an important surveying expedition of the Shenandoah Valley. The next year he was appointed surveyor of Culpeper Co. After Lawrence's death in 1752, Washington managed Mount Vernon, inheriting the estate in 1760.

In 1753 Virginia's Governor Dinwiddie sent Washington on military missions against the French. When the French and Indian War broke out in 1754, Washington served the British side with distinction. At age 23 he was appointed commander in chief of Virginia's colonial troops.

In 1758 Washington returned home and resigned from the military. In Jan. 1759 he married Martha Dandridge Custis, a widow with two children, and settled down to run Mount Vernon. He served in the Virginia House of Burgesses and as justice of the peace. Although he did not support calls for independence at first, he came to oppose severe measures imposed by Britain and became a representative to the First Continental Congress. On June 15, 1775, he was elected commander in chief of the Continental Army.

The American Revolution. When the war for independence began, the forces under Washington's command were poorly trained and armed. In spite of the odds against him, Washington proved to be an able commander and was a constant source of inspiration to his troops. Alliances with France (1778) and Spain (1779) greatly relieved America's position, and the decisive victory against Britain came in Oct. 1781 when Washington and the French joined to defeat General Cornwallis at Yorktown. In Dec. 1783 Washington bid his troops an emotional farewell and went back to Mount Vernon.

A new nation. In 1787 Washington chaired the Constitutional Convention, at which the nation's leaders sought a way to strengthen the weak confederation of states. Under the new constitution, members of the first Electoral College voted Washington president in Feb. 1789.

President. Washington was determined to establish a strong central government. His first administration established a federal judiciary (1789), a national bank (1791), and far-reaching measures by which the national government assumed responsibility for state debts and imposed wide-ranging taxes. In fact, his government assumed responsibilities far greater than some of the nation's founders had intended; the split that developed led to the formation of the first national political parties. Washington reluctantly accepted a second term in 1792. Determined to keep the United States free of foreign influence, he declared it neutral in France's war with Britain and its allies. In spite of this, Washington's second term was largely devoted to foreign affairs, particularly the strained U.S. relations with Britain, France, and Spain. He also had to prove the federal government's power to enforce its laws by putting down the Whiskey Rebellion (1794) against a federal excise tax.

Retirement. Washington refused to accept a third term. He retired to Mount Vernon in Apr. 1797 and died there on Dec. 14, 1799.

See also: Revolutionary War in America.

Washington, Harold (1922-87), U.S. lawyer, politician, first black mayor of Chicago, elected 1983 and 1987. Washington served in the Illinois House of Representatives (1965-76), the Illinois Senate (1976-80), and the U.S. House of Representatives (1981-83). In the racially charged 1983 Democratic primary for mayor he defeated Mayor Jane M. Byrne and Richard M. Daley (son of former mayor and party boss Richard J. Daley) and went on to defeat Republican Bernard E. Epton.

Washington, Martha Custis (1731-1802), wife of President George Washington and first First Lady of the United States. At 17 she married a wealthy planter, Daniel Parke Custis, who died in 1757. She married George Washington in 1759 and moved with her 2 children to Mt. Vernon, which she supervised during Washington's absences.

Washington, Treaty of (1871), agreement between the United States and Great Britain, signed in Washington, D.C., to arbitrate the Alabama claims of the U.S. Civil War and the U.S.-Canadian boundary and fishing disputes. It was largely brought about by Hamilton Fish, U.S. secretary of state.

Washington Cathedral, or National Cathedral, officially, Cathedral Church of Saint Peter and Saint Paul, Episcopal church in Washington, D.C. Built in the early 20th century (starting 1907), it incorporates stones from historic buildings from around the world. It measures 525 ft (160 m) long and 275 ft (84 m) wide at the widest point of its transept.

Washington Conference, post-World War I disarmament meetings convened by Pres. Warren Harding in Washington, D.C., 1921-22. Agreements between the United States, Great Britain, Japan, France, and Italy included a limit on each navy's capital ships, restrictions on submarine warfare, and a ban on the use of poison gas. France, Japan, Great Britain, and the United States also agreed to respect each other's Pacific territories. A 9-power treaty, with the additional signatures of Belgium, China, the Netherlands, and Portugal, guaranteed China's territorial integrity.

Washington Monument, stone obelisk in Washington, D.C., honoring George Washington. Begun in 1848, it was completed in 1884 and opened to the public in 1888. Faced with white marble, it is 555.5 ft (169.3 m) high. Visitors may go to the top by elevator or by climbing 898 steps.

Washington's Birthday, federal holiday celebrated on the third Monday in February in honor of the first president of the United States, George Washington. He was born Feb. 11, 1732, but the 1752 calendar reform changed the date to Feb. 22. In some states the Monday holiday also honors President Abraham Lincoln, who was born on Feb. 12; it is then called *President's Day*.

Wasp, stinging winged insect, banded black and yellow, related to bees and ants in the order Hymenoptera. There are a number of families; most are solitary, but members of the Vespoidea are social, forming true colonies with workers, drones, and queen(s). Most of the solitary species are hunting wasps. These make nest cells in soil or decaying wood, in which they place one or more paralyzed insects before the egg is laid, to act as a living larder for the larva when it hatches. Social wasps congregate to form a permanent colony with both adults and young. The nest is usually constructed of wasp paper, a thick pulp of wood fibers and saliva. The adults feed the developing larvae on dead insects that have been killed by a bite on the neck; the sting, which in solitary wasps is used to paralyze prey, is reserved for defense. Adult wasps feed on carbohydrates: nectar, aphid honeydew, or jam.

Wasserman, August von (1866-1925), German physician and scientist. In 1906 he developed a process, known as the Wasserman test, which indicated syphilis infection through the testing of blood or spinal fluid. Earlier, Wasserman had developed inoculations against cholera, diphtheria, and tuberculosis.
See also: Venereal disease.

Waste disposal, disposal of such matter as animal excreta and the waste products of agricultural, industrial, and domestic processes, where an unacceptable level of environmental pollution would otherwise result. Where an ecological balance exists, wastes are recycled naturally or by technological means before accumulations affect the quality of life or disrupt the ecosystem. The most satisfactory waste disposal methods are therefore probably those that involve recycling, as in manuring fields with dung, reclaiming metals from scrap, or pulping waste paper for remanufacture. Recycling, however, may be inconvenient, uneconomic, or not yet technologically feasible. Many popular waste disposal methods consequently represent either an exchange of one form of environmental pollution for another less troublesome one, at least in the short term—e.g., the dumping or burying of nondegradable garbage or toxic wastes—or a reducing of the rate at which pollutants accumulate—e.g., by compacting or incinerating bulk wastes before dumping. Urban wastes are generally disposed of by means of dumping, sanitary landfill, incineration, and sewage processing. Agricultural, mining, and mineral-processing operations generate most solid wastes—and some of the most intractable waste disposal problems: the "factory" farmer's problem of disposing of surplus organic wastes economically without resorting to incineration or dumping in rivers; the problems created by large mine dumps and open-cast excavations; and the culm dumps that result from the processing of anthracite coal. Another increasingly pressing waste disposal problem is presented by radioactive wastes. Those with a "low" level of radioactivity can be safely packaged and buried; but high-level wastes, produced in the course of reprocessing the fuel elements of nuclear reactors, constitute a permanent hazard. Even the practice of encasing these wastes in thick concrete and dumping them on the ocean bottom is considered by many environmentalists to be an inadequate long-term solution.

Watauga Association, government (1772-75) set up on land leased from the Cherokee along the Watauga River in eastern Tennessee. The settlers, from Virginia and (after suppression of the Regulators) North Carolina, joined North Carolina (1775), became part of the State of Franklin (1784-88), and finally part of Tennessee (1796).

Watch, small, portable timepiece. It is usually worn around the wrist, but may also be carried in a pocket or purse, or be worn as part of jewelry, such as a ring, necklace, or pin. Watches have been in use since the early 1500s when a method was discovered whereby a mainspring could be used to power a clock instead of falling weights; this made it possible to create portable clocks. Most modern watches are electronic, powered by small quartz crystals. After running a year, an electronic watch may be off fewer than 60 seconds.

Water (H_2O), transparent, odorless liquid that in liquid form and solid form (ice) covers about 74% of the earth's surface. Water is essential to life, which began in the oceans. Water is also humanity's most precious natural resource. The advent of desalination technology has made sea water, which accounts for 97% of the total water on earth, available for use as fresh water. Chemically, water is a compound of hydrogen and oxygen. It is a good solvent for many substances, especially ionic and polar compounds; it is ionizing and itself ionizes to give a low concentration of hydroxide and hydrogen ions. It is thus also a better conductor of electricity than most pure liquids. Water is a polar molecule and shows anomalies due to hydrogen bonding, including contraction when heated from 0°C to 4°C (32°F to 39.2°F). Formed when hydrogen or volatile hydrides are burned in oxygen, water oxidizes reactive metals to their ions and reduces fluorine and chlorine. It converts basic oxides to hydroxides and acidic oxides to oxyacids.

Water beetle, any of a number of families of oval insects, in the order Coleoptera, that live in or near water and propel themselves by fringed hind legs. Three of the most common water beetles are the giant water scavenger beetle (family Hydrophilidae), predaceous diving beetle (family Dytiscidae), and whirligig (family Gyrinidae). The predaceous diving beetle and water scavenger beetle feed on small fish and insects.

Water boatman *See:* Water bug.

Water buffalo, any of several oxen in the family Bovidae, most common of which is the Indian buffalo (*Bubalus bubalis*), standing 6-6.5 ft (1.5-2 m) at the shoulder. Bulls have curved horns that may measure as wide as 12 ft (3.7 m) along the curve. The fierce-tempered water buffalo feeds on grass and has very little hair on its dull, bluish-black hide. Domesticated, the water buffalo is a strong and helpful farm animal, used throughout China, southeast Asia, Egypt, Europe, and the Philippines.

Water bug, name given to a number of insects that live on or below the surface of fresh water, especially the giant water bug, which may grow up to 4 in (10 cm) long. Water bugs feed on small aquatic animals, including fish. Backswimmers, water boatmen, and water scorpions are also water bugs.

Waterbury (pop. 221,629), city (inc. 1853) in Connecticut, situated on the Naugatuck River. Once a leading manufacturer of brass products (from the 18th century through World War II), items produced in Waterbury today include timepieces and metal products. Banking and insurance are among its other industries.

Water chestnut, name of 2 different plants that grow in subarctic and temperate wetlands. The Oriental water chestnut (*Eleocharis tuberosa*) is in the sedge family and is native to China. Some of its tubelike stems, which may grow to a height of approximately 5 ft (1.5 m), grow upward out of the soil and water. However, some of the stems grow underground and have small, round, edible bulblike swellings at the end called corms. The water caltrop (genus *Trapa*) also belongs to the water-chestnut family. It is native to tropical and subtropical areas of Africa, Europe, and Asia, and bears edible, nutlike fruits.

Water clock, also called clepsydra, ancient instrument that measured time by the amount of water flowing from it. Used as early as the 14th century B.C. by the Egyptians, it consisted of a hollow container, such as a cylinder or a glass jar, with measuring lines. Water was poured into the container and then allowed to flow out. The lines indicated how much water had escaped, and from this it could be determined how much time had passed. Water clocks were used by Greeks and Romans as well. Among its various purposes was the timing of orators' speeches.

Watercolor, painting technique in which the pigment is mixed with water before application, such as fresco and tempera, but more particularly the aquarelle technique of thin washes. Ancient Egyptians produced watercolor paintings, and the medium was used during and after the Renaissance by, among others, Rembrandt and Van Dyck. The aquarelle technique was mastered by such English artists as John Cotman and J.M.W. Turner around 1800. Watercolor permits powerful effects of transparency, brilliance, and delicacy. Important U.S. watercolorists include Winslow Homer and John Marin.

Water dog *See:* Mudpuppy.

Waterfall, vertical fall of water formed where a river flows from hard rock to an area of more easily eroded rock, or where there has been a rise of the land relative to sea level or a blockage of the river by a landslide. The power of waterfalls often provides energy for the many cities that have sprung up around them. The highest waterfall in the world is Angel Falls, Venezuela (3,212 ft/979 m).

Water flea, any of a group of small animals belonging to the class Branchiopoda. Most species live in fresh water and are anywhere from 1/125-3/4 in (0.2-18 mm) long. Their bodies are covered by a transparent shell, exposing their organs for easy viewing. Water fleas move through water by jumping in jerky motions resembling those of fleas—hence their name.

Waterford (pop. 39,500), port city in southeastern Ireland, located on the River Suir near the point where it flows into the Waterford Harbour. Waterford was first settled in the A.D. 800s by Vikings. It was captured by the English in 1170. Waterford became prominent during the latter part of the 18th century because of the well-known Waterford crystal glassware manufactured there. The city remains an important export center of locally produced items, including canned fruits and meats, beer, paper, chemicals, furniture, and electrical products.
See also: Ireland.

Watergate, series of scandals involving Pres. Richard Nixon and his administration. On June 17, 1972, 5 men from Nixon's reelection committee were arrested as they tried to plant electronic eavesdropping equipment in the headquarters of the Democratic Party national committee in the Watergate office building, Washington, D.C. As a result of their convictions and the suspicions of Judge John Sirica, who tried the case, that a conspiracy was being covered up, investigations were opened that led to Nixon's inner councils. Though Nixon easily won reelection in Nov. 1972, his public support eroded as a televised U.S. Senate investigation continued. Newspaper revelations (notably by Carl Bernstein and Bob Woodward in the *Washington Post*) and testimony of Republican Party and former governmental officials clearly implicated him and his senior aides in a massive abuse of power and the obstruction of justice involving campaign contributions, the CIA, the FBI, the Internal Revenue Service, and other government agencies. The House of Representatives Judiciary Committee voted to impeach Nixon in July 1974, and his ouster from office became inevitable; on Aug. 9, 1974 he resigned—the only U.S. president to do so. One month later he was granted a full pardon by Pres. Gerald Ford. Almost 60 individuals, including former U.S. Attorney General John Mitchell and senior White House staff were convicted of Watergate crimes.
See also: Nixon, Richard Milhous.

Water glass, also known as soluble glass, colorless lump made up of sodium, silicon, and oxygen that resembles glass. Water glass is soluble in water, turning into a thick liquid. It has many industrial uses: as adhesive in fiberboard boxes, glass, and porcelain; to manufacture concrete and cement; and to fireproof and waterproof materials.

Water hyacinth, South American floating plant (*Eichhornia crassipes*). The plants, which have attractive purple or yellow flowers growing on erect stems, float on air-filled bladders, trailing their roots in the water, or in mud where the water is very shallow. Water hyacinths grow wild in South America but have been introduced into other tropical areas. They frequently clog waterways, as in the southern United States.

Water lily, aquatic plant of the genus *Nymphaea* (unrelated to true lilies). They grow in calm, shallow fresh water, with stems rooted in the mud and floating leaves. Many hybrids are used as ornamentals in water gardens. The most well known of the species is the blue or white Egyptian lotus, Egypt's national emblem.

Waterloo, Battle of (June 18, 1815), final engagement of the Napoleonic Wars. Having escaped from exile on Elba and having reinstated himself with a new army, Napoleon returned to face a coalition of Austria, Great Britain, Prussia, and Russia. On the offensive, he advanced into Belgium to prevent an Anglo-Dutch army under Wellington from uniting with the Prussians. After separate battles with the British and Prussians on June 16, the French army, led by Marshall Ney, attacked Wellington's strongly defended position at Waterloo, south of Brussels. The intervention of a Prussian force under Blücher allowed Wellington to take the offensive. The French were routed, losing some 25,000 men. Napoleon abdicated on June 22, 1815.
See also: Napoleon I; Napoleonic Wars.

Watermelon, plant (*Citrullus vulgaris*) and its edible fruit, with a thick rind, juicy pulp, and many seeds. A member of the gourd family native to Africa, the watermelon has been cultivated for at least 4,000 years. Watermelons, so named because more than 90% of their substance is water, may weigh from 5-40 lb (2.3-18.1 kg) or more and are rich in vitamins A and C. They grow on vines and their pulp is red to pink, yellow, or white.

Water meter, device to measure the quantity of water flowing through a pipe or other channel. Such meters, connected with registers that display numerical readings indicating gallons, cubic feet, or other quantities, are used to measure home or business use of water from public water systems or other sources, or to monitor flow in rivers and other moving bodies of water. Quantity may be measured by the water's motion or pressure, or by using magnetism, sound waves, or other energy affected by the rate of flow.

Water moccasin, also called cottonmouth or moccasin snake, poisonous snake in the viper family. This species (*Agkistrodon piscivorus*) lives in the southeastern United States in swampy or marshy areas of rivers, streams, and lakes. It may grow between 3 1/2 ft (107 cm) and 5 ft (1.5 m) long. It is considered a pit viper because of a hollow pit located between the eye and nostril on the side of its head. Its often fatal bite may be preceded by a warning, which involves the exposure of the white, cottonlike inside of its mouth.

Water pipit *See:* Pipit.

Water plant, also called aquatic plant or hydrophyte, any of several plants classified as those that live on the surface or below the surface of water. Water lilies, sedges, and cattails are common water plants. Water bladders, or pores that contain air, are found in submerged water plants to support their upright position. Water plants most often grow in lakes and ponds.

Water pollution, contamination to water systems as a direct result of the discharge of harmful products. There are 3 main sources of water pollution: industrial waste, sewage, and chemical and agricultural wastes. Environmental concern has grown through the years, and government agencies worldwide have helped pass laws that limit the amount of wastes that may be dumped into our waters. Billions of dollars a year are spent to clean up the diseased waters, yet specialists doubt that the natural state of the waters will ever be fully restored. Water pollution has become a grave environmental problem that increasingly threatens lakes, rivers, and oceans.

Water polo, game played in a swimming pool in which 2 teams try to pass or throw a ball into the opponent's goal. The game began in England in the 1870s. Each team consists of 7 players—6 in the field and 1 goalkeeper. Fieldplayers may use head, feet, or 1 hand to manage the ball; goalkeepers may use both hands while in the goal area. The team with the ball is allowed 35 seconds to get the ball across the opponent's goal and score. If the team is unsuccessful, the ball goes to the other team. Water polo is played in an area 66-98 ft (20-30 m) long and 26-66 ft (8-20 m) wide. A men's game lasts 28 minutes, and is divided into 7-minute quarters. A women's game lasts 24 minutes and is divided into 6-minute quarters.

Water power, energy obtained from flowing or falling water used to run machinery or create electrical power. Water has been used to drive devices since ancient times, beginning with the invention of the water wheel. Streaming water flowing over the blades of a wheel caused the wheel to rotate, setting in motion other mechanisms—thus creating the energy that drove the mechanisms. Water was first used to power grinding stones that ground grains. Water power was very important during the Industrial Revolution, when it was used to operate factory machines. The most important modern use of water power is the generating of electricity. Hydroelectric power plants producing electrical energy have been built on rivers in many parts of the world. The largest U.S. power plant is the Grand Coulee on the Columbia River in Washington.
See also: Turbine.

Waters, Ethel (1900-77), African-American singer and actress. She started singing the blues and popular music in clubs when she was 17 and went on to star in musicals, including *Africana* (1927), *At Home Abroad* (1935), and *Cabin in the Sky* (1940). She popularized several songs from the musicals, such as "Heat Wave," and "Taking a Chance on Love." Her singing style was greatly acclaimed, and she recorded with jazz musicians such as Benny Goodman and Duke Ellington. Waters had dramatic roles in several films, including *Pinky* (1949), for which she was nominated for an Academy Award as supporting actress, and *The Member of the Wedding* (1950). She recounted her life in her autobiography, *His Eye Is on the Sparrow* (1951).

Water-skiing, sport in which a person wearing a pair of ski-like runners glides over water while being pulled by a motorboat moving at speeds of 15-35 mph (24-56 kmph). Water skiing is done for recreation as well as for competition events, which include jumping, slalom, and trick riding. In the jumping competition, skiers ski jump off a ramp 24 ft (7.3 m) long and 6 ft (1.8 m) high in an attempt to achieve the greatest distance. In the slalom competition, a skier negotiates through a course of buoys as quickly as possible. For trick skiing, skiers perform intricate actions, such as jumps and turns.

Water snake, any of nearly 80 species of nonvenomous snakes of the genus *Natrix*, including the European grass snake. Water snakes live in fresh waters and feed on fish and amphibians.

Water softening, process of removing calcium and magnesium from hard water. These insoluble minerals, when left in water, form scale in pipes and prevent the dissolution of cleansers, such as soap. Hard water may be softened by adding soda ash and lime to it. The soda ash and lime join with the calcium and magnesium, making them settle to the bottom of the water container. Water may also be softened by filtering it through zeolites, minerals that contain sodium ions. The sodium ions change places with the calcium and magnesium ions, thereby softening the water. When the zeolites become depleted of sodium ions, a strong solution of common salt can be placed in the filter to replenish the sodium.

Waterspout, rotating column of air, or tornado, as it passes over water. A funnel-like cloud of condensed water vapor extends from a parent cumulo-nimbus cloud to the water surface, where it is surrounded by a sheath of spray.

Water wheel, wheel that is turned by flowing water, providing power to operate a device. The running water may come from rivers or waterfalls. Water wheels were used by ancient Romans to grind grain and in time were developed to run other devices, such as machinery. There are 2 basic types: vertical and horizontal. Vertical water wheels often have containers around the wheel. Water usually flows into a container at the top of the wheel, the weight of the water causes the container to fall, and the water flows into the next container, creating a constant motion. Horizontal water wheels have vertical blades. Water strikes the blade on one side of the wheel, causing the wheel to turn to the next blade, thus creating continual motion. Horizontal water wheels are capable of converting more water power into energy and have greater use in the modern world.
See also: Water power.

Watie, Stand (1806-71), Native American brigadier general in the Confederate Army. This Cherokee leader volunteered for the Confederate Army in 1861 and led a Cherokee regiment known as the Cherokee Mounted Rifles.
See also: Civil War, U.S.

Watson, James Dewey (1928-), U.S. biochemist. He shared with Francis Crick and Maurice H.F. Wilkins the 1962 Nobel Prize in physiology or medicine for his work with Crick establishing the double-helix molecular model of DNA. His personalized account of the research, *The Double Helix* (1968), became a best-seller.
See also: Biochemistry; Deoxyribonucleic Acid.

Watson, John Broadus (1878-1958), U.S. psychologist who founded behaviorism, which states that a person's behavior is a result of stimuli in his or her environment. It rejects the idea of inborn emotions, with the exceptions of fear, anger, and love. While Watson's work helped lead to the development of psychology as a science, his views are not widely held today.
See also: Psychology.

Watson, Thomas Edward (1856-1922), U.S. author and political leader from Georgia. He attacked blacks, socialists, Catholics, and Jews. A Farmers' Alliance representative (1891-93) and Democratic U.S. representative (from 1920), he ran as a populist vice presidential and presidential candidate (1896, 1904, respectively).

Watson, Thomas John (1874-1956), U.S. business executive and philanthropist. He took over an ailing computing company (1914), changed its name to International Business Machines Corp. (IBM; 1924), and built it into one of the world's largest corporations. Under his presidency (1914-49) and chairmanship (1949-56), IBM became the leader in electronic data-processing equipment, with sales in 82 countries and assets of more than $600 million at the time of his death.

Watson-Watt, Sir Robert Alexander (1892-1973), Scottish scientist and inventor. His research into radio led to his creation (1935) of a radar device capable of detecting and tracing the movements of flying airplanes.

Watt, James (1736-1819), Scottish engineer and inventor. His first major invention (patented 1769) was an improved steam engine, with a separate condenser air pump, and insulated engine parts. For the manufacture of such engines he entered into partnership with John Roebuck and later (1775), more successfully, with Matthew Boulton. Between 1775 and 1800 he invented the sun-and-planet gear wheel, the double-acting engine, a throttle valve, a pressure gauge, and the centrifugal governor—as well as taking the first steps toward determining the chemical structure of water. He also coined the term *horsepower* and was a founding member of the Lunar Society.
See also: Steam engine.

Watteau, Jean-Antoine (1684-1721), French draftsperson and painter, strongly influenced by Peter Paul Rubens. A masterful colorist, he specialized in small, gay paintings called *fêtes galantes* ("elegant parties") or *fêtes champêtres* ("country parties"). He also painted theater scenes. His works include *The Embarkation for Cythera* (1717), based upon a play of the day, and *Gilles* (c.1718).
See also: Rococo.

Wattmeter, instrument that measures electric power in watts, kilowatts, or megawatts.

Watusi (Swahili: *Watutsi*), Tutsi people of Burundi and Rwanda in central Africa (formerly Ruanda-Urundi). The Watusi, probably originally from Ethiopia, differ ethnically from other African peoples, and many attain a height of over 7 ft (2.13 m). In the 1400s and 1500s the invading Watusi imposed a feudal system on the native Hutu, who revolted in 1959 and drove their cattle-raising rulers to what is now Burundi (the 2 parts became independent nations in 1962). The Tutsi king of Burundi was deposed in 1966. An unsuccessful Hutu rebellion in Burundi in 1972-73 left 10,000 Tutsi and 150,000 Hutu dead. With the outbreak of violence in 1993 and 1994, some 500,000 Hutu and Tutsi were killed in Rwanda.

Waugh, name of 3 English writers, the sons and grandson of journalist and publisher Arthur Waugh (1886-1943). **Alexander Raban (Alec) Waugh** (1898-1981) wrote over 40 novels and travel books, including *Loom of Youth* (1918) and *Island in the Sun* (1956). **Evelyn Arthur St. John Waugh**

(1903-66) wrote mainly satire, both elegant and biting. His conversion to Roman Catholicism in 1930 had a deep affect on his work. His novels include *Decline and Fall* (1928), *Vile Bodies* (1930), *Put Out More Flags* (1942), *Brideshead Revisited* (1945), *The Loved One* (1948), and his World War II trilogy, *The Sword of Honour* (1952-61). Evelyn's son **Auberon Alexander Waugh** (1939-) is a novelist whose works include *Bed of Flowers* (1972).

Wave, in physics, energy that travels in rhythmical motions. Waves may travel on a substance (waves on water), through a substance (the waves of an earthquake through the earth), or in a space devoid of matter (radio waves through space). The top of a wave is the crest, the bottom of a wave is the trough. Wavelength refers to the distance between 2 consecutive crests. There are 3 kinds of waves: transverse, standing, and longitudinal. In transverse waves the energy flows in a steady forward direction and causes the medium through which it travels to move up and down, like water waves. Standing waves are created by 2 identical waves moving in opposite directions, creating a series of loops. Longitudinal waves travel in a forward direction in a series of short back-and-forth motions, like the coils of a spring. *See also:* Physics.

Wavell, Archibald Percival, 1st earl (1883-1950), British field marshal. He was British commander-in-chief in the Middle East during World War II, defeating the Italians in North Africa (1940-41). He served as viceroy and governor general of India from 1943 to 1947.
See also: World War II.

Wax, moldable, water-repellent solid, of which there are several entirely different kinds. *Animal waxes* were the first known: Wool wax when purified yields lanolin; beeswax, from the honeycomb, is used for some candles and as a sculpture medium (by carving or casting); spermaceti wax, from the sperm whale, is used in ointments and cosmetics. *Vegetable waxes*, like animal waxes, are mixtures of esters of long-chain alcohols and carboxylic acids. Carnauba wax, from the leaves of a Brazilian palm tree, is hard and lustrous and is used to make polishes; candelilla wax, from a wild Mexican rush, is similar but more resinous; Japan wax, the coating of sumac berries, is fatty and soft but also tough and kneadable. *Mineral waxes* include montan wax, extracted from lignite, which is bituminous and resinous; ozokerite, an absorbent hydrocarbon wax obtained from wax shales; and paraffin wax, or petroleum wax, the most important commercially, obtained from the residues of petroleum refining by solvent extraction. Some of its uses are to make candles, to coat paper products, in the electrical industry, and to waterproof leather and textiles. Various *synthetic waxes* are made for special uses.

Wax myrtle, tree in bayberry or wax myrtle family. The common wax myrtle (*Myrica cerifera*) grows to about 35 ft (11 m) high. It has thick leaves with small brown dots and small green flowers that bloom between April and June. As an ornamental tree wax myrtle are found along the east coast of the United States.

Waxwing, any of 3 species of starling-sized birds (genus *Bombycilla*) named for the red, waxlike marks on their wings. Found in the Northern Hemisphere, they are the Bohemian waxwing, the cedar waxwing, and the Japanese waxwing (of northeastern Asia). Waxwings feed largely on berries but feed their chicks on insects. They move their nesting grounds from place to place, and in some years migrate en masse southward in the fall.

Wayne, Anthony (1745-96), American Revolutionary general whose daring tactics earned him the name "mad Anthony Wayne." In 1779 he executed the brilliant victory of Stony Point over the British, and he was with Lafayette at the siege of Yorktown (1781). During the wars with Native Americans out West, his success at Fallen Timbers in 1794 led to his negotiation of the Treaty of Greenville (1795) in which most of Ohio was ceded to the U.S. *See also:* Indian wars; Revolutionary War in America.

Wayne, John (Marion Michael Morrison; 1907-79), U.S. film actor, known mostly for his tough hero roles. He acted in low-budget westerns until his big break in 1939 in *Stagecoach*. Over the course of his career, Wayne appeared in over 175 films, including *Red River* (1948), *She Wore a Yellow Ribbon* (1949), *Sands of Iwo Jima* (1950), and *The Quiet Man* (1952). He received an Academy Award for his acting in *True Grit* (1969).

Weakfish, or squeteague, any of a genus (*Cynoscion*) of saltwater fishes used for food, measuring 1-2 ft (30-61 cm) long or more. Its name comes from the fact that it has a weak, fleshy mouth that is easily torn. It is found along the Atlantic and Gulf coasts of the United States.

Weapon, any device used to attack or defend. Throughout human history, weapons have been used to kill animals for food, to protect people in wilderness, and to wage wars. Bows and arrows, slings, swords, blowguns, rifles, guns, bombs, torpedoes, and hand grenades are examples of weapons. As technology has become more sophisticated, destructive power has increased, e.g., nuclear bombs capable of killing millions of people and destroying the planet.

Weasel, small, carnivorous mammal (*Mustela nivalis*) related to the skunk, wolverine, and mink. A slender, lithe, red-brown creature, which often kills prey many times its own size, it measures only up to 10-11 in (25.4-27.9 cm) in the male, 8 in (20.3 cm) in the female. The normal diet is mice, voles, and fledgling birds, though rabbits may be taken. The many races of weasel are distributed throughout Eurasia, Africa, and the Americas.

Weather, variations in atmospheric conditions (temperature, precipitation, wind, humidity, air pressure, and cloudiness) experienced at a given place over a short period of time. Longer periods of data fall under the term *climate*. *See also:* Climate.

Weather Service, National, part of the Environmental Science Services Administration (ESSA), in the U.S. Department of Commerce. Its head office in Washington, D.C., near the National Meteorological Center, is where data from 300 weather stations in the United States and from many other sources, including aircraft, satellites, and balloons, are coordinated and incorporated into charts for distribution to the 30 forecast centers across the country. Here long- and short-range forecasts are prepared and warnings of hurricanes, flooding, and other weather hazards given. Research to improve forecasting accuracy is also undertaken.

Weather vane, instrument used to perceive the direction in which the wind is moving. The vane is built in the form of an arrow, so as to pick up even the smallest breeze. Often the vane has electrical connections by which it can communicate the wind movement to areas that might be far from the device itself.

Weaver, Robert Clifton (1907-), U.S. economist, and secretary of housing and urban development (HUD; 1966-68). He was the administrator of the N.Y. Rent Commission (1955-59) and led the federal Housing and Home Finance Agency (1961-66) before his appointment by Pres. Lyndon Johnson as secretary of the newly formed HUD—a job that made him the first black member of a presidential cabinet.

Weaverbird, small, seed-eating bird (family Ploceidae) of Africa and Asia. Weaverbirds are related to the English sparrow and are usually drab, though during the nesting season many males develop bright plumage. They are named for their elaborate flask-shaped nests, woven from strips of palm fronds or grasses. Weavers live in flocks and are often pests when they descend on crops.

Weaving, process of making a fabric by interlacing 2 or more sets of threads. In plain, or tabby, weave, 1 set of threads (the warp) extends along the length of the fabric; the other set (the woof, or weft) is at right angles to the warp and passes alternately over and under it. Other common weaves include twill, satin, and pile. In basic twill, woof threads pass over 2-4 warp threads, producing diagonal ridges, or wales, as in denim, flannel, and gaberdine. In satin weave, a development of twill, long "float" threads passing under 4 warp threads give the fabric its characteristically lustrous and smooth appearance. Pile fabrics, such as corduroy and velvet, have extra warp or weft threads woven into a ground weave in a series of loops that are then cut to produce the pile. Weaving is usually accomplished by means of a hand- or power-operated machine called a loom. Warp threads are stretched on a frame and passed through eyelet in vertical wires (heddles) supported on a frame (the harness). A space (the shed) between sets of warp threads is made by moving the heddles up or down, and a shuttle containing the woof thread is passed through the shed. A special comb (the reed) then pushes home the newly woven line.

Webb, name of 2 English social reformers and economists. **Beatrice Webb** (née Potter, 1858-1943) studied working life for her *Life and Labour of the People in London* (1891-1903). Her husband, **Sidney James Webb** (1859-1947), was a Labour member of Parliament (1922-29) and held several cabinet posts. The couple were leading intellectuals of the Labour movement and wrote together *The History of Trade Unionism* (1894). They were Fabians and helped found the London School of Economics in 1895 and the left-wing journal *The New Statesman* in 1913.

Weber, Carl Maria von (1786-1826), German composer, pianist, and conductor who established the romantic opera and paved the way in Germany for Richard Wagner. His operas include *Der Freischütz* (*The Marksman*; 1821), *Euryanthe* (1823), and *Oberon* (1826). He wrote a number of orchestral and chamber works, notably for the piano, including the well-known *Invitation to the Dance* (1819).

Weber, Max (1881-1961), U.S. painter. He introduced European modern art movements, such as Fauvism and Cubism, to America by incorporating the styles into his own work. His works between 1912 and 1919 were abstract, becoming more representational from 1919 on. Weber was born in Russia and came to the United States when he was 10. He studied art at the Pratt Institute in Brooklyn, N.Y., at the Académie Julian in Paris, and with the renowned French artist Henri Matisse. Weber was an influential teacher at the Art Students League. Among his students there was Mark Rothko, who later became an important abstract artist.

Weber, Max (1864-1920), German economist and sociologist. His theories contributed to the formation of modern sociological theory. Weber considered bureaucracy the crucial component of society and created an ideal type method for examining different societies. His most influential work, *The Protestant Ethic and the Spirit of Capitalism* (1904-05), deals with Protestantism's economic aspects. Other works include *From Max Weber: Essays in Sociology* and *The Theory of Social and Economic Organization*.

Webern, Anton (1883-1945), Austrian composer. He studied with Arnold Schoenberg and developed 12-tone music. His works include *Five Pieces for Orchestra* (1911-13), 2 symphonies, 3 string quartets, and a number of songs.

Webster, Daniel (1782-1852), U.S. politician, lawyer, and orator whose advocacy of strong central government earned him the name "defender of the Constitution." Early in his career he eloquently defended states' rights and championed New England's interests, first as a New Hampshire member of the House of Representatives (1813-17), and Massachusetts representative (1823-27) and senator (1827-41; 1845-50). As New England's interests changed from shipping to industry, Webster became nationalistic and supported protective tariffs despite his earlier castigation of trade restrictions. His battle against nullification began in 1830 and continued throughout the crisis of 1832-33. In his efforts to preserve the Union, he supported the Compromise of 1850. He was twice secretary of state.

Webster, Noah (1758-1843), U.S. lexicographer whose works—such as *The Elementary Spelling Book*, called the "Blue-Backed Speller" (1829; earlier versions, 1783-87)—helped standardize American spelling. He also compiled a grammar (1784) and a reader (1785). Working on dictionaries from 1803, he published *An American Dictionary of the English Language* (1812), with 70,000 entries and 12,000 new definitions. Today his name is often applied to dictionaries that are in no way based on his work.
See also: Dictionary.

Webster-Ashburton Treaty, 1842 agreement between the United States and Great Britain. It settled boundary disputes between Canada and the United States, established a cooperative effort toward ending the slave trade, and provided for the extradition of criminals. The treaty was signed by Secretary of State Daniel Webster and Lord Ashburton.

Webster, William Hedgecock (1924-), U.S. jurist and director of the Central Intelligence Agency (CIA). Webster was appointed to the U.S.

District Court for the Eastern District of Missouri (1971) by Pres. Richard M. Nixon. In 1973 he began serving in the U.S. Court of Appeals, and in 1978 he was appointed director of the Federal Bureau of Investigation (FBI) by Pres. Jimmy Carter. An expert on terrorist tactics, Webster was made director of the CIA in 1987. He retired in 1991.

Weddell Sea, arm of the Atlantic Ocean in Antarctica between Palmer Land and Coats Land. At its southern end are the Ronne and Filchner ice shelves. It was named for James Weddell, who claimed to have discovered it in 1823. *See also:* Atlantic Ocean.

Wedding anniversary, celebration that takes place at the yearly return of an original wedding date. In Western society it has become common practice to commemorate this event with a characteristic gift, symbolic of the number of years a couple has been married; e.g., silver represents a 25th wedding anniversary; gold, a 50th anniversary.

Wedekind, Frank (1864-1918), German playwright and actor. His work denounced a corrupt bourgeois society that had no interest in the arts or learning, and that was stifling the freedom of individuals. His plays include *The Awakening of Spring* (1895), *Earth Spirit* (1895), and *Pandora's Box* (printed 1904). Although Wedekind was considered scandalous by many in his time, he had a strong following and inspired modern dramatists, including Bertolt Brecht.

Wedge, device with 2 or more surfaces that slope and taper to a thin edge. A wedge may be made of wood, metal, or other material and is used to split something apart. The wedge's thin edge is forced into a narrow opening of the object. The top of the wedge is hammered, driving the wedge further down, thereby piercing the object. A wedge may also be used to move a heavy object.

Wedgwood, Josiah (1730-95), English potter, inventor of Wedgwood ware. Famous for his cream-colored queen's ware, patented in 1765, he frequently employed artists such as John Flaxman for the designs on his blue-and-white jasper ware. Wedgwood, who introduced new materials and machinery to the craft of pottery-making, was the first to acquire steam engines at his factory in Etruria, Staffordshire, and contributed much to improve the standard of living of his workers.

Wedgwood ware, fine English pottery first created by Josiah Wedgwood (1730-95). Wedgwood comes in various styles, including a cream-colored stoneware called creamware (also called queen's ware because Queen Charlotte was so pleased with her set of creamware), a black stoneware called Egyptian black or black basalt, and colored stoneware that often had white designs or figures in relief called Jasperware. Wedgwood ware's durability and beauty made it very popular. Production of it has continued to present time, and it still has a world market.

Weed, any plant that is useless or destructive, or that grows where it is not desired. A plant that grows abundantly in an area where it is not wanted crowds out and takes nutrition, water, and space away from plants that are being cultivated. Injurious plants may be considered weeds. For example, poison ivy and oak can produce a skin rash; goldenrod and ragweed can cause hay fever; and thistles have prickly leaves that can hurt skin. Herbicides and soil cultivation are among methods developed to control the proliferation of weeds.

Weed, Thurlow (1797-1882), U.S. journalist and Whig political leader. He used his Albany *Evening Journal* to promote the Antimasonic party. He supported the presidential campaigns of William Harrison, Henry Clay, and Zachary Taylor, and the career of his friend, William H. Seward. He joined the Republicans in 1855 and under President Lincoln served as a special agent to England.

Weems, Mason Locke (1759-1825), U.S. Anglican Church minister, writer, and traveling bookseller. He wrote popular biographies of noted Americans that were more entertaining than accurate. His biography of George Washington, *The Life and Memorable Actions of George Washington*, contained the fictitious tale about George Washington chopping down a cherry tree.

Weevil, any of 35,000 species of oval- or pear-shaped beetles (from the largest animal family, Curculionidae), having a greatly drawn-out head that ends in a pronounced snout. They feed on hard vegetable matter, seeds, and wood; the larvae, which develop within seeds, are legless. Weevils are pests of such important economic crops as cotton and grain and of stored peas, beans, and flour.

Weight, gravitational force experienced by an object in relation to another massive body (planet). The weight of a body (measured in newtons) is equal to the product of its mass and the local acceleration due to gravity. Weight differs from mass in being a vector quantity.
See also: Gravitation.

Weight, Atomic *See:* Atom.

Weight control, method by which a person maintains a healthy weight. The medical as well as social and emotional well-being of a person is based in part on the maintenance of proper weight. A person must take in 3,500 calories of food to gain 1 lb (0.45 kg). In turn the human body burns up calories during exercise. Therefore food intake and physical exercise are important factors in weight control. Not all weight gain is unhealthy, since exercise often encourages a gain in muscle mass and weight. However, too much weight, based on fat, can cause health problems and, in the extreme, *obesity*—a state of being extremely overweight. Some studies indicate that weight may be related to heredity. In general, underweight people are considered healthy as long as they do not have a disease or serious eating disorder and people who are somewhat overweight are also considered healthy if they maintain a balanced diet and exercise.
See also: Diet.

Weightlessness, condition that arises in the apparent absence of gravitational pull. Experienced by astronauts in space, weightlessness occurs when the centrifugal force of the astronauts and spacecraft in forward motion exactly cancels the force of gravity.

Weight lifting, bodybuilding exercise and competitive sport. As a contest, it has long been popular in Turkey, Egypt, Japan, Europe, and the former USSR, and has been a regular event in the Olympics since 1920. There are 3 basic lifts: the snatch (from the floor to over the head in a single motion); the clean-and-jerk (2 movements—first to the chest and then over the head); and the military, or 2-hand, press (similar to the clean-and-jerk but performed while maintaining a "military" stance).

Weights and measures, units of weight, length, area, and volume commonly used in the home, in commerce, and in industry. Although, like other early peoples, the Hebrews used measures such as the foot, the cubit (the length of the human forearm), and the span, which could easily be realized in practice by using parts of the body, in commerce they also used standard containers and weights. Later, weights were based on the quantity of precious metal in coins. During and after the Middle Ages each region evolved its own system of weights and measures. In the 19th century these were standardized on a national basis, and then in turn were superseded by standards of the metric system. In the Western world, only the British Empire and the United States retained their own systems (the Imperial System and the U.S. Customary System, respectively) into the mid-20th century. With the United Kingdom's adoption of the International System of Units (SI units), the United States remains one of the few countries that does not use metric units, although, as has been the case since 1959, the U.S. customary units are now defined in terms of their metric counterparts and not on the basis of independent standards. In the United States the administration of weights and measures is coordinated by the National Bureau of Standards.

Weil, Simone (1909-43), French philosopher, religious mystic, and left-wing intellectual. She was active in the Spanish Civil War and the French resistance in World War II. She converted from Judaism to Roman Catholicism in 1938. Among her books to be translated into English are *Waiting for God* (1951) and *The Need for Roots* (1952).

Weill, Kurt (1900-50), German-born U.S. composer. His most well-known music is for the 2 satirical operas on which he collaborated with Bertolt Brecht, *The Threepenny Opera* (1928) and *The Rise and Fall of the City of Mahagonny* (1927, rev. 1930). Unpopular with the Nazis, he came to the United States in 1935 and became a successful Broadway composer, creating the music for such musicals as *Knickerbocker Holiday* (1938, with Maxwell Anderson) and *Street Scene* (1947). He was married to singer Lotte Lenya.

Weimar (pop. 63,400), city in east-central Germany, on the Ilm River. Weimar is a center for manufacturing agricultural machinery, electrical equipment, and chemicals. It was capital of the Saxe-Weimar duchy from 1547, and its court became the German cultural and intellectual center in the 18th and 19th centuries. Weimar was the site of the national assembly that established the so-called Weimar Republic in 1919. Buchenwald concentration camp was located nearby (1937-45).

Weimaraner, hunting dog developed in the early 19th century in Weimar, Germany. First used to hunt large animals such as deer, it was later used to hunt game. The Weimaraner has a smooth, short, gray coat and amber eyes.

It weighs 55-85 lb (25-39 kg), and is 23-27 in (58-69 cm) high. Weimaraners are graceful, affectionate, and obedient companions and watchdogs.

Weimar Republic, German government (1919-33) based on the democratic republican constitution adopted at Weimar in 1919. The constitution provided for a parliament of 2 houses and a popularly elected president. President Paul von Hindenburg made Adolf Hitler chancellor in 1933, whereupon Hitler suspended the constitution.

Weinberg, Steven (1933-), U.S. physicist who shared the 1979 Nobel Prize in physics for work demonstrating that 2 of the basic forces of nature, electromagnetism and weak interaction (the cause of radioactive decay in certain atomic nuclei), are aspects of a single interaction.
See also: Physics.

Weinberger, Caspar (1917-   ), U.S. government official. He served as secretary of health, education, and welfare (1973-75) under Pres. Richard M. Nixon and as secretary of defense (1981-87) under Pres. Ronald Reagan.

Weisgard, Leonard (1916-   ), U.S. artist and children's book writer and illustrator. He illustrated over 20 books by Margaret Wise Brown (pseud. Golden MacDonald), including *The Little Island*, for which he won the 1946 Caldecott Medal. Among the books he both wrote and illustrated are *My First Picture Book* (1953) and *The Plymouth Thanksgiving* (1967).

Weismann, August (1834-1914), German biologist. He is renowned for his work on and theories about evolution. Weismann was interested in how a species passed to its offspring various traits, which traits could be inherited, and which could not. He wrote several books, the most famous being *The Germ Plasm: A Theory of Heredity* (1893).
See also: Biology; Evolution.

Weiss, Peter (1916-82), German-Swedish playwright, artist, and filmmaker. He fled Nazi Germany in 1934. With his innovative play *The Persecution and Assassination of Jean Paul Marat as Performed by the Inmates of the Asylum of Charenton Under the Direction of the Marquis de Sade*, or *Marat/Sade* (1964), Weiss was acclaimed the s٠ccessor of Bertolt Brecht. His other dramas include *The Investigation* (1965), and *Trotsky in Exile* (1970).

Weizmann, Chaim (1874-1952), Polish-born scientist and Zionist leader, first president of Israel (1948-52). He emigrated to England in 1904 and became an eminent biochemist and director of the British Admiralty laboratories in 1916. He helped secure the Balfour Declaration (1917), which promised a Jewish state in Palestine. He was head of the World Zionist Organization (1920-29) and of the Jewish Agency (1929-31, 1935-46). He also founded what is known today as the Weizmann Inst. of Science.
See also: Zionism.

Welding, process of bringing pieces of metal together under conditions of heat or pressure, or both, until they coalesce at the joint. The oldest method is forge welding, in which the surfaces to be joined are heated to welding

temperature and then hammered together on an anvil. The most widely used method today is metal-arc welding: An electric arc is struck between an electrode and the pieces to be joined, and molten metal from a "filler rod"—usually the electrode itself—is added. Gas welding, now largely displaced by metal-arc welding, is usually accomplished by means of an oxyacetylene torch, which delivers the necessary heat by burning acetylene in a pure oxygen atmosphere. Sources of heat in other forms of welding include the electrical resistance of the joint (resistance welding), an electric arc at the joint (flash welding), a focused beam of electrons (electron-beam welding), and friction (friction welding). Some more recently applied heat sources include hot plasmas, lasers, ultrasonic vibrations, and explosive impacts.
See also: Soldering.

Welfare, direct government aid to the needy. In the United States various programs, operated by the social security office and by state and local governments, provide aid to the handicapped, aged, poor, and unemployed. Benefits to the aged are more-or-less standardized nationally, but the form of, amount of, and qualifications for other benefits differ from state to state. Benefits fall under many programs, such as veterans' aid and workmen's compensation. All welfare programs are linked to programs that do not give direct financial assistance, such as housing, food stamps, and medical aid. The Reagan administration made significant cuts in federal welfare programs.

Well, manmade hole in the ground used to tap water, gas, or minerals from the earth. Most modern wells are drilled and fitted with a lining, usually of steel, to forestall collapse. Though wells are sunk for natural gas and petroleum oil, the most common type yields water. Such wells may be horizontal or vertical, but all have their innermost end below the water table. If it should be below the permanent water table (the lowest annual level of the water table), the well will yield water throughout the year. Most wells require pumping, but some operate under natural pressure.

Welland Ship Canal, Canadian waterway running 27.6 mi (44.4 km) from Port Colborne on Lake Erie to Port Weller on Lake Ontario to form a major link of the Saint Lawrence Seaway and Great Lakes Waterway. The canal was built 1914-32, modernized in 1972, and has a minimum depth of about 30 ft (9.1 m). It has 8 locks to overcome the 326-ft (99.4-m) difference in height between Lakes Erie and Ontario.
See also: Saint Lawrence Seaway and Great Lakes Waterway.

Weller, Thomas Huckle (1915-), U.S. bacteriologist and virologist who shared with John F. Enders and Frederick C. Robbins the 1954 Nobel Prize in physiology or medicine for their cultivation of poliomyelitis viruses on tissues of human embryos outside the body.
See also: Poliomyelitis.

Welles, Gideon (1802-78), U.S. secretary of the navy in Pres. Abraham Lincoln's cabinet. During the Civil War, he directed the navy to block off the Confederate coast and to patrol the Mississippi River. Originally a newspaper editor, Welles left the Democrats in disagreement over slavery to help found (1856) the Republican Party.

Welles, Orson (1915-85), U.S. actor, director, and producer. In 1938 his realistic radio production of H.G. Well's *War of the Worlds* caused thousands of listeners to panic, fearing the account of the alien attack was a genuine news report. His first motion picture, of which he was director, cowriter, and star, was *Citizen Kane* (1940), loosely modeled on the life of newspaper magnate William R. Hearst. Innovative camera work and film editing continued to characterize his work in such films as *The Magnificent Ambersons* (1942), *The Lady from Shanghai* (1947), *Macbeth* (1948), and *Touch of Evil* (1962).

Wellington (pop. 326,900), capital city of New Zealand since 1865, at the southern end of North Island. Founded in 1840, it is the nation's second-largest city and an important port and transportation center. Manufactures include processed food, transportation equipment, textiles, and clothing.
See also: New Zealand.

Wellington, Arthur Wellesley, 1st duke of (1769-1852), British general and politician, "the Iron Duke," who defeated Napoleon I at the Battle of Waterloo. After distinguished military service in India (1796-1805), he drove the French from Spain and Portugal in the Peninsular War and entered France in 1813. After being created duke, he led the victorious forces at Waterloo (1815). Serving the Tory government (1819-27), he became prime minister (1828-30), and passed the Catholic Emancipation Act; however, he opposed parliamentary reform. In 1842 he became commander-in-chief for life.
See also: Napoleonic Wars.

Wells, Fargo & Company, U.S. banking company. Founded in 1852 by Henry Wells and William G. Fargo as a bank and a delivery company servicing the route from San Francisco to New York, the company expanded with the purchase of the Pony Express (1861) and the Holladay Overland Stage Company (1866), in time servicing the entire West Coast as well as parts of Canada, Mexico, and Central America. Wells Fargo transported passengers, mail, money, and cargo, including gold. In 1905 Wells Fargo gave up its banking operations to the Wells Fargo Nevada National Bank. In 1918 the remainder of the company merged with other companies to form the American Railway Express Company.
See also: Fargo, William George.

Wells, Henry (1805-78), U.S. pioneer businessperson. With William G. Fargo, he founded Wells, Fargo & Co. (1852), which carried people, freight, and mail from New York City to California. With the acquisition of Benjamin Holladay's mail and stagecoach business (1866), Wells, Fargo & Co. became the most powerful firm in the Far West.
See also: Wells, Fargo & Company.

Wells, H. G. (1866-1946), British writer and social reformer. A draper's apprentice, he studied science and became a teacher. After such early science fiction as *The Time Machine* (1895) and *The War of the Worlds* (1898), he wrote novels on the lower middle class, including *Kipps* (1905) and *The History of Mr. Polly* (1910). A founder of the Fabian society, he became a social prophet (*A Modern Utopia*; 1905). After World War I he popularized knowledge in *Outline of History* (1920) and *The Science of Life* (1931).

Wells-Barnett, Ida Bell (1862-1931), African-American reformer and journalist known for her anti-lynching efforts in the late 1800s and early 1900s. In 1909 she helped establish the National Association for the Advancement of Colored People (NAACP). She also participated in the campaign aimed at giving women the right to vote.

Welsbach, Baron von (1858-1929), Viennese chemist and inventor who worked on artificial lighting. He developed the Welsbach mantle (1885), a gas lamp that produced brighter light than previous gas lamps. A few years later, he created the filament for an incandescent lamp that led to the development of the modern light bulb. He also created a metal, called Auer's metal, which, when struck, creates a spark. It is used in modern-day cigarette lighters.
See also: Chemistry.

Welsh *See:* Wales.

Welsh corgi *See:* Cardigan Welsh corgi.

Welsh springer spaniel, breed of dog. This sporting dog can withstand long hours, poor weather, and rough terrain as a retrieving companion to a hunter. Welsh spaniels need careful training, though, because of their tendency to roam. They stand up to 17 in (43 cm) at the shoulder and weigh from 35-45 lb (15.75-20.25 kg). Their fur, including that on their tail, legs, and chest, is white with red patches or spots.

Welsh terrier, small dog native to Wales, used to hunt foxes. The Welsh terrier has a wiry coat with black and reddish-tan markings. It weighs approximately 20 lb (9 kg) and is about 15 in (38 cm) high. The Welsh is a very lively and spirited dog.

Welty, Eudora (1909-   ), U.S. novelist and short-story writer, known for sensitive tales of Mississippi life. She superbly depicted atmosphere and characters in *The Wide Net* (1943), *The Ponder Heart* (1954), *The Optimist's Daughter* (1972; Pulitzer Prize), and others.

Welwitschia, also known as tumboa, family of desert plants (*Welwitschia mirabilis*) that grow in Africa. The Welwitschia is a large, slow-growing plant that lives 100 or more years, and may reach an age of 1,000-2,000 years. Its long main root extends into a short, cone-shaped trunk that spreads to a width of 5-6 ft (1.5-1.8 m). At the base of the trunk grow a pair of leaves 2-3 ft (61-91 cm) wide and 4-6 ft (1.2-1.8 m) long. These leaves, which grow for the entire life of the plant, are usually shredded into thinner strips by strong desert winds and sand.

Wen, or sebaceous cyst, blocked sebaceous gland, often over the scalp or forehead, that forms a cyst containing old sebum under the skin. Should it become infected, its excision is a simple procedure.

Werewolf, in folklore, a man who can supernaturally turn into a wolf and devour humans. The belief dates from Greek legend and was widespread in medieval Europe and in the 19th-century Balkans. The psychiatric condition of lycanthropy involves the belief that one is a werewolf or other beast.

Werfel, Franz (1890-1945), Austrian novelist, poet, and playwright. His early plays and poetry, such as *Der Spiegelmensch* (1920), were important works of German expressionism. He fled Nazi-occupied Austria (1938) and later settled in the United States. His novels include *Embezzled Heaven* (1939), *The Song of Bernadette* (1941), and *Jacobowsky and the Colonel* (1944).

Wergeland, Henrik Arnold (1808-45), Norwegian writer and nationalist. He promoted Norwegian independence from Sweden and inspired Norwegians to feel pride in their own culture. He produced much poetry, drama, and prose, but it is his poetry that received the most acclaim. *Creation, Humanity, and Messiah* (1830), *Jan van Huysum's Flower Piece* (1840), and *The English Pilot* (1844) are some of his best-loved poems. He was dedicated to the causes of liberty, democracy, and international cooperation.

Wertheimer, Max (1880-1943), German psychologist who founded (with Kurt Koffka and Wolfgang Köhler) the school of Gestalt psychology. He taught at Frankfurt and Berlin and emigrated to the United States in 1933. *See also:* Gestalt psychology.

Weser River, major German river whose source is the junction of the Fulda and Werra rivers at Munden. The Weser is about 273 mi (440 km) long and flows into the North Sea near Bremerhaven. About 45 mi (72 km) of the river, from its North Sea mouth to Bremen, is navigable by large ships.

Wesker, Arnold (1932-), English playwright, one of the so-called angry young men to emerge in England in 1956. His early plays, such as the trilogy *Chicken Soup with Barley* (1958), *Roots* (1959), and *I'm Talking About Jerusalem* (1960), are committed to the ideals of socialism. The later, more introspective *Chips with Everything* (1962) and *The Friends* (1970) explore themes of private pain.

Wesley, name of 2 English evangelistic preachers who, with George Whitefield, founded Methodism. **John Wesley** (1703-91) and his brother **Charles** (1707-88) formed an Oxford Holy Club of scholarly Christians, known as Methodists for their "rule and methods." In 1738 the brothers were profoundly influenced by the Moravian Church in Georgia and, John in particular, by Luther's *Preface to the Epistle to the Romans*. Aiming to promote "vital, practical religion," the Wesleys took up evangelistic work by field, or open-air, preaching. Rejected by the Church of England, they were enthusiastically received by the people, and they organized conferences of itinerant lay preachers. Charles composed some 6,500 hymns, including "Hark! The Herald Angels Sing."
See also: Methodists.

Wesleyan Church, U.S. Protestant church formed in 1968 by the merger of the Wesleyan Methodist Church of America and the Pilgrim Holiness Church. Members attempt to live a life free of sin or indulgences such as alcohol or tobacco. The church, headquartered in Marion, Indiana, operates several educational facilities and has missionaries working in areas throughout the world.
See also: Protestantism.

West, Benjamin (1738-1820), U.S.-born painter. After studying in Rome he settled in London (1763) and was appointed the official historical painter (1772) to King George III. He was also a founder of the Royal Academy of Arts. His best-known works are *Death of General Wolfe* (1771) and *Penn's Treaty with the Indians* (1776). Gilbert Stuart and J.S. Copley were among his students.

West, Dame Rebecca (Cicily Isabel Fairfield; 1892-1983), British novelist, critic, and journalist. *Black Lamb and Grey Falcon; A Journey through Yugoslavia* (1941) is perhaps her finest work. Her novels include *The Return of the Soldier* (1918) and *Birds Fall Down* (1966).

West, Jerry (1938-   ), U.S. basketball player and coach. Known for his high scoring as well as ball-handling and defense, he scored 25,192 regular-season points in his National Basketball Association (NBA) career. His achievements include 2 Most Valuable Player awards—1 Playoff (1969) and 1 All-Star (1972)—and appearing in 13 All-Star games. West played for the Los Angeles Lakers (1960-74), leading them to a championship (1972) and, after retiring, became the team's head coach (1976-79) and later, general manager (1982-   ). He was inducted into the Basketball Hall of Fame in 1979.

West, Jessamyn (1907-84), U.S. author. A Quaker whose writings often reflect the ideals of the Quaker religion, West's most famous book is *Friendly Persuasion* (1945), a view of life in a rural Quaker family in the 1800s (she later adapted this book for the 1956 film of the same name). Other works include *The Witch Diggers* (1951), *Cress Delahanty* (1953), and *Except For Thee and Me* (1969), which chronicles the lives of various characters in *Friendly Persuasion*.

West, Mae (1892-1980), U.S. stage and screen actress. This sultry mistress of provocative innuendo and sex symbol of Hollywood films of the 1930s was frequently at odds with the censors. She immortalized the phrase "come up 'n' see me sometime," and starred in such movies as *She Done Him Wrong* (1933), *I'm No Angel* (1933), and *My Little Chickadee* (1940).

West, Nathanael (Nathan Wallenstein Weinstein; 1903-40), U.S. author. His acerbic novels about the American dream include *The Dream Life of Balso Snell* (1931); *Miss Lonelyhearts* (1933), a gloomy satire about a lovelorn columnist; *A Cool Million* (1934), a lampoon of the rags-to-riches theme; and *The Day of the Locust* (1939), a surrealistic view of life and failure in Hollywood.

West, The, western portion of the United States, formerly the region west of the Appalachian Mountains; presently, the territory west of the Mississippi River, in particular the northern part of this area. In U.S. history, the West was a region that lay at the rim of the settled land. This unsettled area was a place where unlimited land was available at a very cheap price to anyone willing to lead a life on the frontier.

West Bank, land to the west of the Dead Sea and the Jordan River, between Israel and Jordan. A part of Palestine, the area was annexed by Jordan following the partition of Palestine and the formation of the state of Israel

(1948). It has been occupied by Israel since 1967, despite a call for withdrawal from the United Nations. Historically known as Judaea and Samaria, the West Bank contains such famous cities as Bethlehem, Jericho, Hebron, and the Old City of Jerusalem. The status of the West Bank, along with that of the Gaza Strip in southwestern Israel, has become an important issue in the Arab-Israeli disputes. The Camp David Agreement of 1978, between Egypt and Israel, specified that the 1.3 million Palestinian Arabs, who are the great majority of inhabitants in the 2 areas, would be given "full autonomy and self-government" for a 5-year period, during which the ultimate sovereignty of the territories would be determined. The parties, however, failed to agree about the details of self-government. At the same time, Israel increased its settlements there. Hostility between Israel and the Palestinians escalated in the late 1980s during the *intifada*, a Palestinian uprising marked by boycotts, demonstrations, and stone-throwing. In 1988 Jordan gave up the West Bank and Jericho attained limited Palestinian self-government in 1994.

West Berlin *See:* Berlin.

Western Australia, largest Australian state (975,290 sq mi/2,527,633 sq km), first settled 1826-29, covering the western third of the country. Beyond the narrow coastal strip and fertile southwest, it is mostly dry plateau with vast desert wastes. Major products are wool, wheat, and lumber, and chief minerals are gold, coal, and iron.

Western European Union (WEU), defensive economic, social, and cultural alliance among Belgium, France, Great Britain, Italy, Luxembourg, the Netherlands, and Germany, formed in 1955. Spain and Portugal joined in 1988 and Greece in 1991. Comprising most of the members of the North Atlantic Treaty Organization (NATO), the organization works to strengthen the European part of NATO.
See also: North Atlantic Treaty Organization.

Western frontier life, folklore and reality of the lives of the men and women who participated in the last phase of the settlement of the U.S. frontier. The western territories of the United States were settled in several stages. After pioneers had settled lands from the Appalachians to the Mississippi and the Old Northwest territory around the Great Lakes, they headed for the Far West, chiefly California and Oregon. The Great Plains, stretching from west of the Mississippi to the Rocky Mountains, were a passage to be crossed, not land to be settled. That changed after the 1850s and, in particular, after the Civil War. The vast expanses of the Great Plains and the intermontane region, between the Rocky Mountains and the Sierra Nevada, were the last frontier, and the area was settled between 1850 and 1890. Within that 40 years, the United States completed its drive to subdue and fill the entire expanse of land between the Atlantic and Pacific oceans. The nation succeeded in fixing and defining its continental boundaries. But the people who did it, the men and women who went out to settle the last frontier, lived lives that would decisively shape the American character. In the process, their lives became the stuff of folklore and the imagination; the land became the setting, the people the characters, and the settlement the taming of the wild west. The 19th century was the age of imperialism. The great European powers, particularly Great Britain, France, and Germany, struggled for markets, territory, and domination in Africa and Asia. The first half of the century had been absorbed with the military ambitions of Napoleon Bonaparte and the political repercussions of the French Revolution. The general failure of the revolutions of 1848 left the industrialized nation states dominated by a socially and politically conservative but ambitious middle class. With Europe temporarily stable, energy was directed outward and fortunes and reputations were sought in the colonies. The United States, was influenced by these developments. Proud of its separation and isolation from Europe, it was not a party to the competition for foreign colonies. The Great Plains remained unsettled and the United States turned to the task with a deliberate sense of itself that took the form of a political purpose and program articulated by the central government and different from the country's previous pioneering efforts. Much more than its earlier pioneering drives, the settlement of the frontier was more frankly driven by the profit motive, more centrally directed by a successful partnership between central government and private enterprise, and inspired by the ideology of Manifest Destiny. While Europeans made their fortunes and reputations in far-off Africa and Asia, U.S. citizens pursued the work and adventure of subduing their country's last frontier.

The people who settled the Great Plains were a varied lot. Most were farmers, skilled and unskilled laborers, miners and prospectors, and, after the Civil War, former soldiers all looking for a better life. Among them were drifters and those with criminal records or a past they wanted to escape. Many were blacks who were attracted to the greater opportunity and freedom from prejudice they hoped to find in the frontier. Among the blacks were men who became well-known cowboys, like the ranchhand Nat Love, famous for his horsemanship, or the former slave, Base Ikard, who rose to become foreman of one of the biggest ranches in Texas. Many European immigrants came to settle the West, too. Some were miners from England or Wales. Many others, especially Germans, came to the United States after the failed revolutions of 1848. Scandinavians also came in large numbers. And in California, the Chinese came to work as laborers on the transcontinental railroad. The major divisions among all these people were the miners and prospectors, the ranchers and cowboys, and the farmers.

The miners and prospectors went west to find gold. The first great gold rush was in the Far West in 1848 triggered by the discovery of gold at Sutter's Mill in California. In succeeding decades, strikes were made farther inland. From 1856 to 1875 silver was found in southern Arizona, then Colorado and Nevada. Eventually, mining prospered in Idaho, Montana, Washington, and the Black Hills of South Dakota. Mining gave rise to boom towns, some of which eventually became stable and prosperous towns and cities, but many of which became ghost towns when the mines gave out. Tucson, Tombstone, Denver, Central City, and Leadville were all, at one time, mining towns.

The ranchers went west to raise cattle. The open plains were ideal for grazing huge herds, and the completion of the transcontinental railroad in 1869 made it possible to ship the cattle to market in large and profitable numbers. Cattle ranching was a tough business that gave the West its cowboys. Cowboys tended the herds while they were grazing, branded them when they were of age, fought off cattle thieves, and managed the long drives of thousands of cattle over hundreds of miles of open prairie to the railroads. They followed well-known trails, like the Chisholm Trail, that have become a part of the landscape of U.S. folklore. The cattle business made towns like Abilene, Kans., and Dodge City. But eventually boom went to bust. The cattle market became glutted, the blizzards of 1886 and 1887 wiped out many ranchers, and competition with farmers for the open range also took its toll.

Farmers had been reluctant, at first, to settle the Great Plains, and the homesteaders formed the last wave of settlers. At first the land was considered unsuitable for farming. There was little water and there were no trees. On top of that, the Native Americans were hostile. But several developments in the 1870s changed the prospects for homesteaders. Barbed wire was invented, so wood was no longer necessary for poling and fencing. New methods of dry farming were invented and windmills were developed to draw water from underground. Homesteaders moved west. They faced harsh conditions. Their houses were built of sod, blocks of compacted soil cut out of the prairie. They had to deal with hot summers and ice-cold winters, infestations of grasshoppers, prairie fires, and possible confrontations with Native Americans. They also had to contend with ranchers, whose herds and livelihoods were threatened when barbed wire put an end to the open range. Bloody range wars pitted ranchers against farmers and in some cases it was necessary for the U.S. army to intervene. But in the end, the farmers prevailed.

Settling the frontier brought out the best and the worst in people. For miners and ranchers, farmers and cowboys, and the skilled and semi-skilled professionals who helped build and settle the towns, life could be harsh, there were few comforts, and a rough-and-ready democracy prevailed. Men who were poor prospectors one day became fabulously rich the next. Many drank or gambled their money away. Some built prosperous farms and ranches, while others were wiped out. In the early days, there were few women and little of the social stability that comes with family life. Those who settled the West lived by a rough-hewn code made up in part of values they brought with them and values that arose from the lives they lived. Men were prized for their self-reliance, survival skills, and reliability. A man's word was more binding than any written law. Though not nearly as violent as one would believe by watching movies or reading Zane Grey, the West saw more than its share of violence and bloodshed and tested man's capacity to fight and endure. These values were rooted in the day-to-day living conditions.

Transportation was uncomfortable and often dangerous. Stagecoaches ran over uneven ground and passengers sat on rough wooden benches for long, dusty, cold rides during which they had often to stay alert for Native Americans or bandits. People traveled by wagon trains before the railroads were completed, and they traveled regularly by horseback. Eventually, the railroads expanded, connecting more towns and improving transport, but in the early days even camels were used for transport over the dry prairies. Communication was no less difficult, though the problem was met with characteristic ingenuity and energy. For 19 months, between Apr. 1860 and Oct. 1861, the Pony Express, a relay system of horseback riders, covered the distance between St. Joseph and Sacramento in about 10 days. The system was replaced by the telegraph.

The 3 great threats to the lives of the settlers on the frontier were nature and the elements, Native Americans, and lawbreakers. Men like Bat Masterson and Wyatt Earp became famous for enforcing the law, and theirs was a daunting task. Everyone was armed and a single lawman was often the only law for 200 or 300 miles around. Judges, like the famous Roy Bean, dispersed law on a circuit and conducted hearings in local saloons with a law book in one hand and a pistol in the other. Desperadoes were not always the colorful or spectacular kind. Most crime had to do with swindles and thefts, the work of claim jumpers, confidence men, card sharps, and rustlers. If caught, these men often faced rough justice, if not at the hands of an individual, then at the hands of vigilantes or a lynch mob. But the Old West had a deep ambivalence about the law. It admired tough and independent characters, gamblers who took chances and won, people who knew how to fight for and keep what was theirs. It admired a tough lawman but was suspicious of government. That ambivalence is apparent in the reputations enjoyed by men like the Dalton boys, Billy the Kid, Sam Bass, and Frank and Jesse James, notorious outlaws who were feared but, in a sense, also admired.

Finally, there were the Native Americans. The Comstock Lode produced $300 million worth of silver ore (1860-80). Cattle ranching made men fortunes. And eventually, farmers turned the Great Plains into the world's greatest bread basket. In this scheme of things there was finally no room for buffalo or tribes of nomadic hunters. The Native Americans occupied the land of the last frontier, presumably protected by treaties, but the treaties gave way to the overwhelming drive for riches, land, and the territorial ambitions of a growing nation-state. The Native Americans resisted and the settlers and the government fought back. The U.S. Army established forts and outposts to protect settlers and subdue the Native Americans. In the process, both fear and greed combined to weave into the ethos of the West the conviction that the only good Indian was a dead Indian. The result was the systematic reduction, the demoralization and decimation, of the Native American peoples, in open warfare or in massacres, like the one near Sand Creek, Col., in 1864. Nonetheless, the Native Americans left a mixed legacy among the people who settled the frontier. There were many who admired their courage and skills and there were those, among them agents of the Indian Bureau, who attempted to mitigate their destruction.

In 1890 the Bureau of the Census declared that the frontier no longer existed. Buffalo Bill Cody began touring with his Wild West Show in 1883. Mark Twain wrote *Roughing It*. Nearly 450 books have been written about Billy the Kid alone, not to mention the works of Zane Grey, Walter Van Tilburg Clark, and A.B. Guthrie. Western frontier life has inspired works in the opera, ballet, and musical theater, and was long a staple of movies that became popular throughout the world. The actual settlement of the frontier was undertaken by individuals and by the country as a whole, driven by the desire for wealth, a better life, and a belief in the country's political destiny. In the process, it shaped people's lives and gave birth to values and a folklore that continue to influence the nation and the people's sense of itself, even though values are critically examined and re-examined, long after the official declaration that the frontier had disappeared.

Western Isles *See:* Hebrides.

Western Reserve, northeastern region of Ohio on the south shore of Lake Erie. In 1786 Connecticut refused to cede this area, which covered 3,667,000 acres (1,483,982 hectares), to the Northwest Territory. In 1792, 500,000 acres were granted to Connecticut citizens whose land was destroyed during the American Revolution. The region joined the Northwest Territory in 1800.

Western Sahara, formerly Spanish Sahara, area in northwest Africa, comprising 100,848 sq mi (252,120 sq km) of mainly desert; bordered by the

Western Samoa

Capital:	Apia
Area:	1,093 sq mi
	(2,831 sq km)
Population:	162,000
Language:	Samoan, English
Government:	Parliamentary
	monarchy in the British
	Commmonwealth
Independent:	1962
Head of gov.:	Prime minister
Per capita:	U.S. $1120
Mon. unit:	1 Tala = 100 sene

Atlantic Ocean in the west, Morocco in the north, Algeria in the northeast, and Mauritania in the east and south. Western Sahara is rich in phosphate deposits. The people are Arabs and Berbers. Western Sahara was a Spanish province from 1958 to 1976, when the territory was transferred to Morocco and Mauritania. Mauritania gave up its claim in 1979, following guerrilla action by nationalists seeking self-government of the Saharans, but Morocco continues to occupy the area, with U.S. arms support. The nationalists have renamed the area the Sacharawi Arab Democratic Republic. In December 1998, a referendum regarding the future status of the country is expected to be held among an electorate of approximately 80,000 voters.

Western Samoa, officially the Independent State of Western Samoa, independent state in the southwestern Pacific Ocean, comprising 2 large islands, Savai'i and Upolu, and 7 smaller islands, only 2 of which are inhabited. Its area is 1,133 sq mi (2,934 sq km).
Land and climate. Most of the islands are mountainous, volcanic, forested, and fertile. The climate is rainy and tropical.
People and economy. The people are Polynesian, and the majority live in Upolu, where Apia, the capital and chief port, stands. Samoans speak probably the oldest Polynesian language in use. The economy is agricultural, the main exports being copra, bananas, and cacao. Tourism is important. The current development program, backed by foreign aid, aims to expand agriculture and encourage modest industrialization (e.g., soap, lumber).
History. The islands were probably discovered by the Dutch explorer Jacob Roggeveen (1722). Germany, Great Britain, and the United States jointly administered the islands (1889-99), and agreed in 1899 that Samoa should be divided between the United States and Germany. In 1914 New Zealand seized German Samoa, later administering it by League of Nations mandate and, later, as a UN Trust Territory. It became independent as Western Samoa in 1962. It joined the UN in 1976. In 1997 parliament agreed to change the country's name to Samoa, despite opposition of American Samoa.

Western Union, shortened name for Western Union Telegraph Company, U.S. communications company. When the company was founded (1851), it telegraphed information from location to location in the eastern half of the

United States. By the end of its first decade, a transcontinental telegraph system was in place. At the turn of the century, transatlantic telegraph cables existed. As a means of communication, telegraphs allowed for immediate transmittal of messages. To keep up with technological advances, Western Union has developed transmitting towers that communicate messages through radio beams (beginning in 1945), satellite communications (beginning in 1974), telex services (beginning in 1982), and an electronic mail service called *EasyLink* (beginning in 1982), which allows computers to communicate with each other. Today this company, based in New Jersey, is called Western Union Corporation (1970).
See also: Telegraph.

West Germany *See:* Germany.

West Highland white terrier, small, white Scottish dog. About 11 in (27.9 cm) high and weighing 13-20 lb (5.9-9.1 kg), its coat is thick and wiry. This terrier was once used to hunt small birds and animals.

West Indies, chain of islands extending about 2,500 mi (4,020 km) from Florida to Venezuela, separating the Caribbean Sea and the Gulf of Mexico from the Atlantic Ocean. An alternative name (excluding the Bahamas) is the Antilles. The West Indies comprises 4 main groups: the Bahamas to the northeast of Cuba and Hispaniola; the Greater Antilles (Cuba, the largest island in the West Indies, Hispaniola, Jamaica, and Puerto Rico); the Lesser Antilles (Leeward and Windward islands, Trinidad and Tobago, and Barbados); and the Netherlands Antilles (Aruba, Bonaire, Curaçao) as well as other islands off the Venezuelan coast. Many of the islands are mountainous and volcanic with lagoons and mangrove swamps on their coastlines. The climate is warm, but there are frequent hurricanes. The principal crop is sugarcane and tourism is an important industry. After Columbus reached the West Indies (1492), they were settled by the Spanish, followed by the English, French, and Dutch, who exploited the spices and sugar, using African slaves. The political status of the islands varies widely.

Westinghouse, George (1846-1914), U.S. engineer, inventor, and manufacturer. In 1869 he founded the Westinghouse Air Brake Company to develop the air brakes he had invented for railroad use. From 1883 he did pioneering work on the safe transmission of natural gas. He also pioneered the use of high-voltage AC electricity and in 1886 founded the Westinghouse Electric Company to develop AC induction motors and transmission equipment. The company was largely responsible for the acceptance of AC in preference to DC for most applications, in spite of opposition from the influential Thomas Edison.
See also: Brake.

Westminster Abbey, officially the Collegiate Church of Saint Peter, English Gothic church in London, a national shrine. The Abbey has been the traditional scene of English coronations since that of William the Conqueror, and is a burial place for English monarchs and famous subjects, including many of England's greatest poets, who lie in the Poets' Corner. The present building, begun in 1245 by Henry III, is on the site of a church built (1065) by Edward the Confessor.

Westminster, Statute of (1931), British parliamentary act abolishing Great Britain's power to legislate for its dominions. It gave the dominions complete independence in the commonwealth of nations, although they owed common allegiance to the British crown.

Westminster Choir, U.S. chorus founded at Dayton Westminster Church, Ohio, in 1921, and since 1932 a part of Westminster Choir College, Princeton, N.J.

Westminster Hall, building that serves as an entranceway to Britain's House of Parliament (Westminster Palace) in London. Westminster Palace was the royal residence before it became the home of Parliament (16th century), and the rulers of Britain held court in its Great Hall. Westminster Hall is all that remains of the Great Hall, which was built in the late 11th century but mostly destroyed by German fire bombs during World War II. Westminster Hall measures 240 ft (73 m) long, 68 ft (21 m) wide, and 89 ft (27 m) high.
See also: Parliament.

Westmoreland, William Childs (1914-), U.S. general, army chief of staff (1968-72). He was superintendent of West Point (1960-63) and the U.S. commander (1964-68) in Vietnam.
See also: Army, U.S.

Weston, Edward (1886-1958), U.S. photographer, winner of the Guggenheim Fellowship (1937). Originally a producer of hazy, unclear pictures, popular in the late 1800s, Weston switched in the 1920s to crisp, focused photographs of simple subjects, a stlye known as straight photography. His pictures emphasized the form and texture of objects and centered predominantly on nature scenes.
See also: Photography.

Westphalia (German, "western plain"), region in Germany, located just east of the Netherlands. Westphalia was first settled c.A.D. 700 by a group of Saxons. It came under the control of the archbishops of Cologne in 1180. During the 18th century, Prussian rulers steadily acquired the region. Napoleon transferred portions of Westphalia to his brother and to the duchy of Berg. However, the Congress of Vienna (1814-15) reestablished Prussian rule of the region. It came under German control in 1946.

West Point, site of, and common name for, the U.S. Military Academy in southeast New York, an institute of higher education that trains officers for the regular army. Established by an Act of Congress in 1802, its training methods and traditions were set down by Col. Sylvanus Thayer, superintendent of the academy from 1817 to 1833. Candidates for entry (since 1976, of either sex) to the academy must be unmarried U.S. citizens age 17-22 and must meet minimum academic requirements. Cadets are enlisted in the regular army on entrance. Graduates are awarded a B.S. degree and a commission as second lieutenant.
See also: United States Military Academy.

West Virginia, state in east-central United States; bordered by Pennsylvania and Maryland to the northeast, Virginia to the east and south, Kentucky to

West Virginia

Capital:	Charleston
Statehood:	June 20, 1863 (35th state)
Familiar name:	Mountain State
Area:	24,231 sq mi (62,759 sq km); ranks 41st
Population:	1,816,000 (1997); ranks 35th
Elevation:	Highest—4,863 ft (1,482 m), Spruce Knob; Lowest—240 ft (73 m), along the Potomac River
Motto:	Montani Semper Liberi (Mountaineers Are Always Free)
Flower:	Rhododendron
Bird:	Cardinal
Tree:	Sugar maple
Songs:	"The West Virginia Hills," "This Is My West Virginia," "West Virginia, My Home, Sweet Home"

the southwest, and the Ohio River (with Ohio on the opposite side) to the west and northwest.

Land and climate. West Virginia has three main land areas. A tiny strip at the state's northeastern corner is part of the Blue Ridge Mountains, a region of fertile slopes and river valleys. In the Appalachian Ridge and Valley Region, which runs in a narrow band along the state's eastern border, high ridges of hard rock are separated by parallel valleys with streams or rivers flowing in them. The Appalachian Plateau, which covers most of the state, is a rugged area of flat highlands, narrow stream valleys, and sloping hills; most of the state's coal deposits are in this region. The Ohio is the state's major river; other important waterways are the Kanawha and the Potomac. There are no large natural lakes; artificial ones have been formed by damming the rivers. Forests covers about four-fifths of the state. West Virginia has warm, humid summers and cold winters. Principal cities are Charleston, Huntington, and Wheeling.

Economy. West Virginia's economy is led by mining, manufacturing, and wholesale and retail trade. Coal is the chief mining product; others are natural gas, crushed stone, sand and gravel, clays, and salt. Chief manufactured goods are chemicals; primary metals; stone, clay, and glass products; plastic and hardwood products; and fabricated metal products. Agriculture accounts for less than half of 1% of West Virginia's gross state product; beef and dairy cattle and hay are the chief agricultural products.

Government. West Virginia's present constitution was adopted in 1872. The governor serves a 4-year term. The state legislature consists of 34 senators serving 4-year terms and 100 delegates serving 2-year terms. In the U.S. Congress, West Virginia is represented by 2 senators and 3 representatives. *History.* West Virginia's history until 1861 is essentially the same as Virginia's, although West Virginia was distinguished by its isolation from the state capital, by the fact that few West Virginians owned slaves, and by its economy (small-scale farming and industries based on mineral resources). In 1861, when a Virginia convention voted to secede from the Union, West Virginians refused to do so. They declared their independence, adopted a constitution (1862), and became the 35th state in 1863. In the early 20th century, West Virginia's rapid expansion in the coal, gas, and steel industries was accompanied by severe labor-management conflicts and by riots. The formation of the National Recovery Administration (1933) improved miners' wages and working conditions. World War II brought industrial growth to the state but, from the 1950s onward, demand for the state's mining products fell. West Virginia remained poor, its land and water resources damaged by strip mining, and many people left the state. The energy shortage of the 1970s temporarily boosted the state's economy, but coal prices dropped in the early 1980s; by the mid-1980s, West Virginia's unemployment rate was the nation's highest. In recent years state leaders have worked to attract tourism and more diverse industries to West Virginia.

Westward movement, in the United States, events and conditions comprising the several major migrations by which the country was settled. The exploration and settlement of the U.S. frontier was an ongoing process that began with the first communities founded on the Atlantic seaboard in the 17th century and ended in the 1890s with the settlement of the Great Plains between the Mississippi River and the Rocky Mountains. Whereas the history of European countries is the story of gradual accretion of territories and extension of authority over centuries, involving many peoples with deep and sharply differing regional loyalties, the establishment and settlement of the territories that now make up the continental United States was swift and dynamic. The previous occupants of the land, the Native Americans, largely nomadic peoples, were unable to mount any long-term effective resistance and, in the end, proved to be more victims than adversaries. The United States was a new land. Its government was revolutionary, its society democratic, its spirit pragmatic and forward looking. All these factors fed into and were fed by its westward expansion.

The first settlers of what was to become the United States came to the Atlantic coast early in the 17th century. Jamestown, Va., was established in 1607, becoming the country's first English settlement. In Massachusetts, other settlers from England founded Plymouth Colony and Boston, and the Dutch established New Amsterdam, later to become New York City.

Colonial America, beginning as it did, at the very edge of a literally uncharted continent, retained close ties with Europe in certain respects while in other ways it began breaking ties from the outset. Many who came to America were religious dissenters, like the Puritans and Quakers. Others came as indentured servants willing to pay their way for the chance for a new life in exchange for their labor. Still others came with royal charters, while black Africans, beginning in 1619, were imported as slaves. In the end, one of the common elements among all these different people and the waves of immigrants who would follow was the attraction of the nearly limitless opportunity of the new continent's open lands. From the original settled towns and communities, the expanding ranks of the colonists spread out, at first along the valleys of the James, York, Rappahannock, and Potomac rivers. By the end of the 17th century, the colonial Americans had expanded from the Atlantic coast to the low hills of the Appalachians. The following century, the 18th century, would culminate in the Revolutionary War, but throughout the century, before the war and after, the colonists would settle the Old West, consisting of the back country of New England, the Piedmont, and the valleys of the Appalachians. With fresh influxes of Germans, Scots-Irish, and Scandinavians, colonists settled the Shenandoah Valley of Virginia, Pennsylvania, North Carolina, South Carolina, and Georgia.

Colonial expansion was both aided and hindered by the British. While still British colonists, the Americans fought in the French and Indian War (1754-63), and Great Britain won territory from France between the Appalachians and the Mississippi. In 1763 Britain put a temporary halt to westward expansion in order to keep peace between the Native Americans and expansionist colonials. Eventually, treaties had to be renegotiated and in any case they proved ineffective in stopping the settlement of Kentucky and Tennessee under the leadership of adventurers like Daniel Boone, who opened the Cumberland Gap in 1775. During the Revolutionary War, America's military successes led it to claim the Old Northwest territories, between the Ohio River and the Great Lakes. After the war, settlers moved to the area and to the old Southwest, including Kentucky, Tennessee, and lands toward the Gulf of Mexico. The U.S. government took an active part in aiding, organizing, and encouraging the settlements.

The Ordinance of 1785 divided the land of the Old Northwest into salable parcels. Large tracts were bought from the government by speculators who then sold them in lots to settlers. The Northwest Ordinance of 1787 settled the political organization of the territories. A territory's original officials would be appointed by Congress. When the population reached 5,000, the adult males elected an assembly and sent a nonvoting representative to Congress. When the population reached 60,000, a territory could apply for statehood. With these ordinances, the U.S. government laid the groundwork for the organized settlement of its expanding territories. Kentucky joined the Union in 1792 and Tennessee in 1796.

As the Old Northwest and the Old Southwest were being rapidly settled, the United States expanded its territory by 827,987 sq mi (2,144,476 sq km) at a cost of $15 million paid to France. The Louisiana Purchase, completed by Thomas Jefferson, expanded U.S. territory from the Mississippi River to the Rocky Mountains. The area would be explored by Merriwether Lewis and William Clark (1803-05), by Zebulon Pike (1806), and by Major Stephen H. Long (1820), but would not actually be settled until the latter half of the 19th century. In the meantime, America fought the British in the War of 1812, bringing an end to British power in America and an end, as well, to effective resistance from Native Americans in the region who had largely sided with the British. The attempt by Tecumseh and his brother, the Shawnee Prophet, to unify the Native Americans from the Great Lakes to the Gulf of Mexico had already been undone by their defeat at the Battle of Tippecanoe in 1811. After the War of 1812, the defeated Native Americans were consigned to an Indian Territory west of the Mississippi in what is present-day Oklahoma. Thousands died of disease and starvation on their way west.

With the threats of the British and the Native Americans eliminated, the Old Northwest was settled rapidly. By 1820 there were 792,000 settlers in the region, and the completion of the Erie Canal in 1825 hastened the development of towns and cities. In the meantime the Adams-Onís Treaty with Spain (1819) opened up Florida, Alabama, and Mississippi. Aided by the river traffic of the Mississippi, the area became home to huge and successful cotton plantations. In the decades before the Civil War, the westward expansion had taken possession of lands from the Great Lakes to the Gulf of Mexico, from Maine to Florida, and from the Atlantic coast to the Mississippi. The last large area of settlement before the Civil War was the Far West.

Originally attracted by the reports and surveys of John C. Fremont in the early 1840s, settlers began moving to California. The first to come were usually trappers and traders, followed by the wagon trains that crossed the prairies over the Oregon Trail that branched into the Santa Fe or Spanish Trails to California. Settlers had already begun moving into Oregon as early as 1835. At first the British were a residual presence in Oregon and contested U.S. expansion, but the Oregon Treaty of 1846 settled all claims between the United States and Britain and established the territory that now comprises the states of Oregon and Washington and the northwestern border with Canada. Two years later, in 1848, gold was discovered at Sutter's Mill in California, and the first gold rush brought California's population from 15,000 in 1848 to 100,000 in 1849. Eventually, gold and silver fever would contribute to the settlement of South Dakota, Montana, Arizona, and Nevada. The decades before the Civil War also saw the settlements of Texas, the Southwest, and Utah.

Originally settled by Stephen F. Austin in the 1820s with the permission of the Mexican government, Texas was Mexican territory. But less than 20 years after Austin's settlement, the settlers were strong enough to contest Mexican authority and, under Samuel Houston, defeat the Mexicans at the Battle of San Jacinto, declaring Texas an independent republic. It joined the union as a state in 1845. Three years later, the United States ended its war with Mexico with the Treaty of Guadalupe Hidalgo and gained California, Nevada, Utah, most of Arizona, and parts of Colorado, New Mexico, and Wyoming. The Gadsden Purchase of 1853 completed the acquisition of the lands that now form the border between Arizona and New Mexico and Mexico.

Within the same period, Utah was settled by Mormons. They first settled the Great Salt Lake region in 1847. By dint of remarkable industry, the Mormons succeeded in settling arid country. Persecuted for their religious beliefs, the Mormons at first proved hostile to other settlers. In order to discourage outsiders, they even disguised themselves as Native Americans and attacked several wagon trains until they were stopped by the U.S. Army.

An anomaly in some ways, the conduct of the Mormons was not completely without precedent. The original colonists had, with few exceptions, fled governments inimical to them. They became self-reliant and self-governing and defeated a major European power in armed struggle over the issue of governance. The Constitutional Convention was marked from beginning to end with a certain hostility toward and suspicion of centralized governments. The settlers carried these same attitudes to the frontier where experience tended to confirm and deepen them. Backwoods and frontier citizens resented the more settled people of the East and, above all, the constraints of authority. The most common grievance was over taxes to be paid to a government that was remote, did little to better their daily lives, and was dominated by people who seemed alien to the plain-spoken, straightforward westerner. That there was much romanticizing and self-serving talk in all of this should not disguise real differences in outlook that bound in common the men who led the Whiskey Rebellion, Sam Houston's Texas Republic, the Mormons in Utah, and the general suspicion of and contempt for Washington, D.C., its politicians and bureaucrats, that has deep roots among western citizens.

Begun before the Civil War and completed by 1890, the last frontier to be settled was the Great Plains, the land west of the Mississippi and extending to the Rocky Mountains, and the intermontane region between the Rocky Mountains and the Sierra Nevada. Gold and silver were the leading inspiration for the last stage of the U.S. westward movement. Rich strikes were made in Nevada and Arizona and also helped open South Dakota, Montana, and Idaho. In the meantime the railroads crossed the plains completing the transcontinental line in 1869. The railroads provided the transport necessary for commerce and the development of towns and cities. But in the beginning, they brought the cattle boom. Taking advantage of the vast stretches of open prairie ideal for grazing livestock, ranchers hurried west to take part in the boom that would last nearly 20 years, 1867-87. At the same time, the U.S. government encouraged settlement with the Homestead Act of 1862. Anyone who would improve the land over 5 years could have 160 acres of it free. At first the farmers had a hard time of it. The Great Plains were treeless and dry. But in the 1870s several developments brought dramatic changes. Barbed wire made it possible to fence off land without wood. Dry farming techniques made raising crops viable, and wind mills provided a means for drawing underground water. The farmers went west. They fought the elements, the Native Americans, and the ranchers, and turned the Great Plains into the country's bread basket.

According to the U.S. census of 1890, there was no more frontier. But it was the last frontier, the last of the westward movement, that would prove in many ways the strongest and most enduring in the country's imagination, peopled with cowboys and outlaws, vigilantes, Native Americans, lawmen, and the cavalry. But for all its robust energy, vitality, and ruthless optimism, the last of the U.S. westward expansion also marked the end of the Native Americans as independent peoples. In the mid-1860s the Sioux were defeated in order to open the Bozeman Trail through their hunting grounds in Wyoming. They were defeated again when gold was discovered in 1874 in the Black Hills of South Dakota. The Arapaho and Cheyenne, the Kiowa, Comanches, and other Native American peoples were in turn subdued, and when they resisted being moved to reservations, they were defeated again in the Red River War of 1874-75. The Indian Territory, which had been established in present-day Oklahoma, proved no more secure than the open plains. Giving in to land-hungry settlers, the government opened the Indian Territory to settlement in 1898. The last armed encounter between the United States and Native Americans occurred in 1890 at Wounded Knee Creek in S. Dak.

In one sense, the entire history of the United States can be seen as a series of westward movements, beginning with the original colonies and ending with the last frontier in 1890. Fed by successive waves of immigrants seeking new lands and new opportunities, these westward movements not only settled the land but also indelibly stamped the character of the people. Energetic, restless, and impatient with authority, they are distinct from the peoples of Europe and Asia. Less regional, they are defined by the nation more than the place, and by ideals and outlooks more than religions or creeds. In many ways, U.S. citizens continue to see themselves in terms whose origins are in its westward movements.

Wetland, area of land where the earth is continuously saturated with water. Three major types of wetlands are bogs, swamps, and marshes, each supporting a different kind of plant life. Bogs, usually located in cooler climates, have acidic soil that appears dry but is not. Bogs are dominated by mosses, which, when they decay, turn into peat. (Peat is valuable because, when dried, it can be burned as a fuel.) Swamps and marshes have mineral soils and are found mostly in warmer climates. Wetlands support a variety of valuable bird and mammal life.

Weymouth (pop. 55,601), city on Massachusetts Bay, southeast of Boston. Founded in 1622 and incorporated in 1635, it is the second-oldest settlement in Massachusetts, after Plymouth. Primarily a residential community, Weymouth has some industry, including the manufacture of fertilizer, lacquers, and electrical equipment.
See also: Massachusetts.

Whale, one of the order Cetacea of large, wholly aquatic mammals. All are highly adapted for life in water, with a torpedo-shaped body, front limbs reduced and modified as steering paddles, and hind limbs absent. They have a tail of 2 transverse flukes and swim by up-and-down movements of this tail. Most species have a fleshy dorsal fin that acts as a stabilizer. The neck is short, the head flowing directly into the trunk. The body is hairless, and the smooth skin lies over a thick layer of blubber that has an insulating function but also acts to smooth out the passage of water over the body in rapid swimming. The nose, or blowhole, is at the top of the head, allowing the animal to breathe as soon as it breaks the surface of the water.
Modern whales divide into 2 suborders, the whalebone whales and the toothed whales. Whalebone whales feed on plankton, straining the enormous quantities they require from the water with special plates of whalebone, or baleen, developed from the mucus membrane of the upper jaw. Whalebone whales—the right, rorqual, and gray whales—are usually large and slow-moving. The group includes the blue whale (*Balaenoptera musulus*), the largest animal of all time (up to 100 ft/30.5 m long). Toothed whales, equipped with conical teeth, feed on fishes and squids. The group includes the dolphins and porpoises, the sperm whale (*Physeter macrocephalus*), and the narwhal (*Mmonodon monoceros*). Many species of whale are endangered.
See also: Whaling.

Whaling, hunting of whales, originally for oil, meat, and baleen (whalebone), practiced since the 10th century. The Basques and Dutch hunted from land and pioneered methods of flensing (stripping of blubber) and boiling whale meat. U.S. whaling started in the 1600s, and whaling ports such as Nantucket and New Bedford, Mass., grew to great size in the 1700s. Whaling became safer for the hunters after the invention (1856) of harpoons with explosive heads that caused instantaneous death and avoided the dangerous pursuit of a wounded whale. From the 1800s whalers moved south in pursuit of the sperm whale. Development of factory ships that processed the catch on board facilitated longer expeditions. In the 20th century whaling has centered on Antarctic waters. Reconnaissance aircraft and electronic aids are now used. Whale products include oils, ambergris, spermaceti, meat, and bone meal. Despite the voluntary restrictions of the International Whaling Convention, whales are still overfished, and many species face extinction.

Wharton, Edith (1862-1937), U.S. novelist, poet, and short-story writer. She wrote subtle and acerbic accounts of society in New York, New England, and Europe, including *The House of Mirth* (1905), *Ethan Frome* (1911), and *The Age of Innocence* (1920; Pulitzer Prize).

Wheat, cereal plant (genus *Triticum*) of the grass family, the world's main cereal crop; about 300 million tons are produced every year, mostly used to make flour for bread and pasta. Wheat has been in cultivation since at least 5000 B.C. and grows best in temperate regions of Europe, North America, China, and Australia. The USSR is the largest producer, followed by the United States and Canada. There are many varieties of wheat, and different parts of the grain are used to produce the various types of flour. Grains comprise an outer husk called bran and a central starchy germ (which is embedded in a protein known as gluten). Wheat is graded as hard or soft depending on how easily the flour can be separated from the bran. Wheat for bread is hard wheat and contains a lot of gluten. Soft wheat flours containing more starch and less protein are used for pastries. There are 2 main types of wheat; these are sown either in the fall (winter wheat) or in the spring (spring wheat). Harvesting is carried out by combine harvesters that cut and thresh the crop in one operation. Wheat is vulnerable to several diseases, including smut, rust, army worm, and Hessian fly.

Wheatley, Phillis (1753?-84), U.S. poet. Brought to Boston from Africa as a slave, she was educated by her owners, John Wheatley and his wife, and began writing poetry. A collection of her verse *Poems on Various Subjects, Religious and Moral* was published in 1773. Her work deals with her joy about converting to Christianity, as well as her concerns about slavery. She is regarded as the first important black U.S. writer.

Wheatstone, Sir Charles (1802-75), British physicist and inventor. He popularized the "Wheatstone bridge" for measuring voltages and, with W.F. Cooke, invented the electric telegraph at about the same time as U.S. inventor Samuel F.B. Morse (1837).
See also: Telegraph.

Wheatstone bridge, electric circuit used for comparing or measuring resistance. Four resistors, including the unknown one, are connected in a square, with a battery between one pair of diagonally opposite corners and a sensitive galvanometer between the other. When no current flows through the meter, the products of opposite pairs of resistances are equal. Similar bridge circuits are used for impedance measurement.
See also: Electric circuit; Wheatstone, Sir Charles.

Wheel and axle, disklike mechanical device consisting of a wheel mounted on an axle of smaller diameter; the wheel and axle turn on the same axis. A first-class lever, it is used to facilitate the movement of heavy objects. The wheel and axle is one of the classic simple machines, along with the pulley and the screw.

Wheelbarrow, boxlike device used to move small loads. The load is carried in a box or tub at the front, below which there is a wheel. The box or tub is lifted and pushed by 2 handles at the rear.

Wheeler, Burton Kendall (1882-1975), U.S. senator from Montana (1923-47). A Democrat, he ran in 1924 as vice presidential candidate, with Robert M. LaFollette, for the Progressive Party. He helped uncover the scandals of Pres. Warren G. Harding's administration. In World War II he advocated isolationism.

Wheeler, Earle Gilmore (1908-75), U.S. Army general. He served in Europe in World War II and in 1962 was appointed army chief of staff by Pres. Lyndon B. Johnson. He was chairman of the Joint Chiefs of Staff (1964-70).
See also: Army, U.S.

Wheeler, William Almon (1819-87), vice president of the United States from 1877 to 1881. A Republican, he served under Pres. Rutherford B. Hayes. He began his career as a lawyer, and from 1861 to 1863 and 1869 to 1877 he represented New York in the House of Representatives. In 1875 he was part of a committee formed to settle a dispute over an election in Louisiana. His "Wheeler Adjustment" was a compromise that gave the Democratic and Republican parties control of the Louisiana state government.

Wheeling (pop. 159,301), city in northern West Virginia, located on the Ohio River. Wheeling is a highly industrial city, producing products such as coal and natural gas, metals, glass, plastics, textiles, and tobacco. The city is also a shipping and educational center. Wheeling College, Bethany College, and West Liberty State College are located in and around the area. Wheeling was founded in 1769 by the Zane family. In time, it became a trading center. During the Civil War, it was the headquarters for Virginians who opposed the withdrawal of the South from the Union.

Wheelwright, William (1798-1873), U.S. businessperson and promoter who opened the first steamship line between South America and Europe. He was responsible for building the first railroad and telegraph lines in Argentina, Chile, and Peru. Shipwrecked near Buenos Aires in 1823, he settled in South America, where he recognized the vast commercial possibilities and natural resources. A native of New England, Wheelwright was born in Newburyport, Mass.

Whelk, spiral-shelled sea snail found worldwide. It feeds off other mollusks and fish caught in commercial traps. The northern whelk, found in North Atlantic waters, has a shell about 3 in (8 cm) long. Most are edible.

Whetstone, natural or artificial abrasive stone used for sharpening and grinding tools. Quartz is the abrasive agent that makes whetstones effective.

Whig Party, English and U.S. political party. In England the term was applied in 1679 to Protestant opponents of the English Crown. The Whigs enjoyed a period of dominance c.1714-60, notably under Robert Walpole. Largely out of office when led by Charles James Fox, they were increasingly associated with Nonconformism, mercantile, industrial, and reforming interests. After the Whig ministries of the 2nd earl Grey and Lord Melbourne (1830-41), during which the Reform Bill of 1832 was passed, the Whigs helped form the Liberal Party in the mid-1800s.

The U.S. Whig Party was formed c.1836 from diverse opponents, including the National Republicans, of Andrew Jackson and the Democrats. Its leaders were Henry Clay and Daniel Webster, and a national economic policy was its principal platform. Whig President William Henry Harrison died after one month in office and was succeeded (1841) by John Tyler, who was disowned by the Whigs when he vetoed their tariff and banking bills. Clay, the next Whig candidate, lost the 1844 election. The second Whig president, Zachary Taylor, died in office (1850) after serving 1 year. He was succeeded by a loyal Whig, Millard Fillmore, but the party was by then divided by the issues of slavery and national expansion; the Compromise of 1850 did not last, and Winfield Scott was heavily defeated in the 1852 election. The party never recovered, and many of the Northern Whigs joined the new Republican Party, while the Cotton (Southern) Whigs joined the Democratic Party.

Whip, in U.S. and British politics, party member of a legislative body chosen to enforce party discipline in attendance and voting. The first U.S. whip, Republican congressperson James E. Watson, was appointed in 1899.

Whiplash, cervical sprain, or neck injury. As a result of the head accidently thrown backward then forward, the muscles and ligaments in the head, neck, and shoulder area may become strained. This strain causes pain and stiffness that may be treated with a neck brace, heat, massage, or pain medicine. It happens most often through automobile accidents, although automobile headrests and shoulder harnesses help prevent or lessen the severity of this injury.

Whippet, greyhoundlike dog possessing great speed. It can run as fast as 35 mph (56 kmph). Whippets weigh 18-23 lb (8-10 kg) and stand 18-22 in (44-57 cm) high. They have short coats of tan, gray, or white, and are used for racing and for rabbit hunting.

Whipple, Abraham (1733-1819), naval officer noted for his successes in the American Revolutionary War. In 1779 he captured 11 ships of the British Jamaica fleet. In 1780 he defended Charleston, S.C., but was captured when the city fell.
See also: Revolutionary War in America.

Whipple, William (1730-85), colonial politician from New Hampshire. He was a signer of the Declaration of Independence and a member of the provincial congress (1775) as well as the Continental Congress (1775-76, 1778). During the Revolution he served as a brigadier general. Afterwards he served his state as a member of its assembly (1780-84), a financial receiver (1782-84), and an associate justice of the superior court (1782-85).

Whippoorwill, nocturnal North American bird (*Caprimulgus vociferus*) known for its odd, deliberate call. They are found in southeastern Canada, the United States, Mexico, and Central America. Whippoorwills are about

10 in (25 cm) long with brown spotted feathers. They assist farmers by feeding on crop-damaging insects.

Whirlaway (1938-53), U.S. Thoroughbred winner of the U.S. Triple Crown (1941). Whirlaway was the winner of 32 of his 60 races; established a Kentucky Derby record for speed; and broke earnings records for racehorses when awarded $500,000. Whirlaway was retired in 1943 after a leg injury.

Whirligig *See:* Water beetle.

Whirlpool, rotary current in water. Permanent whirlpools may arise in the ocean from the interactions of the tides. They occur also in streams or rivers where 2 currents meet or the shape of the channel dictates. Short-lived whirlpools may be created by wind.

Whiskey, strong, distilled spirituous liquor made from grain. When from Scotland or Canada, *whiskey* is spelled without an *e* (whisky). The ingredients and preparation vary. In the United States corn and rye are commonly used: 51% corn for bourbon whiskey and 51% rye for rye whiskey. A grain mash is allowed to ferment, then distilled, diluted, and left to age. Bourbon and rye whiskey stand in oak barrels for 4 years. Irish whiskey uses barley, wheat, oats, and rye, and vessels called potstills for the distilling process. Scotch whisky is the finest form: the best types are pure barley malt or grain whiskies. The secret of its flavor is said to be the peat-flavored water of certain Scottish streams. Manufactured commercially since the 16th century, whiskey is one of the most popular of alcoholic beverages.

Whiskey Rebellion (1794), uprising of mainly Scotch-Irish farmers of western Pennsylvania against the federal excise tax imposed on whiskey by U.S. Secretary of the Treasury Alexander Hamilton in 1791. Federal officers were attacked, some were tarred and feathered, and one had his house burned down. Resistance increased when official measures were taken to obtain the tax. At Hamilton's insistence, President George Washington sent in 13,000 militia to suppress the insurgents. They met no resistance, and Washington pardoned 2 ringleaders convicted of treason. Although Federalists claimed a victory—the federal government had demonstrated the power to enforce its law—the party suffered politically.

Whiskey Ring, U.S. scandal exposed in 1875. Distillers in St. Louis, Chicago, Milwaukee, and elsewhere had evaded taxes through payments to Republican Party funds and individuals. The investigations of Secretary of the Treasury Benjamin Bristow led to 237 indictments (including the chief treasury clerk and the president's private secretary), 110 convictions, and the recovery of over $4 million in taxes. Pres. Ulysses S. Grant was cleared personally, but his party was damaged.

Whistle, device used for signaling, consisting of a tube with a sharp edge or lip that makes a sound when air or steam is blown through it.

Whistler, James Abbott McNeill (1834-1903), U.S. artist. Born in Lowell, Mass., in his youth he lived with his family in Russia. Later he attended the U.S. Military Academy at West Point but failed academically after 3 years.

He resumed his art studies in Paris and moved to London, where he lived until his death. His best-known painting is *Arrangement in Gray and Black No. 1: Portrait of the Artist's Mother* (1872), commonly called "Whistler's Mother." Whistler believed paintings should be abstract responses to the artist's imagination.

White, U.S. family including father and son journalists: **William Allen** (1868-1944) and **William Lindsay** (1900-73). Beginning with the editorial *What's the Matter with Kansas?* (1895) that appeared in his own newspaper, the *Gazette,* William Allen became an important voice in national politics. As a reporter for the *Emporia,* another Kansas newspaper, he won the Pulitzer Prize (1923). His autobiography also won the Pulitzer Prize (1947). William Lindsay worked for a number of newspapers, including the *Gazette* and the *Washington Post.* He was a noted correspondent during World War II. He wrote a book about the war entitled *They Were Expendable* (1942).

White *See:* Color.

White, Andrew Dickson (1832-1918), U.S. educator and diplomat. While serving as chairman of the New York State education committee (1864-67), he founded (with Ezra Cornell) Cornell University on nonsectarian, liberal principles. White served as president of the university from 1867 to 1885. *See also:* Cornell, Ezra.

White, Byron Raymond (1917-), U.S. Supreme Court justice, appointed by President John F. Kennedy (1962). The majority of his decisions have leaned more toward conservatism. These include votes against a person's right to privacy, abortion, fair treatment for criminal suspects, and lifting of the criminal status for homosexuality. Some decisions, though, are considered liberal. These include votes for school desegregation and affirmative action. He was educated in his home state of Colorado (where, as an All-American halfback, he was known as "Whizzer"), in England as a Rhodes Scholar, and at Yale University, where he graduated from the Law School (1946). He was assistant attorney general to Robert Kennedy (1961-62) before his appointment to the Supreme Court. *See also:* Supreme Court of the United States.

White, Edward Douglass (1845-1921), ninth chief justice of the U.S. Supreme Court (1910-21). He was appointed associate justice in 1894. White was known for his conservatism, and is best remembered for his anti-trust views, particularly his "rule of reason" opinions in antitrust cases that mandated the dissolution of the Standard Oil and American Tobacco companies (1911). *See also:* Supreme Court of the United States.

White, Edward Higgins, II (1930-67), U.S. astronaut. On June 3, 1965 he was the first U.S. astronaut to leave his craft, taking a 21-minute walk in outer space. He died Jan. 27, 1967 when a fire occurred during a flight simulation at Cape Kennedy, Florida. Other astronauts who died in the tragedy were Virgil Grissom and Roger Chaffee. *See also:* Astronaut.

White, E(lwyn) B(rooks) (1899-1985), U.S. writer noted for his witty, well-crafted essays in *The New Yorker* magazine. His work includes humorous poems, the satire *Is Sex Necessary?* (1929, with James Thurber), and such children's books as *Stuart Little* (1945) and *Charlotte's Web* (1952).

White ant *See:* Termite.

White, Patrick (1912-90), Australian novelist, winner of the 1973 Nobel Prize in literature. His long novels, set mostly in Australia, include *Voss* (1957), *The Vivisector* (1970), *The Eye of the Storm* (1974), and *The Twyborn Affair* (1980).

White, Paul Dudley (1886-1973), U.S. physician, prominent cardiologist. White was an early advocate of diet and exercise for the prevention of heart attacks, and was one of the first to use electrocardiograms for diagnosis of heart disease. His book *Heart Disease* (1931), in its original and numerous revised editions, became a standard text in the field. He became well known as Dwight D. Eisenhower's cardiologist following the president's heart attack. In 1971 White visited the People's Republic of China to study medicine in that country. *See also:* Cardiology.

White, Peregrine (1620-1703), first U.S. colonist born in New England. His parents travelled from England to North America on the *Mayflower*. Peregrine White was born aboard ship in Cape Cod Bay. His mother, Susanna White, became the first New England bride when after the death of Peregrine's father, William White, she married Edward Winslow.

White, Stanford (1853-1906), U.S. architect and painter in the firm of McKim, Mead & White, a renowned architectural firm. His designs include the Washington Arch (1889-95), the Judson Memorial Church (1891), the campus of Bronx Community College (1892-1901), and the Tiffany Building (1906). Born in New York City, White was shot to death by Harry Thaw, the jealous husband of his lover, Evelyn Nesbit. *See also:* Architecture.

White, T(erence) H(anbury) (1906-64), English novelist, noted for *The Once and Future King* (4 vol., 1939-58), a retelling of the legends of King Arthur, and *The Goshawk* (1951).

White, Walter Francis (1893-1955), U.S. author and a secretary of the National Association for the Advancement of Colored People (1931-55). His works include *Rope and Faggot* (1929), an attack on the lynching of blacks, and his autobiography, *A Man Called White* (1948).

White-eye, common name for about 85 species of small birds (family Zosteropidae) of the Old World tropics that have a white ring around each eye. They feed on insects, flowers, and fruits, and are often pests.

Whitefish, important freshwater food fish found in the northern regions of North America, Europe, and Asia. Whitefish are related to the salmon and trout but have small scales and small, toothless mouths. Among the most valuable species are the lake whitefish (*Coregonus clupeaformis*), the lake herring, or cisco (*C. artedii*), and the mountain whitefish (*Prosopium williamsoni*).

Whitefly, any of a family (Aleyrodidae) of small insects related to the scale insects. Some whiteflies are pests, including the greenhouse whitefly and the citrus whitefly. The latter damages citrus plants by sucking sap and encouraging the growth of a mold.

Whitehead, Alfred North (1861-1947), English mathematician and philosopher. He was coauthor with Bertrand Russell of *Principia Mathematica* (3 vol., 1910-13), a major landmark in the philosophy of mathematics. While teaching at Harvard University (from 1924), Whitehead developed a monumental system of metaphysics, most comprehensively expounded in his book *Process and Reality* (1929).
See also: Metaphysics..

Whitehorse (pop. 15,200), capital of the Yukon Territory, located on the west bank of the Yukon River, 111 mi (179 km) north of Skagway, Alaska. Its economy centers on mining, tourism, transportation, and government services. Whitehorse was the site of the Klondike gold rush of 1897-98.
See also: Yukon Territory.

White House, official home of the president of the United States, in Washington, D.C. It was designed in the manner of an 18th-century English gentleman's country house by James Hoban (1792). John Adams was the first president to live there. It was severely damaged by the British in 1814, but rebuilt and extended (and painted white) by 1818. In 1824 Hoban added the semicircular south portico. The grounds were landscaped in 1850 by Andrew Downing. Major renovations, including the addition of the executive office building, were carried out in the early 20th century by the architectural firm of McKim, Mead & White. From 1948 onward the building was extensively rebuilt.
See also: President of the United States.

White House conference, extended meeting called by the U.S. president in which professional experts, community leaders, and other individuals discuss a specified topic. Similar state-level conferences may be mandated by the president. The topic of the first White House conference, called by Theodore Roosevelt in 1908, was conservation. Many of the more than 60 conferences since then have dealt with children or the aging.

White House hostesses, women who act as hostesses for guests of the U.S. president in place of his wife. The role has generally been filled by daughters or other relatives. During the presidency of Thomas Jefferson (a widower), Dolley Madison, wife of James Madison, distinguished herself as a hostess.

Whiteman, Paul (1891-1967), U.S. orchestra leader known as the "King of Jazz." He introduced a personal style called "symphonic jazz." Whiteman encouraged George Gershwin to compose *Rhapsody in Blue* (1924). Born in Denver, Colo., he spent his later years as a popular musical conductor on radio shows.
See also: Jazz.

White Mountains, section of the Appalachian Mountains covering about 1,000 sq mi (2,590 sq km) in northern New Hampshire and western Maine. They include the Presidential, Sandwich, Carter-Moriah, and Franconia

ranges. The highest peak, Mt. Washington (6,288 ft/1,917 m), is in the Presidential Range. Deep canyons, called *notches*, have been carved out by glaciers. The area is noted for its scenic beauty.
See also: Appalachian Mountains.

White paper, British government report or policy statement on an important issue. The documents are called white papers because they are hastily prepared and submitted without the blue cover used for longer documents.

White Sands Missile Range, main U.S. Army missile-testing site located in south-central New Mexico. It was established as White Sands Proving Ground in 1945 and renamed in 1958. The range extends 120 mi (193 km) from north to south and 40 mi (64 km) east to west. The first atomic bomb was exploded there in 1945.
See also: Army, U.S.

White Sea, arm of the Arctic Ocean, called *Beloye More* in the Soviet Union. It is icebound Sept.-June, but heavy shipping is conducted on it during the summer months.
See also: Atlantic Ocean.

White Sulphur Springs (pop. 3,371), health resort in West Virginia known for its mineral springs, located 120 mi (193 km) east of the state capital, Charleston. It developed as a spa in the 1770s. Its President's Cottage served as the summer residence for a series of U.S. presidents.
See also: West Virginia.

White-tailed deer (*Odocoileus virginianus*), North American deer named for its long white tail, raised as a danger signal when the deer is alarmed.

White walnut *See:* Butternut.

Whitman, Marcus (1802-47), U.S. physician and Presbyterian missionary who established settlements in the Pacific Northwest and encouraged emigration to Oregon. In 1847 his settlers brought an epidemic of measles with them that caused the death of many Cayuse children. Thinking the children had been poisoned, the Native Americans killed Whitman.
See also: Westward movement.

Whitman, Walt (1819-92), major U.S. poet. His *Leaves of Grass* (1855; expanded in successive editions), one of the most influential volumes of poetry in U.S. literary history, was praised by Ralph Waldo Emerson and Henry David Thoreau, but did not achieve popular recognition at the time of its publication. Other works include *Drum-Taps* (1865), a collection of Civil War poems; *Democratic Vistas* (1871), prose studies of U.S. democracy; and the autobiographical *Specimen Days* (1882-83). Whitman rejected regular meter and rhyme in favor of flowing free verse and celebrated erotic love, rugged individualism, democracy, and equality.

Whitman Mission National Historic Site, landmark in southeastern Washington state, near Walla Walla, site of the first mission school in the Pacific Northwest. The mission, established 1836 by Marcus Whitman and his wife, Narcissa Prentiss Whitman, was a landmark on the Oregon Trail. *See also:* Whitman, Marcus.

Whitney, Eli (1765-1825), U.S. inventor of the cotton gin (1793) and pioneer of mass production. In 1798 he contracted with the U.S. government to make 10,000 muskets: He took 8 years to fulfill the 2-year contract, but he showed that with unskilled labor muskets could be put together using parts that were precision-made and thus interchangeable, a benefit not only during production but also in later maintenance.
See also: Cotton gin.

Whitney, Gertrude Vanderbilt (1875-1942), U.S. sculptor. She is best known for her monuments commemorating the victims of World War I and for her fountain sculptures. The Whitney Studio Club, which she established in New York City (1918), was a center for U.S. avant-garde art and led to the founding of the Whitney Museum of American Art (1931).

Whitney, John Hay (1904-82), U.S. diplomat and publisher. He was active in Republican politics and served as ambassador to Great Britain (1957-61). He published the New York *Herald Tribune* (1961-67), served as chairperson of the *International Herald Tribune* (from 1967), and published several prominent U.S. magazines.

Whittier, John Greenleaf (1807-92), U.S. poet born in Haverhill, Mass., to a Quaker family. The themes of his work were the injustice of slavery and the beauty of the New England countryside. He served in the state legislature and was active in the antislavery movement. His political poem, "Ichabod" (1850), attacked Daniel Webster for his role in passing the Compromise of 1850. He attacked what he saw as hypocrisy in a nation that espoused freedom but allowed slavery.

WHO *See:* World Health Organization.

Whooping cough, or pertussis, contagious bacterial disease of children causing upper respiratory symptoms, with a characteristic whoop or inspiratory noise due to inflammation of the larynx. Whooping cough is a serious disease that can lead to pneumonia, brain damage, convulsions, and collapse of the lungs. Vaccination is widely practiced to prevent it.

Whooping crane (*Grus americana*), white wading bird with a red cap on its head. The tallest bird in North America, it reaches a height of about 5 ft (1.5 m). Once widespread, whooping cranes have for several decades been close to extinction and have been preserved only by determined conservation measures.

Wichita (pop. 311,700), city in Kansas, located on the Chisholm Trail. Cowboys used to bring their herds to Wichita on their way to Texas markets. Cattle, along with the Santa Fe Railroad, made this city an important location during 19th-century westward expansion. Today there is still a strong meat industry as well as a large aviation and oil industry. McConnell Air Force Base is located here as well as the domed Century II cultural-convention center and Wichita State University. The city was founded as a trading post

(1864) where European-American settlers traded with the Wichita tribespeople. The legendary western law man Wyatt Earp worked in Wichita in the 1870s.
See also: Kansas.

Wichita Falls (pop. 122,378), city in Texas, located on the Wichita River. With the discovery of oil (1910) near this north-central city, Wichita Falls began to boom. It was founded just 28 years previously. Today it is an oil industry center, the home of North Texas Oil and Gas Association. Manufacturers of electronic components, parts for jet airplanes, jeans, plastic products, and glass also are located here. Sheppard Air Force Base is situated in Wichita Falls.
See also: Texas.

Wicker, material woven from flexible plant fiber or willow twigs. Furniture, especially in hot climates, has been made from wicker since the days of ancient Egypt. Wicker has been appreciated as a durable as well as comfortable and attractive material. Bamboo, rattan, reed, and cane are natural plant fibers used for wicker. Modern synthetic wickers have been developed from materials such as treated twisted paper fibers.

Wiclif, John *See:* Wycliffe, John.

Widgeon *See:* Wigeon.

Wien *See:* Vienna.

Wiener, Norbert (1894-1964), U.S. mathematician noted for his contributions to computer science. He developed the theory of cybernetics. His major book is *Cybernetics: Or Control and Communication in the Animal and the Machine* (1948).
See also: Cybernetics.

Wiesbaden (pop. 261,800), city in southwestern Germany, capital of the German state of Hesse. The word *wiesbaden* translates as "baths on the meadows," and this resort, located in a valley of the Taunus Mountains, is known for its hot springs. The Romans enjoyed this area since the 1st century B.C. and considered it a spa—a resort where mineral springs are often found. People today still come to Wiesbaden for its mineral springs. Tourism is the economic base of the city.
See also: Germany.

Wiesel, Elie (1928-), Romanian-born U.S. novelist. In 1944, with other Jews, he and his family were sent to Auschwitz, where his parents and sister died. He then was sent to Buchenwald, which was liberated in 1945. Wiesel later became the leading spokesperson for survivors of Nazi concentration camps. His autobiographical novel, *Night* (1958), recaptures the horrors he encountered. Other novels include *The Jews of Silence* (1966), *Souls on Fire* (1972), *The Testament* (1980), and *The Fifth Son* (1984). He won the Nobel Peace Prize in 1986.
See also: Concentration camp; Holocaust.

Wiesel, Torsten Nils (1924-), Swedish neurobiologist who shared the 1981 Nobel Prize in physiology or medicine for his research on the brain's processing of visual information.
See also: Brain.

Wiesenthal, Simon (1908-), Austrian hunter of Nazi war criminals. Having lost a large number of relatives in Nazi concentration camps during World War II, he established the Jewish Documentation Center in Vienna, Austria, through which he located more than 1,000 former Nazis accused of war crimes, including Adolf Eichmann.
See also: Holocaust.

Wig, covering for the head of real or artificial hair, worn as a cosmetic device, as a mark of rank or office, as a disguise, or for theatrical portrayals. Known since ancient times, wigs became fashionable in 17th- and 18th-century Europe, when elaborate headpieces for women and full, curled wigs for men came into wide use. The latter are still worn in British law courts. In the 1960s wigs came back into fashion for women. Small hairpieces called *toupees* are worn to conceal baldness.

Wigeon, duck in the family Anatidae. Wigeons found in the United States (*Anas americana*) and those found in northern Europe (*A. penelope*) are the same size, about 19 in (48 cm) long. The U.S. wigeon, also called the *baldpate,* is known for its call, the sound *whew* repeated a number of times. These ducks feed on water plants, using their flat, broad bills. The male heads and throats are marked with white.

Wiggin, Kate Douglas (1856-1923), U.S. author and educator. She pioneered kindergarten classes by organizing the first one on the West Coast in San Francisco (1878). *Rebecca of Sunnybrook Farm* (1903), a book about a young girl's experiences after her father's death, was her most popular novel. She also wrote other children's fiction: *The Birds' Christmas Carol* (1887) and *Mother Carey's Chickens* (1911).
See also: Kindergarten.

Wight, Isle of, diamond-shaped island, 147 sq mi (381 sq km), off the southern coast of England. Its scenery and mild climate make it a popular resort area. Cowes, the chief port, is a well-known yachting center.

Wigner, Eugene Paul (1902-95), Hungarian-born U.S. physicist who worked with Enrico Fermi to produce the first nuclear chain reaction in 1942. Wigner shared the Nobel Prize in physics with J. Hans Jensen and Maria Goeppert in 1963. He was professor of mathematical physics at Princeton University.
See also: Nuclear energy.

Wigwam, kind of dwelling used by Algonquian-speaking Native Americans in the eastern part of North America. Wigwams are usually oval or round and are covered with bark. The term is sometimes used to describe any Native American home, including the conical tepee and wickiup.

Wilberforce, Samuel (1805-73), English priest of the Anglican church. He held important church offices, including bishop of Oxford, dean of Westminster, and chaplain of the House of Lords. Wilberforce mediated a dispute between the Anglo-Catholic and the Evangelical factions of the church. Politically, he fought for prison reform and measures to prevent the abuse of women and children.
See also: Anglicans.

Wilbur, Richard (1921-), U.S. poet and essayist. He won a Pulitzer Prize in poetry for *Things of This World* (1957) and *New and Collected Poems* (1989). In 1987 he received an appointment as poet laureate of the United States.

Wild barley, plant in the grass family. One kind of wild barley, squirreltail (*Hordeum jubatum*), is named because of its prickly, bearded appearance. The seeds of this grass not only spread quickly and destroy other plants, they burrow through to the hide of woolly sheep and cause irritation. In addition the rest of the plant, when chewed, often causes sheep to choke.

Wild canary *See:* Goldfinch.

Wild carrot, also called Queen Anne's lace, plant (*Daucus carota*) in the parsley family. This relative of the edible carrot has a root that looks like the domesticated carrot, but it is inedible. It displays a cluster of lacy white flowers on top of a tall, thin green stalk that grows to about 3 ft (91 cm) high. It is usually a biennial plant—one that lives for 2 years.

Wildcat, name given generally to any small or medium-sized wild cat, such as the Canada lynx (*Lynx canadensis*) and bobcat (*L. rufus*), which are found in North America. The true wildcat (*Felis silvestris*) is a powerful, vicious animal found in Europe and Africa. Wildcats are longer than common house cats and have shorter tails. One type of wildcat, the Egyptian cat, is probably the ancestor of the modern domestic cat.

Wildcat bank, any of numerous unsound state-chartered U.S. banks that issued paper money (wildcat currency) without having adequate assets (1830-63). They proliferated after Pres. Andrew Jackson dismantled the Second Bank of the United States. Many collapsed after Jackson, alarmed by the inflation caused by the wildcat banks, ordered government agents to accept only gold or silver in payment for public lands. The abrupt failures of the wildcat banks resulted in the 1837 financial panic.

Wilde, Oscar (1854-1900), Irish author. He achieved celebrity with the novel *The Picture of Dorian Gray* (1891) and such witty society comedies as *Lady Windermere's Fan* (1892), *An Ideal Husband* (1895), and his masterpiece, *The Importance of Being Earnest* (1895).

Wildebeest *See:* Gnu.

Wilder, Billy (1906-), Austrian-born U.S. screenwriter and film director. Wilder, known for his humorous treatment of serious subject matter, often dealt with topics that had not previously been considered for entertainment purposes, including alcoholism in *The Lost Weekend* (Academy Award; 1945), a prisoner-of-war camp in *Stalag 17* (1953), the Cold War in *One, Two, Three* (1961), and prostitution in *Irma La Douce* (1963). Other works include *Double Indemnity* (1944), *Sunset Boulevard* (Academy Award; 1950), *Some Like It Hot* (1959), *The Apartment* (Academy Award; 1960), and *Fedora* (1979).

Wilder, Laura Ingalls (1867-1957), U.S. children's author best known for her series of 9 popular autobiographical novels, including *Little House on the Prairie* (1935), depicting pioneer life in the Midwest.

Wilder, Thornton Niven (1897-1975), U.S. novelist and playwright. His novels include *The Bridge of San Luis Rey* (1927; Pulitzer Prize) and *The Ides of March* (1948). Wilder experimented with stylized techniques in plays such as *Our Town* (1938; Pulitzer Prize), *The Skin of Our Teeth* (1942; Pulitzer Prize), and *The Matchmaker* (1954).

Wilderness, Battle of the, opening engagement—fought May 5-6, 1864, in central Virginia, 10 mi (16 km) west of Fredericksburg—of the Wilderness Campaign in the U.S. Civil War. Gen. Ulysses S. Grant's 118,000-man Army of the Potomac, advancing to annihilate the Confederate Army in open battle, was met and held in heavily wooded country by 60,000 men under Gen. Robert E. Lee. Both sides suffered heavy losses. Grant then turned to attack Spotsylvania Courthouse (May 8-19). Fighting continued until early June 1864.
See also: Civil War, U.S.

Wilderness Road, early U.S. pioneer route. It ran from Virginia through the Cumberland Gap into the Ohio Valley. Laid out in 1775 by Daniel Boone, it was the main route west until 1840. It became part of U.S. 25 (the Dixie Highway) in 1926, and is now a section of U.S. Route 1.
See also: Pioneer life in America.

Wildlife conservation, organized supervision of the environment that protects the native plant and animal life. Without good environmental management many species would become extinct (killed off) or seriously endangered (greatly diminished in number). Human activities have caused the decline of native species, including hunting and clearing land for crops. Plant life has become endangered through land development and industrial pollution. U.S. National Parks, first developed by President Theodore Roosevelt, protect wilderness areas. The International Union for the Conservation of Nature and Natural Resources (IUCN) has created the Red Data Book, a publication that reports the status of endangered species worldwide. Conservation of plants and animals is important for many reasons: their beauty, their importance in the ecological balance of an area, their scientific and medical value, their economic value to an area.
See also: Endangered species.

Wild rice (*Zizania aquatica*), aquatic plant of the grass family, native to the lakes and streams of North America; also, the cereal grain harvested from the plant. Wild rice is not related to rice. The grain has long been eaten by Native Americans and is now planted to feed wildfowl.

Wilhelm, name of 2 German emperors: **Wilhelm I** (1797-1888) and **Wilhelm II** (1859-1941). The elder became the first emperor of modern Germany—crowned king of Prussia and Wilhelm I (1861)— then kaiser of Germany (1871). With the help of the prime minister, Otto von Bismarck, Germany was unified into an empire with the success of the Franco-Prussian Wars (1870-71). The younger was the grandson of Wilhelm I and the last emperor (kaiser) of Germany. Not only did he make Germany prosperous through growth in manufacturing, trade, and colonization of parts of Africa and the Pacific, he also developed a powerful military force. Expansion and his disruption of an alliance with Russia resulted in World War I (1914-18).

With German defeat eminent, Wilhelm II moved to the neutral Netherlands where he lived out the rest of his days in exile.
See also: Germany.

Wilhelmina (1880-1962), Queen of the Netherlands (1890-1948), having acceded to the throne after the death of her father, King William III. In 1940 she fled to London to escape the German invasion, and from there directed her country's forces against Germany and Japan. Wilhelmina returned home at the end of the war (1945), and 3 years later turned the throne over to her daughter, Juliana.
See also: Netherlands.

Wilkes, Charles (1798-1877), U.S. naval officer. He led a U.S. Navy expedition that identified Antarctica as a continent. He also seized the British ship *Trent* off Cuba (1861) to remove 2 Confederate agents from it—an action that almost caused Britain to support the South in the Civil War (1861-65). His career waned afterwards, and he completed his career writing reports of his explorations.
See also: Antarctica.

Wilkes-Barre (pop. 51,551), city in northeastern Pennsylvania in the Wyoming valley along the Susquehanna River. The area was founded by colonists from Connecticut (1769), suffered near extinction twice because of war in the 19th century, then grew because of the coal industry. The importance of the coal industry lessened in the 1930s and since then other industries have developed an economic base, including publishing, electronics, data processing, and aircraft and military missile parts production. In addition to rebuilding after two fires (1769), the city again suffered severe damage during a storm and subsequent flood (1972).
See also: Pennsylvania.

Wilkins, Maurice Hugh Frederick (1916-   ), British biophysicist. He shared the 1962 Nobel Prize in physiology or medicine with biologists James D. Watson of the United States and Francis H.C. Crick of Great Britain. His research on deoxyribonucleic acid (DNA) led to the model of the molecular structure of DNA. Wilkins also worked on the development of the atomic bomb as part of the Manhattan Project in World War II.
See also: DNA.

Wilkins, Roy (1901-81), U.S. civil rights leader and executive secretary of the National Association for the Advancement of Colored People (NAACP) from 1955 to 1970. Opposed to white supremacy and black separatism, he did much to bring about school desegregation and the 1964 Civil Rights Act.
See also: Civil rights.

Will, legal document by which a person (the testator) gives instructions concerning the disposal of his or her property (bequest, or legacy) after death. Wills are generally prepared by lawyers. Under most jurisdictions a will must be attested in order to be legally valid: Independent witnesses who have nothing to gain under the will must attest that the signature on the will is in fact that of the testator. Wills may be revoked during the life of the testator or altered by codicils. Wills generally appoint executors to administer the estate of the deceased and carry out his or her instructions. When a person dies intestate (without making a will), the property is normally divided among the next of kin.

Willamette River, river located in west-central Oregon, between the Cascade and Coast mountains. It flows northward and empties into the Columbia River near Portland. An annual rainfall of 40 in (1,102 mm) makes the Willamette Valley the richest farming area in Oregon.

Willard, Emma Hart (1787-1870), first U.S. woman to publicly advocate higher education for women. Along with her husband, John Willard, she established a boarding school for girls in Middlebury, Vt. The school was moved to Troy, N.Y., and became known as the Emma Willard School. In 1854 she represented the United States at the World's Educational Convention in London.
See also: Women's movements.

Willard, Frances Elizabeth Caroline (1838-98), U.S. educator, temperance leader, and social reformer. She served as president of the Woman's Christian Temperance Union (WCTU) from 1879. She also worked for woman suffrage and helped found the Prohibition Party (1882).

Willemstad (pop. 100,000), city on the Caribbean island of Curaçao, capital of the Netherlands Antilles. Arawak tribes inhabited this area before Dutch settlers arrived (1634). The island contains the Western Hemisphere's oldest Jewish cemetery (1659) and synagogue (1732). Its harbor is used for crude oil shipment. Oil refinement as well as banking are important to the economic base of Willemstad.

Willet, bird in the sandpiper family. This gray- to white-colored shore bird measures about 16 in (40 cm) long. It has a long, thin bill and long, thin legs. It also is known for its loud call. The eastern willet (*Catoptrophorus semipalmatus*) and the western willet (*C. semipalmatus inornatus*) live in both North and South America.

William, 4 kings of England. **William I**, or **William the Conqueror** (1027?-1087), duke of Normandy from 1035, became the first Norman king in 1066 by defeating Harold in the Battle of Hastings; he suppressed all opposition by 1071. William I was a harsh but capable ruler, reorganizing England's military and land-holding systems, building many castles, and creating a strong feudal government. The Domesday Book, a survey of England, was compiled by his order (1085). His son, **William II** or **Rufus** (c.1056-1100), succeeded him in 1087. Autocratic and brutal, William II put down a rebellion by his own barons in 1088 and invaded Scotland in 1097. He quarreled with St. Anselm over the independence of the Church. He was killed (probably deliberately) by an arrow while hunting. He was succeeded by his brother, Henry I. **William III**, or **William of Orange** (1650-1702), was *stadholder* (ruler) of Holland (1672-1702) and king of England (1689-1702). He married Mary, Protestant daughter of the Roman Catholic king of England, in 1677. English Protestants, unhappy with James II, invited William to invade England, which resulted in the so-called Glorious Revolution (1688). William became coruler of England with his wife after they

accepted the Bill of Rights, which reduced their power (1689). William ruled alone after Mary's death (1694) and was succeeded by Queen Anne. **William IV** (1765-1837) succeeded his brother George IV in 1830. He exercised little political influence and was succeeded by his niece Victoria.
See also: United Kingdom.

William I (1772-1843), king of the Netherlands (1815-40) and son of William V, Prince of Orange and last governor of the Dutch Republic. After the French invaded the Dutch Republic and ousted William V in 1795, William lived in England and Prussia (northern Germany) until 1812. In 1813 the Dutch successfully rebelled against French rule, and in 1815 William was named king of the Netherlands, which then included Belgium, Liege, and the Grand Duchy of Luxembourg. In 1830 the Belgians demanded independence from the Netherlands, but William I refused to accede to the separation. Due in part to public disapproval of his handling of the Belgium question, William I abdicated in 1840.
See also: Netherlands.

William and Mary, College of, coeducational, state university in Williamsburg, Va. Founded in 1693, it is the second-oldest university in the United States. William and Mary was the first college to offer law training and have separate schools of modern language and modern history. The honorary scholastic society Phi Beta Kappa was founded at the university (1776). Famous graduates include Thomas Jefferson and James Monroe.

William I, prince of Orange (1533-84), founder of the present dynasty of the Netherlands. Born in Germany, he supported the Spanish rule of the Netherlands, first under Charles V and then Philip II, until 1568. In that year the Protestant William led a revolt against the Catholic Philip and Spain's policies of religious and political repression in the Netherlands. He worked to unite all of the provinces of the Netherlands, and in 1579 the Dutch Republic consisting of 7 provinces was formed. He was outlawed by Philip II and subsequently assassinated.
See also: Netherlands.

William of Ockham (c.1285-1349), also spelled *Occam,* English philosopher, member of the Franciscan order. Like other great thinkers of the Middle Ages, he was a Scholastic—one who uses reason to understand faith. He broke, though, with other great Scholastics—especially the church-supported St. Thomas Aquinas. Ockham did not believe that reason could deepen understanding of faith. He did advance ideas associated with modern scientific thought in that he believed conclusions should be drawn from things observed by the senses and reasoned through logic. The saying "less is more" describes Ockham's Razor—the belief that a problem should be stated as simply as possible and supported with appropriate evidence. Pope John XXII brought charges of false theological teaching, or heresy, to William of Ockham (1324), which resulted in Ockham's self-imposed exile to Bavaria (1328).
See also: Scholasticism.

Williams, Daniel Hale (1856-1931), African-American surgeon and pioneer in the field of heart surgery. In 1893 he repaired a tear in the pericardium of a patient who then lived for more than 20 years. He founded the first interracial hospital and training school for black nurses and interns, Provident Hospital in Chicago.

Williams, Emlyn (1905-87), Welsh actor and playwright, noted for his semiautobiographical play *The Corn is Green* (1938) and for his concert readings from the works of Dylan Thomas and Charles Dickens. He also wrote *Night Must Fall* (1935).

Williams, Roger (c.1603-83), church leader and founder of the colony of Rhode Island. He came to North America (1631) because of disagreements with the doctrine of the Church of England. His disagreement with the Church became a problem for him in Salem, Mass., also. Because of this he founded Rhode Island (1636) with the help of land granted to him by the Narragansett Native American tribe. In Rhode Island he practiced the belief of religious freedom and separation of church and state—concepts later adopted by the writers of the Constitution. Williams had to journey to England several times to fight for leadership in his colony (1643, 1651). His first trip resulted in his most famous publication, *The Bloudy Tenent of Persecution* (1644). He was president of Rhode Island colony (1654-57).

Williams, Roy Lee (1915-89), U.S. labor leader, president of the International Brotherhood of Teamsters, 1981-83. A truckdriver, Williams became active in the Teamsters organization as business agent in Wichita, Kans. (1948), president of Joint Council 56 (1953-81), and director of the Central Conference (1976). He was an effective bargainer for the membership, but his connections with organized crime forced his resignation. Williams was indicted for criminal offenses 4 times, and finally convicted (1982) for attempted bribery of a U.S. senator. His 55-year prison sentence was reduced to 10 years, of which he served 3 years (1985-88) before being released because of poor health and his willingness to testify in federal crime cases. *See also:* Teamsters Union; Unions, labor.

Williams, Shirley (1930-   ), English political leader. She served as education minister in the Labour government (1976-79), then broke with the party because of its leftward drift; she helped form the Social Democratic Party (SDP) in 1981. In that year she became the first SDP member elected to Parliament.

Williams, Ted (Theodore Samuel Williams; 1918-   ), U.S. baseball player. Considered one of the greatest hitters in baseball history, he was the last major leaguer to achieve a .400 season batting average (.406 in 1941), finishing with a .344 career average. Williams, an outfielder, led the American League in hitting 6 times (1941, 42, 47, 48, 57, 58) and won the Most Valuable Player award twice (1946, 49). He played in the major leagues for the Boston Red Sox (1939-42; 1946-51; 1954-60) and was inducted into the National Baseball Hall of Fame in 1966.

Williams, Tennessee (Thomas Lanier Williams; 1911-83), U.S. playwright. His emotionally intense plays are full of brilliant, poetic dialogue and deal with the effects of failure, loneliness, and futile obsessions on human beings. His first success, *The Glass Menagerie* (1945), was followed by *A Streetcar Named Desire* (1947) and *Cat on a Hot Tin Roof* (1955), both of which received Pulitzer Prizes. Other plays include *Sweet Bird of Youth* (1959) and *The Night of the Iguana* (1961).

Williams, William (1731-1811), colonial politician from Connecticut, a signer of the Declaration of Independence. He served as delegate to the Continental Congress (1776-78); the Congress of Confederation (1783-84), during which time the Articles of Confederation were developed; and the convention for the ratification of the Constitution (1788).

Williams, William Carlos (1883-1963), U.S. poet. Williams was a practicing doctor and specialized in the care of children for over 40 years. He is best known for the long, reflective poem *Paterson* (1946-58) and *Pictures from Breughel* (1963), which won a Pulitzer Prize. He also wrote plays, fiction, and essays, including *In the American Grain* (1925), a study of the American character. Williams wrote hard, clear free verse emphasizing the importance of the subject matter over literary form.

Williamsburg (pop. 9,870), restored colonial city in southeastern Virginia on the James River. The city, which was the capital of Virginia from 1699 to 1779, contains over 500 original or reconstructed 18th-century buildings, including the governor's palace and the capitol, in which the Virginia assembly met. Much of the restoration work, from 1926 onward, was undertaken by the philanthropist John D. Rockefeller, Jr. Williamsburg is the site of William and Mary College, founded in 1693.
See also: Virginia.

Williamson, Hugh (1735-1819), U.S. scientist, doctor, and politician of the American Revolutionary period. A doctor in Philadelphia, Williamson actually assisted in some of Benjamin Franklin's experiments in electricity. Elected to the North Carolina legislature (1782), he served in the Congress of the Confederation (1782-85, 1787-89), and was a North Carolina delegate to the Constitutional Convention (1787) and a signer of the Constitution. After 2 terms in the U.S. House of Representatives (1789-93), he retired from politics to pursue science and writing.

William the Conqueror *See:* William.

Willkie, Wendell Lewis (1892-1944), U.S. political leader. A lawyer, he became president of a giant utility company and led business opposition to the New Deal. A Democrat until the mid-1930s, he was the Republican presidential candidate in 1940, gaining a large popular vote but losing to Franklin D. Roosevelt. His book *One World* (1943) was a plea for international cooperation.

Will-o'-the-wisp, or jack-o-lantern, blue light caused by the natural combustion of gas from decaying matter. It is sometimes visible at night over marshes and graveyards. Also called *ignis fatuus* ("foolish fire"), it was once believed to be an evil spirit that enticed travellers with its elusive glow.

Willow, common name for about 300 species of trees of the genus *Salix*, which occur from the tropics to the Arctic. The leaves are generally swordlike, and male and female catkins are borne on separate plants. The willows of the temperate zone are large, but the dwarf willow, found beyond the tree lines of the Arctic, grows to only about 6 in (15.2 cm). The long, pliable twigs of some species are cut regularly for use in making wicker baskets and furniture. Other species are used for tannins or for their light and durable wood. The ornamental weeping willow is a native of China and southwest Asia.

Willow herb *See:* Fireweed.

Wills, Helen Newington (1906-97), U.S. tennis player. Known for her strength and grace, she won 7 U.S. Open singles titles (1923-25, 27-29, 31), 8 Wimbledon championships (1927-30, 32, 33, 35, 38), and 4 French Open titles (1928-30, 32).

Wilmington (pop. 70,195), largest city in Delaware, seat of New Castle County, in the northern part of the state on the Delaware River. Wilmington, a center of the chemical industry, is the home of E. I. du Pont de Nemours & Co., one of the largest producers of chemicals, plastics, and synthetic fibers and dyes in the United States. Other industries produce leather, textiles, machinery, and paper. The city was first settled in 1638 by Swedish immigrants. The settlement later passed to the Dutch, then to the English, receiving its name in 1739, when it was incorporated as a borough. The Du Pont powder mill was established in 1802.
See also: Delaware.

Wilmot Proviso, congressional proposal to prohibit the extension of slavery into newly acquired U.S. territories. In 1846 President James K. Polk asked Congress to appropriate $2 million for Mexico to settle territorial claims. The Wilmot Proviso was the condition some members of Congress tried to impose in return for this payment. The proposal was defeated by the Senate, and the conflict was not resolved until 1862, when Congress outlawed slavery in all U.S. territories.
See also: Slavery.

Wilson, Angus (1913-91), English novelist and short-story writer who satirizes English class attitudes and social life. His novels include *Hemlock and After* (1952), *Anglo-Saxon Attitudes* (1956), *No Laughing Matter* (1967), and *Setting the World on Fire* (1980).

Wilson, Edmund (1895-1972), U.S. critic and writer who investigated the historical, sociological, and psychological background to literature. His prolific imaginative and critical output includes *Axel's Castle* (1931), a study of symbolism; *To the Finland Station* (1940), on the intellectual sources of the Russian Revolution; *The Wound and the Bow* (1941), on neurosis and literature; the explosive novel *Memoirs of Hecate County* (1949); and *Patriotic Gore* (1962), a study of Civil War literature.

Wilson, Harold (1916-95), prime minister of Great Britain (1964-70, 1974-76). An Oxford economist, he entered Parliament in 1945, became president of the Board of Trade in 1947, and became leader of the Labour Party in 1963. Identified initially with the left wing and known for his tactical skill, he preserved party unity during a period of economic crisis and division over the Common Market. He resigned in 1976 and was knighted that same year. He was named a baron in 1983.
See also: United Kingdom.

Wilson, Henry (1812-75), U.S. senator from Massachusetts (1855-73), a founder of the Republican Party. He was chairperson of the Military Affairs Committee during the Civil War. Wilson devoted his life to the issue of the emancipation of slaves. He served as vice president (1873-75) in the second term of President Ulysses S. Grant.

Wilson, James (1742-98), Scottish-born signer of both the Declaration of Independence and the U.S. Constitution. He believed in a strong national government whose authority was rooted in the will of the people. Wilson served in the Congress of the Confederation (1783, 1785, 1786) and was appointed to the U.S. Supreme Court in 1789.

Wilson, Lanford (1937-   ), U.S. playwright. Known for his realistic themes, Wilson creates dramatic dialogue by combining, and at times over-lapping, conversation and monologue. He was awarded the Pulitzer Prize in 1980 for *Talley's Folly* (1979), a romantic story set in World War II Missouri; the plot deals with the hero's coming to grips with the victimization of his family by anti-Semites. Other works include *The Hot l Baltimore* (1973), *Angels Fall* (1982), and *Burn This* (1987).

Wilson, Woodrow (1856-1924), 28th president of the United States. Wilson's high intellectual qualifications and idealistic fervor made him a forceful leader. Wilson is considered one of the most successful U.S. presidents. His triumphs as a war leader during World War I and his eloquence in the cause of freedom made him the idol of millions around the world. His successes form a sharp contrast to his failure to achieve a League of Nations—one of the deepest personal tragedies in U.S. politics.

Early life. Thomas Woodrow Wilson (he later dropped the first name) was born Dec. 29, 1856, in Staunton, Va. He attended Davidson College in North Carolina, then Princeton University, from which he graduated in 1879. After law school and a brief, unsuccessful law practice, he attended graduate school at Johns Hopkins University. In 1885 Wilson married Ellen Louise Axson; they had three children. Mrs. Wilson died in Aug. 1914. In 1915 Wilson married Edith Bolling Galt, a widow.

From education to politics. Wilson taught at Bryn Mawr (1885-88), Wesleyan University (1888-90), and Princeton (1890-1910), and was elected president of Princeton University in 1902. In 1910 he was elected governor of New Jersey (1911-13). In 1912 Wilson won the Democratic Party's

Woodrow Wilson

28th president of the United States

Born:	Staunton, Va.; Dec. 29, 1856.
Term:	Mar. 1913-Mar. 1921.
Vice president:	Thomas R. Marshall.
Political party:	Democratic.
Spouses:	Ellen Louise Axson Wilson; Edith Bolling Galt Wilson.
Children:	3.
Died:	Washington, D.C.; Feb. 3, 1924.

nomination and presidential election, aided by the Republicans' split between William Howard Taft and Theodore Roosevelt.

President. In the first years of his presidency, Wilson enjoyed the support of a Democratic-controlled Congress, which led to a remarkable succession of legislative achievements, including the Underwood Tariff Act, which made significant reductions in customs duties; a graduated income tax; and the Federal Reserve Act, which overhauled the nation's banking and credit system and placed it under public control. The Clayton Antitrust Act strengthened the government's power against monopolies and exempted unions from the antitrust law; the Federal Trade Commission (FTC) was established to control "unfair business practices"; and the Adamson Act established an eight-hour work day for railroad employees, while the Child-Labor Act limited children's work hours.

In foreign affairs the United States under Wilson took control of Nicaragua's financial and foreign affairs, and U.S. troops intervened in Mexico, Haiti, and the Dominican Republic. After World War I broke out in 1914, Wilson declared the United States neutral. In 1916 he was reelected by a narrow margin with the slogan, "He kept us out of war." But after Germany sank four U.S. ships, Wilson asked Congress to declare war in Apr. 1917.

Still, Wilson pushed for peace. On Jan. 8, 1918, he proposed a basis for peace negotiations—his famous "Fourteen Points." Germany finally agreed to them and, on Nov. 11, 1918, the armistice ending the war was signed.

In 1919 Wilson attended the Versailles Peace Conference. He believed that the only hope for a lasting peace lay in a League of Nations. Back home, he campaigned hard for its establishment.

In Oct. 1919 Wilson was permanently invalided by a stroke. Yet, aided by his wife and cabinet members, he retained executive powers.

The Senate rejected the treaty that would have established the League of Nations—a bitter failure for Wilson. He did not run for reelection in 1920.

Retirement. Wilson left the presidency a sick and saddened man; winning the 1919 Nobel Peace Prize was little consolation to him. He died in Washington, D.C., on Feb. 3, 1924.

Wilson cloud chamber, instrument that makes radiation visible and measurable. This device is made out of a container, a piston, and water-concentrated gas. It works on the same principle as natural cloud formation—that is, when more than 100% humidity occurs and water cools, water droplets become apparent either in the form of a cloud in the sky or, in the case of the Wilson cloud chamber, as tracks of charged particles. Particles with an electric charge within the chamber join with molecules of the cooled gas to form the visible tracks. Alpha and beta rays emitted from radioactive materials form these visible streaks.
See also: Radiation.

Wilt, condition where plants droop and wither due to lack of water in their cells. This can be caused by lack of available moisture, physiological disorders, or fungi or bacteria damaging water-conducting tissues inside roots or stems.

Wimbledon *See:* Tennis.

Winch, device facilitating the hoisting or hauling of loads. It comprises a rotatable drum around which is wound a rope or cable attached to the load. The drum is turned by means of a hand-operated crank or a motor.

Winchester (pop. 93,700), English town, site of the famous 14th-century Winchester Cathedral, the longest church (556 ft/169 m) in England. During the reign of Alfred the Great (871-899) Winchester became a center of learning. It was the seat of government for the Danish king Canute (1016-35). Today Winchester is a prosperous religious, service, and light industry center.

Winckelmann, Johann Joachim (1717-68), German scholar, founder of archeology and art history. He demonstrated that art can reveal the history of a culture just as writing does. As a youngster he studied Greek and Latin in order to read Homer and other classical writers. His principal work, *The History of Ancient Art* (1764), is still used by art historians.
See also: Archeology.

Wind, body of air moving in relation to the earth's surface. The world's major wind systems are set up to counter the equal heating of the earth's surface and are modified by the rotation of the earth.

Wind Cave National Park, area of 28,292 acres (11,449 hectares) in the Black Hills in southwestern South Dakota. Established in 1903, it surrounds a cavern with alternating air current and unusual crystal formations.

Wind chill, index that determines the relative temperature, based on the effects of wind on exposed human flesh. An increase in wind speed increases the rate at which a person becomes chilled. Thus, the temperature will seem to be colder when there is wind than when there is not. Wind chill measurements are not exact, but they do reflect more how a person feels the cold than a thermometer reading of temperature alone.

Windermere, lake in the northwestern Cumbria section of England, better known as the Lake District. This, the largest lake in England, measures 10.5 mi (16.9 km) long and 1 mi (1.6 km) at its widest point, with a total area of 5.69 sq mi (14.7 sq km). It is a popular resort area described in the poetry of the 19th-century English romantic poets William Wordsworth and Samuel Coleridge, among others.

Windhoek (pop. 114,500), capital and largest city of Namibia, as well as its commercial, administrative, and communications center. Windhoek was originally called Aigams ("hot water")—a reference to the area's hot springs. In the late 1880s Germany occupied the city, but it was taken over by South African forces in World War I. Until Namibia's independence in 1990, the white government of South Africa ruled Namibia, and apartheid was strictly enforced. While the population of Windhoek is mostly black, the whites controlled the politics and economy of the city until 1990.
See also: Namibia.

Wind instrument, any of the musical instruments whose sound is produced by blowing air into a tube, causing a vibration within it. In *woodwind* instruments the vibration is made either by blowing across or into a specially shaped mouthpiece, as with the flute, piccolo, recorder, and flageolet, or by blowing against a single or double reed, as in the clarinet, saxophone, oboe, English horn, and bassoon. The pitch is altered by opening and closing holes set into the tube. In *brass* instruments the vibration is made by the player's lips on the mouthpiece. The bugle and various types of posthorn have a single, unbroken tube. The cornet, French horn, trumpet, and tuba have valves to vary the effective tube length and increase the range of notes; the trombone has a slide mechanism for the same purpose.

Windlass, compound machine made from a rope or chain wound around a cylinder shape attached to a crank. This wheel and axle design is commonly used to lift water from wells. A container attached to the end of the rope or chain collects the well water. Human power or machine power hoists up the container and line.

Windmill, machine that performs work by harnessing wind power. In the traditional windmill the power applied to a horizontal shaft by 4 large radiating sails is transmitted to milling or pumping machinery housed in a sizable supporting structure. The windmill's modern counterpart is the wind turbine, often seen in rural areas. Here a multibladed turbine wheel mounted on a steel derrick or mast and pointed into the wind by a fantail drives a pump or electric generator.

Window, building openings for air and light. Some windows open inward or outward from the opening, and these are called *casement* or *hinged* windows. Many windows are double-hung and are opened by lifting them up or pushing them down, and these are called *double-hung* windows. Double-hung windows were a Dutch invention (1800s). The arrangement of windows—known as *fenestration*—in a building is an important part of its overall design. Stained-glass windows, in which colored bits of glass within metal frames create a picture or pattern, were an important part of church design from the Middle Ages.

Windsor (pop. 262,100), city in southern Ontario, Canada, on the opposite bank of the Detroit River from Detroit, Mich. Like Detroit, Windsor is an important automotive manufacturing center. Originally inhabited by the Huron and Iroquois tribes, it was settled by the French (early 18th century) and later the English (1790s). In its early days a ferry connected the cities of Windsor and Detroit, whereas a bridge and tunnel connect them today.

Windsor, name of the ruling dynasty of the United Kingdom of Great Britain and Northern Ireland, adopted by King George V in 1917 to replace the royal family's German name, Saxe-Coburg-Gotha (from Albert Wettin, Queen Victoria's husband), when anti-German feeling was high.
See also: United Kingdom.

Windsor, Duke of *See:* Edward.

Windsor Castle, principal residence of British sovereigns since the 11th century. Begun by William I, it stands about 20 mi (32 km) west of London. The Round Tower, built in 1180, is the castle's center, and St. George's Chapel (1528) is a fine example of English Perpendicular architecture.

Windsurfing, water sport in which an individual rides a *sailboard*, a surfboard with a central mast to which a sail is attached. The sail is turned by the

207

rider to steer. The *sailsurfer* uses a board up to 7 ft (2.1 m) long, riding waves as in surfing. The *sailboarder* uses a longer board (up to 12 ft/3.7 m) and depends on wind as in sailing.

Wind tunnel, structure in which a controlled stream of air is produced in order to observe the effects on scale models or full-size components of airplanes, missiles, automobiles, or such structures as bridges and skyscrapers. An important research tool in aerodynamics, the wind tunnel enables a design to be accurately tested without the risks attached to full-scale trials. Hypersonic wind tunnels, operating on an impulse principle, can simulate the frictional effects of flight at over 5 times the speed of sound.
See also: Aerodynamics.

Windward Islands, group of islands in the Lesser Antilles, West Indies, stretching toward Venezuela. They include St. Lucia, St. Vincent, the Grenadines, Grenada, and Martinique. The area is about 950 sq mi (2,461 sq km) and the islands produce bananas, cacao, limes, nutmeg, and cotton. Tourism is an important industry.

Wine, alcoholic beverage made from fermented grape juice; wines made from other fruits are always named accordingly. Table wines are red, rosé, or white in color; red wines are made from dark grapes, the skins being left in the fermenting mixture; white wines may be made from dark or pale grapes, the skins being removed. The grapes—normally varieties of *Vitis vinifera*—are allowed to ripen until they attain suitable sugar content—18% or more—and acidity (in cool years or northern areas, sugar may have to be added). After crushing, they undergo fermentation in large tanks, during which time a small amount of sulfur dioxide is added to inhibit growth of wild yeasts and bacteria. When the alcohol and sugar content is right, the wine is cellared, racked off the lees (from which argol is obtained), clarified by filtration or fining (adding absorbent substances such as bentonite, gelatin, and isinglass), aged in the wood, and bottled. Sweet wines contain residual sugar; dry wines little or none. The alcohol content of table wines varies from 8% to 14% by volume. Sparkling wines—notably Champagne—are made by secondary fermentation under pressure, in bottles or in tanks. Fortified wines, or dessert wines—including sherry, port, and Madeira—have brandy added during or after fermentation and contain about 20% alcohol. Vermouth is a fortified wine flavored with wormwood and other herbs. Major wine-producing areas of the world include France, Germany, Spain, Portugal, Italy, and California.

Winged bull, mythic beast of ancient Assyria, frequently appearing in paintings and statues. The beast, which originated c.1000 B.C., had a man's head on a winged bull's body. Enormous portal statues of winged bulls were used as guardians of palaces, to frighten away enemies and evil spirits.
See also: Mythology.

Winged lion, mythic beast of ancient Babylonia and Assyria, represented in paintings and statues. The beast had a man's head on a winged lion's body. Enormous winged lion statues were placed at a city's gate or the entranceway to a palace to frighten off harmful spirits or humans.
See also: Mythology.

Winged Victory, Greek sculpture dated c.180 B.C. depicting Nike, the goddess of victory, bringing a message of victory from the gods. The sculptor is unknown. In 1863 the statue, broken into 118 pieces, was discovered by a French archeologist. The statue was reconstructed; it stands today in the Louvre Museum in Paris.

Winnebago, Siouan-speaking Native Americans from eastern Wisconsin. Buffalo hunters and farmers, they were related to the Eastern Woodlands group. Once friendly to the French and English, they joined in the Black Hawk War (1832) against U.S. troups and were removed to reservations in Nebraska and Wisconsin. They now number about 2,000.

Winnemucca, Sarah, or Thoc-me-tony ("Shell Flower"; 1844?-91), U.S. advocate for Native American rights. A member of the Paiute tribe in the Nevada area, she worked as a guide and interpreter. In 1870 she began speaking out against abuses of the Paiute, and in 1880 met with President Rutherford B. Hayes to plead on behalf of the tribe. She then became a writer (*Life Among the Paiutes: Their Claims and Wrongs*, 1883) and lecturer, and founded 2 schools for Native American children.

Winnetka Plan, system of individualized instruction introduced in the public elementary and junior high schools of Winnetka, Ill., in 1919. It grew as a reaction to the uniform grading of students, which held them to the same rate of progress. In the plan, pupils develop particular abilities at their own pace. The curriculum is divided into 2 sections: basic tasks learned by students individually, and creative activities, such as art, literature, music, where achievement is not measured.

Winnipeg (pop. 652,300), capital city of Manitoba, Canada, on the Red and Assiniboine rivers. The Canadian transcontinental railroad goes through this city in the center of the country. Along with a network of highways, this made Winnipeg an important distribution location for Canada in the past. At the time of French settlement (1738), fur trading was the base of the Winnipeg economy. Because of its location in the wheat belt, the city became home to Canada's grain market. Early in the 20th century, with cross-continental access, the population of the area grew. At the same time it developed as a major manufacturing center. Today the city is a center for culture and finance as well as trade and industry, with a symphony orchestra, theater center, art museum, and planetarium. The city was originally inhabited by Cree and Assiniboine Native Americans, and the population of Winnipeg today contains a large number of people of Native American ancestry. *See also:* Manitoba.

Winnipeg River, part of the Saskatchewan-Nelson river system that rises in western Ontario, Canada, and empties into Hudson Bay. The 140-mi (225-km)-long river was the route traveled by French explorers and fur traders to the Northwest in the 1700s. Today hydroelectric plants on the Winnipeg River provide power for most of Manitoba.

Winslow, Edward (1595-1655), one of the original settlers of Plymouth, Mass., who came from England on the *Mayflower* and served as governor of the colony for 3 years. He and his wife, Susanna White, were the first to marry in the new colony. A friend of the neighboring tribes, he arranged the first treaty with Chief Massasoit. In 1646 he returned to England, where he served in the government of Oliver Cromwell until his death.

Winterberry, shrub in the holly family. The winterberry (*Ilex verticillata*) displays red berries in November. It grows between 6 and 12 ft (2 and 4 m), usually in swampy areas in the eastern United States.

Wintergreen, plant in the heath family. This ground creeper shows pink globe-shaped flowers or bright red berries. The shiny leaves are grouped at the end of upright red-colored branches, whose leaves remain green year round. Oil extracted from the plant is used as flavoring in foods, medicines, and chewing gum.

Winthrop, name of 3 distinguished American colonists. **John Winthrop** (1588-1649), led the English Great Migration to Salem in 1630, founded Boston, and was 12 times elected governor of the Massachusetts Bay Colony. His journal, *The History of New England*, is an important historical source. His eldest son, **John Winthrop** (1606-76), went to Massachusetts Bay in 1631. After being named commissioner general of the new colony at Saybrook in 1633, he became governor of Connecticut (1657, 1659-76), receiving in 1662 a charter from Charles II uniting New Haven and Connecticut. His son **Fitz-John Winthrop** (1638-1707), left Massachusetts to join Oliver Cromwell's army in England, returning (1663) to fight the Dutch, the French, and the Native Americans. He was Connecticut's agent in London (1693-97) and a popular governor of Connecticut (1698-1707).

Wire, length of metal that has been drawn out into a thread. Wire is usually flexible, circular in cross-section, and uniform in diameter. Wire diameters generally range from about 0.001 to 0.5 in (0.025-12.7 mm). To manufacture wire, a hot-rolled metal rod pointed at one end is coated with a lubricant, threaded through a tungsten, carbide, or diamond die, and attached to a drum called a *draw block*. The draw block is rotated and wire—its diameter (gauge) determined by the diameter of the die—is drawn until the entire metal rod is reduced to steel. Steel, iron, aluminum, copper, and bronze are the metals most widely used for wire making, although others, including gold, platinum, and silver, are used as well. Copper and aluminum are preferred for electrical wiring because they combine high ductility with low resistance to electric current.

Wire glass, glass with wire mesh embedded in it to provide reinforcement for use in doors and windows. Usually 1/4-3/4 in (6-18 mm) thick, it may be produced by pressing the wire between 2 sheets of glass (Appert process), by pressing the wire into a single sheet (Shuman process), or by pouring molten glass over the mesh.

Wirehaired pointing griffon, hunting dog first bred in the Netherlands in the late 1800s. A slow, deliberate hunter, it points its body toward the location of the game. The griffon stands 19-23 in (48-58 cm) high and weighs 50-60 lb (23-27 kg). Its rough coat is steel gray and chestnut brown in color.

Wiretapping, interception of telephone conversations without the knowledge of those communicating. Wiretapping and the use of other "bugging" devices by private citizens are prohibited by U.S., federal, and state laws, but there has always been argument about whether police and other government officials should be able to use wiretapping to detect crimes and collect evidence. In 1968 Congress passed a law allowing wiretapping to be used in cases involving national security and certain serious crimes, provided that a court order is first obtained.

Wireworm, larva of the click beetle, which is often a serious pest. Wireworms are brown and hardskinned and are found in the soil. There is a wireworm pest for nearly every crop: They eat newly planted seeds or burrow into the roots and underground parts of stems. Because they spend several years in the soil before pupating, it is difficult to free the ground of wireworms.

Wirz, Henry (d. 1865), Confederate army officer in the U.S. Civil War, director of the Andersonville prison camp, in which Northern prisoners were crowded into a too-small stockade and abused and neglected. Wirz was tried by a military tribunal and hanged, the only Confederate soldier to be executed for war crimes. *See also:* Civil War, U.S.

Wisconsin, state in the Great Lakes region of north-central United States; considered a Midwestern state; bordered by Lake Superior and Michigan to the north, Lake Michigan to the east, Illinois to the south, and the Mississippi River (with Iowa and Minnesota on the opposite side), the St. Croix River, and Minnesota to the west.

Land and climate. Wisconsin has five main land regions. The Eastern Ridges and Lowlands region, in the east along Lake Michigan, is a gently rolling plain that is the state's most fertile area. The Central Plain covers much of the state's center; above it lie the Northern Highland, an area of forested hills and hundreds of small lakes, and the flat plain of the Lake Superior Lowland. Below the Central Plain lies the Western Upland, an area of steep hills, bluffs, and ridges that borders the Mississippi River. Wisconsin has about 15,000 lakes, most small, and hundreds of waterfalls. The state's major rivers are the Wisconsin, Black, St. Croix, Fox, Menominee, and Mississippi. Forests covers about 50% of the state. Wisconsin has relatively short but warm and humid summers and long, cold winters. Principal cities are Milwaukee and Madison.

Economy. Wisconsin's economy is led by manufacturing and by wholesale and retail trade and other service industries. Chief manufactured goods are nonelectrical machinery, processed foods, paper products, electrical machinery and equipment, fabricated metal products, and transportation equipment. Agriculture and mining account for a small fraction of Wisconsin's state gross product. Milk and dairy products earn the most agricultural income; other leading livestock products are beef cattle and hogs; chief crops are corn, hay, oats, barley, wheat, and soybeans. Chief mining products are crushed stone, sand and gravel, and lime.

Government. Wisconsin's constitution was adopted in 1848. The governor serves a 4-year term. The state legislature consists of 33 senators serving 4-year terms and 99 assembly members serving 2-year terms. In the U.S. Congress, Wisconsin is represented by 2 senators and 9 representatives.

History. The Wisconsin area was home to Dakota, Menominee, and Winnebago Native Americans when the first Europeans—led by French explorer Jean Nicolet— arrived in 1634. Other Native American tribes moved into the area in the late 1600s. Wisconsin's European-American settlers battled

Wisconsin

Capital:	Madison
Statehood:	May 29, 1848 (30th state)
Familiar name:	Badger State
Area:	56,153 sq mi (145,436 sq km); ranks 26th
Population:	5,170,000 (1997); ranks 18th
Elevation:	Highest—1,952 ft (595 m), Timms Hill; Lowest—581 ft (177 m), along the Lake Michigan shore
Motto:	Forward
Flower:	Wood violet
Bird:	Robin
Tree:	Sugar maple
Song:	"On, Wisconsin!"

the Fox Native Americans (1690-1740); the area came under British control in 1763 and became part of the United States in 1783. In the early 1800s European-American settlement grew rapidly; resistance by the Fox and Sauk was crushed in the 1832 Black Hawk War. In 1836 Congress created the Wisconsin Territory; in 1848 Wisconsin became the 30th state. In the early 1900s Wisconsin acquired a reputation for progressivism under Governor Robert M. La Follette, Sr. (elected in 1901). In the 1920s the state became predominantly urban. In 1932 Wisconsin became the first state to pass a state unemployment-compensation act. Manufacturing and agriculture remain important in Wisconsin, although the state's economy has suffered from the auto industry's decline (1980s) and the shrinking number and size of farms. Wisconsin's leaders are seeking more diverse industries and solutions to its problems of high education costs, water pollution, conservation of natural resources, and farm debt.

Wisconsin Dells *See:* Dalles.

Wisconsin River, longest river in Wisconsin, rising in the north near the Michigan border and flowing 430 mi (692 km) south and southwest to empty into the Mississippi River near Prairie du Chien. Near the town of Wisconsin Dells, the river has carved a 7-mi (11-km) scenic canyon. The river was once an important link on the trade route between the Great Lakes and the Mississippi. Today it provides considerable hydroelectric power.

Wisdom of Solomon, book of the Old Testament Apocrypha, traditionally ascribed to Solomon but probably written in the 2nd or 1st century B.C. An

example of wisdom literature (pre-Christian Jewish philosophical writings), it praises wisdom and outlines God's care for the Jews.
See also: Old Testament.

Wise, Isaac Mayer (1819-1900), religious leader, Jewish rabbi, and founder of the Reform Judaism movement in the United States. He helped organize the Union of American Hebrew Congregations (1873). Two years later Wise founded a school in Cincinnati to train rabbis, Hebrew Union College (1875), at which he served as president. The Central Conference of American Rabbis (founded in 1889) was headed by him until 1900. He came to the United States (1846) from his birthplace of Bohemia, an area of modern-day Czechoslovakia.
See also: Judaism.

Wise, Stephen Samuel (1874-1949), religious leader, Jewish rabbi, and author. He presided as rabbi at the Free Synagogue in New York City, which was founded by him (1922). As a strong supporter of *Zionism*—belief in the establishment of the Jewish state of Israel—he founded the Federation of American Zionists. Other organizations he helped establish are the Jewish Institute for Religion and the American Jewish Congress. He wrote books—*How to Face Life* (1917) and *The Challenging Years* (1949), among others—and edited *Opinion,* a magazine.
See also: Zionism.

Wisteria, plant in the pea family. Blue- to white-colored clusters of flowers blossom on this lacy-looking vine, which may grow to more than 35 ft (11 m) long. The Chinese wisteria (*Wisteria sinensis*) is commonly found in gardens throughout the United States while other species of this vine are native to the eastern portion of the country.

Witchcraft, manipulation of supernatural forces, usually toward evil ends. It has existed in most cultures throughout history and still has its devotees in modern society. In the Christian West witchcraft developed from surviving pagan beliefs. Witches were held responsible for disease and misfortune and were believed to acquire their evil power from the devil, whom they worshiped in obscene ritual (satanism, or devil worship, is not synonymous with witchcraft). From the 14th to the 18th century a witch-hunting epidemic prevailed in Europe, and many thousands of innocent people were tortured and executed in fanatical and hysterical persecutions.

Witch hazel, low tree or shrub (genus *Hamamelis*) growing in eastern North America and eastern Asia. It produces its small, yellow flowers in the autumn, when the leaves have fallen. A year later the seeds ripen and are thrown 20 ft (6.2 m) or more when the pods dry up and contract suddenly. Extracts from its bark and leaves are used in aftershave lotions and lotions for treating bruises.

Witenagemot, group of counselors to the Anglo-Saxon king. Before the king's court (*curia regis*) was established by the Norman conquerors of England (1066), these men partook in decisions to make war, grant lands, make important appointments in the court or church, and so on. They even had the power to dethrone a king during conflicts involving various claims to the throne. *Thanes,* or followers, of the king along with earls, bishops, and abbots were members of the witenagemot, which in translation means "a meeting of wise men."

Witherspoon, John (1723-94), Scottish-born American educator and clergyman who was one of the signers of the Declaration of Independence. He was a member of the Continental Congress. Prior to the American Revolution, he came to America to serve as president of what is now Princeton University. He resumed his post after the end of the war.

Witness, individual who testifies under oath in a legal proceeding or acts as a signer of a legal document. In giving testimony, a witness provides a court of law with information about persons or events relating to a particular case. A witness is criminally liable if he or she fails to appear in court or lies under oath. Certain individuals, such as children, are exempted from giving testimony.

Wittgenstein, Ludwig (1889-1951), Austrian philosopher whose two chief works, *Tractatus Logico-philosophicus* (1921) and the posthumous *Philosophical Investigations* (1953), have profoundly influenced the course of much British and U.S. philosophy. The *Tractatus* dwells on the logical nature and limits of language, understood as "picturing" reality. The *Investigations* rejects the assumption in the *Tractatus* that all representations must share a common logical form and instead relates the meanings of sentences to their uses in particular contexts: Philosophical problems are attributed to misuses of language. Wittgenstein was professor of philosophy at Cambridge University, England (1929-47).
See also: Philosophy.

Witwatersrand, or the Rand, gold-bearing rocky ridge in southern Transvaal, South Africa. It produces one-third of the world's gold output and is South Africa's major industrial region, with Johannesburg located at its center. Soweto township also lies in the Rand.
See also: South Africa.

Wodehouse, P.G. (Sir Pelham Grenville Wodehouse; 1881-1975), English writer of humorous novels and short stories. His writings, set in the early 1900-1920s, portray life in the upper class. Wodehouse's best-known novels, *Carry On Jeeves* (1925) and *The Code of the Woosters* (1938), relate the humorous predicaments of the dim-witted Bertie Wooster and his ever-sensible valet, Jeeves. Other works include *A Pelican at Blandings* (1969) and lyrics for such musical comedies as *Leave It to Jane* (1917) and *Rosalie* (1928). Wodehouse became a U.S. citizen (1955) and was knighted in England (1975).

Woden *See:* Odin.

Wöhler, Friedrich (1800-82), German chemist, the first to synthesize an organic substance (urea) from inorganic chemicals. He isolated the element beryllium, and was the first to measure the gravity of aluminum. Along with chemist Justus von Liebig, he developed an early theory of the structure of organic compounds.
See also: Chemistry.

Wolcott 214

Wolcott, name of a prominent Connecticut family. **Roger Wolcott** (1679-1767) became chief justice and governor of the colony (1751-54). His *Poetical Meditations* (1725) was the first book of verse published in Connecticut. His son **Oliver Wolcott** (1726-97) served in the Continental Congress (1775-78, 1780-84), was a signer of the Declaration of Independence, and was governor of Connecticut (1796-97). **Oliver Wolcott, Jr.** (1760-1833) was U.S. comptroller (1791-95), secretary of the treasury (1795-1800), and governor of Connecticut (1817-27).

Wolf (*Canis lupus*), powerful carnivore ranging throughout the deciduous and coniferous forests and tundra of the Northern Hemisphere. Broad-chested, with small, pointed ears and long legs, wolves are pack hunters, preying on the huge northern moose, deer, and elk herds. In the summer, with the onset of the breeding season and with small-mammal prey more readily available, the packs break up into smaller groups. Wolf packs have distinct territories, and within the pack there is a complex social structure under a top male and female.

Wolfe, James (1727-59), British general whose capture of Quebec was the decisive victory in the last of the French and Indian Wars. He fought in the War of the Austrian Succession (1742-45) and at Falkirk and Culloden Moor in the Jacobite rebellion (1745-46). Second in command under Amherst (1758), he distinguished himself in the capture of Louisburg and was chosen to lead the attack on Quebec. By brilliant strategy, aided by good luck, he routed the French but died during the battle.
See also: Quebec, Battle of; French and Indian Wars.

Wolfe, Thomas Clayton (1900-38), U.S. novelist whose works constitute an autobiographical epic. *Look Homeward, Angel* (1929), *Of Time and the River* (1935), and the posthumous works *The Web and the Rock* (1939) and *You Can't Go Home Again* (1940) are rich in detail and characterization and capture the author's vividly felt sense of place.

Wolffish, fish belonging to the Anarhichadidae family that lives in the northern Atlantic and Pacific oceans. It is known for its strong jaws and teeth, and for attacking its capturers, causing painful injury. The Atlantic wolffish measures up to 3 ft (91 cm) in length; the Pacific variety can grow to almost 8 ft (2.4 m) in length. It is a popular eating fish, and its tough skin is sometimes used for leather-type goods.

Wolfhound, family of hunting dogs consisting of three breeds. The borzoi, or Russian wolfhound, was first used by 17th-century Russian tsars to hunt wolves. The Irish wolfhound was first bred by the Celts and later imported to Ireland by the Romans. The Scottish deerhound, a descendent of the staghound, was once used for hunting deer. Wolfhounds are fiercely loyal and can make good companion dogs if they are given enough space for long, unrestricted runs.

Wolfram *See:* Tungsten.

Wolframite, brownish-black mineral derived from tungsten. It is commonly found in the veins in and around granite. Major ore deposits are located in

England, the former USSR, China, and Australia. Wolframite is used commercially in the production of electronic and industrial equipment.

Wollongong (pop. 238,200), city located in the state of New South Wales on the southeast coast of Australia. Founded in 1816, it achieved status as a city in 1942. Because of nearby coal deposits, it has become a major industrial and shipping center; its industries include coal mining, iron and steel production, chemicals, and processed foods. The city includes many examples of 19th-century Victorian and Georgian architecture.

Wollstonecraft, Mary (1759-97), British author and feminist. Her influential book, *A Vindication of the Rights of Woman* (1792), was based on the egalitarian principles of the French Revolution and promoted the cause of equal rights for women. She also wrote other essays, translations, and stories that focused attention on the role of women in society. Harshly critical of the notion that women were intellectually inferior to men, she was a strong believer in equal educational opportunities for women. She died shortly after the birth of her daughter, Mary Wollstonecraft Shelley, author of the novel *Frankenstein.*

Wolsey, Thomas (1473?-1530), Roman Catholic cardinal and politician. He became a political power during the reign of King Henry VIII, wielding great influence in both church and state matters; however, he fell into sudden disrepute due to his disapproval of Henry VIII's decision to divorce Catherine of Aragon and marry Anne Boleyn. Criticisms of his opulent way of life contributed to a growing desire for clerical reform.

Wolverine (*Gulo gulo*), large terrestrial carnivore of the weasel family, weighing up to 54 lb (24.5 kg). They live in tundra regions, the males defending a home range of up to 100 sq mi (259 sq km). Fierce animals, wolverines feed on insects, fish, small mammals, and carrion, although they have been known to attack big game, such as elk.

Wolverine State *See:* Michigan.

Woman's Relief Corps, National, U.S. patriotic organization. It became the women's auxiliary of the Grand Army of the Republic (Union veterans of the Civil War) in 1883. Its purposes include memorializing the war dead, assistance to veterans, and child welfare.

Woman suffrage, women's lawful right to vote. Under the U.S. Constitution, states initially gave voting rights to land-holding white men only. By 1830, although all states had abolished property requirements for white men, no state allowed women to vote. In the 19th century, as a result of changing social conditions and new ideas about equality, the movement for woman suffrage took shape; however, the efforts of such activists as Elizabeth Cady Stanton and Susan B. Anthony were strongly opposed. The 15th Amendment, which gave the vote to black men, still did not grant voting rights to women. During the early 20th century, an extensive and highly organized campaign to win congressional support for woman suffrage began. By 1920 more than half the states had granted either full or partial voting rights to women. With the passage of the 19th Amendment in 1920, women in the United States were given full voting rights. Women in 27 countries were also

granted voting rights during the period following World War I. In 1952 the United Nations Convention on the Voting Rights of Women resolved that all women be entitled to vote in all elections.
See also: Women's movements.

Wombat, heavy, stockily built, burrowing marsupial of Australia, closely related to the koala. Wombats share many anatomical features with placental, burrowing rodents. Nocturnal animals, they emerge from their holes to feed on grasses and roots.

Women's American ORT, affiliate of ORT (Organization for Rehabilitation through Training), an international nonprofit agency established in 1880 to provide education and job skills to Jews in many countries throughout the world. The ORT, which receives private and government funding, supports more than 800 facilities in over 20 countries. The Women's American ORT has a membership of about 145,000.

Women's Bureau, agency of the U.S. Department of Labor established in 1920 to deal with working conditions, needs, and opportunities of wage-earning women. The bureau acts as an information resource, advisory body, and advocacy group, helping employees, employers, institutions, government bodies, and international organizations with such issues as job training, placement and advancement, childcare, and sex discrimination.

Women's Christian Temperance Union (WCTU), U.S. organization seeking legislation against the consumption of alcohol. Founded in 1874, it became a worldwide organization in 1883 through the efforts of Frances Willard. It also conducts research into tobacco and narcotics.

Women's movements, organized attempts to achieve political, legal, economic, and social equality for women. Following the English common law, the U.S. legal system long assigned women a special and inferior status. Although the Constitution did not use the words "men" and "women" but always "people," "persons," and "citizens," the courts did not interpret these terms to include women. Rather, they classified women with children and imbeciles as incapable of managing their own affairs. Women were denied educations, barred from certain occupations and professions, and excluded from juries and public offices. Married women were virtually the property of their husbands. They were limited in their ability to own property, sign contracts, obtain credit, go into business, control their earnings, or write wills. The law regarded home and family as the special province of women, and it did all it could to confine them there in the belief that this was in the best interests of women themselves and of society as a whole.
Early in the 19th century, educated upper-class women began to enter public life through participation in the many reform movements of the period, especially the abolitionist crusade, often in the face of male hostility. The rebuff of women at a World Antislavery Convention in London in 1840 led directly to the organization of a U.S. women's rights movement at Seneca Falls, N.Y., in 1848.
From the start, a prime objective of the movement was to win for women the right to vote. After the Civil War, the 14th Amendment, in extending the status of citizen to former slaves, introduced the word "male" into the

Constitution as a qualification for voting. The 15th Amendment, which enfranchised the former slaves, provided that the right to vote should not be denied or abridged "on account of race, color, or previous condition of servitude," but not on account of sex. When women sought the right to vote on the basis of the 14th Amendment's "privileges and immunities" and "equal protection" clauses, the courts upheld the states' authority to fix voter qualifications.

The states, however, acted to improve the position of women. During the second half of the 19th century, all the states passed Married Women's Property Acts, which largely ended the subordination of women under the common law by dissolving the legal unity of husband and wife. Married women thereby acquired control over their own property and earnings. By 1900 women enjoyed many of the legal advantages of citizenship, the most significant exception being the right to vote. Chivalrous legislators still exempted them from certain responsibilities of citizenship, such as jury duty and poll and property taxes. This benign attitude underlay decisions of the courts early in the 20th century upholding the constitutionality of a number of state and federal laws intended to protect working women—but not men—by regulating their hours, pay, and working conditions.

In 1890 Wyoming entered the union with a state constitution providing for woman suffrage. In the next two decades many states gave women partial voting privileges. Twelve states had given women the unqualified right to vote by 1920 when ratification of the 19th Amendment secured the vote for women nationwide and established the principle of equal political rights for women.

The suffrage did not immediately bring about the removal of gender-based classifications, which, in the guise of protecting women, actually confined them to their traditional "separate place." It was, rather, the social changes resulting from 2 world wars, a major depression, and, more recently, unprecedented national affluence that revolutionized the lives of women and gave new impetus to the feminist movement. Two developments were of particular importance: The development of new and widely accessible birth-control methods liberated women from the necessity of functioning largely as child-bearers and child-rearers; and the rising flood of women into the labor force, mostly into low-paying "women's work," made women of all classes conscious of the disadvantages of their "separate place."

Feminists now perceive all gender-based classifications as discriminatory, including the legislation intended to protect women in the workplace. Not only was that legislation based on the "separate place" doctrine, but experience showed that it prevented women who wanted to do so from working overtime at premium pay, taking higher-paying jobs that required heavy work, and getting promoted to supervisory positions. A series of federal laws and executive orders has now largely nullified that protective legislation. The Equal Pay Act of 1963 legally ended discrimination on the basis of sex in the payment of wages (though in actual practice this discrimination persists). The Civil Rights Act of 1964 ended discrimination in private employment on the basis of sex as well as race, color, religion, and national origin. Executive orders have made it illegal for the federal government and for federal contractors and subcontractors to discriminate on the basis of sex.

But other legal, economic, and social inequities remain. To remove these is the goal of the modern women's movement, whose origin is usually traced to the founding of the National Organization for Women (NOW) in 1966.

NOW was soon joined by numerous other women's organizations reflecting a variety of women's interests, including those of black, Hispanic, working, and poor women as well as abortion advocates and lesbians. The presence of these latter groups in the women's rights coalition provided a convenient target for opponents of the movement, who believed it to be the work of an elite of radical and professional women contemptuous of traditional values of home, family, and religion shared by many other women. As a result, by the 1970s, the women's movement in the United States was faced with a determined opposition. Progressives, following the mainstream of the traditional women's movement, continue to pursue greater individual autonomy, the elimination of all gender-based discrimination, and greater freedom and self-determination for women. Conservatives, representing a radical departure from and reversal of the goals and outlooks of the traditional women's movement, seek to maintain the traditional roles of men and women and to neutralize or reverse changes, particularly in the law, which they contend threaten the moral authority of the family. The conflict is strongest over the issue of a woman's right to have an abortion.
See also: Feminism.

Wonder, Stevie (Stevland Judkins, or Morris; 1950-), U.S. composer, keyboard player, and singer of popular music, leading Motown musician of the 1970s. "Little Stevie Wonder"'s first recorded hit, "Fingertips," became number 1 on the pop charts when he was 13. Among his many successful albums was *Songs in the Key of Life* (1976). His music combines elements of gospel, soul, jazz, and African and Jamaican music. Blind from an early age, he progressed from the harmonica to keyboards, to become a highly skilled performer on synthesizers. In 1996 he received 3 Grammy's, which made a total of 19 Grammy awards he received during his career.

Wood, hard, dead tissue obtained from the trunks and branches of trees and shrubs. Woody tissue is also found in some herbaceous plants. Botanically, wood consists of xylem tissue, which is responsible for the conduction of water around the plant. A living tree trunk is composed of (beginning from the center): the pith (remains of the primary growth); wood (xylem); cambium (a band of living cells that divide to produce new wood and phloem); phloem (conducting nutrients made in the leaves); and bark. The wood nearest the cambium is termed *sapwood* because it is capable of conducting water. However, the bulk of the wood is heartwood, in which the xylem is impregnated with lignin, which gives the cells extra strength but prevents them from conducting water. In temperate regions, a tree's age can be found by counting its annual rings. Commercially, wood is divided into hardwood (from deciduous angiosperm trees) and softwood (from gymnosperms).

Wood, Grant (1891-1942), U.S. painter, exponent of the 1930s movement known as regionalism. Influenced by Gothic and Early Renaissance painting, he realistically depicted the people and places of Iowa, as in his best-known painting, *American Gothic* (1930).

Wood alcohol *See:* Methanol.

Woodcarving, old art form involving the chiseling of wood to create designs or figures. Woodcarving has played a significant role in the religious and cultural life of many of the world's great civilizations. Notable woodcarvers throughout history have achieved status as artists. Today woodcarving involves a variety of tools, including chisels of many sizes and shapes, gouges with different types of cutting edges, and parting tools for deeper cutting. Some woodcarving is done by machine on high-speed cutters.

Woodchuck, or groundhog (*Marmota monax*), familiar ground squirrel of the woodlands of North America. A large rodent, up to 2 ft (61 cm) long, with a short, bushy tail, the woodchuck is diurnal and feeds on water animals.

Woodcock, large game bird of the snipe family. One species lives in eastern North America and another in Europe and Asia. Woodcocks are very well camouflaged and are difficult to see against the forest floor. They become active at dusk, and the males fly up and down regular routes, croaking and whistling to establish a territory. They feed mainly on earthworms that they catch by thrusting their bills into the soil, opening just the tip to seize the worm.

Woodcock, Leonard (1911-), U.S. labor leader, president of the United Automobile Workers (1970-77). In 1977 he was named the first U.S. chief of mission to Communist China and served as ambassador 1979-81. *See also:* United Automobile Workers.

Woodcut and wood engraving, techniques for producing pictures by incising a design on a block of wood, inking the design, and then pressing the inked block onto paper. Those parts of the design that are to be white are cut away and not inked, leaving in relief the areas to be printed. Woodcut is the older method, originating in China and Japan, and used in Europe from the 14th century, particularly for book illustration. Eminent artists in the medium include Albrecht Dürer, Gauguin, and Maillol. In wood engraving the artist uses a tool called a *burin*, producing a design of white lines on a black background. It became popular in the 18th and 19th centuries.

Wood duck, bird belonging to the Anatidae family and found in the wet woodlands of southern Canada and the United States. It searches for seeds and insects in the shallow waters of swamps and ponds. It is about 20 in (51 cm) in length. The male of the species has bright multicolored feathers, while the female has feathers of yellowish brown.

Wooden, John (1910-), U.S. basketball player and coach. Between 1964-75, he led the University of California at Los Angeles (UCLA) to an unprecedented 10 National Collegiate Athletic Association (NCAA) championships, including a record 7 straight titles (1967-73) and an 88-game winning streak (1971-74). Wooden coached at Indiana State (1947-48) and UCLA (1949-75), compiling 664 career wins. A former star basketball player at the University of Purdue, he was inducted into the Basketball Hall of Fame in 1960 as both a player and a coach.

Wooden horse *See:* Trojan War.

Woodhull, Victoria Claflin (1838-1927), social reformer and first woman to run for the U.S. presidency (1872). She won support for her stand on voting rights for women, but was criticized by some suffragists for her less conven-

0

tional beliefs, which included free love, communal living, and mysticism. In 1866 she and her sister Tennessee established the first female-owned brokerage firm. They also founded a weekly newspaper, which in 1872 published the first English-language translation of the *Communist Manifesto*.

Wood ibis (*Mycteria americana*), large wading bird found in the swamps of South and Central America and the southern United States. The wood ibis is not a true ibis, but a stork. It has a curved bill and feeds on water animals.

Wood louse, land-living crustacean. It has a flattened body and 7 pairs of legs. Wood lice live in moist places, under bark or stones, and come out at night to feed. Moisture is essential to wood lice, and they often bunch together to reduce evaporation. Pill wood lice can roll into a ball for protection against spiders and other predators.

Woodpecker, one of the family Picidae of birds specialized in obtaining insects from the trunks and branches of trees. The 210 species occur worldwide, except in Australasia. All have wedge-shaped tails that may be pressed against the trunk of a tree as a prop. The bill is strong and straight, and the muscles and structure of head and neck are adapted for driving the bill powerfully forward into tree bark and absorbing the shock of the blow. The tongue is long and slender for picking out insects. One group, the sapsuckers, also feeds on tree sap. Woodpeckers also use the bill during courtship "drumming" and to hack out nesting holes in tree trunks.

Wood pewee, or Eastern pewee, woodland bird belonging to the flycatcher family. It lives in southern Canada and the eastern United States in the summer and migrates to Central America for the winter. It is a small, gray-brown bird with white bars on its wings. Its name is a reference to its distinctive song, which it sings at dawn and at dusk. The pewee feeds on insects that are known to destroy plants and crops.

Wood rat, or pack rat, any of 22 rat species belonging to the Cricetidae family and found in the mountains and deserts of North and Central America. It resembles the house rat but has softer fur, longer ears, and a furry tail. Its name derives from its habit of picking up small articles of interest and carrying them back to its den. Also known as *trade rat*, it will typically drop one object in favor of a more attractive one.

Woods, Granville T. (1856-1910), black U.S. inventor. Woods was largely self-taught but studied some engineering. His most important invention was a railway telegraph system (1887) for communication between moving trains and between trains and stations. Other inventions included a steam boiler furnace, an automatic air brake, and a galvanic battery. Many of his inventions were sold to General Electric and other large companies.

Woods Hole Oceanographic Institution, research center for marine science located at the southwest tip of Cape Cod, Mass. Its facilities include laboratories as well as deep-sea vessels. Scientists conduct research in areas such as marine biology, physics, engineering, and chemistry. Established in 1930 as a nonprofit, independent institution, it offers programs for undergraduate, doctoral, and postdoctoral students.

Woodson, Carter Goodwin (1875-1950), U.S. historian and educator who popularized African-American studies and founded the Association for the Study of Negro Life and History (1915), which trained African-American historians, collected historical documentation, and issued *The Journal of Negro History*. Woodson's works include *The Negro in Our History* (1922).

Wood sorrel *See:* Shamrock.

Woodward, Robert Burns (1917-79), U.S. chemist who won the 1965 Nobel Prize for his contributions in the field of synthetic organic chemistry. His work involved developing methods for the artificial synthesis of various chemical compounds found in nature, such as quinine, cortisone, cholesterol, and vitamin B_{12}. He was a faculty member at Harvard University from 1941 to 1979.
See also: Organic chemistry.

Woodworking, process of making objects from wood. Such objects can be of any size and may be utilitarian (houses, furniture) or purely decorative. Many wooden objects are produced at home, and woodworking is often pursued as a hobby. By the Middle Ages the status of woodworking as a profession was formalized in organizations known as craft guilds. The use of tools to work in wood dates to about 8000 B.C. The wide variety of materials and hand tools now in use includes measuring tools (rules, squares, gauges), cutting tools (saws, chisels, planes), tools for fastening (screws, glues, hammers), and finishing tools (sandpaper, paint). Modern woodworkers such as carpenters and cabinetmakers also use power drills, saws, and other electricity-driven tools. According to the requirements of a woodworking project, wood is chosen for its hardness, pliability, durability, appearance (grain, color), and availability.
See also: Carpentry.

Wool, animal fiber that forms the fleece, or protective coat, of sheep. Coarser than most vegetable or synthetic fibers, wool fibers are wavy and vary in color from the usual white to brown or black. Wool is composed of the protein keratin, whose molecules are long, coiled chains, giving wool elasticity and resilience. Reactive side groups result in good affinity for dyes and enable new, desirable properties to be chemically imparted. Wool lasts if well cared for but is liable to be damaged by some insect larvae (which eat it), by heat, sunlight, alkalis, and hot water. It chars and smolders when burned but is not inflammable. Wool strongly absorbs moisture from the air. It is weakened when wet and liable to form felt if mechanically agitated in water. Wool has been used since ancient times to make cloth. Sheep are shorn, usually annually, and the fleeces are cleaned—the wool wax removed is the source of lanolin—and sorted, blended, carded (which disentangles the fibers and removes any foreign bodies), and combed if necessary to remove shorter fibers. A rope of woolen fibers (roving) is thus produced and is spun. The woolen yarn is woven into cloth, knitted, or made into carpets or blankets. The main wool-producing countries are Australia, New Zealand, the USSR, and India. Because the supply of new (virgin) wool is inadequate, some textiles are made of reprocessed wool.

Woolf, Virginia (1882-1941), English novelist and essayist. The daughter of Sir Leslie Stephen, she married the critic Leonard Sidney Woolf (1880-

1969), and they established the Hogarth Press (1917). Their home was the center of the Bloomsbury group. Her novels *Mrs. Dalloway* (1925), *To the Lighthouse* (1927), and *The Waves* (1931) display—using the technique of stream of consciousness—her characters' thoughts and feelings about common experiences. Some of her brilliant criticism was published in *The Common Reader* (1925). She also wrote feminist tracts, including *A Room of One's Own* (1929). Subject to fits of mental instability, she drowned herself.
See also: Bloomsbury group.

Woolly monkey, or woolly spider monkey, either of two species of monkey belonging to the New World monkey family and found in the Amazon rain forest. It is a large, heavy monkey with dark, thick fur and a prehensile tail. It moves through the trees in groups of about 12, subsisting on fruit, seeds, and leaves. Its existence is threatened due to deforestation; the yellow-tailed variety is already considered very rare.

Woolworth, name of two brothers who cofounded the F.W. Woolworth Company, an extensive chain of "5-and-10-cent" stores. **Frank Winfield Woolworth** (1852-1919) was the principal founder and **Charles S. Woolworth** (1856-1947) served as vice president and later as chairman of the board. The venture, which began in Utica, N.Y., grew out of the idea that profits could be made by selling a large assortment of goods at fixed, low prices. The company later went on to operate stores in Canada, Germany, France, and Cuba.

Worcester (pop. 436,905), city in central Massachusetts on the Blackstone River. The city was established as a town in 1684, on the site of what was previously a settlement of the Nipmuc Native Americans. Colonists named the village to commemorate an English Civil War battle in which King Charles II was defeated. The city became an important industrial center in the 1800s, and its many factories attracted immigrants from all over the world. Today its hundreds of manufacturing plants produce a wide variety of products including chemicals, plastics, machinery, fabricated metals, textiles, clothing, paper, and leather. The city is also the site of many important educational, historical, and cultural institutions for the New England region.

Worden, Alfred Merrill (1932-), U.S. astronaut who piloted the *Apollo 15* command module on its journey to the moon. During the 1971 mission, he orbited the moon while astronauts David R. Scott and James B. Irwin explored its surface. On their return to earth, Worden took the first "space walk" in history, leaving the spacecraft for 20 minutes to retrieve materials from the rear of the module.
See also: Astronaut.

Word processing, use of electronic equipment to write, edit, and print documents. A word processor is basically an electronic typewriter with information storage devices similar to those of a computer and a cathode-ray-tube screen on which text is displayed. This makes it possible to edit or correct the text before it is printed out; the processor "remembers" the corrections and prints out the final version. The processor can also make the right-hand margins even (justify them) and produce documents in any desired format. The documents can be stored on magnetic disk or tape for later use. In many newspaper offices the word-processing equipment is connected directly to electronic typesetting machines.

Wordsworth, William (1770-1850), considered to be the greatest poet of the English romantic period. Known for his descriptions of nature, he derived much of his inspiration from the northern English countryside where he lived. Along with close friend and collaborator Samuel Taylor Coleridge, he believed that poetry could come out of actual experience and be written in the language of the common person. Together, they wrote *Lyrical Ballads* (1798), a collection of poems regarded as the first great works of the romantic movement. Wordsworth completed his great autobiographical poem, *The Prelude: Growth of a Poet's Mind,* in 1805, but subjected it to constant revision for the rest of his life. The author of more than 500 sonnets, he was appointed poet laureate in 1843.

Work, in physics, alternative name for energy, used particularly in discussing mechanical processes. Work of 1 joule is done when a force of 1 newton acts through a distance of 1 meter.
See also: Joule, James Prescott.

Worker's compensation, provision by employers of medical, cash, and sometimes rehabilitation benefits for workers who are injured in accidents at work. In the United States all states (Wisconsin was the first) have had worker's compensation laws since 1949, but 20% of all workers are unprotected. Railroad employees and merchant seamen are covered by other legislation. Before the first effective U.S. compensation acts, passed in 1908-11, injured employees were dependent on their employers' financial goodwill or on winning a negligence suit against them. Present laws are based on the principle of "liability without fault," which assumes that accidents are inevitable and that their costs are a legitimate business expense.

Works Progress Administration *See:* New Deal.

World, term used in various ways to designate a comprehensive unity. The idea or concept of a world is ancient. Numerous cultures have proposed models for the unity of all things signified by the idea of a world. In its simplest form, the idea is suggested by the containment of a horizon, with a dome of sky above, and the ground of earth below. In pre-modern cultures, the idea of a world is never far removed from religious concerns. It is usually understood as animate and many ancient mythologies tell stories of the marriage of earth and sky. In higher cultures, animism takes on the more distinct characteristics of individual deities or spirits, gods and goddesses, and attempts are then made to explain what appears in the world, the sun and the moon, the stars, and various creatures, including humans, in terms of the workings of occult forces with which the world is understood to be infused. Another aspect of the idea of a world in its earlier forms is that it attempts to unite and explain the visible and the invisible. Most importantly, it includes a realm of the dead. In Egyptian culture, this conception took the literal form of a necropolis, or city of the dead, on the western banks of the Nile, corresponding to the city of the living on the eastern bank. Some early concepts of a world are relatively static, others dynamic and even cataclysmic. The Mayans, speculating in astronomical expanses of time, proposed the growth, fiery destruction, and birth of many worlds over the aeons. The ancient Chinese conceived of the world as the result of a ceaseless dynamic that moved according to internal laws. All of these ancient concepts of a world were graphically symbolized, many in the form of maps. Their conceptualization and elaboration was the work of many generations and inspired the arts.

The Greeks also had mythopoetic conceptions of the world peopled by gods and goddesses, but they were the first to decisively depart from the mystical and magical conceptions of the world. Greek thinkers were the first to look for reasonable answers to why the world was as it was and how things came to be. In doing so, they rejected occult explanations and put forth questions to the world, believing that the world itself was somehow reasonably organized or directed by an intelligence, resembling human intelligence. Not coincidentally, it was a Greek who worked out a reasonable approximation of the earth's circumference, and a Greek who devised star and planet charts that used to be the basis of Western astronomy until modern times. To the practical Romans, Greek concerns were too speculative. Nonetheless, the Romans further altered the content of the concept of world by conquering and organizing a vast empire. Their work as soldiers, engineers, administrators, and legislators contributed to a very practical sense of the world that was in many ways the forerunner of the modern sensibility. But the Romans were not wholly without religion; in fact, they tended to be superstitious, and as the empire aged, religion played a more and more dominant part in people's conception of the world. The most important distinction between the idea of the world in pre-modern times and the modern conception is that the Old World view had always to account for the visible and the invisible, this world and the next. The spiritualism and dualism that characterized the ancient view of the world in the West came to an end with Columbus and Copernicus.

Columbus's discovery of the New World radically changed people's conception of place. It wasn't only the matter of having discovered hitherto unknown continents, but the challenge this discovery posed to all previous knowledge and the demands it made to know and measure the world as it actually was. Working within Columbus's lifetime, the Polish astronomer Nicholas Copernicus (1473-1543) reported that the earth was not the center of the universe, but rather one of several planets revolving about the central sun. The very meaning of the word *world*, in its most fundamental sense for modern peoples, begins with Columbus and Copernicus. Modern science continued to add to the concept. The idea of world retained the ancient sense of unity, but with scientific skepticism and knowledge, the world and its societal ideas were radically separated from religions and spiritual concerns. The world was no longer divided between the visible and invisible, but rather between the known and the unknown. The work of science further altered the common sense of the world thanks to Darwin. His theory of natural selection offered an explanation for the variety of life on the planet, including *Homo sapiens*, that was radically different. In absorbing the new knowledge, humans had to reconsider their position in relation to other animals.

Not only modern science but modern institutions changed people's sense of the world. Modern capital and commerce made international business possible and by the 17th century, markets in Amsterdam and London could be affected by events half a world away. Nation-states changed the way people thought of the world as well. In old Europe there had been a binding force in the ideas of a common Christendom and the Holy Roman Empire. The nation-states substituted for these ideals clearly defined territorial entities measured accurately and administered with ruthless rationalism. Printing presses and the modern printed media spread information rapidly and universally, bringing people closer to one another in their calculations and concerns.

Both the Industrial Revolution and imperialism in the 18th and 19th centuries brought to people's attention for the first time certain economic forces and conditions working on a worldwide scale. The theories of Karl Marx were an attempt to formulate the laws inherent in those forces and, combined with international socialism, to promote an understanding of the world that was opposed to the limited views and interests of nation-states and nationalism. Finally, drawing upon 2 centuries of industrial and technological development, World War I and World War II gave birth to a world united by a sense of common peril, a world with the technical capacity to utterly annihilate itself.

The modern conception of world can be considered a framework or canister for holding an ever-accumulating body of data. In 1992 there were some 5 1/3 billion people on earth and, at current rates of reproduction, there are likely to be more than 6 billion by the year 2000. Numerous species of plants and animals have become extinct, and, as pressure increases in the competition with humans for living space and food, more and more species face extinction. Currently the world consists of 192 countries and some 45 dependencies, but boundaries are changeable and, in many places in the world, volatile. Until the early 1990s it was a common convention to divide the world's nations among the First World, consisting of the prosperous industrialized societies; the Second World, the Soviet Union; and the Third World, consisting of all the less-developed countries. Most of the Third World is concentrated in Africa, South America, and the Asian subcontinent, the southern half of the world. Some 3,000 languages are spoken the world over, though 12 are the most widely used. The 12, in order of the numbers of people who use them, are Chinese, English, Russian, Spanish, Hindi, Arabic, Bengali, Portuguese, Japanese, German, Malay-Indonesian, and French. The 8 major religions of the world are Christianity, Islam, Buddhism, Confucianism, Hinduism, Shinto, Taoism, and Judaism. The world, as a framework or container for the data that has already been accumulated and that continues to accumulate, is virtually infinite. At the same time that it has this property of never-ending expansion, it also seems incredibly small and contracted. Modern communications and media have made it possible to connect any 2 points on the globe instantly, for business or pleasure. Modern transport puts the entire planet within reasonable traveling distance. Common concerns suggest there may be a basis for a more genuine unity in coming to terms with overpopulation, shrinking resources, and the threat posed by a degraded environment. There are as many indications that divisions will deepen and multiply. Still we use the term *world* in numerous ways and continue to find it useful, in fact, indispensable, no matter how unstable the notion of unity it contains.

World Bank, officially the International Bank for Reconstruction and Development, specialized agency of the United Nations, founded in 1945. Its headquarters is in Washington, D.C. From capital (limited to $24 billion) it lends money to its 176 member states for investment, foreign trade, and repayment of debts. Members own shares of $100,000 and belong to the International Monetary Fund. The bank is self-sustaining and profit-making. In 1960 it set up the International Development Association.

World Council of Churches, international association of about 300 Protestant, Anglican, Eastern Orthodox, and Old Catholic churches in some 90 countries. Founded 1948, with headquarters in Geneva, it promotes Christian unity, religious liberty, missionary cooperation, interfaith doctrinal study, and service projects such as refugee relief.
See also: Christianity.

World Court *See:* International Court of Justice.

World government, theoretical organization with the authority and power to maintain law order throughout the world. The idea first began in the 1300s and the massive destruction caused by World Wars I (1914-18) and II (1939-45) has led to a revival of the concept. Supporters see the creation and effective leadership of the United Nations as a positive model and test case for a world government.

World Health Organization (WHO), specialized agency of the United Nations founded in 1948 and based in Geneva. Its services are available to all nations and territories. WHO advises countries on how to develop health services, combat epidemics, and promote health education and standards of nutrition. It also coordinates the standardization of drugs and health statistics and studies pollution.

World Intellectual Property Organization (WIPO), international agency, part of the United Nations (UN), that protects the legal rights of intellectual property, such as inventions, trademarks, literary and artistic works, and other original ideas. Founded in 1967, WIPO became part of the UN in 1974 and has a membership of over 110 countries. Its headquarters are located in Geneva, Switzerland.

World Jewish Congress, international body, representing Jewish organizations from over 70 countries, whose goals are to maintain Jewish unity, culture, and religion. Founded in 1936, the congress was active during World War II (1939-45), helping Jews escape Nazi persecution, and in the 1970s, securing the release of thousands of Jews from the USSR. Its headquarters are located in New York City.
See also: Jews.

World Meteorological Organization (WMO), specialized agency of the United Nations, established in Geneva in 1951 to promote international meteorological observation and standardization.

World's fair, international exposition of science and technology, entertainment, and culture. The first such fair was the Great Exhibition of 1851 in London. World's fairs have frequently displayed new inventions and feats of engineering, such as the telephone (Philadelphia, 1876), the Eiffel Tower (Paris, 1889), the automobile (St. Louis, 1904), and television (New York, 1939). More recently, fairs have had central themes such as outer space or the oceans. World's fairs have been held all over the world.

World Trade Center, twin towers (each 110 stories) rising 1,350 ft (411 m) over lower Manhattan in New York City. Completed in 1973, they were the tallest buildings in the world until 1974, when they were surpassed by the Sears Tower in Chicago. The center was designed by Minoru Yamasaki and Emery Roth and cost $750 million to build.
See also: Skyscraper.

World War I, global conflict waged from 1914 to 1918 that caused more destruction and involved more participants than any other conflict up to that time. The war's spread was facilitated by an interlocking system of military alliances that Europe had forged during the previous decades, ostensibly to keep the peace. These alliances comprised the Central Powers (primarily Germany and Austria-Hungary) and the Allies (primarily Russia, France, and Great Britain). Later, other nations joined one or the other of the blocks.
Causes of the war. The underlying causes of the conflict involved the rise of nationalism in Europe, the military buildup pursued by parties of both alliances, and the competition among various European countries for colonies. The immediate cause of the war was the assassination of Austrian Crown Prince Francis Ferdinand at Sarajevo on June 28, 1914, by a Serbian nationalist. Austria, looking for a pretext to suppress Slavic nationalist aspirations in the Austro-Hungarian Empire, declared war on Serbia (July 28), with the approval of Germany. Russia announced full mobilization (July 30), and France rejected a German demand that she declare herself neutral.
The two fronts. Germany declared war on Russia (Aug. 1) and on France (Aug. 3) and invaded neutral Belgium, the shortest route to Paris, in search of a quick victory in the west before Russia had time to muster all its forces in the east. The invasion prompted Britain to enter the war (Aug. 4) in support of Belgium and France. All the major members of the alliances were now committed to war.
The western front. German armies gained initial successes, sweeping through Belgium and into France. They were halted at the Marne River (First Battle of the Marne, Sept. 6-9, 1914) by French forces led by Gen. Joseph Joffre. This battle ended German hopes of quickly overrunning its opponents in the west, and by late Nov. 1914 war on the western front settled into a dreadful stalemate. For the next $3^1/2$ years, terrible trench warfare raged along a 450-mile (724-km)-long front extending across Belgium and northeastern France to the Swiss border.
The eastern front. In late Aug. 1914 the Russians invaded East Prussia, but were defeated by the Germans in the battles of Tannenberg and the Masurian Lakes, suffering about 250,000 Russian casualties. Austria-Hungary was less successful, failing to capture Serbia and losing its province of Galicia to the Russians. In Oct. 1914 Turkey joined the Central Powers against Russia. In a vain attempt to aid the Russians, the Allies in early 1915 sent a fleet to the Dardanelles and ground forces to the Gallipoli Peninsula. The thrust proved unsuccessful, and troops were evacuated in Dec. 1915 with losses of about 250,000.
Outside Europe. After the Gallipoli disaster, the Allies attacked Turkey through her empire in the Middle East, and were largely successful, leaving her in possession of little more than Anatolia. Farther afield, British, French, and South African troops overran Germany's African possessions, while the Japanese (who had entered the war in Sept. 1914) and Australasian troops captured German possessions in the Far East and the Pacific.

Attrition in the West. In 1915 Italy joined the Allies and engaged the Austrian army in the Alps. In 1916 German forces were repulsed in their attempt to take the French city of Verdun with fearful losses on both sides (about 315,000 casualties for the French and 280,000 for the Germans). Paul von Hindenburg and Erich Ludendorff, the heroic leaders of German forces in the east, took command in the west, Hindenburg as chief of general staff with Ludendorff his aide.

An Allied offensive late in the year (the Battle of the Somme), led principally by the British, was also unsuccessful, and by its end it had cost the Germans over 600,000 casualties, the British over 400,000, and the French nearly 200,000. Britain maintained a naval blockade of the continent while German submarines harassed Allied mercantile shipping. An attempt by the German fleet to lift the blockade at Jutland (May 1916) failed.

The final stages. In Mar. 1917 the Russian people, sick of the war that had cost them dearly, revolted and overthrew Tsar Nicholas II. In Apr. 1917 V.I. Lenin returned to Russia from his exile in Switzerland, and 7 months later, as head of the revolutionary Bolshevik government, sued for peace with Germany. The Germans dictated a harsh peace between the 2 nations in Mar. 1918 at Brest-Litovsk. The sinking of 3 U.S. merchant ships in Mar. 1917 together with the discovery of a German plan to try to persuade Mexico to go to war against the United States (the "Zimmermann Telegram") caused the United States to declare war on the Central Powers in Apr. 1917. The American Expeditionary Forces, led by Gen. John J. Pershing, began arriving in France in mid-1917. Despite a massive final German offensive in 1918 that drove the Allies back to the Marne, Allied forces, boosted by U.S. contingents, eventually began to tell. In September the Hindenburg Line was breached. The Central Powers sued for peace, and an armistice went into effect on Nov. 11, 1918. The Treaty of Versailles (June 28, 1919), imposed on Germany, formalized the Allied victory. The dead on both sides totaled about 10 million.

Aftermath of the war. Europe had spent much of its economic resources on the war and was exhausted and in debt. The dissolution of old empires in Europe and Turkey spawned a host of new countries and allegiances, and the United States, unscathed in the war, emerged as the economic world power. An era of European dominance was clearly coming to an end, and a new, but very unsettled, world order was in the making.

World War II, second global conflict lasting from 1939 to 1945 that involved civilian populations on an unprecedented scale. Military deaths probably amounted to some 17 million, but civilian deaths were undoubtedly much higher because of mass bombing of cities, starvation, epidemics, massacres, and other war-related causes. The parties to the conflict involved nearly every major power in the world, divided into 2 groups: the Allies (principally Great Britain, the United States, the Soviet Union, and China) and the Axis Powers (principally Germany, Italy, and Japan). The development—and use—of the atomic bomb late in the war ushered in the nuclear age.

Causes of the war. The conflict arose because of the increasing military might of the aggressive, totalitarian regimes in Germany, Italy, and Japan following World War I. The harsh terms of the Treaty of Versailles after World War I had left Germany bitter and unstable, and hard economic times plagued much of the world in the 1920s and 1930s. These conditions fostered fascistic dictatorships in Germany and Italy, and Japan became aggressively militaristic and expansionist in Asia. Attempts to contain the aggressive impulses of these states through the League of Nations (which the U.S. did not join) proved ineffectual. With the rise of Hitler and Nazism to power in Germany (1933), the Versailles arrangements began to crumble. Germany rearmed and, on the pretext of defending German ethnic nationals in certain neighboring countries, laid claim to some of their territories. Hitler annexed Austria in Mar. 1938 (the *Anschluss*) and obtained the Sudetenland (in Czechoslovakia) through the Munich Pact (Sept. 1938). The policy of appeasement practiced at Munich failed, however, as Germany in Mar. 1939 occupied the rest of Czechoslovakia. On Aug. 23, 1939, Germany signed a non-aggression pact with its former arch enemy the Soviet Union, clearing the way for Hitler to move westward.

Outbreak of the war. Germany invaded Poland on Sept. 1, 1939. France and Britain responded by declaring war on Germany (Sept. 3). Germany, using the blitzkrieg strategy of speed and surprise, soon overran most of Poland, and on Sept. 17 Soviet forces invaded Poland from the east. By the end of September the Soviets had occupied the eastern third of Poland while Germany held all the rest. The Soviet Union continued with invasions of Finland and the Baltic states, as Germany went on to swift conquests of Denmark and Norway (Apr. 1940), and in May overran the Low Countries and invaded France. By June German troops had swept through France to the English Channel. British forces, almost trapped by the Germans, effected a desperate evacuation from Dunkirk back to England. France accepted an armistice on June 11, although Free French forces led by Gen. Charles de Gaulle continued the struggle. With Germany and Italy dominant on the continent, Hitler turned his sights on Britain, and attempted to bomb the nation into submission. Inspired by their leader, Winston Churchill, the British held firm and the Royal Air Force thwarted the effort in the Battle of Britain. In May 1941 Hitler broke off the massive air attack and began rebuilding his depleted air force. He continued, however, to harass British shipping with submarine warfare in the North Atlantic principally. On June 22 Germany invaded the Soviet Union, bringing that country, under its leader Joseph Stalin, into the war. Surprised, the Soviet forces initially suffered heavy losses. However, with Moscow and Leningrad surrounded and under siege, resistance stiffened. Also, a severe winter in 1941 caused enormous hardship for the German army, and they were never able to fully capture either city. Late in 1941 Germany and Italy found a new ally in Japan, whose aggressive militarism was bent on the conquest of Eastern Asia and the Western Pacific. On Dec. 7, 1941, Japan surprised and crippled the U.S. fleet at Pearl Harbor, Hawaii. President Franklin Roosevelt asked for, and obtained, an immediate U.S. declaration of war.

Turn of the tide. Though the United States initially fared badly in the Pacific, its first major victories were recorded at Coral Sea and Midway (June 1942). In North Africa, Allied supremacy was established at the Battle of El Alamein (Oct.-Nov. 1942). On the eastern front the Germans lost an army at the siege of Stalingrad (early 1943), and Soviet forces began to push the invader back. Sicily fell to Anglo-American forces in July 1943, and the Italian dictator Benito Mussolini was driven from power.

D-Day (June 6, 1944) signaled the last phase of the war in Europe, as Allied troops stormed across the Channel and invaded Normandy. By Sept. 1944 German forces, already expelled from the Soviet Union, had been driven out of France and Belgium. The Battle of the Bulge (Dec. 1944) proved to be the final German counteroffensive. By Jan. 1945 the Allies resumed their drive into Germany; the Russians captured East Germany, and the Allies broke the Siegfried Line in March. As Russian forces at last entered Berlin, Hitler committed suicide (Apr. 30, 1945) and 8 days later all German resistance ended. The fate of conquered Europe was subsequently settled at the Yalta Conference and the Potsdam Conference, although Germany itself was not reunited into one country until 1990.

Defeat of Japan. Since 1943 Allied forces had been eroding Japanese power in the Pacific and Asia. By mid-1945 island-hopping assaults by U.S. forces, culminating in Iwo Jima and Okinawa, had largely swept Japan from the Western Pacific. The Soviet Union declared war on Japan and occupied Manchuria, and U.S. and Allied forces were massing in the Pacific for an invasion of the Japanese homeland. President Harry Truman ordered the dropping of the atomic bomb on Hiroshima and Nagasaki (Aug. 6 and 9), and on Aug. 14 Japan accepted unconditional terms of surrender.

Aftermath of the war. The stupendous destruction of World War II left much of the world in ruins, with the Soviet Union and the United States emerging as the 2 world superpowers. A struggle, known as the Cold War, soon developed between the Communist world, led by the Soviet Union, and the non-Communist world, led by the United States. Perhaps most important of all, the horror of nuclear devastation was introduced as a possibility in any future global conflict.

Worm, term used for any elongate, cylindrical invertebrate, such as the earthworm, roundworm, hairworm, or acorn worm. The word has no taxonomic validity; animals commonly referred to as worms belong to many related phyla: Chordata, Annelida, and Platyhelminthes. However, the term is sometimes restricted to the phylum Annelida.

Worms (pop. 71,827), city in southwestern Germany, situated on the Rhine River. Its main industries include the manufacture of chemicals, furniture, leather goods, and machinery. It is also a famous wine producer. Founded in 14 B.C. by Roman soldiers, Worms has a Romanesque cathedral that dates from the 1000s, and what may be Europe's oldest Jewish cemetery, also from the 1000s.

Worms, Edict of, civil decree issued at Worms, Germany, in 1521, denouncing religious reformer Martin Luther as a heretic, banning his writings, and calling for his capture. The question of whether or not to enforce the edict was a subject of great controversy until a truce was declared in 1555 with the Peace of Augsburg.
See also: Luther, Martin; Reformation.

Wormwood, group of herbs and shrubs in the composite family, found chiefly in arid regions of the Northern Hemisphere. Wormwood is grown commercially to provide an essential oil that has a variety of medicinal uses. The leaves of another type of wormwood, tarragon, is used as a seasoning. Common wormwood, or mugwort, is used in medicines and in the manufacture of absinthe.

Worsted, type of yarn known for its strength and its smooth, shiny texture. It was first produced in Worsted, England. It is made by combing the wool fibers into parallel layers before they are spun. Worsted yarns are frequently used in knitting. The term *worsted* also refers to any fabric made with worsted yarns.

Wouk, Herman (1915-   ), U.S. author of novels and plays. His work often draws on his own naval experiences during World War II. In 1952 he won the Pulitzer Prize in fiction for his war novel, *The Caine Mutiny* (1951), which was later adapted for stage and screen. Other popular novels that were adapted for the screen include *Marjorie Morningstar* (1955), *The Winds of War* (1971), and *War and Remembrance* (1978). In 1993 *The Hope* was published.

Wounded Knee, Battle of, massacre by U.S. soldiers of more than 200 Sioux men, women, and children at Wounded Knee Creek, S.D., on Dec. 29, 1890, in the last major battle of the Indian Wars. In 1973, 200 members of the American Indian Movement (AIM) occupied the Wounded Knee Reservation for 69 days, demanding a Senate investigation into the conditions of Native Americans. *See also:* Indian wars.

Wovoka (1858?-1932), also known as Jack Wilson, Nevada-born Paiute Native American who originated the ghost-dance religion practiced by Native Americans of the West. In 1889, while ill with a fever, he had a prophetic vision during a solar eclipse. In the vision, the Great Spirit told him that if his people lived in harmony and performed certain rituals, the foreign settlers would leave, Paiute ancestors would be brought back to life, and they would live long, happy lives. Wovoka, the son of a Paiute prophet, was adopted as a boy by David Wilson, a European-American settler.

WPA *See:* New Deal.

Wrangel Island, island belonging to Russia and located in the Arctic Ocean, about 90 miles north of Siberia. Whalers from the United States discovered the uninhabited island in 1867. Despite the claims of the United States and Canada, the USSR sent settlers there in 1926. The land is icy and barren during most of the year. Polar bears, walruses, and birds can be found there. It is inhabited by about 50 people who fish and hunt for a living.

Wrangell-St. Elias National Park, largest U.S. national park, located in southeastern Alaska. The park measures about 14,000 sq mi (36,000 sq km). Its terrain includes numerous glaciers and some of the tallest mountain peaks in North America. Animal life includes bears, caribou, moose, sea otters, and trumpeter swans.

Wren, name of several groups of small birds. The true wrens are the Troglodytidae, a family of 60 species of small perching birds. The name is also used for some 80 species (family Malurinae) of warblers of Australia and New Guinea, and the New Zealand wrens (family Xenicidae). True wrens are small, compact birds with short to long tails cocked upward. They occur in Central and North America.

Wren, Sir Christopher (1632-1723), English architect, astronomer, mathematician. Wren is best remembered as architect of St. Paul's Cathedral (1710) and over 50 other churches that were rebuilt after having been destroyed by the Great Fire of London (1666). A widely respected astronomer, he was appointed professor of Gresham College, London (1657), served on the faculty of Oxford University (1661-73), and was a founder of the Royal Society (1660). *See also:* Architecture; Astronomy.

Wrestling, in the West, sport in which 2 persons grapple and try to pin one another's shoulders to the floor by means of various holds. An ancient Greek sport, wrestling became a recognized Olympic sport in 1904. In the United States the preferred form is the free-style, or catch-as-catch-can. The Greco-Roman form, popular in Europe, forbids holds below the waist. Bouts are divided into 3 periods of 3 minutes each. The match is over when a wrestler pins both his opponent's shoulders for the count of 3 (a fall). Matches can also be won on points awarded by the referee for skilled maneuvers.

Wright, Frances (1795-1852), Scottish-born U.S. reformer for women's rights, public education, and the abolition of slavery. Wright lectured on women's right to divorce and birth control. She also founded the short-lived Nashoba community (1825-27) near Memphis, Tenn., where slaves worked to buy their freedom. A member of the utopian New Harmony community in Indiana, Wright was coeditor of its magazine the *Gazette* and also coedited the *Free Enquirer* of New York City. *See also:* Women's movements.

Wright, Frank Lloyd (1869-1959), 20th-century U.S. architect. He studied engineering, joined the architect Louis Sullivan, and was influenced by the Arts and Crafts movement. His pioneering "prairie style" (Robie House; 1908-09)—strong, horizontal lines; low-pitched, hipped roofs; open plan; and change of internal levels—influenced De Stijl. He articulated massive forms clearly (Larkin Building, 1904) and, though he liked natural materials and locations, was innovative in his use of reinforced concrete, dramatic cantilevering, and screen walls (Kaufmann House, or Falling Water, 1936-37; Johnson's Wax Building, 1936-49; Guggenheim Museum, 1946-59). *See also:* Architecture.

Wright, Quincy (1890-1970), U.S. political scientist, an expert on international law. He was a supporter of the League of Nations and United Nations. His books include *A Study of War* (2 vol., 1942) and *The Study of International Relations* (1955).

Wright, Richard (1908-60), U.S. novelist and social critic. His works include *Uncle Tom's Children* (1938), stories of Southern racial prejudice; *Native Son* (1940), about a victimized black in Chicago; and *Black Boy* (1945), his autobiography.

Wright brothers, name of two U.S. inventors; designers and builders of the world's first successful airplane (1903). Inspired by the work of Otto Lilienthal, who did pioneering work with gliders in the 1890s, the Wrights, **Wilbur** (1867-1912) and **Orville** (1871-1948), conducted experiments with kites and gliders (1899-1902) to develop and test theories of control and lift. Their powered airplane was first tested Dec. 17, 1903, at Kill Devil Hill, near Kitty Hawk, N.C. The machine weighed 750 lb (340 kg), with wings 40 ft (12 m) long. The Wrights continued experimental flights, receiving little attention in the United States but arranging for production of planes in France and Germany. After Wilbur Wright's death, his brother continued work to perfect the airplane. The Wrights were elected posthumously to the Hall of Fame for Great Americans. Their original plane is now exhibited in the National Air and Space Museum, Washington, D.C. *See also:* Airplane.

234 *Wroclaw*

Wrist, or carpus, particularly in humans, joint between the hand and forearm, along with the connecting 8 small carpal bones. The wrist joint connects the long *radius* bone of the forearm to the carpal bones of the hand. The tendons and muscles that connect the arm to the finger bones control movement of the fingers..A joint connects the *ulna* of the forearm to the parallel radius rather than to the carpal bones, allowing the free rotation of the wrist.

Writ, written order of a court of law. Under English common law, a writ had to be issued before any legal action could be initiated. Most ancient writs have been replaced by summonses and declarations, but some—such as writs of certiorari, habeas corpus, and mandamus—survive.

Writing, in business, career in such diverse areas as technical-writing, journalism, fiction and poetry, and screenplay and script writing. *Staff writers* have salaried jobs with newspapers and magazines, in company public relations departments, at advertising agencies, and elsewhere. However, writing services are largely provided by *freelance writers* who are hired for particular projects (e.g., computer manuals, encyclopedia articles) or who create their own articles, scripts, and so on, which they then attempt to sell to various publishers and producers. Writers, particularly those already well established, may work through a *literary agent* to place a manuscript with a buyer. Only a small percentage of fiction writers and a handful of poets actually make a living from their creative writing.

Writing, visual representation of human language and other communication according to social convention. Early writing included marks used for counting and pictures representing situations and objects. Pictures developed into *ideographs*, symbolic representations of ideas rather than of speech. The more advanced and abstract *logographs*, which represent actual elements of speech, were first developed by the Sumerians c.3500 B.C. The Sumerians also began to develop phonetic representations, or *syllabograms*. While this *cuneiform* writing of the Sumerians spread through the Middle East, the Egyptians developed *hieroglyphics*. The complex Chinese system of writing developed c.1500 B.C. Further developments led to the Phoenician alphabet, representing consonants, the Greek alphabet, representing consonants and vowels, and the Japanese alphabet, representing consonant-vowel combinations.

Writ of assistance, general search warrant issued to customs officers by American colonial courts from 1751. Their use to enforce import duties was imposed by the 1767 Townshend Acts and caused a major furor among the colonists. By 1772 many colonial courts were refusing to issue them. These writs were mentioned by the Declaration of Independence as one of the grievances of the colonies against England.

Wroclaw (German: *Breslau*; pop. 640,700), city in southwestern Poland, capital of Wroclaw province; located in the region of Dolny lsk (Lower Silesia) on the Oder River. The trade center of Wroclaw was established in the 10th century on the site of a Stone Age settlement. Originally Polish, the city came under control of Austria in 1526 and Prussia in 1742. Under the name of Breslau it was a part of Germany from 1871 to 1945, when it was returned to Poland. Modern Wroclaw is an industrial, transportation, and communication center. Manufactures include machinery, electronics; textiles, and food products. *See also:* Poland.

Wryneck, jynx, or snakebird (genus *Jynx*), small, gray-brown, insect-eating bird of the Eastern Hemisphere, named for the snakelike hissing and movement of its head and neck when it is threatened. The 2 species, often considered members of the woodpecker family, are the Eurasian wryneck (*J. torquilla*) and the African red-breasted wryneck (*J. ruficollis*).

Wu, Chien-shiung (1912?-), U.S. experimental physicist. In 1957 her experiments in particle physics disproved the law of the conservation of parity, a long-held theory that the direction in which beta particles are emitted from a radioactive nucleus is not related to the direction of spin of the nucleus. Her work confirmed the theory of physicists Tsung Dao Lee and Chen Ning Yang (who shared the 1957 Nobel Prize in physics) that the direction of spin affects the predominant direction of such emissions. Her experimental work also helped confirm theoretical work of Richard P. Feynman and Murray Gell-Mann. Wu emigrated from China to study at the University of California, Berkeley. She worked at Columbia University from 1944, first in the Division of War Research and after 1957 as a professor.
See also: Parity; Physics.

Wuchang *See:* Wuhan.

Wuhan (pop. 3,750,000), city in east-central China comprised of the former cities of Hankou, Hanyang, and Wuchang. Located at the confluence of the Yangtze and Han rivers, Wuhan is a major commercial, transportation, and industrial (iron and steel production) center.
See also: China.

Wundt, Wilhelm (1832-1920), German psychologist and philosopher. He thought that research psychologists should combine laboratory work with an examination of their own thoughts and feelings. In 1879 he started a laboratory in which his ideas on experimental psychology were practiced.
See also: Psychology.

Wyatt, Sir Thomas (1503?-42), English poet of the early Renaissance. He and Henry Howard, earl of Surrey, translated and introduced Italian poetry and poetic forms to English literature. They are generally credited with having written the first sonnets in English. Wyatt, a lover of Anne Boleyn before her marriage, was known for his wit and charm in the court of King Henry VIII, and served his country as a diplomat to the European continent. In addition to sonnets, he wrote lyrics for lute accompaniment, epigrams, and satires. His poems were first published in Tottel's *Miscellany*, a famous early Renaissance collection.
See also: Renaissance.

Wycliffe, John (1328?-84), British religious reformer, created first English translation of the Latin Bible. He lived during a time that saw the roles of church and state seriously questioned. Siding with the common people against both corrupt church and civil rulers, he claimed that obedience was due only to God. For his beliefs and writings on this subject, he was tried several times, unsuccessfully. Protected by England's royal family, he wrote vehement attacks against the church, fighting in large part against its hypocrisy and in favor of the rights of the poor. Subsequent religious reformers, including the Protestants of the Reformation in the 16th century, considered Wycliffe a major influence. *See also:* Reformation.

Wyeth, Andrew (1917-), U.S. painter. His work depicts scenes of strange, lonely rural life in a highly detailed style that seems almost photographic. His best-known picture is *Christina's World* (1948).

Wyler, William (1902-81), U.S. film director. He won Academy Awards for *Mrs. Miniver* (1942), *The Best Years of Our Lives (1946)*, and *Ben Hur* (1958). His other films include *Wuthering Heights* (1939), *Friendly Persuasion* (1956), and *Funny Girl* (1968).

Wylie, Elinor (1885-1928), U.S. poet and novelist. Her well-crafted verse appeared in 4 volumes during the 1920s and included *Nets to Catch the Wind* (1921), *Black Armour* (1923), *Trivial Breath* (1928), and *Angels and Earthly Creatures* (posthumously published in 1929). She usually wrote in traditional forms, including the sonnet. She also wrote 4 historical novels, including *Jennifer Lorn* (1923).

Wyoming, state in the Rocky Mountain region of northwestern United States; bordered by Montana to the north, South Dakota and Nebraska to the east, Colorado to the south, Utah to the south and west, and Utah, Idaho, and Montana to the west.
Land and climate. Wyoming has the second-highest average elevation of any state (Colorado's is highest). Part of the Continental Divide runs northwest to southeast through central Wyoming. Wyoming has three major land regions. The Rocky Mountains in western, central, and southeastern Wyoming. The Rocky Mountains region is separated in central and northern Wyoming by the Intermontane Basins, which are relatively flat, treeless areas separating various sections of high mountain peaks. The Great Plains, in eastern Wyoming, is a region consisting of flat or gently rolling grassland. Three major river systems rise in the Rocky Mountains of Wyoming: the Missouri, the Colorado, and the Columbia. Forests cover about one-sixth of the state. Yellowstone National Park, in the state's northwestern corner, has the world's largest geyser, magnificent waterfalls, and deep canyons. Wyoming's climate is dry, with warm, brief summers and long, cold winters. Principal cities are Casper and Cheyenne.
Economy. Mining and service industries (including tourism) lead Wyoming's economy. Chief mining products are petroleum, natural gas, coal, uranium, sodium carbonate, clays, Portland cement, and crushed stone. Manufacturing and agriculture account for only a small share of the gross state product. Chief manufactured goods are chemicals, nonelectrical machinery, processed foods, lumber and wood products, refined petroleum products, and stone, clay, and glass products. Ranching is the leading agricultural activity; chief livestock products are beef cattle, milk, sheep, and wool; chief crops are hay, barley, wheat, sugar beets, corn, and beans.
Government. Wyoming's constitution was adopted in 1889. The governor serves a 4-year term. The state legislature consists of 30 senators serving 4-year terms and 64 representatives serving 2-year terms. In the U.S. Congress, Wyoming is represented by 2 senators and 1 representative.
History. Native American hunters were the area's first residents; the first Europeans—French fur trappers—arrived in the mid-1700s. John Colter,

Wyoming

Capital:	Cheyenne
Statehood:	July 10, 1890 (44th state)
Familiar name:	Equality State
Area:	97,809 sq mi (253,326 sq km); ranks 9th
Population:	480,000 (1997); ranks 50th
Elevation:	Highest—13,804 ft (4,207 m), Gannett Peak; Lowest—3,100 ft (945 m), Belle Fourche River
Motto:	Equal Rights
Flower:	Indian paintbrush
Bird:	Meadowlark
Tree:	Cottonwood
Song:	"Wyoming"

an American trapper, made the first records of the Yellowstone region in 1807. Over the next 30 years, the fur trade developed and European-American can settlers passed through Wyoming on the Oregon Trail. Native Americans fought foreign encroachment on their lands (1849-76) until the U.S. Army wiped out or divided their forces. The Territory of Wyoming was created by Congress in 1868; in 1869 it became the first state or territory to give women the right to vote. Cattle and oil industries developed in the 1880s; in 1890 Wyoming became the 44th state. In 1892 the bitter Johnson County War broke out between cattle ranchers and sheep herders; tensions and occasio-

nal violence lasted into the early 1900s. Federal homestead acts brought new waves of settlers to the state in the early 1900s; 1912 brought the state's first oil boom. In 1924 Wyoming elected the nation's first woman governor, Nellie Tayloe Ross. Wyoming was hard hit by the Dust Bowl and the Great Depression of the 1930s but, since World War II, uranium and tourist industries have prospered; the state's population grew by 42% from 1970 to 1980. The 1980s brought economic decline and a drop-off in population. Wyoming's leaders are seeking more diverse industries to revive its economy.

Wyoming Valley, valley in northeastern Pennsylvania and scene of a bloody battle during the Revolutionary War. The valley, which is rich with hard coal, is about 20 mi (32 km) long and 3 mi (5 km) wide. On July 3, 1778, 200 British loyalists together with 600 Native Americans raided the valley and killed almost 200 settlers.

Wyoming Valley Massacre, event in the American Revolutionary War. A force of Loyalists, Butler's Rangers, and Iroquois led by John Butler defeated a band of 300 Connecticut settlers led by Zebulon Butler in Wyoming Valley, Pa., in July 1778. A massacre ensued in which the Iroquois butchered the survivors.

237   *Xavier, Saint Francis*

The incident horrified both sides; it made the English wary of Native American allies and prompted George Washington to attack the Iroquois (1779).
See also: Revolutionary War in America.

Wyss family, authors of and models for the famous children's story *The Swiss Family Robinson*. The story of a family's life and survival alone on an island was first created and written down by **Johann David Wyss** (1743-1818) as an entertainment for his children. Many years later in 1812, one of his sons, **Johann Rudolf** (1781-1830), who was at the time a well-known Swiss editor of folklore, edited and published his father's account. The novel was an instant success and was translated into English in 1814. The book, now available in many languages, is still a popular children's book.
See also: Children's literature.

Wyszynski, Stefan Cardinal (1901-81), Polish Catholic cardinal, archbishop of Warsaw, and primate of Poland. Arrested for his attacks on the Communist government's persecution of the church in 1953, he was released after Wladyslaw Gomulka's rise to power (1956). His funeral was a national event attended by Pope John Paul II.
See also: Poland.

Wythe, George (1726-1806), judge, friend of Thomas Jefferson and first U.S. law professor at the College of William and Mary (1779-90). A member of the Second Continental Congress (1775-77) and a signer of the Declaration of Independence, he was judge of the Virginia high court of chancery (1788-1806).

X

X, 24th letter of the English alphabet, corresponding to the 21st letter of the Latin alphabet, which was itself derived from a letter of the western subdivision of the ancient Greek alphabet representing the sound "ks." The same letter in the eastern Greek alphabet represented "ch" or "kh," and as such passed into the later Greek and Cyrillic alphabets. X represents 10 in Roman numerals, and in algebra and in the sciences it is used as the symbol for an unknown quantity.

X and Y chromosomes, or sex chromosomes, cell nuclei that determine the sex of a person (as well as carrying some genetic information not related to sex determination). Sex chromosomes are inherited in the same way as the other 22 human chromosome pairs, normal persons being either XX (female) or XY (male). The Y chromosome carries little genetic information, and it is largely the properties of the X chromosome that determine sex-linked characteristics in males. Sex-linked characteristics include hemophilia and color blindness, which are carried as recessive genes in females.
See also: Chromosome.

Xavier, Saint Francis (Spanish: Francisco Javier; 1506-52), Spanish missionary. A friend of St. Ignatius of Loyola, he helped him found the order of Jesuits. In 1541 he set out as a missionary, reaching the East Indies, Goa, India, Malacca, and Ceylon. In 1549 he established a Jesuit mission in Japan and in 1552 sought to extend his work to China, but died on Shangchuan while waiting for permission to enter the country. His feast day is Dec. 3. *See also:* Jesuits.

Xenakis, Yannis (1922-), Greek avant-garde composer who developed "stochastic" music using computer-programmed sequences based on mathematical probability, as in *Métastaseis* (1953-54) and *Achorripsis* (1958).

Xenon, chemical element, symbol Xe; for physical constants, see Periodic Table. Xenon was discovered by Sir William Ramsay and Morris W. Travers in 1898. It occurs in the atmosphere to the extent of one part in 20 million. It is obtained from liquid air residues and from the gases evolved from certain mineral springs. Xenon is a colorless, odorless, and chemically inert gas. It is a member of the noble or "inert" gases. The noble gases do not normally combine with other elements, but the existence of many xenon compounds has been established. Xenon difluoride, tetrafluoride, hexafluoride, and others have been prepared. It is used in special electric lamps.

Xenophanes (570-480 B.C.), Greek poet and pre-Socratic philosopher. An Ionian who emigrated to South Italy, he wrote satires and ridiculed the idea that the gods had human attributes, positing a single, all-embracing divine being. Only some 40 fragments of his works survive.
See also: Pre-Socratic philosophy.

Xenophon (431-355 B.C.), Greek soldier and author. An Athenian and admirer of Socrates, he joined the Greek expedition supporting Cyrus the Younger (401) and after its defeat led the Greeks back in a heroic 1,500-mi (2,414-km) march recounted in his famous *Anabasis*. He later fought for Sparta, whose conservative militarism he admired. Retiring to the country, he wrote his famous volumes of Greek history, memoirs of Socrates, a romanticized account of Cyrus the Great's education, and works on horsemanship and politics.
See also: Greece, Ancient.

Xerography *See:* Photocopying.

Xerxes, name of two kings of ancient Persia. **Xerxes I** (r.486-465 B.C.) continued the war against Greece started by his father, Darius I. His vast army crossed the Hellespont in 480 B.C., and despite a defeat at Thermopylae, destroyed Athens. However, his fleet was defeated at Salamis (480), and he returned to Persia, leaving his army, which was defeated at Plataea (479). He was murdered in a court intrigue. **Xerxes II**, his grandson, was murdered by his half brother, Sogdianus, in 424 B.C., after ruling for 45 days.
See also: Persia, Ancient.

Xhosa, group of related tribes (formerly called *Kafir*) predominantly living in Transkei, South Africa. Bantu-speaking, they are mainly agriculturists, though some cattle are raised. The Xhosa are organized in patrilineal clans. Many now work as migrant laborers in Johannesburg.

Xiamen (pop. 588,000), Hsia-men, or Amoy, port city in Fujian province, southeastern China, located on Amoy and Ku-lang islands, on the Strait of

Formosa at the mouth of the Chiu-lung Chiang (river). The city has a history of contact with Western nations, beginning in 1544 with the arrival of Portuguese traders, who were soon expelled. The port was visited by Dutch, Spanish, and British ships during the 17th and 18th centuries, but foreign trade restrictions were imposed in 1757. As a result of a treaty following the Opium War of 1839-42, Xiamen and 4 other ports were reopened to the British, and foreigners were allowed residence. During the 19th century the port was a center of the tea trade. It was held by the Japanese from 1938 to 1945. It remains a shipping center, with industries including food processing, shipbuilding, and engineering. Xiamen is now connected to the mainland by a causeway. It has had close ties with nearby Taiwan, and has a large emigrant Chinese population.
See also: China.

Xi Jiang (also Hsi Chiang), longest river of southern China. Originating in the highlands of Yunnan province, it flows some 1,500 mi (2,414 km) southeast to the South China Sea. There, along with several other rivers, it forms a delta on which is located the large Chinese city of Guangzhou.

Xinjiang, large, northwestern province of China, bordered on the northwest by Kazachstan. Most of the region's inhabitants are of Middle Eastern origin, including Turkish. The main religion is Islam. The region has been under Chinese rule off and on since the Han dynasty (202 B.C.-A.D. 220). It was officially made a province by the Chinese in 1884. The region's economy is based primarily on herding (cattle, sheep, and goats) and farming (corn, cotton, wheat, and rice). Ürümqi is its capital.
See also: China.

Xochimilco *See:* Lake Xochimilco.

X ray, type of radiation of higher frequency than visible light but lower than a gamma ray. Discovered by the German physicist Wilhem Conrad Roentgen in 1895, X rays are usually produced by high-energy electrons impinging upon a metal target. X rays are often used in medicine to make radiographs (X-ray pictures) of the bones and internal organs of the body.
See also: Roentgen, Wilhelm Conrad.

Xunzi, or Hsun Tzu (340?-245? B.C.), Chinese philosopher. He is considered a follower of Kongfuzi (Confucius; 551-479 B.C.). Whereas Mengzi (Mencius), the "Second Sage" (4th century B.C.), interpreted Kongfuzi in an optimistic light, teaching the intrinsic goodness of human nature, Xunzi taught that human nature is intrinsically evil and that morality must be taught and reinforced by society. His teachings are articulated in the book *Xunzi*.
See also: Philosophy.

Xylophone, percussion instrument consisting of a series of tuned wooden blocks set in a frame and struck with special hammers. Of ancient origin, it was widespread in Asia and Africa before being introduced in Europe.

XYZ Affair, diplomatic incident that nearly led to open war between the United States and France in 1798. President John Adams sent John Marshall, Elbridge Gerry, and C. C. Pinckney to settle disputes with France following

Jay's Treaty. They were met by three unnamed agents, later called X, Y, and Z, who demanded U.S. loans and bribes before opening negotiations. When this was announced in Congress, there was an uproar, but Adams averted war and reopened negotiations with Talleyrand, the French foreign minister. Later, the agents were identified as Jean Conrad Hottinguer (X), a U.S. banker in Hamburg named Bellamy (Y), and Lucien Hauteval (Z).

Y

Y, 25th letter of the English alphabet. Like *u*, *v*, and *w*, it derives from the ancient Semitic letter *waw* (meaning "hook"), itself adapted from an Egyptian hieroglyphic. It passed into the Greek alphabet as the letter *upsilon* and was later used in the Roman alphabet only for words of Greek origin. In Old and Middle English, *y* was often used instead of *i*, a usage that is part of our language today. In chemistry, *y* is used as the symbol for the element *yttrium*.

Yablonovyy Mountains, mountain range in Russia and northern Mongolia. The range, which extends 1,000 mi (1,600 km), is a watershed, dividing those rivers that flow into the Arctic Ocean from those that flow into the Pacific. Its highest peak is Mt. Sokhondo (8,199 ft/2,499 m). There are large tin mines in the mountains. The range is crossed by the Trans-Siberian Railroad at Yablonovo.

Yachts and yachting, popular international sport and pastime of racing or cruising in yachts. Yachting developed in the early 19th century as steam began to supplant sails in commercial vessels. It became established on an organized basis with the setting up of the New York Yacht Club in 1844. In 1851 the first race for the *America's Cup* took place, and subsequent races for the cup played a major role in the evolution of yacht design. After World War I the trend moved away from large, expensive yachts, and popular "one-design" classes emerged, with the Bermuda rig predominating. Small-keep yachts and catboats are now raced and sailed for pleasure throughout the world. Ocean racing is also popular, and recently single-handed transatlantic and round-the-world races have attracted enormous public attention.
See also: Sailing.

Yahweh *See:* Jehovah.

Yak (*Bos grunniens*), shaggy ox of the high plateau of Tibet. Yaks are distinguished by the long fringe of hair on shoulders, flanks, thighs, and tail, and the long in-curved horns. Wild yaks are large animals, up to 7 ft (2.1 m) at the shoulder, with black coats. Domestic yaks, kept as beasts of burden and for their milk, are smaller and may be any of several colors.

Yakima (pop. 188,823), city in south-central Washington state, seat of Yakima County, located on the Yakima River, at the eastern edge of Mt. Rainier National Park. The city was established as a railroad depot in 1886, and began to flourish after the introduction of irrigation (1891) made the Yakima Valley an important agricultural area. Industry includes lumber and the processing of agricultural products. Native Americans of the Yakima

confederation, the group of tribes originally living in the area, now live on a nearby reservation.
See also: Washington.

Yakima, Native Americans belonging to the Sahapin-Chinook language family. They lived along the Columbia and Yakima rivers in Washington. In 1859 they were settled on a Washington reservation after a 3-year war against European-American settlers (1855-58).

Yale, Elihu (1649-1721), American-born English merchant who made a fortune in India (1670-99). In 1718 he made a donation to the collegiate school at New Haven, which was renamed Yale College (now Yale University).

Yale, Linus, Jr. (1821-68), U.S. inventor and manufacturer of locks. He developed the Yale Infallible Bank Lock (1851) and other bank locks, the combination lock (1861), and the key-operated cylinder pin-tumbler lock (patents 1861 and 1865), developed from a design used in ancient Egypt and now commonly used on doors of residences. Yale and partners Henry Towne and Henry Robinson Towne founded the Yale Lock Manufacturing Company in 1868.

Yale University, U.S. university chartered in 1701 as the Collegiate School, first at Killingworth, Milford, and Saybrook, Conn., then (1716) at New Haven, Conn., its present site. Renamed Yale College in 1718 in honor of Elihu Yale (1649-1721), it expanded greatly in the 19th century, awarded the first Ph.D. in the United States in 1861, and was renamed Yale University in 1887.

Yalow, Rosalyn Sussman (1921-), U.S. medical researcher who shared the 1977 Nobel Prize in physiology or medicine for helping develop *radioimmunoassay*, a technique for measuring minute amounts of hormones, vitamins, or enzymes that could not be detected by other means.
See also: Physiology.

Yalta (pop. 85,000), winter and health resort on the Black Sea, in southern Crimea, Ukraine. It was site of the 1945 Yalta Conference between U.S. president Roosevelt, British prime minister Churchill, and Soviet premier Stalin.
See also: Union of Soviet Socialist Republics.

Yalta Conference, meeting held near Yalta (Crimea, Ukraine), Feb. 4-11, 1945, between Winston Churchill, Franklin Roosevelt, and Joseph Stalin, representing the major Allied powers in World War II. Plans were drawn up for the treatment of Germany after the war, including its division into occupation zones, the elimination of its war industries, and the prosecution of war criminals. The foundation of a new Polish state was decided upon, and the creation of the United Nations was discussed. The USSR agreed to join in the war against Japan after Germany's defeat, receiving occupation areas in eastern Europe in return.
See also: World War II.

Yalu River (Chinese: *Ya-Lu Chiang*; Korean: *Amnok-Kang*), river forming most of the boundary between North Korea and Manchuria, China. It rises in the Changbai Shan (Long White Mountains) of Manchuria and flows southeast 500 mi (800 km) to Korea Bay (Yellow Sea). The crossing of the river by Chinese Communist troops to help North Korea (Oct. 1950) was an important event of the Korean War.

Yam (genus *Dioscorea*), plant of the yam family with a flowering vine and a large tuber, similar to a sweet potato but of a different botanical family. The name "yam" often refers to the yellow- or white-fleshed tuber of edible species (e.g., *D. alata* and *D. rotundata*). The tuber is actually an enlarged underground portion of the stem, weighing as much as 100 lb (45 kg), in which the plant stores starch, water, and some sugar. Some varieties contain toxic substances that can only be eliminated by cooking, and cortisone and other drugs are derived from *saponin* compounds found in certain wild yams. Yams grow in warm, moist climates, and are an important food crop in West Africa, India, Southeast Asia, and the Caribbean area.

Yamamoto, Isoroku (1884-1943), commander of the Japanese fleet in World War II. He planned and commanded the attack on Pearl Harbor (1941) and Midway Island (1941). He was reported killed in an air ambush.
See also: World War II.

Yamasaki, Minoru (1912-86), U.S. architect. The Lambert-St. Louis air terminal (1951), the McGregor Conference Center at Wayne University, Detroit (1956), and the U.S. science pavilion at the Seattle Exposition (1962) reveal his mastery of ornamental and sculptural form. He was also the architect, with Emery Roth, of the World Trade Center in New York.
See also: Architecture.

Yamasee, Native Americans of the Muskogean language family. Living in southern Georgia and northern Florida, they were driven into South Carolina by the Spanish (1687) and back into Florida (1715) by the British, who in 1727 destroyed their village near St. Augustine. The survivors eventually assimilated with the Seminole and Creek.

Yamashita, Tomoyuki (1885-1946), Japanese army commander in World War II. His forces overran Malaya and captured Singapore (1942). He later commanded Japanese forces in the Philippines, surrendering in 1945. He was hanged by the Allies for the atrocities committed by his troops.
See also: World War II.

Yamato period, portion of Japanese history (c.A.D. 200-646) during which the imperial center was Yamato, the area around current-day Nara, near Osaka. During this time the Japanese empire included much of central Japan and parts of southern Korea. The period was characterized by the influence of Chinese culture on Japanese arts and government, and the transmission of the Buddhist religion from China to Japan (although the primary popular religion remained Shinto).
See also: Japan.

Yam bean *See:* Jicama.

Yancey, William Lowndes (1814-63), U.S. proslavery politician and advocate of secession. A lawyer and U.S. senator (1844-46), he drafted the

proslavery "Alabama platform" (1848) in reply to the Wilmot proviso, became a leading "fire-eater," wrote the Alabama ordinance of secession (1860), and served the Confederate government in the Civil War as commissioner to England and France (1861-62).
See also: Slavery; Civil War, U.S.

Yang, Chen Ning (1922-), Chinese-born U.S. physicist who shared with Tsung Dao Lee the 1957 Nobel Prize in physics for their studies of violations of the conservation of parity.
See also: Parity; Physics.

Yangon (pop. 2,458,700; formerly Rangoon), capital, largest city, and chief port of Myanmar (Burma), on the Rangoon River. It is a commercial and manufacturing center, with textile, sawmilling, food-processing, and petroleum industries. Its gold-domed Shwe Dagon Pagoda is the country's principal Buddhist shrine. Yangon was founded in 1753 as the Burmese capital. It was occupied by the British (1824-26) and retaken by them in 1852, after which it developed as a modern city. During World War II Yangon was occupied by the Japanese and suffered heavy damage.

Yangtze River, or Chang River, China's longest river. It rises in the Kunlun Mountains of Tibet and flows 3,434 mi (5,526 km) into the East China Sea, draining an area (about 750,000 sq mi/1,942,500 sq km) that includes China's richest agricultural land along its lower reaches. Its main tributaries are the Min, Wu, and Han. It is navigable for oceangoing ships for some 600 mi (966 km), as far as Wuhan.

Yank, World War II weekly magazine produced by U.S. Army personnel for U.S. soldiers around the world. Contributors included both soldier correspondents, photographers, and artists and enlistees, whose work for the magazine was unpaid. Information helpful to those in the armed forces as well as soldiers' comments and complaints were printed in the regular feature "Mail Call." *Yank* appeared from June 17, 1942 until the end of the war in 1945, and contained many exclusive articles on the progress of the war.
See also: World War II.

Yankee, slang term of uncertain origin, probably Dutch. Outside the United States, it refers to anyone from the United States; inside the country, it normally refers to a New Englander, especially someone descended from colonists. In the South it refers to Northerners, a tradition dating from the Civil War.

Yankee Doodle, song popular among American troops in the Revolutionary War. It probably originated among the British during the French and Indian Wars as a song making fun of the Americans, who later adopted it for themselves.

Yaoundé, or Yaunde (pop. 649,000), capital city of Cameroon, located in the south-central part of the country between the Nyong and Sanaga rivers. It was founded in 1888 by the Germans, under whom Cameroon was a protectorate. When the area was divided in 1922, the city became the capital of French East Cameroon. In 1960 it was made capital of the newly inde-

pendent Republic of Cameroon. Yaoundé is a center for transportation, light industry, and education.
See also: Cameroon.

Yap Islands, in the western Pacific Ocean, part of the Caroline Islands, consisting of 4 large and 10 small islands, surrounded by a coral reef. The Micronesian population fishes and grows yams, taro, bananas, and coconuts.

Yaqui, tribe of Native Americans living in Sonora, northern Mexico, and in Arizona and California. In ancient times the Yaqui lived by farming, hunting, and gathering. They defeated the invading Spaniards (1533 and 1609). After making peace, they arranged for the Jesuit missionaries to live with them and teach them European agricultural methods. As a result, the Yaqui culture blends Roman Catholicism and ancient Yaqui custom. Starting in the 1730s the Yaqui rebelled against Spanish colonial rule. Fighting continued into the 1900s, and many Yaqui fled to the United States. Modern Yaqui are primarily subsistence farmers.

Yawning, involuntary gaping of the mouth, often accompanied by involuntary stretching of the muscles and accompanied by a deep inspiration. It usually occurs during the drowsy state produced by fatigue or boredom and is often a prelude to sleep.

Yaws, disease caused by an organism related to that which causes syphilis. Common in the tropics, it occurs often in children and consists of a local lesion on the limbs; there is also mild systemic disease. Chronic, destructive lesions of skin, bone, and cartilage may develop later. When the Wassermann test is positive, that indicates the disease is present, and penicillin is the treatment of choice.

Yazoo Fraud, 1795 scandal in which the Georgia state legislature was bribed to sell 35 million acres (14.2 million hectares) of land along the Yazoo River to 4 land companies. In 1796 a new legislature rescinded the act. In a historic 1810 decision the U.S. Supreme Court declared the rescinding unconstitutional and awarded compensation to investors who had suffered.

Yazoo River, tributary of the Mississippi River, in the state of Mississippi. It begins near Greenwood and flows southwest 188 mi (303 km) to join the Mississippi near Vicksburg. A system of dams and reservoirs on the Yazoo and its tributaries has reduced flooding in the fertile cotton-growing region.

Yeager, Chuck (Charles Elwood Yeager; 1923-), U.S. fighter pilot in World War II, test pilot, first person to fly faster than the speed of sound (Oct. 14, 1947). Yeager set a second record by flying 2 1/2 times the speed of sound, or 1,650 mph (2,655 kmph) on Dec. 12, 1953. He retired from the military as a brigadier general (1975), later serving on the presidential commission investigating the 1986 explosion of the *Challenger* space shuttle. He told his life story in *Yeager* (1985), coauthored by Leo Janos, and his exploits as a test pilot are celebrated in Tom Wolfe's *The Right Stuff* (1979).

Year, name of various units of time, all depending on the revolution of the earth about the sun. The *sidereal year* (365.256636 mean solar days) is the average time the earth takes to complete one revolution measured with respect to a fixed direction in space. The *tropical year* (365.24220 mean solar days), the year measured by the changing seasons, is that in which the mean longitude of the sun moves through 360°. The *anomalistic year* (365.25964 mean solar days) is the average interval between successive terrestrial perihelions. The *civil year* is a period of variable duration, usually 365 or 366 days (leap year), depending on the type of calendar in use.

Yeast, any of single-celled plants classified with the fungi. Some cause diseases of the skin and mucous membranes, while others, notably the strains of *Saccharomyces cerevisiae* (baker's yeast), are used in baking, brewing, and winemaking. Yeasts employ either or both of 2 metabolic processes: Fermentation involves the anaerobic decomposition of hexose sugars to yield alcohol (ethanol) and carbon dioxide; "respiration" involves the exothermic decomposition of various sugars in the presence of oxygen to give carbon dioxide and water. Yeasts are also grown as a source of food rich in B-complex vitamins.

Yeats, William Butler (1865-1939), Irish poet and dramatist, leader of the Celtic Renaissance in Ireland and one of the world's greatest lyric poets. Nationalism was a major element in his early poetry, such as *The Wanderings of Oisin* (1889), which drew on Irish legend. Yeats cofounded (1898) Dublin's Irish Literary Theatre, later the Abbey Theatre. His mature poetic works, often symbolic and mystical, treated universal themes. They include *The Wild Swans at Coole* (1917), *The Tower* (1928), and *Last Poems* (1940). Yeats was awarded the Nobel Prize in literature in 1923.

Yeh Chien-Ying, or Ye Jianying (1899-1985), Chinese minister of defense (1971-78). A planner of the Long March and a Central Committee member from 1945, his seniority and military connections assured his continued position within the inner circle of leadership after the death of Mao Tse-tung (Mao Zedong).
See also: China.

Yellow *See:* Color.

Yellow daisy *See:* Black-eyed Susan.

Yellow-dog contract, pledge signed by prospective employees that they will not join a union. U.S. Supreme Court decisions (1908, 1915) upheld their legality, and they were widely used by antiunion employers in the 1920s. The Norris-La Guardia Act (1932) finally outlawed them.

Yellow fever, infectious disease caused by a virus carried by mosquitos of the genus *Aëdes* and occurring in tropical Americas and Africa. The disease consists of fever, headache, backache, prostration, and vomiting of sudden onset. Protein loss in the urine, kidney failure, and liver disorder with jaundice are also frequent. Hemorrhage from mucous membranes, especially in the gastrointestinal tract, is also common. A moderate number of cases are fatal, but a mild form of the disease is also recognized. Vaccination to induce immunity is important and effective as no specific therapy is available; mosquito control provides a similarly important preventive measure.

Yellowhammer, or yellow-shafted flicker (*Colaptes auratus auratus*), bird of the woodpecker family, subspecies of the common flicker, native to North America; also, the yellow bunting (German: *Ammer*, "bunting"; *Emberiza citrinella*), finch of Europe and Asia.

Yellow jacket, one of a genus (*Vespula*) of hornets, social wasps of the family Vespidae, common in North America. They usually construct an underground nest of paper, frequently in or near human habitation. Yellow jackets can inflict a painful sting.

Yellow journalism, vulgar and sensational newspaper reporting whose sole aim is to attract readers. The term originated with the "Yellow Kid" comic strip in the Sunday supplement of Joseph Pulitzer's New York *World* (1896). This began a "yellow journalism" circulation war in the city with William Randolph Hearst's *Journal*.It is still evident today.

Yellowknife (pop. 11,800), capital and largest city of Northwest Territories, in north-central Canada, on Yellowknife Bay of Great Slave Lake. The city was founded in 1935 after the discovery of gold nearby, and was relocated in 1945. The economy is supported by gold prospecting, mining, and tourism. *See also:* Northwest Territories.

Yellowlegs (genus *Tringa*), migrating shore bird of the sandpiper family, native to the Western Hemisphere and identified by dark wings, white belly and tail, and long yellow legs. The 2 species are the greater yellowlegs (*T. melanoleuca*), measuring 13-15 in (34-38 cm), and the lesser yellowlegs (*T. flavipes*), measuring about 10 in (25 cm). The birds nest in Canada and winter in the southern United States, around the Gulf of Mexico, and as far south as Chile.

Yellow poplar, or tulip tree (*Liriodendron tulipifera*), tall hardwood tree of the magnolia family, native to eastern North America. It is the tallest broadleaf tree of eastern North America, its straight trunk growing to a height of 200 ft (60 m) and a diameter of 10 ft (3 m). The light-colored wood is widely used for furniture, veneer, plywood, and crates. Nectar from its tulip-shaped yellow and green flowers is an important source of honey.

Yellow River, or Hwang Ho, river of northern China, flowing 2,903 mi (4,672 km) from the Kunlun Mountains, generally east to the Yellow Sea. It is named for its fertile yellow silt and is often nicknamed China's Sorrow because of terrible floods and destructive changes of course. In 1955 a major 50-year flood-control and hydroelectric project was begun on the river.

Yellow Sea, or Huang Hai, western arm of the Pacific Ocean between Korea and northeast China. It opens in the south into the East China Sea. The name arises from the color of its waters, which receive yellow silt from the Yellow and other rivers.
See also: Pacific Ocean.

Yellowstone National Park, oldest and largest U.S. national park, created in 1872 and covering 3,472 sq mi (8,992 sq km), mostly in northwestern Wyoming. It contains some of the most spectacular wonders in the United

States, including Old Faithful geyser, thousands of hot springs and mud pools, petrified forests, black grass cliffs, and the Grand Canyon of the Yellowstone River. Wildlife abounds in the forests covering most of the park.

Yellowstone River, river flowing 671 mi (1,080 km) from northwestern Wyoming north and east through Montana to join the Missouri River at the North Dakota state line. It rises in the Rocky Mountains, flowing into Yellowstone Lake in Yellowstone National Park, emptying by a dramatic drop of over 420 ft (128 m) into Yellowstone Canyon. It then flows northeast through the Great Plains of Montana. The river system, including the tributaries Bighorn, Tongue, and Powder, drains 70,000 sq mi (181,000 sq km). The river is visited for its natural beauty and is used for irrigation.

Yellowthroat (*Geothlypis trichas*), small, migratory bird of the wood warbler family native to North America. Yellowthroats are olive-green with white and buff breasts and measure about 5 in (13 cm) long; males have black masks. They are found in the tall grasses of marshes and other wet areas.

Yeltsin, Boris Nikolayevich, (1931-   ), president of the Russian Federation (1990-   ). He joined the Communist Party in 1961. Yeltsin was a member of the Politburo, the policy-making organ of the party, and was President Mikhail Gorbachev's chief rival. After he was elected president of the Russian republic, Yeltsin resigned from the Communist Party. In 1991, after a general election, he retained the presidency of the Russian Federation. In 1993 he suppressed a rebellion of communist and nationalist members of parliament. He tried to shake off the communist past by discontinuing a number of communist organizations. In 1995 he temporarily left politics because of health problems. However, in 1996 he won the presidential elections with an ample majority.

Yemen, officially the Republic of Yemen, formerly divided into Yemen (Sana), also known as North Yemen, and Yemen (Aden), also known as South Yemen, now united into a single republic occupying the southwest corner of the Arabian peninsula and including the islands of Kamaran, Perim, and Socotra. With a combined area of 207,232 sq mi (536,870 sq km), Yemen is bordered by Saudi Arabia to the north and northeast, the Gulf of Aden to the south, Oman to the east, and the Red Sea to the west.
Land and climate. Beyond the Red Sea coast with its coral reefs and low-lying beaches is the Tihamah, a dry coastal plain, and, farther inland, a foothill region scored by valleys, known as *wadis*. The coastal plain along the Gulf of Aden is hot and arid with palm oases. The lowlands along both shores give way to a mountainous interior with some peaks exceeding 12,000 ft (3,658 m). Among the mountains is a mosaic of plateaus, upland plains, and fertile valleys. The mountains eventually give way in the north and east to the Rub'al-Khali desert. The highlands of Yemen enjoy the best climate on the Arabian peninsula, with annual rainfall of some 16-32 in (41-81 cm).
People. The people of what was formerly South Yemen consist of various tribes of Arabs and are either farmers or nomads. The people of what was formerly Yemen are mostly south Arabians, but there are African influences in the people living along the Red Sea coast and toward the south. Though the people are Muslim, they are divided about equally between Sunni and Shi'te Muslims. The religious differences translated into significant social

Yemen

Capital:	San'a'
Area:	207,232 sq mi
	(536,870 sq km)
Population:	15,272,000
Language:	Arabic
Government:	Republic
Independent:	since 1990 (united)
Head of gov.:	Prime minister
Per capita:	U.S. $260
Mon. unit:	1 Rial = 100 fils

and political divisions in the former Yemen Arab Republic, and are now part of the United Republic of Yemen as well. The official language of Yemen is Arabic. *History.* The histories of North Yemen and South Yemen have, since antiquity, sometimes blended, sometimes gone their separate ways, and at other times collided. Formerly known as Al-Yaman, the land of South Yemen was once home to the Minaean, Sabaean, and Himyarite kingdoms. Conquered by Arabs in the 8th century A.D., it became part of the Ottoman Empire during the 16th century. Known as Aden under British control from the 1830s, South Yemen became fully independent in 1967 following the collapse of the Federation of South Arabia. Governed by the Marxist National Liberation Front, it was known as the People's Democratic Republic of Yemen.

Neighboring North Yemen was once part of the Sabaean kingdom and was incorporated into the Muslim caliphate in the 7th century A.D. Various foreign powers have exercised nominal suzerainty over North Yemen, including the Ottoman Turks from the 1500s to 1918. But effective power from the 9th to the 20th centuries lay in the hands of competing local imams. In 1962 an army coup led to the proclamation of a republic. In the ensuing civil war, Saudi Arabia backed the royalist tribes, while Egypt supported the republicans. The conflict ended with a mediated settlement in 1970 from which the republicans emerged in control of the fledgling Yemen Arab Republic.

In 1972 war erupted between the Yemen Arab Republic and the People's Democratic Republic of Yemen. A ceasefire was followed by an agreement to unify North Yemen and South Yemen, but hostilities flared again in 1979. Finally, on May 22, 1990, the two countries were united as the Republic of Yemen under the interim presidency of Ali Abdallah Salih. Yemen abstained from a vote in the Arab League to condemn Saddam Hussein's invasion of Kuwait and earned the immediate enmity of its powerful neighbor, Saudi Arabia, at considerable cost to its already troubled economy. After the 1993 elections tensions between the north and the south increased. The ensuing civil war of 1994 was won by the north. In 1995 there was an armed conflict with Eritrea regarding some small islands in the strait which gives entrance to the Red Sea.

Yenisey River, major river of Siberia, flowing 2,500 mi (4,000 km) from the Sayan Mountains west and north to the Kara Sea (Arctic Ocean). The river is navigable by ocean steamers for 400 mi (640 km) to the port of Igarka, and is an important source of hydroelectric power.

Yeoman, Middle English word denoting a king's or nobleman's retainer or officer, or a freehold farmer cultivating his own land, ranking below the gentry. Yeoman now refers to a naval petty officer performing clerical duties.

Yerevan, or Erevan (pop. 1,202,000), capital city of Armenia, on the Razdan River, in southeastern Europe, near Turkey. Archeological remains indicate a settlement on the site dating from before 2000 B.C., and a fortress from the 8th century B.C.
The city was often under siege and destroyed by rival powers, particularly, during the 15th-19th centuries, the Persians and Ottomans. It was established as capital of the Armenian republic in 1920. Hydroelectric power from the Razdan River has helped the city become a center for chemical, engineering, and other industries. It is also a center for culture and higher education.
See also: Armenia.

Yerkes Observatory, observatory of the University of Chicago. It was set up in 1892 on the shores of Lake Geneva, Wis., by the astronomer George Hale and financed by Charles Yerkes. The observatory contains the world's largest refracting telescope (built 1897), its lens 40 in (102 cm) in diameter, together with several reflecting telescopes.
See also: Astronomy; Hale, George Ellery.

Yevtushenko, Yevgeny (1933-), Russian poet who became a spokesperson for "liberal" forces in Soviet literature in the early 1960s. His best-known poems include "Babi-Yar" (1961), dealing with the Nazis' massacre of Soviet Jews in 1941, and "The Heirs of Stalin" (1962), warning of the persistence of Stalinism.

Yew, any of several species of evergreen trees and shrubs of genus *Taxus* native to the Northern Hemisphere. Yews are often grown as ornamental plants. They have flat, dark-green needles and red-brown bark. Their wood, which is hard and dense, was once valued for its use in archery bows and furniture. The bark, needles, and seeds are poisonous and can be fatal to livestock. Yews native to North America include the western, or Pacific, yew (*T. brevifolia*), used for cabinetry; the Japanese yew (*T. cuspidata*), an ornamental shrub; and the American yew, or ground hemlock (*T. canadensis*), which grows along the ground.

Yiddish, language spoken by Jewish people, developed during the A.D. 900s and 1000s. Yiddish has roots in several languages, including German, Hebrew, Aramaic, French, and Italian. After World War II (1939-45), in which the Nazis exterminated over 6 million Jews, the use of Yiddish declined considerably.

Yiddish literature, body of written works that developed in the late 1200s and remained strongly connected to Jewish religious tradition until the 1800s, when modern Jewish literature had its beginnings through a cultural literary movement called the *Haskalah* (Enlightenment). The humorist Solomon Rabinowitz, who wrote under the name Sholom Aleichem, Shalom Jacob

Abramovich, whose pen name was Mendele the Bookseller, and Isaac Leibush Peretz stand out as major exponents of Yiddish literature during much of the 1800s and 1900s. Some of the common themes underlying most works of this time include the hardships involved with living in a non-Jewish world and the social conflicts within the Jewish community.

The flowering of Yiddish literature took place during the period of 1914-18 in Poland, the Soviet Union, and the United States. During this period, Sholem Asch in Poland, David Bergelson in the Soviet Union, and Moishe Leib Halpern in the United States ranked as the most important figures in Yiddish literature. During World War II (1939-45), many notable Yiddish writers perished along with the 6 million Jews that were exterminated by the Nazis. Isaac Bashevis Singer, a Polish-born U.S. author, became the first Yiddish writer to win the Nobel Prize in literature (1978).

Yin and yang, two principles in Chinese philosophy, representing the passive and the active forces of the universe. Yin stands for earth, female, passive, dark, and receiving; yang, for heaven, male, active, light, and generative. All things exist through their interaction. The symbol for yin-yang is a circle divided into 2 curved forms, one dark, the other light.
See also: Philosophy.

YMCA *See:* Young Men's Christian Association (YMCA).

Yoga (Sanskrit, "union"), forms of spiritual discipline practiced in Buddhism and Hinduism. Through these disciplines the yogi (one who follows yoga) strives to free the mind from attachment to the senses and to achieve *samadhi*—or union with *Brahma*, the deity—and fusion into oneness. In Hindu tradition there are three varieties of yoga: *karma yoga*, salvation through action; *jnana yoga*, salvation through knowledge; and *bhakti yoga*, salvation through devotion. In each the student passes through 8 levels of attainment, supervised by a guru, or teacher. The practice of *hatha yoga*, based on physical postures and control, has become increasingly popular in the West.
See also: Hinduism.

Yogurt, or yoghurt, semisolid, cultured milk food made by inoculating pasteurized milk with a culture of *Streptococcus thermophilus* and *Lactobacillus bulgaricus* and incubating until the desired acidity is achieved. Various fruits can be added.

Yokohama (pop. 2,250,500), city in Japan on the western shore of Tokyo Bay, a leading national seaport and part of Tokyo's industrial belt in southern Honshu Island. It is a trading center and supports large shipbuilding, iron, steel, chemical, machinery, and oil industries. It also has several universities. Yokohama was a fishing village when visited by Commodore Matthew Perry in 1854. Its growth began in 1859, when it became a foreign-trade port.
See also: Japan.

Yom Kippur, Jewish Day of Atonement, the most sacred day in the Jewish religious calendar. It falls on the 10th day after the Jewish New Year (Rosh Hashanah) and is marked by repentance, prayers, and abstention from food, drink, sex, and work.
See also: Judaism.

Yonkers (pop. 195,351), city in southeastern New York State just north of New York City, between the Bronx and Hudson rivers. The area, once inhabited by the Manhattan tribe, was granted in 1646 to a Dutch nobleman, Adriaen Van der Donck, known as "the Young Gentleman," or De Jonkheer, thus the name Yonkers. The farming village of Yonkers developed after Frederick Philipse (who acquired land in 1693) and his heirs rented land to farmers. In the mid-19th century the area was connected by rail to New York City and the first industry, Otis Elevator, was established. Industrial development attracted immigrants during the 20th century, and the city's population peaked in 1970. Current industry includes chemicals, food products, and electronics. St. Joseph's College and Elizabeth Seton College are located in Yonkers, and the Yonkers Museum has an important collection of paintings of the Hudson River school.
See also: New York.

York (pop. 107,700), city in northern England. Built on the site of a Roman fort, it emerged during the early Middle Ages as an important religious capital and trade center. Today York, with its many museums and historic buildings and churches, thrives primarily on tourism. The Cathedral of St. Peter, known as Minster Cathedral, and the National Railway Museum are of special interest. It also supports several industries, including the manufacture of precision instruments.
See also: England.

York, ruling dynasty of England (1461-85), a branch of the Plantagenet family, whose symbol was the white rose. The three Yorkist kings were **Edward IV** (r.1461-83), his son **Edward V** (r.April-June 1483), and **Richard III** (r.1483-85), who was killed at the Battle of Bosworth Field by Henry Tudor (Henry VII), who established the House of Tudor as the ruling family.
See also: United Kingdom.

Yorkshire terrier, breed of toy dog developed in Yorkshire and Lancashire, England, in the mid-19th century to hunt rats. Yorkies stand 8-9 in (20-23 cm) at the shoulder and weigh 4-8 lb (2-2.3 kg). Their long, straight, silky coat is bluish gray, with tan on the head and chest.

Yorktown (pop. 450), town in southeastern Virginia, seat of York County, on the York River, and site of the last campaign of the Revolutionary War. In 1781, 16,000 American and French troops, led by Generals Washington and Rochambeau, laid siege to 7,000 British troops under Lord Cornwallis in Yorktown. With British naval reinforcements defeated by U.S. Admiral de Grasse and escape impossible, Cornwallis surrendered.
See also: Virginia.

Yorktown, Battle of *See:* Revolutionary War in America.

Yoruba, African people in southwest Nigeria, characteristically urban dwellers. Yoruba culture exists also in Cuba and Brazil because of large slave importations.

Yosemite Falls, North America's highest waterfalls, in Yosemite National Park, central California. Here Yosemite Creek descends in 2 dramatic drops:

the Upper Falls (1,430 ft/436 m), and the Lower Falls (320 ft/98 m). In between the waters fall in cascades, for a total descent of 2,425 ft (739 m).

Yosemite National Park, national park in eastern California, established in 1890, 1,189 sq mi (3,000 sq km) of spectacular mountain scenery formed during the last glacial period, on the western slopes of the Sierra Nevada. Its chief attractions are the Yosemite Valley; Yosemite Falls, the highest falls in North America; and the Mariposa Grove of 200 giant sequoias.

Youmans, Vincent (1898-1946), U.S. composer of popular musical comedies of the 1920s, among them *No, No, Nanette* and *Hit the Deck*. His songs included "Tea for Two," "Without a Song," and "I Want to Be Happy."

Young, Andrew Jackson, Jr. (1932-   ), U.S. clergyman and civil rights leader. He helped draft the civil rights and voting rights acts (1964, 1965) and served in the U.S. House of Representatives (1971-76). As the first black U.S. ambassador to the UN (1977-79), he stirred up frequent controversy with undiplomatic public statements. In 1981 he was elected mayor of Atlanta.

Young, Brigham (1801-77), U.S. Mormon leader. He joined the Mormons in 1832 and quickly rose to prominence. After 3 years as a missionary in England, he assumed leadership of the Mormons following the death of Joseph Smith (1844) and led them to Salt Lake City, Utah, in 1846. Young established a thriving city on a sound commercial basis and became first governor of Utah in 1850. He may have had as many as 27 wives.
See also: Mormons.

Young, Cy (Denton True Young; 1867-1955), U.S. baseball player. Considered one of the greatest pitchers of all time, he holds the record for career wins (511) and innings pitched (7,356), he pitched no-hit games (1897 and 1908) and pitched one perfect game (May 5, 1904). Young played for the Cleveland Spiders (1890-98), St. Louis Nationals (1898-1900), Boston Red Sox (1901-08), Cleveland Indians (1909-11), and Boston Braves (1911) and was inducted into the National Baseball Hall of Fame in 1937. The Cy Young Award is given each year to the leading pitcher of each league.

Young, John Watts (1930-), U.S. astronaut. Young was a U.S. Navy test pilot (1952-62), setting 2 world altitude records, before becoming an astronaut in 1962. He made more space flights than any other astronaut. His missions included the first *Gemini* mission with Virgil I. Grissom on Mar. 23, 1965, and the command of the Apr. 1972 *Apollo 16* flight and lunar landing. Chief of the National Aeronautics and Space Administration's (NASA's) astronaut office at Johnson Space Center, Houston, Tex., Young was the commander of the *Columbia* in Apr. 1981, the first space-shuttle flight.
See also: Astronaut.

Young, Lester Willis (1909-59), U.S. tenor saxophonist, one of the most influential jazz musicians. Young grew up in New Orleans, playing in his father's carnival band, first as drummer and then saxophonist. He was active in Kansas City jazz, playing with "King" Oliver and other bands. Young (or

"Prez" as he became known) played with Count Basie from 1935 to 1944 and on tour with "Jazz at the Philharmonic" in the 1940s and 1950s. He helped develop the "cool" jazz style of the 1940s, using the saxophone to create new sounds and employing expressive silences.
See also: Jazz.

Young, Owen D. (1874-1962), U.S. lawyer, industrial executive, and diplomat. An extrenely successful businessperson, he is chiefly remembered as an international diplomat. Young presided at the 1929 Paris Reparations Conference and produced the Young Plan, a schedule for German World War I reparations payments, which was considered a triumph of diplomacy.

Young, Whitney Moore, Jr. (1921-71), U.S. civil rights leader. As director of the National Urban League (1961-71), he worked for better job and housing conditions for blacks in the United States and was one of the most influential black leaders of the 1960s.

Young Men's Christian Association (YMCA), worldwide organization that seeks, through programs of sport, religious and current-affairs study groups, and summer camps, to promote a healthy way of life based on Christian ideals. It was begun in England in 1844.

Youngstown (pop. 115,436), city in northeastern Ohio, seat of Mahoning County, located on the Mahoning River near Pennsylvania. John Young bought the original land site in 1797. The area gradually became important for the production of iron with the opening of a nearby iron furnace (1805), the discovery of local coal for use in smelting, and the availability of Great Lakes iron ore via the Sault Ste. Marie Canal (1855). Youngstown's first steel mill opened in 1891, and the city was a leading steel center until dramatic declines in the steel industry forced closing of all its steel mills (1977-81). Aluminum, textile, and paper products, automotive parts, and other industries are still active. Among Youngstown's many city parks is its well-known Mill Creek Park.
See also: Ohio.

Young Women's Christian Association (YWCA), international organization that promotes a Christian way of life through educational and recreational activities and social work. The movement started in the United States in 1858.

Yourcenar, Marguerite (1903-87), pen name of Marguerite de Crayencour, Belgian-born French author who became a U.S. citizen in the 1940s. The first woman elected to the Académie Française (1980), she is best known for the historical novel *Memoirs of Hadrian* (1951) and *The Abyss* (1968).

Youth hostel, inexpensive, supervised overnight lodging, particularly for young people but generally accommodating all members of such hosteling organizations as the International Youth Hostel Federation and the American Youth Hostels. Hostels provide dormitory-style sleeping and a communal kitchen, but little in the way of bedding and services. Length of stay is often limited to 1-3 nights. The first hostel was founded in Westphalia, Germany, in 1910. Hostels spread rapidly in Europe after World War I. The first U.S. hostel was founded in Northfield, Mass., in 1934.

Ypres (Flemish, "Ieper"; pop. 34,800), city in West Flanders, western Belgium, on the Yperlee River. The city was a major textile center in the Middle Ages, and the main political power of Flanders in the 13th century. It declined in the 15th-18th centuries due to a succession of civil wars, religious strife, and military domination by the French and Dutch. It was nearly destroyed during World War I (battles of Ypres) and was again the scene of fighting in World War II. The city, with many of its medieval buildings, was rebuilt, and it is now a center for linen and lace-making and agricultural products.
See also: Belgium.

Ytterbium, chemical element, symbol Yb; for physical constants, see Periodic Table. Ytterbium was discovered by Jean de Marignac in 1878. It occurs in the minerals xenotime, polycrase, gadolinite, and monazite, the principal source of the element. It is prepared by reducing the anhydrous fluoride with calcium. Ytterbium is a silvery, soft, malleable, ductile, reactive metal belonging to the series of elements known as the rare-earth metals. Ion-exchange and solvent extraction techniques have led to much easier isolation of the rare-earth elements. Ytterbium has strong magnetic properties and a characteristic spectrum. It has possible use as a stainless steel additive. Ytterbium and its compounds are used in carbon-arc lighting, glass, and ceramics. Radioactive ytterbium is used as a portable X-ray source.

Yttrium, chemical element, symbol Y; for physical constants, see Periodic Table. Yttria, an earth (oxide) containing yttrium, was discovered in 1794 by John Gadolin. Yttrium was first isolated by Friedrich Wöhler in 1828. Yttrium occurs in nature as xenotime (yttrium phosphate), and other minerals, monazite being the commercial source. It is obtained by the reduction of the fluoride with calcium metal. Yttrium is a silvery-white, soft, reactive metal. Although not a member of the rare-earth series of metals, it is chemically similar and often considered with them. Yttrium and its compounds are used in phosphors for color televisions, in yttrium aluminum garnets used in YAG-lasers, and in mantles for incandescent lamps. In 1843 Carl Gustav Mosander divided the earth yttria into three earths, which then were named yttria, erbia, and terbia.

Yüan Shih-k'ai, or Yuan Shikai (1859-1916), Chinese soldier and president of China (1912-16). His efforts to check Japan in Korea led to the Sino-Japanese War of 1894-95. He supported the dowager empress Tz'u Hsi and helped suppress the Boxer movement (1900). Supported by his army during the revolution of 1911, he emerged as president but was unable to attain his goal of establishing himself emperor.
See also: China.

Yucatán Peninsula, peninsula (c.70,000 sq mi/c.181,200 sq km) dividing the Gulf of Mexico from the Caribbean Sea. It is comprised of Belize, El Petén (part of Guatemala), and 3 Mexican states. The climate is hot and humid, and farming and forestry are the main activities. The northern region is the leading producer of henequen (fiber used for twine). The people are of Maya stock and Chichén Itza, a famed Mayan site, is on the peninsula.
See also: Mexico.

Yucca, genus of plants of the Lily family found in desert regions of Mexico and the southwestern United States. The Joshua tree is a small tree, but other yuccas are shrubs or low plants bearing clusters of sword-shaped leaves and white, waxy flowers. All depend on the yucca moth for pollination.

Yugoslavia, Until 1991 the Socialist Federal Republic of Yugoslavia, republic with six constituent republics: Serbia, Croatia, Bosnia and Hercegovina, Macedonia, Slovenia and Montenegro.

Land and climate. Yugoslavia was made up of four geographical areas. A mostly mountainous country, it has an Alpine region in the nortwest, but also fertile northern plains. The south rugged mountainous region and there is also the island-studded Dalmatian coast. Most of Yugoslavia is drained by the Danude river, which flows southeast from the Hungarian border across the northern plains. The climate varies from being continental in the north to Mediterranean in the south.

People. Yugoslavia was a federation of many different peoples, principly Serbs, Croats, Slovenes, Macedonians and Montenegrins, but also including many minority groups. The various peoples also profess several different religions. Roman Catholics comprise some 30% of the population, and most of them are Croats and Slovenes. Members of the Eastern Orthodox Church make up about 40% of the population and they are chiefly Serbs, Macedonians, and Montenegrins. The Roman Catholics use the Roman alphabet, whereas the Eastern Orthodox use the Cyrillic alphabet. Finally some 10% of the people are Muslims. Serbs and Croats speak Serbo-Croatian. Each of the other ethnic groups has its own language. About 40% of the people live in cities, the federal capital is Belgrade.

History. Once dominated by the Ottoman Empire, most of Yugoslavia subsequently came under the Austro-Hungarian monarchy, including Croatia, Slovenia, and Bosnia and Hercegovina. By 1914 only Serbia and Montenegro were independent. Serbia sought unification of the country, and it was a Serbian nationalist who assassinated Archduke Francis Ferdinand of Austria and his wife, Sophie, in 1914, setting off the chain of events that led directly to World War I. In 1918 the "Kingdom of the Serbs, Croats, and Slovenes" was created. Its name was changed to Yugoslavia in 1929, but separatist pressures were strong from the very start, particularly among Croats and Macedonians. The Germans invaded in 1941, and two rival resistance groups were organized, one the royalist Dra a Mihailovic and the other the communist resistance under Josip Tito. In 1943, even before the war had ended, the rival resistance groups were fighting one another; backed by Great Britain and the USSR, Tito prevailed. In 1945 he proclaimed Yugoslavia a federal republic of six states and established a communist government. Yugoslavia was expelled from the Comanform in 1948, and relations between the Yugoslavians and Soviets were strained. President Tito charted a policy of "independent national communism" for Yugoslavia and successfully withstood Soviet pressure. Tito's regime continued to have to deal with internal tensions, which were centered on the nationalist aspirations of the constituent republics, most notably from Croatia. The regime was also challenged on issues of intellectual freedom. Following Tito's death in 1980, a collective state presidency was established. Despite attempts to maintain the federal system and the country's unity, the collapse of communist regimes throughout eastern Europe, beginning in 1989, has had profound repercussions in Yugoslavia. Separatism could not be contained, and in 1991 Slovenia and Croatia were the first republics to claim independence. Macedonia and Bosnia Hercegovina followed, and Serbia and Montenegro amalgamated into a new Federal Republic of Yugoslavia. Not all inhabitants of the

Federal Republic Yugoslavia

Capital:	Belgrade
Area:	39,499 sq mi
	(102,173 sq km)
Population:	10,597,000
Language:	Serbian
Government:	Federal republic
Independent:	1992
Head of gov.:	Prime minister
Per capita:	U.S. $3035
Mon. unit:	1 new dinar = 100 para

newly independent countries complied with the new situation, and many protested violently, resulting in civil wars in both Bosnia Hercegovina and Croatia. *See also:* Tito, Josip Broz.

Yugoslavia, Federal Republic of, independent country in southeastern Europe, bordered by Croatiaon the west and the north, Bosnia Hercegovina on the west, Hungary on the north, Romania and Bulgaria on the east, and Macedonia and Albania in the south. The Federal Republic consists of Montenegro in the south and the dominant republic Serbia in the north.

Land and climate. Serbia's landscape is varied, with fertile plains and woody hills. Montenegro is mainly mountainous. Along the coast the climate is Mediterranean, while the interior has a continental climate.

People. About two-thirds of the population is Serbian. Montenegrans constitute 5% of the population. Many Albanians live in the Kosovo province (17%). The official language is Serbian. The major religions are: the Serbian Orthodox Church (44%), the Roman Catholic Church (31%), and the Islam (12%).

Economy. Because of the wars against Croatia and in Bosnia and the UN trade boycott, the economy suffered severely. In the early 1990s tourism collapsed. Agriculture and mining are currently on the increase.

History. Although Serbia was a dominant republic in the former Socialist Federal Republic of Yugoslavia, it could not prevent the separation of the prosperous republics Slovenia and Croatia in the early 1990s. Serbia then amalgamated with Montenegro to form a new Federal Republic of Yugoslavia. Serbian troops were involved in the civil war that followed the collapse of Yugoslavia in 1991. In 1998 tensions in Kosovo resulted in a civil war in that province.

Yukawa, Hideki (1907-81), Japanese physicist who postulated the meson as the agent bonding the atomic nucleus. In fact, the mu-meson (now called *muon*), discovered shortly afterward (in 1936) by Carl D. Anderson, does not fulfill this role, and Yukawa had to wait until Cecil F. Powell discovered the pi-meson (now called *pion*) in 1947 for vindication of his theory. He received the 1949 Nobel Prize in physics.
See also: Meson.

Yukon River, sixth-longest river in North America, flowing from northern British Columbia for 1,979 mi (3,185 km) through Yukon Territory into Alaska, then southwest to the Norton Sound on the Bering Sea. It is navigable for about 1,770 mi (2,848 km).

Yukon Territory, subarctic territory in northwestern Canada. Covering 207,076 sq mi (536,327 sq km), the Yukon is bordered by the Arctic Ocean to the north, the Northwest Territories to the east, British Columbia and Alaska to the west.

Land and climate. The mountainous Yukon Territory includes the Rocky Mountains and, in the southwest, the St. Elias Range. The latter includes Canada's highest mountain, Mount Logan (19,850 ft/ 6,050 m). The territory has 8 other peaks over 15,000 ft (4,572 m) high. A large central basin, or plateau, is heavily forested. The Yukon River drains over one-half the region and is navigable for about 1,770 mi (2,848 km). The inhabited valleys and plateaus of the Yukon have a subarctic climate with long, cold winters and summers about 4 months long. winter temperatures can drop as low as –50°F/–°58C.

People. The Yukon is the original home of about 2,500 Native Americans, who live principally as trappers and hunters. The majority of the territory's population is concentrated in the warmer southern and central valleys. Whitehorse, the largest city, has been the capital since 1956.

Economy. Mining, the Yukon's principal industry, centers on the production of silver, lead, gold, and zinc, and provides jobs for most of the territory's inhabitants. During the 1960s, mining operations expanded to include the production of copper and asbestos; potential reserves of oil and iron ore remain to be developed.

History. The Yukon territory was first explored by the fur traders Robert Campbell and John Bell of the Hudson's Bay Company between 1840 and 1848. Canada acquired the territory from the Hudson's Bay Company in 1870. In the 1860s and 1870s prospectors began mining gold in the area. In 1897 the famous Klondike gold rush began after gold was discovered in several tributaries of the Klondike River. Between 1897 and 1904, an estimated $100 million worth of gold was obtained from deposits in the region. In 1898 the Yukon achieved separate territorial status, but the mines were soon depleted and between 1901 and 1911 the population dropped from 27,219 to 8,512. The decline of the territory was arrested during World War II. The construction of airports on the staging route to Alaska, and the Alaska Highway, brought a new influx of people to the Yukon. Since then, the expansion of mining and new transportation facilities has brought a slow but steady increase in growth to the territory.

See also: Canada.

Yuma (pop. 106,895), city in southwestern Arizona, seat of Yuma County, situated on the Colorado River at the mouth of the Gila River. The location, an important river crossing, was visited by European explorers perhaps as early as 1540, but the town (originally Colorado City) was not founded until 1854. The development of irrigation systems in the early 1900s made the region an important agricultural area. Marine and army installations and tourism help support Yuma's economy.

See also: Arizona.

Yurok, Native Americans who lived along the Klamath River and in nearby coastal aresa of nortwestn California. In 1770 their number was estimated approximately 2,500. The spoke an Algonquian language.
See also: Native Americans.

YWCA *See:* Young Women's Christian Association (YWCA).

Z

Z, 26th and last letter of the English alphabet, corresponding to the ancient Semitic letter *zayin*, meaning "weapon." The Greeks adopted the familiar *z* form for *zeta*, the sixth letter of their alphabet. The Romans used the letter only for words of Greek origin. In Old French, the letter was called *zède* or *zé*, hence the name *zed* used in Great Britain and Canada, and the name *zee* commonly used in the United States. In Old English, the *z* sound was represented by the letter.

Zadkine, Ossip (1890-1967), Russian-born French sculptor. Came to Paris in 1909. He was influenced by Rodin and African art. His often large works in bronze, wood, and stone include *The Destruction of Rotterdam* (1954),

Zagreb (pop. 706,800), capital of the republic of Croatia. Zagreb occupies the site of an early Roman settlement that was also home to Slavic tribes from c.A.D. 600. The present city of Zagreb grew from the merger of 2 earlier towns, Kaptol and Gradac, in the 16th century. It was part of the Austro-Hungarian Empire until 1918, when Croatia, Dalmatia, and Slovenia declared themselves independent. It is a cultural and industrial center, supplying machinery, leather, pharmaceuticals and chemicals, textiles, metal, and paper. Zagreb is characterized by parks and open squares, and is home to Zagreb University, a national theater, and various galleries and museums.
See also: Yugoslavia; Croatia.

Zaharias, Babe Didrikson (1913-1956), U.S. athlete. Considered the greatest woman athlete in history, between 1930-32 she won national hurdles, javelin, baseball throw, broad- and high-jump titles, and set an Olympic 80-m hurdles and javelin records (1932). A top U.S. woman golfer, she won the U.S. Women's Open 3 times (1948, 50, 54).

Zaïre, formerly the Belgian Congo and the Democratic Republic of the Congo, officially Zaïre since 1971, nation in west-central Africa. With an area of 905,446 sq mi (2,345,095 sq km), Zaïre is bordered by Angola on the southwest; the Congo Republic on the west; the Central African Republic and Sudan on the north; Uganda, Rwanda, Burundi, and Tanzania on the east; and Zambia on the southeast.
Land and climate. Central Zaïre, which straddles the equator, is a large, low plateau covered by rain forest. There is a higher, drier plateau in the southeast. In the east, on the border with Uganda, are the mountains of the Ruwenzori Range and lakes Albert, Edward, and Tanganyika. The Congo (Zaïre) River, one of the largest in Africa, flows west to the Atlantic, where the country narrows to a 25-mi (40-km) wide coastline. Zaïre has a hot, rainy climate.

Zaïre (Congo)

Capital:	Kinshasa
Area:	905,446 sq mi
	(2,345,095 sq km)
Population:	49,001,000
Language:	French
Government:	Presidential republic
Independent:	1960
Head of gov.:	Prime minister
Per capita:	U.S. $120
Mon. unit:	1 nouveau zaire = 100
	makuta

People. The population is divided among many groups, among which the Kongo are the most numerous. Other important peoples include the Mongo, Luba, and Zande. There are Nilotic-speaking peoples living primarily in the north, and Pygmies live in the east. About 200 languages are spoken, most of them in the Bantu family of languages. French is the official language, but Lingola and Swahili are common. Most of the people are Christians , but sizable minorities adhere to traditional African religions. The capital of the country is Kinshasa.

Economy. The mainstay of Zaïre's economy is mining. The country has 65% of the world's reserves of cobalt and copper, the principal exports. Zaire is also a leading diamond producer. Zaïre has a diversified industrial sector including food processing, chemicals, cement, and textiles. Its farms produce cash crops of coffee, rubber, palm oil, cocoa, and tea.

History. First Pygmies and later Bantus were the original black African inhabitants of the region. The first Europeans in the area were Portuguese following in the wake of Diogo Cão, who came in 1482. In 1885 King Leopold II of Belgium took control of an area he called the Congo Free State; in 1908 it became the Belgian Congo and was a rich and profitable colony. The Belgian Congo became independent in 1960 and, as the Republic of the Congo, had Joseph Kasavubu as president and Patrice Lumumba as premier. The fledgling state was unable to maintain either stability or unity, and shortly after independence Moïse Tshombe urged the secession of the mineral-rich province of Katanga (now Shaba). Before Katanga rejoined the nation in 1963, the UN and Belgium sent troops and both the United States and the USSR had taken sides in the conflict. In 1965, following continuing unrest, Maj. Gen. Joseph Mobotu, later Mobuto Sese Seko, took control and has been president since 1970. The Democratic Republic of the Congo was renamed Zaïre in 1971 and adopted its current constitution in 1978. Although Zaïre is rich in mineral resources, mismanagment and decreases in world-market prices have led to severe economic problems. Political liberalization in the 1990s did not solve the problems. In 1997 Mobutu was ousted by Désiré Kabila, who in turn had to deal with rebellious Tutsi soldiers in 1998. After Kabila became the new president, the country's name was changed into Democratic Republic of Congo.

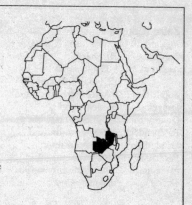

Zambia

Capital:	Lusaka
Area:	290,586 sq mi
	(752,614 sq km)
Population:	9,461,000
Language:	English
Government:	Presidential republic
Independent:	1964
Head of gov.:	President
Per capita:	U.S. $400
Mon. unit:	1 kwacha = 100 ngwee

Zambezi River, river in southeast Africa, fourth-largest in Africa. Rising in northwest Zambia, it flows about 1,700 mi (about 2,736 km) south, then east along the Zambia-Zimbabwe border, through Mozambique to enter the Mozambique Channel of the Indian Ocean through a 2,500-sq mi (6,475-sq km) delta.

Zambia, formerly Northern Rhodesia, officially the Republic of Zambia, independent republic in south-central Africa. With an area of 290,584 sq mi (752,614 sq km), Zambia is bordered by Zaïre on the north; Tanzania on the northeast; Malawi and Mozambique on the east; Zimbabwe, Botswana, and Namibia on the south; and Angola on the west.

Land and climate. The country occupies a mostly flat plateau some 3,000 to 4,500 ft (914 to 1,372 m) above sea level and broken by deep valleys formed by the Luangwa and Zambezi rivers. The plateau is largely savanna and open woodland, and the course of the Zambezi includes Victoria Falls and Lake Kariba, formed by the Kariba Dam. Both Victoria Falls and Lake Kariba are on Zambia's border with Zimbabwe. In the northeast part of the country, the Muchinga Mountains rise some 7,000 ft (2,124 m). Zambia's climate is tropical, but its effects are moderated by altitude.

People. The Zambian people are black Africans, mostly Bantu peoples, with over 70 different tribes and a variety of languages. There are also European and Asian minorities. More than half the people follow animist beliefs. The balance profess Christianity, either Roman Catholicism or Protestantism. While English is the official language, many Bantu languages are also spoken. The capital of Zambia is Lusaka.

Economy. The majority of Zambia's people are engaged in subsistence farming, but the country is also one of the world's major producers of copper, which accounts for the bulk of its export earnings. Cobalt is the second-largest export earner and Zambia also supports lead, zinc, manganese, and sulfur. The agricultural sector produces cash crops, including tobacco, sugarcane, and wheat. Despite its resources, Zambia underwent considerable economic dislocation as a result of its active opposition to Southern Rhodesia in the 1960s and 1970s. In the 1980s the country faced severe food shortages principally due to drought.

History. Present-day Zambians are descendants of Bantu peoples who migrated to the region between the 16th and 18th centuries. European traders and missionaries came in the 19th century, most notably David Livingstone, who came in 1851. In 1888 Cecil Rhodes led the way for British commercial interests. As Northern Rhodesia the area became a British protectorate in 1911. Copper deposits were discovered in the 1920s, leading to rapid and lucrative development but at the expense of the native inhabitants. A nationalist movement arose in 1946, and despite its rigorous opposition to the plan, Northern Rhodesia was combined by the British into the Federation of Rhodesia and Nyasaland, which included Southern Rhodesia (now Zimbabwe) and Nyasaland (now Malawi). Northern Rhodesia and Nyasaland left the federation in 1963 and Northern Rhodesia became the independent Republic of Zambia in 1964, under the presidency of Kenneth Kaunda. The fledgling country protested against and eventually opposed the white regime of Ian Smith in Southern Rhodesia. Though contributing to the isolation of the Smith regime and the eventual emergence of Zimbabwe, the policy proved costly. After more than 25 years Kaunda was defeated in democratic elections in 1991, and was succeeded by Frederik Chiluba. In 1997 the military tried to overthrow the government but failed.

Zamboanga (pop. 343,722), Philippine city on the extreme western tip of Mindanao Island, capital of Zamboanga del Sur Province. Zamboanga is the major port and trade center of the Sulu Archipelago and exports hardwoods, rice, abaca, rubber, copra, fish, and sugar. Settled by Spain in 1635, much of the city was destroyed in World War II and was subsequently rebuilt. *See also:* Philippines.

Zane, Ebenezer (1747-1812), American pioneer. A Quaker, he cofounded (1769) Zanesburg (now in West Virginia; renamed Wheeling in 1806) and blazed a trail to Maysville, Ky., known as Zane's Trace. *See also:* Pioneer life in America.

Zanuck, Darryl F. (1902-79), U.S. film producer. He cofounded 20th Century Pictures, which merged with Fox Films (1935) to form 20th Century-Fox, was its production head (1935-52), and its president (1962-71).

Zanzibar, island, part of Tanzania, off eastern Africa. It was a center of an Omani Arab sultanate (1700) with extensive mainland territories. Zanzibar became a British protectorate (1890-93), part of German East Africa (1893), an independent sultanate (1963), and a republic (1964). It then united (1964) with nearby Pemba and with Tanganyika to form Tanzania. The chief exports are cloves and copra. *See also:* Tanzania.

Zapata, Emiliano (1879?-1919), Mexican revolutionary whose chief ambition was to return Mexican land to the native population. Zapata joined the successful forces of Francisco Madero against the dictatorship of President Porfirio Díaz (1910) and led the insurrectionists of Morelos, his native state. After Díaz's overthrow, Zapata refused to recognize Madero or his successor, Victoriano Huerta, for their failure to redistribute land to the people. Together with Pancho Villa, he renewed his revolutionary endeavors. On 3 occasions (1914-15), Zapata occupied Mexico City. He was assassinated (1919).

Zapotec, ancient native people of southeast Oaxaca, Mexico, and their descendants. They created a formative pre-Columbian culture about 2,000 years ago. Monte Alban, west of Oaxaca city, contains magnificent ruins of tombs, stelae, temples, and plazas.

Zarathustra *See:* Zoroastrianism.

Zealots, Jewish religious and political fanatics in Palestine about the time of Jesus. Led by Judas of Galilee and Zadock the priest, they resisted Rome and its collaborator Herod the Great, but they later perished (A.D. 70) with the destruction of Jerusalem. St. Simon the Apostle may have been a Zealot.

Zebra, 3 species of striped horses (genus *Equus*) of Africa. The zebra's black-and-white striped coat makes the animal inconspicuous at long range. The 3 species—plains zebra, mountain zebra, and Grévy's zebra—differ in stripe pattern, habitat, and behavior. Plains and mountain zebras live in permanent, nonterritorial stallion groups, but mountain zebras are adapted to life in more arid regions. Grévy's zebras, with very narrow stripes, are territorial animals.

Zebu, or Brahman ox (*Bos indicus*), ox found in India, Africa, and Asia. It has a hump on its shoulders and a dewlap under the chin. The horns are large, up to 5 ft (1.5 m) in the *ankole* cattle of Uganda. Zebus are used as draft animals and for milk and meat. They react to heat well and have been introduced to many areas with hot climates, including the southern United States, where they are immune to the Texas fever carried by cattle ticks.

Zebulun, one of the 12 tribes of Israel and one of the 10 lost tribes removed from Palestine by the conquering Assyrians (721 B.C.) and dispersed. Zebulun was part of the Northern Kingdom of Israel and occupied lands northeast of the Plain of Jezreel. The tribe name comes from the sixth son born to Jacob and Leah (Genesis 30:20).

Zechariah, Book of, Old Testament book named for 1 of the 12 minor prophets. Zechariah (or Zacharias), an associate of the prophet Haggai, prophesied from 520 B.C.-518 B.C., and, after the Jews returned to Palestine from exile, advocated rebuilding the Temple. The Book of Zechariah has 14 chapters. The first 8, attributed to Zechariah himself, record a series of visions showing hope for a new order in Jerusalem and the plans for its establishment and organization. The last 6 chapters, attributed to a later author or group of authors, elaborate on Zechariah's themes of the restoration of the Davidic royal line, the intervention of a messiah, and Jerusalem's exiles returned and forgiven.
See also: Bible; Old Testament.

Zeeman effect, changes in the energy levels of atoms that may be observed by the splitting of spectral lines when a light source is placed in a magnetic field. The line separations are expressed as differences of frequency and increase in direct proportion to the strength of the magnetic field. They occur when an atom's electron moves from one energy level, corresponding to the concentric orbits the electron makes around the atomic nucleus, to another. The effect was discovered (1896) by Pieter Zeeman, a Dutch physicist, and was the first indication that electrons are negatively charged particles. It is used by astronomers and physicists to study the properties of nuclei, atoms, and molecules.
See also: Atom; Electron.

Zeiss, Carl (1816-88), German optical manufacturer who founded a famous workshop at Jena in 1846. Realizing that optical technology had much to gain from scientific research, in the mid-1860s he formed a fruitful association with the physicist Ernest Abbe.
See also: Optics.

Zen (Chinese: *Ch'an*, meaning "meditation"), form of Buddhism that developed in China from c.500 A.D. and spread to Japan, exerting great influence on Japanese culture. Zen differs markedly from traditional Buddhism in its abhorrance of images and ritual, scriptures and metaphysics. Rinzai Zen uses *koan* (paradoxical riddles) to shock into sudden enlightenment; Soto Zen stresses contemplation.
See also: Buddhism.

Zenger, John Peter (1697-1745), colonial publisher and journalist whose trial for libel (1735) furthered freedom of the press. As opponents of the English governor, William Cosby, and his party, Zenger and a group of colleagues established the *New York Weekly Journal* (1733) to provide a dissident political voice. The paper consistently criticized the governor, and Zenger was arrested (1734) for criminal libel. Determined to secure Zenger's conviction, the authorities disbarred his attorneys, but his case was eventually defended by Andrew Hamilton of Philadelphia, who argued that Zenger's articles were not libelous because they were based on fact. Zenger was acquitted (1735) and published a verbatim account of the trial as *A Brief Narrative of the Case and Trial of John Peter Zenger* (1736).*See also:* Press.

Zenith, in astronomy, point on the celestial sphere directly above an observer and exactly 90° from the celestial horizon. It is directly opposite to the nadir.
See also: Astronomy; Nadir.

Zeno of Citium (335?-265? B.C.), Cypriot philosopher who founded the Stoic school of philosophy in Athens (301 B.C.). A wealthy merchant forced by shipwreck to remain in Athens, Zeno became fascinated with the life of Socrates and the writings of the Cynics, and abandoned trade for philosophy. After years of study he established his own school. Zeno saw the cosmos as the reference point for human ethics, with a divine intelligence guiding both nature and humanity toward "the city of Zeus," that is, toward goodness. He felt that natural law superseded civil law, and that the practice of acceptance and moderation were characteristics of a virtuous life. He defined morality as surrender to divine governance. At his death, the Athenian Assembly gave him citizenship and voted him a statue and gold crown.
See also: Stoicism.

Zeno of Elea (490?-430 B.C.), Greek philosopher who studied under Parmenides and defended his teacher's theories. Zeno used indirect argumentation to try to prove his philosophy and is considered the inventor of pre-Socratic dialectic. He based his arguments on 4 propositions: that all things belong to one unchanging reality as opposed to many; that nothing can be proved by human reason; that empty space is not real because the One fills all voids; that motion is not real because it assumes movement from someplace to empty space, which does not exist. Zeno is known for his book of about 40 paradoxes (of which 8 survive), particularly the 4 concerning

motion, which were the beginnings of modern mathematical concepts of infinity and continuity.
See also: Pre-Socratic philosophy.

Zephaniah, Book of, Old Testament book written c.640-630 B.C. during the reign of Josiah (638-608 B.C.) and after the Scythian invasion of Palestine. The dominant themes of the book are condemnation of the Judeans for adopting foreign idols and customs, and a catastrophic day of judgement, the "day of the Lord," when only the few faithful will be saved. This element evolved into the popular notion of the judgement day prominent in Biblical prophecy.
See also: Bible; Old Testament.

Zeppelin *See:* Airship.

Zeppelin, Ferdinand von (1838-1917), German aeronautical engineer who designed and built almost 100 powered balloons.

Zero-base budgeting (ZBB), annual economic planning that justifies expenditure on actual cost or need rather than on increments of the previous year's budget. ZBB assumes a base of zero dollars and asks managers to prepare outlines showing expected high and low spending levels. Budgeting for the coming year is based on these outlines. Introduced in the 1960s by the electronics manufacturer, Texas Instruments, Incorporated, ZBB is used by government and business as a means of controlling spending.
See also: Sunset laws.

Zero population growth, close approximation in numbers of births and deaths needed to stabilize a nation's population and prevent annual increases. To stabilize the U.S. population at its present level, the replacement ratio for families (excluding illegitimate births) is 2.54 children per fertile married woman. Zero Population Growth is also the name of an organization formed in 1968 by Richard Bowers, Paul Ehrlich, and Charles Remington to inform the public and legislators of the disadvantages of continued population growth.

Zeus, supreme god of Greek mythology. His mother, Rhea, saved him from his jealous father, Cronus, and he was brother and husband of Hera. He led the Olympian gods in overthrowing Cronus and the other Titans. By lot he became god of earth and sky (Poseidon won the sea, Hades the underworld). Zeus's Roman counterpart is Jupiter.
See also: Mythology.

Zhao Ziyang (1919-   ), premier of China (1980-87), successor to Hua Kuo-feng (Hua Guofeng). Purged during the Cultural Revolution, Zhao was later "rehabilitated." He was appointed governor of Szechwan (Sichuan) province in 1975 and elected to the politburo in 1979. Party leader from 1987-89. In 1989 he was removed from office.

Zhou dynasty (also Chou), China's third and longest-ruling (1122 B.C.-256 B.C.) royal house. The Zhou people were seminomadic tribes who overturned the Shang dynasty, expanded their territory by conquering neighboring tribes, and established a feudal society of separate states ruled by a central government. Their control corresponded to the flowering of Chinese culture. Under Zhou governance, the merchant class emerged, coinage replaced trade by barter, education flourished, and the family became the focus of society. Iron implements, including the traction plow, were introduced, and irrigation improved farming. Confucius, Mencius, and Laozi lived during the Zhou dynasty, and Buddhism was introduced to China in that period.

Zhou Enlai, or **Chou En Lai** (1898-1976), Chinese Communist leader, premier and foreign minister of China (1949-59). Zhou began his political activity (1919) when he was imprisoned for a year for demonstrating against the Treaty of Versailles. He was a leader in the labor revolts of Nanchang and Shanghai (1927) and helped establish the Red Army, of which he succeeded Mao Zedong as commissar (1932). In the 1940s he was a leader in the struggle for control of China and was instrumental in the ouster of Chiang Kai-shek. He became prime minister of the Chinese People's Republic (1949), and after his removal (1959) remained influential in Chinese foreign affairs.
See also: China.

Zhuangzi (Chuang Tsu or Chuang-Tzo; 377?-286 B.C.), Chinese scholar and Taoist philosopher, to whom the book *Zhuangzi*, the first Chinese book dealing only with spiritual matters, is attributed. Zhuangzi was a minor official who several times rejected public office. He advocated a life of simplicity, submissive to and at one with nature, and renounced government, science, and even education as of no help in understanding that unity. The *Zhuangzi*, an interpretation of the *Tao*, has as its primary theme unending and inevitable change. The work was important in the development of Zen Buddhism.
See also: Taoism.

Zhukov, Georgi Konstantinovich (1896-1974), Soviet general, hero of the battles at Stalingrad (1943) and Berlin (1945). After the death of Stalin (who had blocked his career), Zhukov was defense minister (1955-57) and briefly a full member of the Communist Party Presidium (1957).
See also: World War II.

Ziegfeld, Florenz (1869-1932), U.S. theatrical producer. In 1907 he launched the Ziegfeld Follies, an annual revue famous for its spectacular staging, beautiful women, and star performers; under his direction it ran for 24 years. Ziegfeld also produced musicals, including *Sally* (1920) and *Show Boat* (1927).

Zimbabwe, officially the Republic of Zimbabwe, formerly Southern Rhodesia under the British, and Rhodesia under Ian Smith, a landlocked republic in south central Africa. With an area of 150,873 sq mi (390,759 sq km), Zimbabwe is bordered by Zambia to the north, Mozambique to the northeast and east, and Botswana to the southwest and west.
Land and climate. Zimbabwe is situated astride a high plateau between the Zambezi and Limpopo rivers. The plateau is divided into three distinct zones. The High Veld is over 4,000 ft (1,219 m) above sea level and extends across the country from the southwest to the northeast. The Middle Veld is most

Zimbabwe

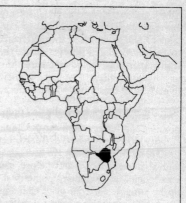

Capital:	Harare
Area:	150,873 sq mi
	(390,759 sq km)
Population:	11,044,000
Language:	English
Government:	Presidential republic
Independent:	1980
Head of gov.:	President
Per capita:	U.S. $570
Mon. unit:	1 Zimbabwean dollar =
	100 cents

extensive in the northwest and rises 3,000-4,000 ft (914-1,219 m) above sea level. The Low Veld occupies land near river basins in the north and south and is 3,000 ft (914 m) below sea level. In the east, the highlands include Mt. Inyangani which rises to 8,503 ft (2,592 m). Zimbabwe's climate varies with the altitude.

People. The people of Zimbabwe are overwhelmingly black Africans, principally Bantus of the Shona or Ndebele groups. Other important tribes include the Tonga, Sena, Hlengwe, Venda, and Sotho. About 5% of the population consists of whites, coloreds (descendants of whites and black Africans), and Asians. The majority of the people is Christian, about 45% follow traditional animist beliefs, and there are Hindus among the small Asian minority. English is the official language, but Shona and Ndebele are widely spoken.

Economy. Most of the people of Zimbabwe work as subsistence farmers. But the country's agricultural sector was a major food exporter to the South African region. The principal cash crop is tobacco. Zimbabwe is also rich in mineral resources. Gold is the country's major export, but other valuable minerals include iron ore, asbestos, chrome, copper, and nickel. The country also has an expanding and diversified industrial sector.

History. Bushmen paintings and tools indicate that Zimbabwe had Stone Age inhabitants. Bantu peoples settled the area about A.D. 400, and during the 15th century, the Shona civilization established an empire; the capital was called Zimbabwe. In 1889, Cecil Rhodes obtained a charter from Britain to colonize and administer the area, and in 1923 it became the self-governing British colony of Southern Rhodesia. In 1953 the British combined Southern Rhodesia with Northern Rhodesia (now Zambia) and Nyasaland (now Malawi) to form the Federation of Rhodesia and Nyasaland. The federation dissolved in 1963 and in the face of growing demands from black Africans for self-determination, white conservatives led by Prime Minister Ian Smith declared independence from Britain in 1965. Britain refused to recognize the all-white regime and white Rhodesia was beset by international pressure and an armed insurgency. Rebel forces were headed by Robert Mugabe and Joshua Nkomo. In a negotiated settlement, the country gained its independence and black majority rule in 1980, and its name was changed from Rhodesia to Zimbabwe. Rivalry between elements loyal to Robert Mugabe, who was elected president, and Joshua Nkomo threatened the new country's unity, but by the late 1980s the worst excesses of the internal fighting seemed to be under control. In the early 1990s land reforms were carried out, intended to lessen the difference in landownership between black and white. However, they were not entirely succesful.

Zimbalist, Efrem (1889-1985), Russian-born U.S. virtuoso violinist. He directed the Curtis Institute of Music in Philadelphia (1941-68) and composed several pieces for violin and orchestra.

Zinc, chemical element, symbol Zn; for physical constants, see Periodic Table. Zinc ores were used for making brass centuries before zinc was recognized as a distinct element. The metal was prepared in India in the 13th century by reducing calamine with organic substances such as wool. It occurs in nature principally as sphalerite (zinc sulfide). It is produced by reduction of the oxide with carbon. Zinc is a bluish-white, lustrous, brittle, reactive metal. It is used in many important metal alloys, including bronze, Babbitt metal, and German silver. Zinc is an essential growth element for humans and animals. The uses of the metal and its compounds are numerous, including in pigments, dry cell batteries, pharmaceuticals, and television screens.

Zinjanthropus, humanlike creature that probably lived about 1,750,000 years ago. Its skull was discovered (1959) at Olduvai Gorge, Tanzania, by Mary D. Leakey. The skull belonged to a creature about 17 years of age with a low brow and large, flat teeth. *Zinjanthropus* was probably chiefly herbivorous and had a brain about one-third the size of a modern human. It may have used stone tools. It became extinct about 1 million years ago. *Zinjanthropus* was renamed (1967) *Australopithecus boisei*.
See also: Australopithecus.

Zinneman, Fred (1907-97), film director and winner of Academy Awards for *That Mothers Might Live* (1938), *From Here to Eternity* (1953), and *A Man for All Seasons* (1966). Zinneman studied film making in France before moving to the United States in 1929. Other works include *High Noon* (1952) and *The Nun's Story* (1958). In 1992 his autobiography *A Life in the Movies* was published.

Zion, in the Old Testament, ancient citadel of David, on the southeast hill of Jerusalem. In a wider sense it symbolizes the whole of Jerusalem and the Jewish people and their aspirations.

Zionism, movement to establish a Jewish national home in Palestine. After the destruction of their state in A.D. 70, the Jews retained their identity and kept alive their dream of an eventual return from exile. The dream turned into a political movement in the 19th century, largely in response to the persecution of Jews in the USSR and Austria, and Jewish farmers and artisans began to settle in Palestine. The decisive impetus came in 1897, when Theodore Herzl organized the first World Zionist Congress, after which Zionist groups were established all over the world. In 1903 the British government offered the Jews a home in Uganda, but this was rejected. Leadership of the Zionist movement was assumed by Chaim Weizmann, who was largely responsible for the Balfour Declaration (1917).
See also: Herzl, Theodor.

Zion National Park, established in 1919 and covering 147,035 acres (59,528 hectares) in southwest Utah. It is noted for its canyons and multicolored rock formations.

ZIP Code, acronym for Zone Improvement Plan, a 5-digit code implemented (1963) to speed sorting and delivery of domestic mail. An optional extra 4 digits were added in 1981. The first number of the code identifies 1 of 10 large geographical areas in the United States where the mail will be delivered. The second 2 numbers indicate the metropolitan area, and the last 2 numbers represent the addressee's local post office. The ZIP code facilitates mechanical mail processing.

Zircon, silicate mineral, zirconium silicate ($ZrSiO_4$), used chiefly as a gemstone and as the main source of the metals zirconium and hafnium, in industry and research. Zircon crystals are widespread in igneous deposits such as granite, in some metamorphic rock, and in beach sands. They occur in Australia, Asia, Europe, and North America, and may be clear, red-brown, green, yellow, or blue.

Zirconium, chemical element, symbol Zr; for physical constants, see Periodic Table. Zirconium is mentioned in biblical writings as the mineral zircon. In 1789 Martin Heinrich Klaproth isolated the oxide of zirconium from zircon. The impure metal was first isolated by Jöns J. Berzelius in 1824. Zircon (zirconium silicate) is the principal ore of zirconium. Zirconium is produced commercially by reduction of the chloride with magnesium. It is a grayish-white, lustrous metal resistant to corrosion by acids, alkalis, sea water, and other agents. It is superconductive at low temperatures. The metal has a low absorption cross section for neutrons. Most zirconium is used in nuclear reactors. Zirconium oxide is a refractory material and is used in furnaces and in the glass and ceramic industries.

Zodiac, band of the heavens whose outer limits lie 9° on each side of the ecliptic. The 12 main constellations near the eclipse, corresponding to the 12 signs of the zodiac, are Aries; Taurus; Gemini; Cancer; Leo; Virgo; Libra; Scorpio; Sagittarius; Capricorn; Aquarius; Pisces. The orbits of all the planets except Pluto lie within the zodiac, and their positions, as that of the sun, are important in astronomy and astrology. The 12 signs are each equivalent to 30° of arc along the zodiac.
See also: Astrology; Constellation.

Zodiacal light, faint cone of light visible in the night sky just before dawn or after sunset. The luminosity extends along the plane of the zodiac or ecliptic and can best be seen at a point 30° to 90° from the sun, though there is some zodiacal light in all parts of the sky. Scientists explain zodiacal light as dust particles from comets and asteroids dispersed over a vast area and reflecting sunlight.

Zog (Ahmedi Bey Zogu; 1895-1961), king of Albania (1928-46). After serving in the Austrian army he was made premier (1922-24) and president (1925-28), whereupon he proclaimed himself king. He fled when the Italians invaded, and he spent the rest of his life in exile.
See also: Albania.

Zola, Émile (1840-1902), French novelist and founder of naturalism. His works proclaim a "scientific" vision of life determined entirely by heredity and environment. His first success, *Thérèse Raquin* (1867), was followed by the *Rougon-Macquart* cycle (20 vol., 1871-93), depicting, with powerful and often lurid realism, the fortunes of a contemporary family. It includes his celebrated studies of alcoholism (*The Dram Shop*, 1877), prostitution (*Nana*, 1880), and life in a mining community (*Germinal*, 1885). In 1898 Zola threw himself into the Dreyfus affair with the pamphlet "J'accuse," attacking the army.
See also: Naturalism.

Zoogeography, study of the geographical distribution of animal species and populations. Physical barriers—such as wide oceans and mountain ranges, major climatic extremes, or intense heat or cold—may prevent the spread of a species into new areas or may separate 2 previously like populations, allowing them to develop into distinct species. The effect of these barriers on movement and interbreeding, both now and in the past, are reflected in the distributions and, later, adaptive radiations of animal species, resulting in the zoogeographical distributions we find today.

Zoology, scientific study of animal life. Originally concerned with the classification of animal groups, comparative anatomy, and physiology, the science now embraces studies of evolution, genetics, embryology, biochemistry, animal behavior, and ecology.

Zoroastrianism, Persian religion based on the teachings of Zoroaster (Greek form of *Zarathustra*), a sage who lived in the 6th century B.C. It was founded on the old Aryan folk religion but abolished its polytheism, establishing 2 predominant spirits: Ahura-Mazda (Ormazd), the spirit of light and good; and Ahriman, the spirit of evil and darkness. Zoroastrianism includes the belief in eternal reward or punishment after death according to man's deeds. Its scriptures are the *Zend-Avesta*. Almost wiped out in the 7th century by the Muslim conquest of Persia, Zoroastrianism survives among the Parsees (Parsis) of India.
See also: Persia, Ancient.

Zukerman, Pinchas (1948-), Israeli-born violinist, violist, and conductor who came to New York (1962) as a protégé of Isaac Stern. He performed with orchestras throughout the world and made his conducting debut in 1974.

Zulu, South African Bantu people who settled what is now Natal Province early in the 17th century. Under King Shaka (or Chaka), the Zulus conquered neighboring tribes and expanded their domain (1818-20). Shaka was friendly to Europeans, but his half-brother and successor, Dingaan, fought with Boer settlers (1838) in a cattle dispute. The British invaded Zulu territory (1879) and, after losing a battle at Isandhlwana, defeated the Zulus at Ulundi. There was political unrest until 1910 when the Union of South Africa absorbed the Zulu province. Traditionally cattle and grain farmers, the Zulus live in a patriarchal clan society and the clan chief is the genealogically senior male. They practice polygyny. Zulu religion was based on ancestor worship and the belief in a divine creator, though now many Zulus have adopted Christianity.

Zululand, former semi-autonomous homeland in Natal, South Africa. It borders on Mozambique, the Indian Ocean, Swaziland, and the Buffalo and Tugela rivers. It produces sugarcane, cotton, and maize. Cattle raising is the traditional occupation of the Zulus, a Bantu people who comprise most of the population. Traditionally they live in beehive-shaped huts in fenced compounds called *kraals*. Zululand was annexed by the British in 1887 after prolonged Zulu resistance to white conquest. Many Zulu men now work as migrant laborers in mines and in cities.
See also: South Africa.

Zuñi, Native Americans of the Zuñian linguistic stock, in New Mexico. The Zuñi live mainly by agriculture and produce fine jewelry and sculpture. They have retained their ancient religion, which they celebrate in magnificent festivals noted for their dancing and costumes.

Zürich (pop. 343,100), city in northern Switzerland, capital of Zürich canton, and the nation's financial and education center. The Romans settled Zürich c.A.D. 100 as the fortified Turicum. It joined the Swiss Confederation that became modern Switzerland (1351). Zürich is a tourist and cultural center, home to the University of Zürich; the National Museum; 2 11th-century churches, the Grossmünster and the Fraumünster; and the 15th-century Wasserkirche. Industrial products include precision machinery, textiles, food, paper, and tobacco. The world's banking and gold-trade centers are located in Zürich.
See also: Switzerland.

Zweig, Arnold (1887-1968), German novelist. He wrote an 8-volume epic that includes his best-known novel, *The Case of Sergeant Grischa* (1927), which powerfully indicted militarism in its description of World War I and its effects on German society.

Zweig, Stefan (1881-1942), Austrian biographer and novelist. He is best known for his psychological studies of such historical figures and writers as Erasmus, Mary, Queen of Scots, and Honoré Balzac. He wrote of European culture in *The Tide of Fortune* (1928).

Zwicky, Fritz (1898-1974), Swiss-born U.S. astronomer and astrophysicist best known for his studies of supernovas, which he showed to be quite distinct from, and much rarer than, novas. He also did pioneering work on jet propulsion.
See also: Astronomy; Supernova.

Zworykin, Vladimir Kosma (1889-1982), Russian-born U.S. electronic engineer regarded as the father of modern television: His kinescope (patented 1924), little adapted, is our modern picture tube; and his iconoscope, though now obsolete, represents the basis of the first practical television camera. He also made important contributions to the electron microscope.
See also: Television.